The
Kennebeck
Proprietors

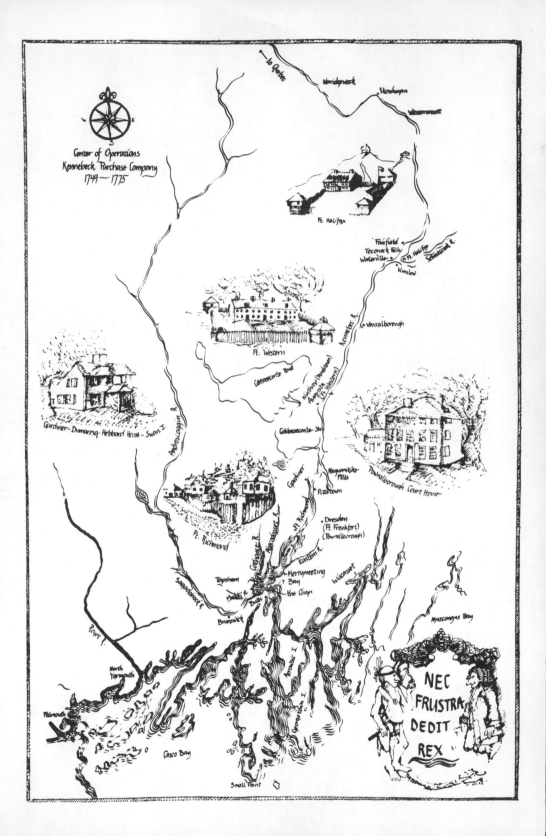

Center of Operations
Kennebeck Purchase Company
1749 — 1775

Ft. Halifax

Norridgewock
Skowhegan
Wesserunsett

Fairfield
Teconock Falls
Waterville
@ Ft. Halifax
Sebasticook R.
Winslow

Kennebec R.
to Vassalborough

Ft. Western

Cobbosseecontee Pond

Hallowell (Fondtown)
Augusta
(Ft. Western)

Gardiner-Dumaresq-Hebbard House - Swan I.

Androscoggin R.

Cobbosseecontee Stm.

Pownalborough Court House

Gardiner

Mequumkike
Falls

Pittstown

Dresden
(Ft. Frankfort)
(Pownalborough)

Ft. Richmond

Eastern R.

Wiscasset

Topsham
Merrymeeting
Bay
the Chops

Cathance R.
Abagadasset R.
Muddy R.

Bath

Brunswick

Sagadahoc R.

Sasanoa R.

Arrowsic I.

Muscongus Bay

Tory I.

North
Yarmouth

Georgetown I.

Falmouth

NEC
FRUSTRA
DEDIT
REX

Casco Bay

Small Point

"Gentlemen of Large Property & Judicious Men"

THE KENNEBECK PROPRIETORS

1749-1775

By Gordon E. Kershaw

NEW HAMPSHIRE PUBLISHING COMPANY—Somersworth

MAINE HISTORICAL SOCIETY—Portland

1975

For My
Father and Mother

Contents

Illustrations

Preface

In 1629, when the Pilgrims obtained their patent from the Council for New England for land along the Kennebec River, their goal was immediate and simple: the development of a profitable fur trade. Their legal descendants, the Kennebeck proprietors, who revived the almost defunct claim over one hundred years later, were men of a different breed. Wealthy Boston merchants for the most part, they formed a speculative land company to develop the wilderness areas of central Maine. They possessed the means to expand their holdings methodically, defend their controversial title in the courts, and await the enormous riches that would eventually accrue from their investment. As stalwart Whigs in the eighteenth century tradition, these Kennebeck proprietors held the rights of property supreme. Their methods of operation would have proved instructive to the nineteenth century "Robber Barons." Unfortunately for them, the American Revolution thwarted the complete realization of their dreams. Nevertheless, in the long run, the Kennebeck proprietors demonstrated, if unwillingly, that aggrandizement for private gain might not necessarily run counter to the public interest.

One of the greatest pleasures of historical research derives from the acquaintances one makes along the way. In this respect, I have been particularly fortunate in meeting individuals who not only have shown a genuine interest in my research, but have given unstintingly of their time and resources to further it. My debt to Richard S. Dunn dates back to the writing of the dissertation from which this book has emerged. It has continued into the present through his friendly advice and innumerable suggestions.

Robert E. Moody provided a kindly, never-ending source of ideas and encouragement. I owe special thanks to the late Gwendolyn Flagg Drew, whose shrewd speculations concerning the movements of one of her ancestors during the Stamp Act crisis sparked one of the theories explored in this work. Equally valuable were the suggestions of William F. Royall in reference to Governor William Shirley's mysterious land grant from the Kennebeck proprietors. I owe much to Marcia Sewall, who drew the pictorial map of the Kennebec River area. Several colleagues and friends were kind enough to read and criticize the entire manuscript; these include: Harry Stegmaier, Jr., David Dean, Helen McIntyre, Constance Murray, Judith Thelen, Roger Ray, Mildred Burrage, Martha Vaughan, and Margaret Guild. I am grateful to the staffs of the following institutions for their interest and kindnesses: the Maine Historical Society; the American Antiquarian Society, the Massachusetts Historical Society; the Houghton and Baker Libraries, Harvard; the Wiscassett Public Library; Special Collections, the Bowdoin College Library; the New Hampshire Archives; and the Lincoln County Cultural and Historical Association. I will always remember having tea and conversation, if not sympathy, with Mr. and Mrs. Leo Flaherty of the Massachusetts Archives at the end of a tiring day poring over microfilm.

My thanks to the editors of the *New England Quarterly*, the *American Neptune*, and the Maine Historical Society *Newsletter*, who have generously permitted the reappearance here of material that was originally published in their journals. I am most grateful to Robert Albion, Edmund S. Morgan, and John A. Schutz, who were good enough to read and criticize chapters of the manuscript of a complete stranger to them. This book has profited immensely from the efforts of a succession of able editors: Frances Russell, Martha Dean, and Richard Plumer, who, though unsparing with the blue pencil, never harrassed me more than I deserved. Mary Margaret Birmingham typed the final draft of the manuscript under the pressures of a very tight schedule. Finally, but not least, my gratitude to Gerald Morris of the Maine Historical Society and his inspired team of readers, Charles Clark and James Leamon, who by their penetrating comments and suggestions did much to mold this work.

Gordon E. Kershaw
Frostburg, Maryland
October, 1974

Introduction

The casual summer visitor, attracted by a modest sign pointing the direction to the old Pownalborough Court House in Dresden, Maine, will follow a narrow country road for nearly a mile before turning off to a meadow rich in high grass. Beyond lies the courthouse, a severely plain but dignified clapboard structure rising for three full stories with its small-paned windows sparkling in the sun. Wandering inside the Georgian building, the curious will peer into the unassuming, sparsely furnished rooms, glance into the commodious second-story courtroom where John Adams once practiced law, poke into the stifling attic with its massive exposed beams, and perhaps even climb a narrow staircase to look out from the scuttle in the roof. From here he will see the Kennebec—at this point broad and slow-moving and within a few yards of the courthouse. In the history of central Maine, both the river and the Pownalborough Court House are symbols of the resources, vigor, and authority of the proprietors of the Kennebeck Purchase Company in the decades just before the American Revolution.

Speculative land companies were operating in nearly every British mainland colony in the eighteenth century. George Washington held shares in several such companies, as did Benjamin Franklin. In New York, investment groups schemed to gain control of the upper Hudson and the Mohawk Valley. For Virginians, there was the lure of the Ohio. In New England, the proprietors, usually merchants, speculated in the undeveloped lands of western Massachusetts, Connecticut, Vermont, New Hampshire, and Maine. Historians have provided several well-documented studies of such speculative land companies of colonial America, the best known of them the Susquehannah Company, a Connecticut-based organization which developed northern Pennsylvania, and the Ohio Company of Virginia. Surprisingly enough, although materials are readily available, historians have neglected to study the land companies of northern New England.

The purpose of this work is to inquire into the nature, leadership, and significance of perhaps the most powerful land company in northern New England—the Kennebeck Purchase Company. This enterprise was a decisive force because its proprietors were strategically entrenched in the economic, political, and religious spheres of colonial Massachusetts and were prepared to use their positions, and perhaps even issues of the approaching American Revolution, to corporate advantage. Ironically, the Revolution contributed to the permanent decline of Company fortunes.

The Kennebeck Purchase Company came into being in 1749, when an association of Boston merchant-speculators revived interest in an old Pilgrim grant on the Kennebec River in Maine. Organizing as "The Proprietors of the Kennebeck Purchase from the late Colony of New-Plymouth," they proceeded to develop their tract during the twenty-five years preceding the Revolution. As claimants to a patent encompassing approximately three thousand square miles, they were "great proprietors" indeed, functioning on the grand scale. They are not to be compared with the mere proprietors of New England townships, although their powers and rights before the law were substantially the same. Dazzled by the opportunity to engross large amounts of land, they pushed back the wilderness as they built two forts and a courthouse, planted a dozen towns, settled hundreds of families on the Kennebec, and created landed estates for themselves.

The proprietors operated almost as an independent force in Massachusetts politics during those years. They spent money freely, influenced the General Court, and intrigued with royal governors. They clashed wth John Wentworth, governor of New Hampshire and surveyor-general of the King's Woods, over ownership of the royal mast trees within their territory. They became embroiled in the religious conflict between Congregationalists and Anglicans that had been simmering in the colonies for decades. The Company frequently made bitter enemies, both on the great river and back in Boston, as the proprietors battled individual farmers, rival land companies, and the king's agents. They evicted settlers and foreclosed on householders as they extended their claims. Company lawyers were ever before the bar and often won their cases, thanks in part to proprietary influence in high places.

As the American Revolution approached, the proprietors struggled to maintain a united front in spite of divisions caused by party strife. By 1775, however, they represented every political shade between the extremes of Whig and Tory. Incorporation of towns began to lead to the establishment of self-government in many places. This, combined with the democratizing aspects of the Revolution and increasing lawlessness, began to erode proprietary control. After the battle of Lexington, the proprietors went their separate ways and Company operations halted. No longer a secure investment opportunity nor an impetus to frontier expansion, the Kennebeck Purchase Company began to fade into the background and was finally dissolved in 1816.

There are several major reasons for studying the history of the Kennebeck Purchase Company, 1749-1775. First, the quality of its leadership was extraordinary. The vivid, aggressive personalities of Dr. Silvester Gardiner, Company moderator; James Bowdoin, treasurer; and such shareholders as Thomas Hancock, Charles Apthorp, William Brattle, James Pitts, and William Bowdoin dominated the social, economic, and political arenas of their day. Indeed, the roles several of them played in the coming Revolution seem to have directed attention from their superlative entrepreneurial talents. Proprietors like Dr. Gardiner were of the stuff from which legends are made, and legendary they have remained on the Kennebec. Second, the Kennebeck Company merits a close examination because its records are unusually complete and shed new light on colonial economics. Successive Company clerks hoarded not only the records of proprietary meetings but also letter books, day books, waste books, pamphlets, and newspaper clippings. They kept copies of provincial laws, petitions, and Indian treaties, as well as every scrap of paper relating to corporate operations, no matter how insignificant. Even the first drafts and original envelopes of the polished versions of Company correspondence were preserved. Collections of deeds and depositions dating back to the 1660s are filed away with the original plan for a Company fort and the deerskin pouch used to carry proprietary documents. Correspondence of the Bowdoin, Gardiner, Vassall, Hancock, Goodwin, and Jeffries families, available elsewhere, and the John Wentworth letter books further round out land company activities and provide glimpses into the personal affairs of its proprietors. Records of the Pejepscot Company, rival of the Kennebeck propriety, expand the scope of a potentially narrow study. Finally, the decisions and actions of the Kennebeck proprietors have had an enduring influence upon the lives of Maine people. For this reason alone, the Company merits attention. Although most of its activities were motivated by vested interests of its proprietors, the Kennebeck Purchase Company transformed the river valley into a center of population and one of the most economically important regions of what is now the state of Maine. A study of this speculative land company and its enterprising proprietors is therefore basic to the understanding of the fundamental political interests, cultural patterns, and psychology of central Maine.

THE
KENNEBECK
PROPRIETORS

SEAL OF PROPRIETORS
KENNEBEC PURCHASE

I

The Lure Of The Valley

The Kennebec—winding its way for nearly one hundred and fifty miles from its origins in the depths of mighty Moosehead Lake—rushes onward, crashing over falls, at times moving sluggishly, ever changing as it flows majestically toward the seacoast, dividing before islands and filling inlets and harbors until it is finally lost in the waters of the Atlantic. The river already possessed a rich and varied past when, in 1749, an aggressive group of land speculators formed the Kennebeck Purchase Company and "Applyed themselves vigorously for the further settling [of] their Kennebeck Tract."[1] The proprietors soon learned that this could be a cruel river, bleak and icy in winter and monstrous in flood time, but one generous in its resources, its waters and tree-crowded shores abounding with fish and furs as well as timber for building and masts for the Royal Navy. As they began to develop its resources and to clear the wilderness, the proprietors became increasingly conscious of the poorly defined bounds of their valuable grant. With more at stake than just curiosity about the origins of their tract, they traced boundaries and accumulated evidence to strengthen their claims. The early history of the Maine river, interlaced with romance and legend, both fascinated and frustrated the Kennebeck proprietors, as it does present-day historians.

The great river valley had long been a land of enchantment. In 1604, Samuel de Champlain was so enthralled that he braved

stormy weather to sail among the coastal islands, and returned
the next year to explore the lower river. In 1607, Captain George
Popham entered the lower Kennebec, which the Indians then
called the Sagadahock. A member of Popham's expedition reported that " we Sailled up into this ryver 14 Leags and found ytt
to be a most gallant ryver very brod & of a good depth we never
had Lesse Wattr than 3 fetham when we had Least & abundance
of greatt fyshes in ytt Leaping above the Wattr on each Syd of us
as we Sailled."[2] The next month twenty men pushed farther up
the river, this time reaching the rapids that mark the present location of Augusta. The first night out, the explorers camped on a
small island, probably Cushnoc, which was remarkable for its
"good and sweett" grapes. They described being awakened by
"sartain Salvages Callinge unto us in broken inglyshe we
answered them aggain So for this time they dept [departed]."[3]
These natives were a branch of the Algonquin Indians.

The Norridgewocks or Kennebecs occupied the river from
Merrymeeting Bay near its mouth to Moosehead Lake far to the
north.[4] Their traditional center of government and culture was
Swan Island, an island nearly seven miles long dominating the
middle of the river a few miles above Merrymeeting Bay. When
the Europeans arrived in the early seventeenth century, Sachem
Kenebis, a powerful chieftain, ruled all the lands on both sides of
the river. Like other Indians of northern New England, the Kennebecs moved with the seasons, sheltered by conical huts of
birch bark or woven mats that could be easily dismantled as the
tribes temporarily abandoned semipermanent villages to take advantage of the resources of the moment. In the spring they
hunted game and feasted on salmon. In summer the Indians
planted corn and then moved to the seashore to harvest fresh oys-
ters, clams, and lobsters. In the fall they returned to the villages
to reap their crops and hunt. Here they remained for the winter,
drawing from stores of corn, game, and dried seafood. Each season held its own delight and usually its own sufficiency.[5] The idyl-
lic existence of the Kennebecs, a peaceful tribe, came to an end
soon after the appearance of the English in their valley.

The English settlers who began to invade the Kennebec in the
early 1600s slaughtered or drove away the game, built permanent
farmsteads, and repeatedly violated treaties they made with the
Indians. Thus, when the French and English came to blows in
America, it was natural for the Kennebecs to side with the more

sympathetic French; and this they often did, usually to their detriment. Indian villages were burned and tribes were scattered in the course of these wars. For a time, however, remnants of the tribes were held together through the efforts of Father Sebastian Rasle, a French Jesuit. The destruction of the Indian village of Norridgewock in 1724 by Massachusetts provincial forces broke the remaining Indian strength, for Father Rasle was killed during the attack. By the early 1700s, famine, disease, and continued warfare had cut the Maine Indian population, earlier estimated at nearly three thousand, to a few hundred. Only a handful lived in the lower areas of the Kennebec River. In 1726 Captain John Giles, released after many years of Indian captivity, estimated that there were only 289 warriors remaining in all of Maine, of which the Kennebecs numbered forty.[6] The Kennebec Indians, a mere handful, were no real threat to the English settlers who began cautiously to work their way up the river valley in the early eighteenth century.

As the Kennebeck proprietors searched out the boundaries of their patent, they located ancient landmarks named by the Indians, whose custom was to assign a special name for a part of a river rather than for an entire waterway. The lower river flowing into the Atlantic they called the Sagadahock. Directly above this lies a beautiful but lonesome section which they named the Kennebec, for it was the country of Kenebis, their native ruler. They also called it the Snake, because the seething appearance caused by the converging of several important rivers suggested the writhing of a serpent beneath the surface. Another Indian name for this bay area of the river was Quabacook, "the duck water place."[7] The name is singularly appropriate even today, as hunters are aware, for waterfowl in the region still feed upon a kind of wild rice which grows in the sand beds of the bay's center. The English called this body of water Merrymeeting Bay. It is connected to the Sagadahock by a narrow pass, the entrance to which is named the Chops because the strong currents there make it dangerous for navigation. Swan Island, home of the legendary Kenebis, lies a few miles above the Bay in the center of the river. Cabbosaconteag (Cobboseconte), "The place where sturgeon is found," is a name applied to a lake and a stream not far from the middle Kennebec. Teconnett, "a place to cross" (Waterville) is on the fall line. Caratunk, fifty miles farther up the river, is "a narrow strip of land between two rivers." It offers access to the Chaudiere River and passage to Canada.[8] These Indian place names, so literal in their translations, were of inestimable value to the proprietors in fixing many of their boundaries.

Several rivers that pour into Merrymeeting Bay were of similar significance. Greatest of these is the Androscoggin, which swings northward before flowing south to join the lower Kennebec. The smaller and unnavigable Cathance River assumed importance as the southern boundary of what became the proprietors' claim on the western side of the Kennebec. The Abacadasset, above the Cathance, was another useful landmark in locating that boundary. The Eastern River served a similar purpose to the northeast. It rises from a small pond nearly twenty miles away, flows past Swan Island, and enters the upper reaches of the Bay.[9] This river is navigable for some distance. Descriptive but prosaic place names, Sand Pond, Long Pond, and Muddy River, began to appear—sure indications that by this time the Englishman was beginning to have his say in designating important landmarks. Though the Englishman lacked the music of the Indian, he was capable of flights of fancy, as evidenced by his designations of Upper Hell and Purgatory.

The Kennebec Valley looks today much as it did nearly three hundred years ago, though the middle river, Swan Island to Augusta, is now the location of several quiet river towns founded in the years immediately preceding the American Revolution. Facing the west side of Swan Island is Richmond, site of an early fort and Indian trading post. On the east side of the river lies Dresden. Ascending the river, one passes on the east side the little town of Pittston and, on the west, Gardiner. Until the early 1900s, these two places were centers for lumbering and the ice industry. Ice was shipped to Baltimore, Savannah, New Orleans, and the West Indies.[10] Today there is some activity in lumbering, leather, and textiles along this part of the river, but the Federal and Greek Revival mansions along the bank suggest a greater past prosperity. Ahead lies Augusta, capital of the state, which had its beginnings in 1629 as the trading post of Cushnoc. Its furs saved the Plymouth Colony from financial ruin. Above this site lies the fall line, making only limited navigation possible. Here one blockhouse remains of old Fort Halifax (Winslow), which for many years marked the northern boundary of the frontier. Today it stands next to a bustling business intersection, but the river itself nearby is placid, tree-lined, and unmarked by signs of commerce.

The lands of the upper Kennebec were of strategic importance at the beginning of the French and Indian War, last of the historic conflicts in America between the two Old World rivals, France and England. It was from Fort Halifax that General John Winslow deployed his little army in 1755, searching for the enemy he believed secreted somewhere in the unknown forests ahead. Beyond present-day Skowhegan and up past Norridgewock Falls, the men marched, beyond Sandy River, on past Caratunk. Finally, slower now, they turned to the west fork of the Kennebec and reached their goal, the Great Carrying Place, five miles across. Here Winslow's militia halted, not caring to continue its pursuit or to trace the northern branch of the Kennebec to Moosehead, the legendary habitation of the fur-bearing animals so eagerly sought by the white man. From the Atlantic to Moosehead Lake—this was the region where the storied Kennebec flowed, where the eighteenth century proprietors hoped to extend their sway.

The history of the Kennebeck proprietors in the river valley begins with the patent conveyed to the Pilgrims by the Council for New England in 1629. The grant at Plymouth on which the Pilgrims had settled was small, and lacked sufficient resources and arable lands to support a population that had slowly climbed to three hundred by the end of a decade in the New World. In debt to English backers for nearly £1800,[11] William Bradford and his associates petitioned the Council for New England for a land grant on the Kennebec to the eastward. A foothold along this great river leading to the interior's fabled riches in furs proved a means for solving the colony's financial problems. The Pilgrims were latecomers among the fur traders in an industry, highly competitive and already over-exploited, which was soon to move westward. Nevertheless, they determined to "farm" the fur resources of the upper Kennebec to advantage. At least one early historian believed that the Pilgrims' original intention in coming to America had been to establish a factory (trading post or truck house), not to plant the colony that they were now trying to make self-sustaining by the augmentation of assets from another patent.[12] The Council for New England ceded them some carelessly delineated lands along the Kennebec, a patent which would remain controversial until long after the American Revolution.

The Pilgrims, already familiar with the area, had themselves selected these lands and had sent Isaac Allerton to England to act as their agent in securing them. Bradford's records show that Allerton had orders "to procure a patente for a fitt trading place in the river Kennebec."[13] The concession with which Allerton returned was the hoped-for tract along the Kennebec.

The deed Allerton delivered to the colonists was not an official royal charter, however, for it did not bear the mandatory Great Seal. Moreover, the land Allerton obtained was not well suited to its purpose. The Pilgrims, feeling that "it was so strait and ill-bounded,"[14] in 1630 petitioned the Council for New England for a second patent and received one. While its terms were more lavish than those of the first, they were also indefinite. Bradford and his associates, acting for the Plymouth Colony, were granted "all that Tract of Land or part of New England . . . Which lyeth Within or between and Extendeth itself from the Utmost Limits of Cobbiseconte, alias Comisseconte, Which Adjoineth to the River of Kennebeckike, towards the Western Ocean, and a Place called the Falls, at Neguamkike . . . and the Space of Fifteen English Miles on Each Side of the Said River Commonly Called Kennebeck that Lies Within the Said Limits, and bounds Eastward, Westward, Northward, or Southward."[15] The patent also included mineral and fishing rights within the area. This was a generous gift indeed, but one whose vagueness and reliance on uncertain boundaries would cause endless litigation for the eighteenth century proprietors of the Kennebeck Purchase Company.

The Bradford associates were probably not concerned with the positive identification of boundaries (which were likely well-known in their own day), but their primary purpose was not to settle the land but to make a profit from the fur trade and reduce the crushing debt of the Plymouth Colony. They immediately established a truck house at Cushnoc on the river, a decidedly convenient point, for it lay below the fall line where easy water transportation was assured, yet high enough up the river to attract the tribes of the interior for trading. The post at Cushnoc became a part of the burgeoning Pilgrim fur trade operation which eventually included truck houses at Aptuxcet (Bourne) on Cape Cod, several stations in southern New England, and even a branch on the distant Penobscot River in Maine.[16] For a time, Governor Bradford and his associates enjoyed a monopoly of the New England fur trade.[17]

Pilgrim success in fur trading was rapid but temporary. Their canny use of Indian wampum as a means of exchange, a secret they had learned from the Dutch as early as 1630,[18] gave them a fleeting advantage. It was several years before rival trading companies discovered a source of supply. The year 1636 seems to have been the peak year in the colony's fur trading venture. In that year, according to a journal entry made by William Bradford, "They sent [to England] in beaver 3366 pounds weight, and much of it coat beaver, which yielded 20. s. per pound, and some of it above; and of other skines 346 sould also at a good price."[19] Much of this cargo must have come from the Kennebec. But the New England fur trade began to decline the next year; and after 1640, no Pilgrim merchants engaged in the overseas export trade.[20] In spite of their profitable trading years, because of high expenses the Pilgrim debt to London merchants had only been reduced to £1200 by 1647.[21]

Several factors combined to force the Pilgrims into increasing financial embarrassment. The cost of truck house operations had multiplied; the Bradford group faced competition from one of their own apostate members, Isaac Allerton; and the Penobscot trading post had been looted by the French of several hundred pounds' worth of goods. In desperation, the Pilgrims decided that their faltering economy could be corrected by direct governmental control over the Kennebec tract, for that could eliminate competing trading companies, or at least regulate their actions. This control had been provided for in the 1629 patent,[22] but the prevailing Parliamentary rule in England had terminated the earlier powers granted the Council of Plymouth by King James I. It was thus necessary to petition the existing government to secure approval of the government control clause. Accordingly, in 1652, Edward Winslow, representing the Plymouth Colony in England, petitioned Oliver Cromwell's Parliament for a patent for the entire river as well as permission to form a government on the Kennebec. His grounds were that "not having the whole of the river under their grant and government, many excesses and wickednesses have been committed."[23] On March 8, 1652, the Parliamentary Committee for Foreign Affairs recommended that the Plymouth Colony be granted governing authority over the entire

Kennebec region for a probationary period of seven years.[24] The recommendation was approved by the Council of State in May. The Pilgrims immediately extended their domain over the river and began to act on violations of their jurisdiction.

To implement the new policy, the Plymouth General Court proceeded to establish a local government for the Kennebec area which included the heads of sixteen households then living along the river. Following their instructions, the settlers assembled at the home of Thomas Ashley of Merrymeeting Bay on May 15, 1654, to take an oath of allegiance to Plymouth. At this meeting the sixteen settlers chose Thomas Purchas to serve as their official representative to the Plymouth Council and a constable and a clerk.[25] Thus was launched the government that was to meet the needs of the inhabitants of the Kennebec for the next few years. Its brief existence held special significance for the later proprietors, as did an earlier incident of violence upon the river.

The trouble began in 1634 when John Hocking, an agent at Piscataqua Plantation for the Lord Say and Sele and Lord Brooke, highly influential Puritan leaders in England, attempted to violate the Pilgrims' decree against trading in their private preserve. John Howland, the Pilgrim commander at Cushnoc, ordered Hocking to sail downstream and sent his men to cut Hocking's ship cables. At this juncture Hocking shot Moses Talbot, a Plymouth Colony employee, and in turn was killed by one of the Pilgrims.[26] John Alden, an eyewitness aboard a nearby ship, was seized by the Puritans as a hostage and imprisoned at Boston to await the trial of Hocking's slayer, a trial which never materialized, as both the Puritans and the Pilgrims feared repercussions from England. Both sides suspected, as Governor John Winthrop pointed out, that the tragedy "would give occasion to the kind to send a general governor over."[27] The affair was therefore smoothed over and Alden was released, all parties agreeing that Hocking's death had been brought about by his own wayward actions.[28] Governor Bradford wrote at length of the episode in his *History*.

In the eighteenth century, the Kennebeck proprietors used the settlers' submission to the Plymouth government and the Hocking incident to advantage. They cited the former in detail in their "Brief State of the Kennebeck Proprietors Title to the Kennebeck Purchase," drawn up to support their position in a legal test with John Wentworth, Surveyor-General of the King's Woods, over ownership of mast trees in their territory. In this document they showed that one of the signers of the Pilgrim oath of allegiance, Thomas Parker, lived at Parker's Island; that another, John Richards, lived at Richards' Island; and that a third, Thomas Atkins, lived at Atkins' Bay.[29] Each of these places is within six miles of the mouth of the Kennebec River, so the Pilgrims' oath was helpful to the proprietors in proving that the Pilgrims, their predecessors, had at one time controlled the entire river valley.

The events of May 15, 1654, proved valuable in another way. In November, 1752, the inhabitants and proprietors of the Kennebeck Purchase tract petitioned the Massachusetts General Court to be set off as a county apart from York County, then the only administrative unit in Maine. They cited as a precedent the fact that the river settlers had been governed by Plymouth nearly a century before, and blandly hinted that their ownership of the old Pilgrim holding gave them special rights to the local government formerly enjoyed. The proprietors did not gain county status at that time, but did a few years later. Ironically, when they did, the benefits they received from the government were no more a stabilizing force in their tract than they had been for the Pilgrims a century before.

The new proprietors found the Hocking story useful because Hocking had invaded Pilgrim territory by sailing *above* Cushnoc. In doing so, he had established a precedent that the proprietors could cite in setting the upper limit of their patent. Unfortunately, the narrative implied that Hocking would have been safe had he remained *below* Cushnoc, thus invalidating the Kennebeck Company's claims that its patent extended to the sea. Later Company actions imply that the proprietors realized this implication and dropped the argument. Nevertheless, the proprietors' copy of the Hocking story, painstakingly transcribed from Bradford's *History,* was carefully filed away in Company papers.

The Pilgrims, benefiting from the establishment of local government on the Kennebec, bent their efforts to exploiting what was left of the fur trade. Their way was difficult, because the supply of fur-bearing animals declined and, with it, the fortunes of the trading post at Cushnoc. In 1655 moving to stimulate the traffic, the General Court of Plymouth leased the truck house to William Bradford, Thomas Prence, and Captain Thomas Willett for seven years at a rate of £35 per year.[30] The lease was to run until 1662, two years after the colony's seven-year trial period of government would lapse. The Pilgrims had become reconciled to a tiny but dependable income from their Kennebec holdings. Nevertheless, the fur trade continued to diminish, and its operation was further complicated by increasing Indian troubles. In 1659, acknowledging the financial difficulties of the fur "farmers," the General Court voted to return to the Bradford associates the £35 yearly rental fee for the Cushnoc truck house, and further provide that the rental for the next year, 1660, would be lowered to £10. This would be the last year of truck house operation, for the General Court also decreed that the colony would consider itself free to dispose of its tract on the Kennebec after November 1, 1660.[31]

The decision was a realistic one, prompted by changing conditions on the Kennebec, the unsettled Indian situation, and perhaps the likelihood of purchasers for the Kennebec lands. With the disappearance of the beaver from central Maine, the interests and occupations of some three hundred inhabitants scattered from the coast to Cushnoc had begun to diversify. The settlers began to concentrate on agriculture, cattle raising, fishing, and lumbering. For their part, the Plymouth leaders looked for a new way to meet their heavy obligations. On June 3, 1660, a committee of the Plymouth General Court presented a resolution that "if five hundred pounds sterling could be obtained, for the Countrey's interest there [on the Kennebec], it should be sold."[32] The General Court voted to accept the resolution. Its decision was well-timed; in a few years, increasing Indian raids on the frontier would have made it extremely difficult to find a buyer for the unpromising tract.

Prospective purchasers were not lacking. In 1661, four Boston merchants bought the whole territory for £400, £100 less than the asking price but still an attractive figure. The new partners were Antipas Boyes (Boyce), Edward Tyng, Thomas Brattle, and John Winslow, each a solid member of the town's rising merchant class. The indenture signed by the Plymouth General Court and the Boston buyers is dated October 27/November 5, 1661, the two dates suggesting that the two groups, one in Plymouth and the other in Boston, signed the deed at different times, or perhaps that both Old Style and New Style calendar dates were included. (See Appendix II.) The new owners, although equally wealthy, had quite different backgrounds.

John Winslow had arrived in America in 1623 and had joined his brother, Edward, a leader in the Plymouth Colony's operation of the Maine grant. John had also been active on behalf of the Colony, serving as agent on the river from 1651 to 1654.[33] In 1655 his business interests took him to Boston, where he remained until his death in 1674.[34] Here he must have met Tyng, Brattle, and Boyes and described the merits of the Plymouth tract to them. Only he of the four merchant purchasers could have had first-hand knowledge of the situation on the Kennebec River in 1661. His previous experience in Maine could have been put to good use, but he did not take an active part in the managing of the territory. Indeed, soon after purchasing his quarter interest, he closed most of it out. It is recorded that on July 3, 1668, Winslow sold 20% of the whole tract to Sir Thomas Temple, sometime governor of Nova Scotia, and John Joliff, a Boston merchant, for a paltry £50.[35] Whether this represented an actual loss is difficult to determine, considering the troubled state of Massachusetts' currency. Only a 5% interest then remained in the Winslow family.

Edward Tyng and his brother, William, emigrated to Massachusetts from London in 1636 and had become merchant traders in Boston and Dunstable. Edward, recognizing the growing importance of land and the opportunities provided by a broadened economic base, included land speculation and brewing in his business operations and soon accumulated a fortune. Edward and William Tyng founded an enduring local dynasty, for Tyng children later married into the Bradstreet, Wharton, Brattle, Dudley, Savage, Usher, and Gibbons families, thus establishing connections also with the Hutchinson, Shrimpton, Stoddard, Winthrop, Browne, and Corwin clans.[36]. Each of these families contributed substantially to the economic, social, political, and even religious leadership of the Bay Colony. Edward Tyng had already achieved political power by the time he bought into the Plymouth holding, for he had served as a selectman in Boston as early as 1648.[37] Later he began to take a more active role in Massachusetts politics and in 1675 was raised from the House to become a member of Governor Leverett's Council.[38]. Somehow he also found time to inspect his Kennebec River lands. He apparently liked what he saw in Maine; for during the 1680s, he held land at Falmouth (Portland), where his family lived and his son Edward was born in 1683.[39] In his willingness to cast his nets wide in search of profit, Edward Tyng typified a new entrepreneurial breed that had arisen in the American colonies. It was his interest in land speculation that led him to buy shares in a tract which was later to become the Kennebeck Purchase Company. His judicious investment in the Maine patent foreshadowed the interests of the great land speculators of the eighteenth century.

Captain Thomas Brattle, founder of the Old South Church (Third Church) in Boston, had married a daughter of William Tyng, perhaps the reason he now joined Edward in the Plymouth purchase. One of the Brattle children, another William, became a noted preacher. Other children contributed to the dynasty begun by Edward and William Tyng by marrying into the Oliver, Mico, and Winthrop families.[40] Captain Brattle, like Edward Tyng, became prominent in Boston political circles, serving as selectman from 1675 until 1683.[41] When he died in 1683, his estate was valued at £7,227.16.10 and reckoned to be one of the largest of the period.[42] His family continued to be influential in Massachusetts until the start of the American Revolution.

Antipas Boyes took little interest in developing his lands in Maine, possibly because he also invested in lands at Dover, New Hampshire, with Valentine Hill, his brother-in-law, the same year that he bought into the old Plymouth patent. When he died in 1669, he left his entire estate of £1,708.10.3 to his "only sonn and beloved Antipas Boyse."[43] The son took no part in furthering his father's landed interests and soon disappeared from the Boston scene, dying in Barbados, a bachelor. On August 3, 1719, the *Boston News-Letter* advertised for heirs who might be of closer blood relationship than Captain Nathaniel Hill of Oyster River Parish at Dover, New Hampshire, the proposed administrator of the estate of Antipas Boyes, Jr.[44] Two heirs, Antipas and Samuel Marshall, perhaps cousins of Antipas Boyes, appeared, and in due time succeeded to ownership of one-fourth of the Plymouth tract.[45] During the next thirty years, the Marshalls and their heirs sold off nearly all of their share. Nevertheless, like other descendants of the purchasers of 1661, they would continue to exercise an influence over development of the patent.

The four new owners of the Plymouth Colony patent and their descendants or assigns can be properly termed "proprietors." During the colonial period in New England, the term was applied on several levels. An individual might be the proprietor of a farm, a business, a township, or a large initially undeveloped but well-defined land area. Land proprietors recognized by the colonial legislature were empowered to survey their holdings, lay out townships and individual lots, and make grants to new settlers, imposing any conditions on the grants which were mutually acceptable. Until all the lands were granted and a conventional town government established, the proprietors' word was law. Even after the town meeting system was introduced, they could subtly control town affairs through such devices as mortgages and mill rights.[46] Proprietors of large land companies, such as that purchased from the Plymouth Colony, differed from proprietors of a new township only in that the magnitude of ownership, domination, and expense involved was greater. Thus for the new partners, land proprietorship carried both prestige and an opportunity to profit from their investment.

The partners would gain prestige from their new status as extensive landowners as well as from their authority. The tradition that merchants who invested in land could pave a pathway to gentility was well established in the British Isles, and was spreading in the American colonies, where the acquisition of large estates was much easier. Many New England merchants were engaged in remunerative but highly speculative and hazardous commerce and wished to reinvest their profits. Relatively few types of investment were open to them, however, and banks did not exist. Surplus silver coins could be melted down and converted into useful household plate, but such articles did not bring an income. Rather than sink all their gains back into shipping, which would seem to be tempting fate, they turned to investments in land. The land would endure, regardless of the hazards of Indian wars, and it would rapidly rise in value once developed. To the four partners, the risk of speculation in Maine lands must have seemed little greater, if any, than in shipping. They could also have been attracted by the prospect of becoming members of the landed gentry, their origins in trade thus soon forgotten.[47]

In any case, the purchase of wilderness lands along the Kennebec must have seemed a wise investment to the affluent Boston merchants. The fur trade was dwindling rapidly, it is true, but farm lands would appreciate as new settlers arrived on the river. Of more importance than rising land values, however, were the immediate profits that could be made in marketing timber and in building shipyards. Mast trees were also a potential source of in-

come, for the Royal Navy was aware that choice New Hampshire pines were dwindling and was already interested in Maine's
tall trees.[48] It was evident that Maine would soon develop a flour-
ishing mast industry. Although the Boston investors were primarily interested in long-term profits, they turned to each of these
sources of income to make their project self-sustaining during its
development.

The new proprietors began by salvaging what they could of
the fur trade. Early records reveal that the year after the purchase "the said Boyes, Tyng, Brattle, and Winslow, Build [Built] a
Fortification at Mousequite, to Supply the Indians, and were concerned in a considerable trade at Arrowsic, which is Five Miles
above the Mouth of Kennebeck River at the Sea."[49] Unlike the Pilgrims, the new owners were moving closer to the sea in their
search for furs. By doing so they might tap the catches of the
eastern tribes. They must have been no more successful at managing a truck house than their predecessors had been, for in 1669
they leased the trading post, but not the entire tract as had the Pilgrims, to the partnership of Naylor and Walker for four years at
£60 a year.[50] The terms indicated that the proprietors were more
skillful at bargaining than the Pilgrims had been. Disregarding
inflationary trends, if the contract was carried to completion under the proprietors' terms, they made a return on their investment of more than half the purchase price within the four-year
period alone. This must have been augmented by additional income from other lands within their purchase. Any plans they had
for further exploitation, however, were halted by the beginning
of King Philip's War in New England in 1675.

Within a year, the Maine frontier was under attack. As all the
Kennebec River settlements were wiped out, those owners of the
former Plymouth tract lost all control of their lands. They were
fortunate. Other traders on the river lost their lives, as did Captain Lake of Clark and Lake, a Boston-based partnership whose
fort on Arrowsic Island at the mouth of the Kennebec was taken
by surprise. Captain Lake, the father-in-law of the Reverend Increase Mather of Boston, had little opportunity to defend himself
in the sudden attack. His friend, Sylvanus Davis, found refuge
on a nearby island.[51] With the loss of the Kennebec River line,
the frontier retreated southward to Falmouth, where it held
temporarily.

Here in 1690, at Fort Loyal, Captain Edward Tyng for a short time tried to hold off the Indians, who were now allies of the French. Tyng may have unintentionally brought on the major Indian attack that led to the fall of the fort, for he had given the order to move some captives to Boston. This move was bitterly resented by the Indians, who swore revenge. Probably because he recognized that conditions at Falmouth were becoming precarious, Tyng sailed back to Boston with his family and other settlers. The durable Captain Sylvanus Davis, who had already survived the sacking of one fort, now took command. Tyng's defection was well-timed.[52] On May 20, after five days of steady attack, the fort fell.[53] Most of the garrison was slaughtered; Captain Davis and the survivors were carried as prisoners to Quebec, where the captain was ransomed in October, 1690.[54] After the capture of Fort Loyal, the towns of Berwick, Wells, and York in the south were the only outposts remaining in Maine, and these were often under attack. The proprietors were now completely isolated from their Kennebeck tract, where weeds grew up in the ruins of their former truck houses and farmsteads. For many years to come it would be impossible to benefit from the proprietary holding.

During those years, discouraging though conditions were, speculators showed a mild interest in the Maine tract. Future development would depend entirely on British success in military operations against the French. For the time being, inaccessible land went begging at any price in many areas of northern New England. This was true of the proprietary lands on the Kennebec, but nevertheless a limited trading in shares went on. The value of the shares fluctuated, apparently reflecting frontier conditions of the moment. The four portions purchased by Tyng, Brattle, Boyes, and Winslow were splintered repeatedly by purchase or inheritance. Low prices may have indicated forced sales or near gifts as well as unstable frontier conditions, however. Amounts received in the transfers did rise somewhat over the years, though probably not because conditions stabilized. The rise seems best explained by the galloping inflation that afflicted Massachusetts during the early decades of the 1700s.[55] Thus it is hard to judge the real value of such sales as those made by Martha Balstone (Boylston) and the Marshall family, both of Boston.

On December 3, 1729, Mrs. Balston, a widow and the daughter of John Joliff, who with Sir Thomas Temple had earlier bought out the Winslow share, sold extensive lands to James Bowdoin I, a Boston merchant. The land included 1000 acres on the Kennebunk River in southern Maine near Wells, "And also my one Half of the fifth part of the Plymouth Purchase so called . . . ."[56] The total purchase price was only £50. Because the Kennebunk River lands were conveniently located for immediate use, one may conclude that the 1/10th interest in the old Plymouth tract was thrown in as an inducement.

In contrast, in 1735, just six years later, members of the Marshall family, owners of most of the old Boyes share, sold Phineas Jones of Boston "seven eighth Parts of one eighth Part" of the Kennebeck lands for £254.[57] This figure would put a full value on the tract in excess of £2323 in inflated provincial currency. Jones was the surveyor who in 1731 had been employed by the scattered proprietors to begin mapping their holdings.[58] This surveying, suggestive of developmental plans to come, may have raised the going rate. The price must have been somewhat in line with real values, for Jones, more aware of the potential of these lands than the average proprietor, would not have bought in ignorance. But prices were relative. Maine farmland, even in more settled areas, sold at much lower rates than in Massachusetts. As land was worth only what one could get for it and prices fluctuated widely, the descendants of the Brattles and Tyngs apparently bought and sold their shares for the most part for the meager profit of the moment.

After the turn of the eighteenth century, improved prospects for peace led to a stirring of corporate activity among land companies whose aspirations often competed with those of the New Plymouth Company, the name informally applied to descendants of the four original purchasers of 1661. Most of these companies held patents from the Council for New England, which had issued nearly two dozen in addition to the Plymouth Colony grant of 1629. A few holdings had been created by purchases from the Indians. The most important of these companies was the Pejepscot Company, whose activities were centered at the mouth of the Kennebec. The Pejepscot patent, originally granted to Thomas Purchas and George Way by the Council, and later enlarged by Indian deeds, was acquired in the 1680s by the ambitious Richard Wharton, a titan among Boston merchants of his day. With his death in 1689, coincident with the beginning of King William's War, a war characterized by the fiercest of frontier fighting, interest in this land company declined. In 1714, the year following the treaty with France ending Queen Anne's War, Wharton's patent fell into the hands of eight influential merchants who organized as the Company of Pejepscot Proprietors. These entrepreneurs were Thomas Hutchinson, father of the future royal governor of Massachusetts; John Wentworth, the later lieutenant governor of New Hampshire and progenitor of two royal governors; John Watts; David Jeffries, father of the later Kennebeck Company proprietor of the same name; Adam Winthrop; Stephen Minot; Oliver Noyes; and John Rusk.[59] The Pejepscot proprietors had every intention of developing their patent and employed Joseph Heath to survey the lower Kennebec River.

Upon the completion of the survey in 1719, these proprietors claimed land on both sides of the river as far up as the conjunction of Cobboseconte Stream above Swan Island. In the same year, they reinforced their position by building Fort Richmond on their northern boundary opposite Swan Island.[60] This stronghold was conveniently garrisoned and maintained by Provincial forces as an encouragement and protection to new settlers. By their timely action, the Pejepscot proprietors had preempted lands eventually to be claimed by the New Plymouth Company. After building the fort, the Pejepscot proprietors proceeded to establish the towns of Brunswick and Topsham on the nearby Androscoggin River. The settlement of these towns was expensive and, because of occasional Indian attacks, extremely hazardous.[61] The poorly organized New Plymouth proprietors looked on helplessly, attempting neither to emulate the Pejepscot Company nor to contest its claims.

The time was not yet ripe for New Plymouth Company expansion. Any settlements of that day would have placed the company in conflict with the Pejepscot proprietors unless they had been located up the river beyond Fort Richmond, still uncontested Indian territory. Precarious frontier conditions made it unlikely that settlers could be induced to move into the region, however attractive the lands. The New Plymouth proprietors, disorganized as a group and singularly unambitious men anyway, neither moved against the Pejepscot Company nor improved their own lands. The inheritances of the children and grandchildren of the land speculators of 1661 remained in this undeveloped state for the first four decades of the eighteenth century. During that period, Brunswick and Topsham grew slowly, other towns such as Georgetown and Woolwich began to appear near the mouth of the Kennebec, and their populations gradually rose. When the New Plymouth proprietors did regain interest, it was not due to the initiative of a Tyng or a Brattle. Samuel Goodwin, a new minor proprietor of humble background, struck by the economic opportunities awaiting on the river more than by its romantic past, spurred the proprietors to action.

NOTES

CHAPTER I

1 "A brief State of the Kennebeck Proprietors' Title to the Kennebeck Purchase from the late Colony of New Plymouth," c. 1771, Kennebeck Purchase Papers, Letter Book I, 63, Maine Historical Society, Portland, Me., hereafter cited as K.P.P.

2 Henry O. Thayer, ed., *The Sagadahock Colony, Comprising the Relation of a Voyage into New England* (Portland, Me., 1892), 65.

3 *Ibid.*, 75.

4 Charles E. Allen, *History of Dresden* (Copyright by Bertram E. Packard, Augusta, Me., 1931), 21.

5 Charles C. Willoughby, *Antiquities of the New England Indians* (Cambridge, Mass., 1935), 276-297.

6 Stanwood C. Gilman and Margaret C. Gilman, *Land of the Kennebec* (Boston, Mass., 1966), 71.

7 *Ibid.*, 13.

8 John W. Hanson, *History of Gardiner, Pittston, and West Gardiner* (Gardiner, Me., 1852), 20-21.

9 James Sullivan, *History of the District of Maine* (Boston, 1795), 30.

10 Jennie G. Everson, *Tidewater Ice of the Kennebec River* (Freeport, Me., 1970), 122-123.

11 Bernard Bailyn, *The New England Merchants in the Seventeenth Century* (Cambridge, Mass., 1955), 23.

12 Thomas Hutchinson, *The History of the Colony and Province of Massachusetts-Bay,* ed. Lawrence S. Mayo (Cambridge, Mass., 1936), II, 359. Hutchinson based his view on the belief that before leaving England the Pilgrims "had no notion of cultivating any more ground than would afford their own necessary provisions, but proposed that their chief secular employment should be commerce with the natives . . . ."

13 William Bradford, *Of Plymouth Plantation,* ed. Samuel E. Morison (New York, 1970), 193.

14 *Ibid.,* 101-102.

15 Plymouth (Kennebeck) Company Forms for a Grant, Jan. 24, 1753, K.P.P., Records, I, 172-182. This description of the original grant from the Council for New England was cited as authority in grants of the Kennebeck Purchase Company to its proprietors and also in individual grants made to small tract holders, and appears many times in Company records. The original patent, still preserved in its container, is now in the Registry of Deeds at Plymouth, Mass. The full terms of the grant can be found in the *Farnham Papers, Maine Historical Society Publication,* I, 108-116. See also Appendix I.

16 George D. Langdon, Jr., *Pilgrim Colony: A History of New Plymouth* (New Haven, 1966), 36.

17 *Ibid.,* 36; 142.

18 Bradford, *Of Plymouth Plantation,* 263.

19 *Ibid.,* 268.

20 Bailyn, *New England Merchants,* 24.

21 *Ibid.,* 25.

22 *A Patent for Plymouth in New-England, To which is annexed Extracts from the Records of that Colony, &c.* (Boston, 1751), 5. This pamphlet of 20 pp. was printed by the Kennebeck Purchase Company. The pertinent passage authorized Bradford and his associates to "frame and make Orders, Ordinances and Constitutions as well as for the better Government of their Affairs here . . . provided that the said

Laws and Orders be not repugnant to the Laws of England,
or the Frame of Government by the said President and Council [for New England] hereafter to be established."

23 Order of the Council of State, Mar. 8, 1652, *Calendar of
State Papers, Colonial Series, America and the West Indies,
1574-1660* (London, 1860), XI, 376.

24 Order of the Council of State, Mar. 16, 1653, *Calendar of
State Papers, Colonial Series, America and the West Indies,
1574-1660* (London, 1860), XII, 401.

25 Nathaniel B. Shurtleff and David Pulsifer, eds., *Records of
the Colony of New Plymouth* (Boston, 1855-1860), III, 44-45.
The oath of office was administered by Thomas Prence of the
Plymouth government. Prence had been charged with the following instructions by the General Court:

"1.   That upon theire appearance att his summons, hee tender and require them to take the oath of fidelitie for the
State of England and this present government of New Plymouth.

2.   That hee acquaint them with the body of laws of this government; our intention being not to expect theire strict ob-
servance of every thing peculiare to ourselves, but considering the distance of the place, we doe allow them libertie to
make choise of such to bee assistant to our commissioner
as hee shall approve of for the making of such further orders
wee may best conduce to their welfare.

3.   That none bee allowed for inhabitants theire but such as
will take the oath of fidellitie as above said.

4.   That such persons onely as have taken the said oath of
fidellitie shall acte in the choise of such as may be assistant
to our commissioner as aforesaid in making and executing
such orders as may be thought fitt to bee established amongst them; and the said assistants to acte as if they were actually freemen for the present, untill further orders bee tak-
en."

26 Bradford, *Of Plymouth Plantation*, 263.

27 Henry S. Burrage, *The Beginnings of Colonial Maine, 1602-
1658* (Portland, Me., 1914), 248.

28 Bradford, *Of Plymouth Plantation*, 267-268.

29 See Note 1.

30 Shurtleff and Pulsifer, eds., *Records of the Colony of New Plymouth*, III, 95-96. An inventory of the period signed by Prence, Thomas Southward, and William Davis shows that in 1658 the group had a cash balance of £1135.3.11. "Inventory of the Estate att Cushnock & Neumkeek & att Boston, being in partnership, between Mr. Tho. Prence & Co. in equall parts." Winslow Papers (1638-1759), Mass. Hist. Soc., hereafter cited as M.H.S.

31 Shurtleff and Pulsifer, eds., *Records of the Colony of New Plymouth*, III, 170-171.

32 *Ibid.*, 194.

33 George F. Willison, *Saints and Strangers* (New York, 1945), 446.

34 *Ibid.*, Winslow's descendants remained active in Mass. history until the American Revolution. His namesake, Gen. John Winslow, fought at Louisburg in 1745. He built Ft. Halifax in 1754 and, with James Otis and others, became a proprietor of the town of Winslow in the Kennebeck Purchase.

35 *York Deeds*, X, Fol. 136.

36 Bailyn, *New England Merchants*, 135-137.

37 Justin Winsor, ed., *The Memorial History of Boston, 1630-1880, (Including Suffolk County, Massachusetts)* (Boston, 1880), I, 56.

38 *Ibid.*, 312.

39 William Goold, *Portland in the Past* (Portland, Me., 1886), 247.

40 Winsor, ed., *Memorial History of Boston*, I, 580.

41 *Ibid.*, 562.

42 James North, *History of Augusta* (Augusta, Me., 1870), 282.

43 *Ibid.*

44 *New England Historical and Genealogical Register*, XLI, 92.

45 North, *History of Augusta*, 282.

46 Roy H. Akagi, *The Town Proprietors of the New England Colonies* (Philadelphia, 1924), 3.

47 Bailyn, *New England Merchants,* 102-103.

48 Joseph J. Malone, *Pine Trees and Politics: The Naval Stores and Forest Policy in Colonial New England, 1691-1775* (Seattle, 1964), 3; 10.

49 "A Brief State . . . ," K.P.P., Letter Book I, 61. The location of Mousequite is uncertain; the site at Arrowsic was cited by the later proprietors as proof that Boyes and his associates, like the Pilgrims, controlled the Kennebec River down to the sea. The phrase, "concerned in a considerable trade," however, seems to imply that the new proprietors cooperated in a trading operation with other fur companies, such as Clark and Lake, as the Pilgrims had done earlier.

50 "The State of the Case Relating to the Kennebeck Propriety," Pejepscot Papers, Records, IV, 389, Maine Historical Society, Portland, Me., hereafter cited as P.P. The Kennebeck Purchase Company and its rival, the Pejepscot Company, carried on a pamphlet war for several years, during which time each company tried to assemble as complete a history of its rival's activities as possible.

51 Goold, *Portland in the Past,* 122.

52 Robert E. Moody, *The Maine Frontier, 1607-1763* (unpubl. Ph.D. diss. Yale University, 1933), 231-232.

53 Goold, *Portland in the Past,* 247.

54 *Ibid.,* 148-150.

55 Joseph B. Felt, *An Historical Account of Massachusetts Currency* (Boston, 1839), 83. As an example, Provincial paper money valued at 8 shillings per ounce of silver in 1710 depreciated to 17 shillings per ounce by 1727. Widows, orphans, clergymen, and others living on fixed incomes suffered much hardship, as did creditors generally.

56 Deed of Martha Balstone to James Bowdoin, Dec. 3, 1729, *York Deeds,* XIII, Fol. 147.

57 Deed of Samuel Marshall *et al.* to Phineas Jones, Sept. 3, 1735, *York Deeds,* XVII, Fol. 204.

58 "Claim of the Company exhibited to the Commissioners," c. 1800, K.P.P., Records, V. 31.

59 Akagi, *Town Proprietors,* 245-246. Leading Pejepscot pro-

prietors of the next generation included Belcher Noyes, Benning Wentworth, and Issac Royall.

60 North, *Augusta,* 18-19.

61 George A. Wheeler, *History of Brunswick, Topsham, and Harpswell, Maine* (Boston, 1878), 37. Brunswick, founded by the Pejepscot proprietors in 1717, was nearly wiped out in 1722 during Lovewell's War. The town was resettled in 1730.

II

Opportunities On The Frontier

The old Plymouth patent setting forth the "meets and bounds" of the Kennebec River tract had mysteriously disappeared several decades before Samuel Goodwin of Charlestown became intrigued by the history and potential of a tiny gift from his father, only one-half of his father's purchase of one-third of one-quarter share from Elizabeth Franklin in 1721.[1] Goodwin knew that a thorough search for the patent had been conducted in 1727, when the document had been needed to help resolve the settlement of a boundary dispute between Massachusetts and Rhode Island, and again in 1733 and 1739.[2] Continuing the search in 1741 must have seemed a formidable task as Goodwin began to follow every clue. If this now almost legendary patent could be found, it might provide the legal basis and inspiration for the revitalization of the New Plymouth Company and the development of its holdings.

Samuel Goodwin was not alone in his interest in the missing patent. It is likely that the state of the dormant patent and ways to reactivate it were discussed when the shareholders of the New Plymouth Company living in Boston met during a casual promenade across the Common, after the Thursday Lecture, or on the bustling wharves. The latest French war, low market prices for frontier lands, difficulties in procuring settlers, and the perplexing problem of shipping timber from the wilderness were probably among their excuses for inaction, but the missing patent was also mentioned. Without Goodwin's persistence, it might never have come to light.

Goodwin's search led him to Perez Bradford, a sometime resident of Falmouth and North Yarmouth in Maine and, in 1744, a member of the Massachusetts House for Swansea. This descendant of the Pilgrims had the answer. Bradford had found the old parchment in the possession of Samuel Welles, who had obtained it while serving as a commissioner in settling the old Plymouth Colony boundary with Rhode Island in 1741. According to legend, the patent was given to Welles by an old lady who had hidden it in her home, hoping that it would eventually be ransomed at a great price.[3] Welles only explained that it had been "designedly concealed."[4] This was all the proprietors ever learned, as they explained in a letter written in 1752 to Paschal Nelson, a shareholder living in England: "[It] was stole about forty years ago and but lately found, at Newport on Rod island but by whom it was Carried away Whether by Proprietors of Indian deeds or Others we know not."[5] In spite of his sworn deposition, there are some indications that Welles himself may have hidden the patent for his own purposes. The discovery created a flurry among New Plymouth Company proprietors; all must have been as excited as Goodwin was.

Samuel Goodwin's good luck in laying his hands on the patent coincided with the most favorable conditions for Maine development that had prevailed for several generations. In 1748, British and French representatives had signed the Treaty of Aix-la-Chapelle, inaugurating an uneasy peace that would last until 1754. The Indians beyond Maine's frontier, temporarily deserted by their French allies, were quiescent. Goodwin was now joined by Captain Robert Temple, an Irish-born nephew of Sir Thomas Temple, in his efforts to galvanize the other proprietors into action. As a consequence, the New Plymouth Company came alive in 1749. The course of the new land company did not run smooth, but after the initial problems of reorganization, incorporation, and long-range planning were solved, the proprietors were able to embark upon a highly successful period of corporate activity which, by 1775, had made several men rich and others well-to-do. Much of the Company's achievement was due to the enterprise of the new leaders.

The second-generation descendants of the Winslows, Brattles, and Tyngs now consisted of ministers, old ladies, widows, orphans, and businessmen largely occupied with interests other than the New Plymouth Company and Samuel Goodwin's vision for it. New faces, such as Captain Robert Temple, showed more promise for molding an enterprising proprietary board and developing company policy. In the early 1720s, Temple, then a proprietor in the Pejepscot Company, had tried to settle a colony of Scotch-Irish near present-day Bath. He had failed and, soon after, closed out his Pejepscot share. Inspired by Goodwin's imagination and curiosity, he sought support that would ensure the success of a second land venture.

William Lithgow, Provincial commander of Fort Richmond, later recalled that "being in Company with old Robert Temple, Esq., and Major [Arthur] Noble, at Temple's House, Temple told us that he was concerned in an old Patent, by virtue of which he and Four or Five more Gentlemen were entitled to a Tract of Land lying between Nee-quam-kee and Caw-besse-con-teague . . . Temple told them he should be glad to have Three or Four more substantial partners to make the Number Seven or Eight good men."[6] By 1751, Temple had encouraged Dr. Silvester Gardiner, James Bowdoin, Benjamin Hallowell, Thomas Hancock, Charles Apthorp, and James Pitts to take active roles in Company expansion. These ambitious personalities formed the nucleus of a proprietary board which formulated an aggressive, comprehensive Company policy. The older, less venturesome shareholders, unwilling or unable to underwrite corporate expenses and not interested in radical schemes, dropped out of the Company. Some of them sold their shares, and others merely failed to pay proprietary assessments. As Massachusetts law prescribed, these shares were sold at public auction, often at very low prices because of an absence of interested buyers. This indication of public distrust worked to the advantage of the new Company leaders, for they were able to buy additional rights at low prices. As Goodwin, Temple, and associates set about reactivating the Company, they closely followed the letter of the law.

The activities of speculative land companies had been regulated to some extent by the Massachusetts General Court since 1698.[7] In 1713, the General Court, in an "act directing how proprietors of lands lying in Common may be called," had decreed that five proprietors had the power to apply to a justice of the peace for a warrant to hold a company meeting, provided that sufficient public notice was given two weeks in advance. At such a meeting the proprietors could choose a moderator, treasurer, clerk, and a standing committee and vote any action deemed necessary to develop their lands.[8] In 1749, Temple and his fellow associates called for a proprietors' meeting as the act directed.[9]

When the initial meeting was held on September 21, 1749, at three o'clock, at the Royal Exchange Tavern in Boston, with nine proprietors or their attorneys in attendance, the enabling warrant followed a conventional pattern. It empowered those present to "choose a Clerk and Committee or to do anything that the major part of the . . . Proprietors shall think necessary in order to settle or divide the . . . tract of land."[10] This brief statement left the Company free to transact almost any kind of business. The first meeting was repeatedly adjourned in an effort to complete an agenda for action. When its business was finished nearly a year later, a new warrant was called for, and new officers were elected. At the meeting on September 21, however, the proprietors did manage to agree on Edward Winslow for moderator and Joseph Gooch for clerk. But Winslow's share in the Company was small and his interest fleeting. Gooch was only acting as an attorney for an absent shareholder. It was not surprising, then, that in 1752 when the "new breed" of proprietors went to work, these first two officeholders were not in evidence. Gooch resigned at the second meeting, and Winslow dropped out of the Company late in 1751. Their replacements were abler men with grander plans, and within a year, the newly reorganized land company was a going concern.

Those first nine active proprietors did set an important precedent for the new leaders, for they commenced operations by hiring a skillful lawyer to determine the limits of the Company lands and to initiate lawsuits against squatters and competitors. The Company also began to survey the lands to prepare the way for laying out townships. On December 19, 1749, Benjamin Prat was hired as legal counsel.[11] He would prove to be only the first in a long time of eminent Company lawyers, which would include Robert Auchmuty, James Otis, Jr., and John Adams. Prat's appointment was soon followed by the selection of a committee to "Treet with and Examine the Deeds and Claims of the Pejepscot Company and with all other Claims that is within the . . . propriete."[12] This was the basis on which the Company proceeded in 1750.

Samuel Goodwin, Gooch's replacement as clerk, was delegated to secure the allegiance of settlers of coastal towns such as Brunswick, Woolwich, and Georgetown. In return, the settlers were to be given Company quitclaims for lands long in their possession. Accordingly, Goodwin was the first of the proprietors to move to the Kennebec to expedite Company policies. To rivals of the New Plymouth Company, he soon became notorious for his threatening, cajoling, and coercing of local farmers. The Pejepscot proprietors immediately opposed him, charging that he was intimidating their grantees. In response to this threat, for a time the New Plymouth proprietors held back and canceled projected surveys within lands claimed by the Pejepscot propriety.[13] Eventually, however, the proprietors became bolder and passed new resolutions that called for surveying the whole area of the patent as they interpreted it. Although they were harsh and uncompromising and used the courts to their own advantage, the proprietors tried to stay within the limits of the law.

Accordingly, when a new Massachusetts law of 1752 made incorporation possible for speculative land companies, the Plymouth proprietors were quick to incorporate. At the same time, they adopted an official title for their company. Before this, it appears to have been referred to carelessly as the Plymouth Company, or the New Plymouth Company. This title led to confusion with the earlier Plymouth Colony, though it had been useful in preserving the continuity and authority which stemmed from the old Plymouth Colony patent. In June, 1753, combining the new with the old, the shareholders incorporated their land company under the official designation of "The Proprietors of the Kennebeck Purchase from the late Colony of New Plymouth."[14] This title was valuable in a legal sense, for it described the Company's pedigree. It proved cumbersome for most purposes, however, so "Plymouth Company," "Kennebeck Company," and "Kennebeck Purchase Company" were more often used.[15]

Ambitious for their Company and proud of its early historical associations, the Kennebeck proprietors soon created their own official seal. The design, cut by Thomas Johnston, an engraver and painter, is described in Company records as "An Anker with a Cod Fish, across the same."[16] Around this design is the Latin inscription, *Nec Frustra, Dedit Rex* (The King Never Gave in Vain), an obvious reference to the original grant from King James I to the Council for New England, which in turn had granted the patent of 1629 to the Pilgrims. The inscription also suggests that the revived company was fulfilling its expectations. In 1753, this was more optimistic than truthful—an optimism which would do much to make the motto a prophecy during the years of Company expansion. Little could be done, however, until the proprietors determined an exact ratio for their shares. Once this was established, each member would receive lands and Company assessments in correct proportion to his investment.

In April, 1754, the Kennebeck proprietors voted that "one Twenty fourth part of the Kennebeck purchase from the late Colony of New Plymouth shall hereafter be understood to be One full Share of said purchase."[17] It was necessary to go further than this, however, for shares had been splintered by sale and inheritance. Recognizing that it was imperative to calculate the individual proprietary holdings in *fractions* of shares, they determined that 192nds was the most convenient unit, with 8/192nds representing a full share. Some of the great proprietors owned several full shares. They continued to buy, sell, and will their proportions, so it is difficult to determine just how large a holding a proprietor owned at a given moment. There is information available for 1764. In that year, Silvester Gardiner, Benjamin Hallowell, Thomas Hancock, James Bowdoin, William Bowdoin, and James Pitts each owned a double share.[18] The heirs of Sir Thomas Temple then collectively owned 13/192nds. Florentius Vassall, Charles Ward Apthorp, John Jones, and Samuel Goodwin each owned a share, and the children of Mary (Bowdoin) Bayard owned one share together. These great proprietors were trailed by a succession of small ones. Some, such as William Brattle, formerly a multiple shareholder, then owned as little as 1/192nd. The size of a proprietor's share had much to do with his importance in the Company.

During twenty-five years of corporate activity, the various proprietary offices were held by many shareholders, but not as the result of democratic elections.[19] Proprietors, like modern-day investors, voted in proportion to the shares they held; the smallest shareholders voted mere fractions, thus having little voice in Company business. It became the unwritten rule that moderator, treasurer, and members of the Standing Committee would be chosen from among the large shareholders, and the position of Company clerk from among the small investors. Eventually, however, the Company decided to hire an outsider for clerk, probably because a disinterested person would be easier to control than even a small proprietor. With little voice in policy-making, the small proprietors were often negligent in attending meetings. They did generally respond to calls to meetings where land divisions were to take place, for personal interests were then at stake. Nevertheless, innumerable meetings were adjourned for lack of a quorum. This was especially true of gatherings called in the spring, when travel was difficult, and during the summer months, when the wealthy proprietors fled the hot city to take refuge at their country estates.

During periods of inaction, the proprietors might not meet for several months. When the agenda was long and important or decisions had to be made hurriedly, meetings might be scheduled weekly. The Standing Committee handled routine matters, so the irregularity of the general proprietors' meetings did not curtail Company business. The Boston grandees owning double shares dominated this decision-making group.

Membership in the Standing Committee constituted special privilege and prestige in the Kennebeck Company, but it also entailed giving personal bonds for raising large sums of money to finance corporate policies. The major advantage of a committee whose members all lived in Boston was that a meeting could be called on short notice. Records indicate that the matters discussed by the Committee were mostly mundane: plans for surveys, cases of trespass, and mortgage foreclosures. Dramatic and perhaps confidential issues may have been discussed, but not written into the record. In contrast to the tavern-like atmosphere of the general meetings, those of the councils of the Standing Committee were intimate. These meetings, held in the home of a member, resembled social gatherings. The members of this select group enjoyed the hospitality of Charles Apthorp in his elegant King Street house, dinner with Thomas Hancock at his somewhat isolated but sumptuous mansion on Beacon Hill, and collations at James Bowdoin's handsome house at the corner of present-day Beacon and Bowdoin streets.[20] The meetings were held only when business was pressing. During the period, February 15, 1758, to May 22, 1765, the Committee met only twenty-five times—an average of little more than three times a year.[21] There was a limit beyond which the Standing Committee did not venture. The New England political tradition was one of consensus. Thus, whenever the Standing Committee was to make any really important decisions, it took the precaution of calling together the entire propriety for approval of what must have been previously decided policy. The proprietors of the Standing Committee had the votes to push through their decisions in any case, but they preferred to preserve the semblance of Company unity through open discussion and voting in their general meetings.

The decision to raise money for corporate purposes by assessment of the membership was invariably reached in the regular proprietary meetings, thereby giving dissenters a chance to be heard. As expected by Company strategists, developing the tract involved enormous expenses. As early as December 13, 1753, operating expenses totaled £2800.[22] By 1771, the proprietors claimed that they had invested a total of £8200 sterling in improving Company holdings.[23] Many shareholders spent additional sums on their own grants from the Company, so their private expenses had also been high. As these grants were of all-consuming interest to the proprietors, and the *raison d'être* of the Kennebeck Purchase Company, there was at most only grudging resistance to increasing expenses.

Proprietors increased their personal holdings during five general land divisions which had been voted and implemented by 1795. In these divisions, the proprietors drew for lots grouped by sizes ranging from 200 to 3200 acres. Some lots were rich, wooded, or partly cleared and ready for use. Others were infertile, hilly, or swampy. Theoretically the proprietors took their chances on the worth of the lots drawn.[24] In this era, when water transportation was essential, lands bordering on the Kennebec or even a lesser river were most prized. The amount of land received by some proprietors were staggering. By 1795, a proprietor with a double share (1/12th) held a total of 20,360 acres; 1/24th, 10,180 acres; 1/48th, 5,090 acres; and so on.[25] Even the smallest shareholder received at least 1600 acres. Generally, the longer a lot was held, the more it appreciated. The best sections had substantially increased in market value by 1795.

Just how much Kennebeck Purchase lands were really worth is difficult to determine, for in the Province there were many variables affecting land values. The ruinous inflation in Massachusetts, which had nearly doubled prices in the early 1700s, had continued almost unchecked. Therefore, prices quoted for Maine farmlands by the 1770s may have represented accrued value or simply an adjustment necessary to meet the increased cost of living. Too, until the Treaty of Paris ending the French and Indian War was signed in 1763, the net worth of frontier lands fluctuated, and was sometimes almost negligible. During the intervals of peace, if Kennebec River lands were partly cleared and otherwise improved with farm buildings or if they contained valuable timber, their market value might be considerable, particularly if they were accessible to water transportation. On the other hand, wild lands located in remote areas were worth, even in peacetime, only whatever a purchaser would pay. Nevertheless, it is possible to set a minimum value of two shillings per acre on all but the worst land.[26] Provincial financial crises also affected the situation. The decade of the 1750s was a harsh one for the people of Massachusetts, especially for those living on a fixed income. During this period, several proprietors were forced to forfeit their holdings for whatever the market would bring.

The plight of Jabez Fox, a proprietor living in Falmouth, Maine, is a case in point. Although a member of the Massachusetts Council, Fox was encumbered with many debts, and his merchandising and surveying activities did not begin to meet his expenses and obligations. By the early 1750s, his situation was desperate, and he had to sell a part of his Kennebeck Company holding. On March 28, 1752, he sold a half share (4/192nds) to James Bowdoin for £133.6.8[27] The price was low, indicating a buyer's market, and inflation and debts soon melted it away. On Fox's death in 1755, his estate was insolvent. He was not alone in his financial dilemma. Some proprietors lacked the ready cash to keep up their Company assessments. Others felt that paying their rates after 1754 in the face of renewed French and Indian warfare was merely sending good money after bad. In any event, many Kennebeck Company shares went on the market.

In contrast, other proprietors, even very small shareholders—though they too were struggling to survive amid inflationary prices—realized the future worth of the Kennebeck Purchase lands and tried to keep them. Henry Lloyd II of Boston, an heir of Sir Thomas Temple, wrote to his father in 1755 that the family proportion of the latest £2800 assessment was £28.11.5 lawful money. He commented that ". . . my part is 2/9 & amounts to

£6.7.6 which I intend to pay & shall leave my Brethren to Act for themselves, but would let them know the interest is too valuable to be neglected."[28] The Temple heirs kept their Company payments up to date and retained their interest. Other proprietors did not have the money to do so.

On November 9, 1757, in Boston, the Kennebeck Company held its first sale of delinquent proprietors' shares. Most of the holdings offered were bought by the wealthier proprietors or their agents to swell their own shares. As the law provided, shares offered at auction could be redeemed later if the original owners had the means to do so. At this sale, a going rate seemed to prevail for Company shares. William Brattle's 6/192nd part brought "£149 Lawful Money," while the 6/192nd part of John Goodwin's heirs sold for £154. It is a satisfaction to know that the Goodwins, who had done so much to stimulate Company reorganization, later found the money to redeem their portion. A 1/192nd portion owned by Sarah Smith went for £27.[29] These auction prices seem to establish a value for Kennebeck shares in 1757 at around £216 each, not a very impressive figure, but a good one in view of the hard times. The country was at war, and the Kennebeck tract was endangered. It must be remembered also that, even considering the effects of inflation, a little money went a long way. At that time, an artisan could feed a family on £50 sterling a year, and even a wealthy merchant could live very comfortably on £500.[30] Thus the going price of £216 for a Kennebeck share in 1757 was not an inconsiderable amount.

Upon his death in 1758, Charles Apthorp, a Boston merchant prince, left numerous properties, including a full share in the Kennebeck Company. It is instructive to compare the values set for real estate in the Boston area with those of lands on the Kennebec River. Apthorp's elaborate mansion in Boston (later the Custom House) was appraised at £2300 and a rental of £80 per year, 100 acres of woodland in Braintree at £280, ten acres near Milton Meeting House at £100, and twenty acres of upland in Dorchester at £165.6.8. His Kennebeck share was estimated to be worth £390, considerably higher than the prices received at auction the year before.[31] The share could not have been esteemed very highly by Mr. Apthorp in proportion to the rest of his estate, although he had been faithful in his attendance at Company meetings. Nevertheless, the £390 probably represents a close approximation of the real value of the land, even though it was still largely unimproved and undivided.[32] Land development soon changed this picture considerably.

Later inventories and land sales show that the price of Kennebeck shares rose in Boston speculative circles, especially during the years immediately preceding and following the American Revolution. The 1770s were quite different from the 1750s in terms of the development of the propriety. By that time, the French wars were concluded, the Indian threat was eliminated, several towns had been laid out in the tract, small industry was developing, and much of the Company land had been distributed to its shareholders. In September, 1773, an inventory was made of the estate of the late William Bowdoin, holder of a double Company share. His total estate, valued at £20,192.55.32, included houses and lands in Boston, Needham, Hadley, Ashburnham, and elsewhere, in addition to his Kennebeck Purchase lands. These lands, listed as "One Twelfth part of the Kennebeck purchase from the late Colony of New Plymouth being in the County of Lincoln," were appraised at £2,666.13.4 (£1,333.6.10 for a single share) and represent over one-sixth of his total property.[33] His Maine lands, it is clear, were a substantial proportion of this largely landed estate. Company lands had become very valuable and desirable holdings.

Another example, this one drawn from the post-revolutionary period, bears out the continued appreciation of Kennebeck Purchase lands. William Vassall, owner of a proprietary half-share, was, like William Bowdoin, a very rich man. He held extensive plantations in Jamaica as well as land in New England. Vassall set great store by his Kennebeck holdings. Even though they constituted only one-fifth of his total estate, Vassall clung to them tenaciously after fleeing to England when the American Revolution erupted and, after 1783, spent large sums in a successful attempt to recover those that had been confiscated. In 1794, he engaged Judge Jonathan Bowman of Pownalborough, Maine, to itemize and appraise his Kennebeck estates. Bowman found that the Vassall holdings included 8100 acres of good and bad land valued at from nine to twenty-four shillings per acre, which totaled £4,450. In addition, the judge listed "1/45th of the undivided Lands Supposed to be about 3500 [acres]. Suppose at the low value of 6/Acre—£1050."[34] The total value set on Vassall's half share was thus £5,500—a considerable sum for those days and well worth the litigation involved.[35] The Bowdoin and Vassall estates cited here are evidence of the confidence the owners had in the protracted development of Kennebeck Company lands.

Speculation in the Kennebeck Purchase did not mean the same thing to all proprietors. To enterprising leaders like Silvester Gardiner and James Bowdoin, attending to the Company lands became an agreeable and profitable, if increasingly time-consuming, occupation. For Samuel Goodwin, Nathaniel Thwing, and Jonathan Reed, who emigrated to the proprietary tract, the Kennebeck Purchase Company meant a new way of life. To small shareholders such as Habijah Weld and Nathan Stone, Congregational ministers living in rural areas, Maine investments provided a welcome addition to their narrow incomes. Wealthy merchants like Thomas Hancock, Charles Apthorp, and James Pitts considered their speculative venture to be of substantial but not critical importance. Whatever the motive for investment and the degree of participation in Company affairs, each proprietor received an ample if not remarkable return from his Kennebeck investment during the years 1749-1775, and even greater profits afterward.

During those twenty-five years of activity, the proprietors accomplished much. In 1749, the great river above Fort Richmond had been an untouched wilderness. By 1775, the new Lincoln County had been established, with the Company town of Pownalborough as county seat, and the proprietors had erected the Pownalborough Court House at their own expense. Winthrop, Hallowell, Vassalborough, Bowdoinham, and Winslow had been incorporated by the Massachusetts General Court, and the foundations had been laid for many other towns. Even as early as 1771, the proprietors insisted that they had brought a total of 950 families into the territory.[36] Each of these achievements, although motivated purely by prospects for financial gain, was impressive. The proprietors had come close to realizing their dreams of great wealth as they saw their towns, several named for prominent leaders among them, rise along the river banks, watched their gristmills and sawmills roll into operation, saw their logs glide swiftly down the river, and collected their rentals and mortgage payments.

By 1775, the Kennebeck Purchase Company had risen to far greater heights than Samuel Goodwin and Captain Robert Temple must have hoped. So many hurdles, elements of chance, and responses to unforeseen circumstances influenced the fortunes of the Company, it is doubtful that these two Company activists could have anticipated its prospects. Although they had inspired the interest of newer proprietors in reviving the hopes of the New Plymouth Company, it was for these new men who had the will, ability, and imagination to continue the direction of the Company. The turning point of Company fortunes came at a proprietary meeting held on December 6, 1751, when the new leadership announced plans to build the first Company town—plans which embarked the propriety on a course of action which it followed until the opening guns of revolution sounded.

NOTES

CHAPTER II

1 Deed of John Goodwin to Samuel Goodwin, July 18, 1749, *York Deeds*, XVII, Fol. 80-81. Samuel Goodwin later either purchased or assumed management of other family claims.

2 "A Brief State . . .," Letter Book I, 62. The old Plymouth Colony, whose southern boundary was contiguous with northern Rhode Island, had merged with Massachusetts Bay in 1691. The missing patent was needed because it made mention of that Rhode Island boundary.

3 Clifford Shipton, *Sibley's Harvard Graduates*, VI, 7. "In this body [the House] his only notable service was to find the original Plymouth Colony Charter which had been carefully hidden many years before." North, *Augusta*, 40.

4 Testimony of Samuel Welles, May 22, 1765, Suffolk County Court Files (86326-86585), 9. Welles' deposition was taken as evidence to be used in the Jeffries-Donnell case, an important land controversy. Welles had served on the earlier boundary commission of 1733, but denied finding the patent at that time.

5 Committee of the Kennebeck proprietors to Paschal Nelson of London, May 11, 1752, K.P.P., Loose Papers, 1690-1753.

The proprietors prided themselves that their own patent was not based on Indian deeds but upon a grant by the Council for New England.

6 Testimony of William Lithgow, June 7, 1766, "Appendix to the Appellant's Case," 14, K.P.P., Printed Papers.

7 Akagi, *Town Proprietors,* 55-56. The organization of town proprietorships began in 1652 at Plymouth, and in 1698 in Massachusetts Bay Colony. The latter was also responsible in 1713 for a definitive law "directing how meetings of proprietors of lands lying in common may be called." (Mass. Acts and Resolves, I, 334, Sec. 3, which was reinforced by an act of 1753, Mass. Acts and Resolves, III, 669-670). The Kennebeck proprietors kept a copy of this act in their Company files.

8 *Ibid.*

9 William Parker to David Jeffries, Aug., 1748, David Jeffries Papers, XIII, 41, Massachusetts Historical Society, hereafter cited as M.H.S. Jeffries, a sometime clerk of the Kennebeck Company, consulted Parker, a Portsmouth, N.H., attorney, on the mechanics of calling for a first meeting of a proprietorship.

10 First Warrant, Aug., 17, 1749, K.P.P., I, 1-2.

11 Resolution, Dec. 19, 1749, K.P.P., Records, I, 7.

12 Resolution, Apr. 3, 1750, K.P.P., Records, I, 20.

13 Resolution, Apr. 23, 1750, K.P.P., Records, I, 24. At a meeting on this date it was voted that "Their Should be only a Survey taken of part of our Lands aforesaid at or from Cobbaconte Downwards on the West Side of Kennebec River to the Southernmost part of the River Next to and below Richmond fort . . . ."

14 North, *Augusta,* 285; Hanson, *Gardiner,* 41.

15 In this study, the land company after its sale to the four proprietors (1661-1752) is termed the "New Plymouth Company," and after its 1753 incorporation, the "Kennebeck Company," "Kennebeck Purchase," and "Kennebeck Purchase Company." Shareholders after this date are referred to as the "Kennebeck proprietors."

16 Resolution, Jan. 24, 1753, K.P.P., Records, I, 172. The

seal's impression in red wax protected with white paper appeared on all Company deeds. The original is now in the M. H.S.

17 Resolution, Apr. 10, 1754, K.P.P., Records, II, 60.

18 "Shares and Proportions of the Proprietors in the Kennebeck Purchase on Dec. 13, 1753; May 5, 1756; and Nov. 14, 1764," K.P.P., Records, II (Titles Traced; Land Accounts; Money Accounts), 1-15.

19 Charles S. Grant, *Democracy in the Connecticut Frontier Town of Kent* (New York, 1961), 152-153. Grant showed that a similar situation existed during the same period in the proprietary town of Kent, Conn. This was probably true in most proprietary towns, as well as in the larger land company proprietorships. Each investor voted according to the number of shares he controlled. If he had enough votes, he dominated the company.

20 Minute Book of the Committee of the Kennebeck Proprietors (Feb. 15, 1758-May 22, 1765), K.P.P., 1-3. This is the only minute book of the Standing Committee which survives. Probably there had been one earlier and at least one later record.

21 *Ibid.*, 1-17.

22 "Shares and Proportions . . . ," 1-15.

23 "A Brief State . . . ," K.P.P., Letter Book I, 69.

24 _____, *A Strange Account of the Rising and Breaking of a Great Bubble* [*With Amendments and Enlargements*]. *Re-Printed and Sold at my Office, at the Sign of the Tree of Liberty on Sagadahock River, 1767.* Reprinted in *The Magazine of History*, Extra Edition, 1928, 249-268. James Flagg, son of Gershom Flagg, a proprietor, was the probable author, and Edes and Gill the probable printers. This pamphlet has significant value as a contemporary, though hostile, view of Kennebeck Company activities, and will be cited in relation to several episodes of its history. In reference to land divisions, the author stated that Dr. Gardiner took advantage of his fellow proprietors ". . . by employing Surveyors to take a particular Notice so as to be able to furnish him with Intelligence of all valuable Places that should come within their observation. When the Meeting[s] were for drawing

Lots, he would refuse to draw his Lot with his Partners, and pitch on those Places he had set his Mark on."

25 "Memoranda of the Lands drawn or granted to the Several Proprietors of the Kennebeck Purchase from the late Colony of New Plymouth from the 11 December 1754 to the 3d June 1795 Inclusive," Loose Papers, K.P.P.

26 "An Account of Dr. Gardiner's Holdings in the Kennebeck Purchase to 28 Feb. 1768," K.P.P., Loose Papers, 1760-1790. In this letter Gardiner spoke of a grant to him by the Company in April, 1754, of undeveloped lands on the Sheepscot River ". . . then not worth more than 2/ per Acre . . . ."

27 Silas Adams, *History of the Town of Bowdoinham, 1762-1912* (Fairfield, Me., 1912), 14.

28 Henry Lloyd II to Henry Lloyd, Jan. 20, 1754, *Papers of the Lloyd Family of Lloyd's Neck, New York, New York Historical Society Collections* (New York, 1927), II, 515-516.

29 Sale of Delinquent Proprietors' Lands, Nov. 9, 1757, K.P.P., Records, II, 136-137.

30 Jackson T. Main, *The Social Structure of Colonial America* (Princeton, 1965), 133; 138.

31 "Inventory of the Real Estate of Charles Apthorp, Esq., deceased," probated May 25, 1759, Suffolk County Probate Records, LVI, LXVIII (No. 11871). The value placed on Apthorp's share probably represents a more accurate assessment than auction prices of the previous year.

32 Compare this with the £192 received at auction for the full share of Edward Tyng at the second sale of Delinquent Proprietors' Lands, May 10, 1758, K.P.P., Records, II, 166.

33 "Inventory of the Real and Personal Estate of William Bowdoin late of Roxbury . . . ," Sept. 10, 1773, Suffolk County Probate Records, LXXIII, 85-87; 99-101. In contrast, no value was set on the share owned by Benjamin Hallowell, who willed all of his Kennebeck lands to his children. "Inventory of the Estate of Benjamin Hallowell late of Boston Esq., decd . . . ," March, 1773, Suffolk County Probate Records, LXXII, 290-292.

34 "A List of Land belonging to Wm. Vassall on Kennebeck Riv-

er," July 22, 1794, Lloyd, Vassall; Borland Papers, Houghton Library, Harvard, hereafter cited as H.L.

35 Vassall later sold a portion or all of his Kennebeck holding for £3090 sterling. William Vassall to James Lloyd, Aug. 7, 1797, Lloyd, Vassall; Borland Papers, H.L.

36 "A Brief State . . . ," K.P.P., Letter Book I, 69.

III

The Propriety: Leading Lights

After more than two years of preparation, the Kennebeck propriety, spurred on by the enthusiasm of Dr. Silvester Gardiner, Nathaniel Thwing, and William Bowdoin, was ready to begin settlement of its tract in Maine. The occasion was momentous. The faces of the proprietors assembled in the low-ceilinged room of Samuel Wetherhead's Boston inn for that meeting on Friday, December 6, 1751, undoubtedly mirrored excitement. Proprietary action must be quick if the opportunity of the moment was to be captured. Attendance was fair considering the difficulties of winter travel. Most of those present lived in Boston, but others, attracted by the enthusiasm generated by the impending proposal, traveled some distance. Samuel Goodwin journeyed all the way from Kennebec River to give a firsthand report on conditions there. In addition to Gardiner, Thwing, Bowdoin, and Goodwin, heavy shareholders in attendance included Edward Winslow, Thomas Marshall, Jacob Wendell, William Brattle, James Pitts, David Jeffries, and John Tufts. One can imagine the proprietors seated around a massive gateleg table, with pipes, ale cans, and punch cups much in evidence. Edward Winslow called the meeting to order, and Thomas Marshall, acting as temporary clerk for the Company, read the roll. Without further ceremony, Winslow proceeded to the important business at hand.

These great proprietors and their lesser fellows were united in their desire to wrest wealth from their Kennebeck Patent, and formed a cohesive working organization. A clear-cut majority acted quickly to accept motions that would provide a basis for early Company activities on the Kennebec; the first proprietary town would be laid out on the east side of the river opposite Fort Richmond, each settler would receive one hundred acres in two sections, a "Defencable House of 400 feet Square" would be built for the "Greater Security of the Settlers,"[1] and a group of German Protestants who had recently arrived in Boston would be encouraged to migrate to the new lands. The membership also appointed Gardiner, Thwing, and Bowdoin, the three who had proposed the undertaking and had been instrumental in bringing it to a head, to set the conditions of settlement, supply the immigrants with provisions, and otherwise assist them during their first year on the river.[2] Undoubtedly there was much discussion and some spirited argument before the motions carried. Predictions of exorbitant expenses, the dangers of planting a new town in harsh winter weather, and the possibility that German immigrants fresh to the wilderness would make poor settlers, were important enough issues to have created a division of opinion and defeat the proposal. The leaders' boldness, coupled with their compelling arguments, ambition, and assurance, enabled them to carry the day at the proprietary meeting, and they moved ahead with their plans to plant the town of Frankfort. Control of corporate affairs was now in the hands of a new clique among the great proprietors.

Edward Winslow (1714-1784) soon disassociated himself from this clique. Although only thirty-seven and at the peak of his powers, he resigned as moderator after this meeting and became inactive in the Company.[3] He may have disapproved of the proceedings or simply have been more interested in the Plymouth scene than in Boston affairs. As a fourth-generation descendant and namesake of Governor Edward Winslow, he was highly respected in the old Pilgrim town, where he served as Clerk of the Court of Common Pleas for the Port of Plymouth and lived in style on £300 a year.[4] In 1751 he was appointed Justice of the Peace at Plymouth, probably one of the reasons for his retirement from Company activities that would have taken him frequently to Boston. Later he accepted the post of Deputy Collector for the Port of Boston, residing in Plymouth. Fortune smiled on Edward Winslow during these years, but it would not always. His position as Deputy Collector for the Port of Boston and the

Loyalist activities of his oldest son, Ned, pushed him into the Tory camp in the late 1760s. When the forces of the Revolution were unleashed, he endured mobbing and intimidation until 1781, when he fled to British lines in New York City. During the evacuation of the city two years later, he took his family to Halifax, where he died in 1784.[5]

In contrast, Dr. Silvester Gardiner (1707-1786) made an immediate impact on his associates at the December 6 meeting, as is evident from his appointment to the committee for Frankfort. He went on to become the most active and influential of the proprietors. This was Gardiner's first shareholders' meeting, but his important appointment suggests that he had been working behind the scenes on this venture for some time. He was soon elected to the Standing Committee, a position which enabled him to dominate Company meetings. As a contemporary observed some years later, "Dr. Gardiner . . . was then the mainspring and acted as the mouth of the Company."[6] He became moderator when William Bowdoin relinquished the post in 1764, and held this place of honor with evident enjoyment until the beginning of the Revolution.[7] A man of conviction, he remained a devout member of the Church of England and clung tenaciously to his allegiance to the mother country. When the war occurred, he sacrificed a fortune because of his Loyalist adherence and was forced into exile. This man's personality shaped the Kennebeck Company's character during its most active period. Neither the Company nor the doctor regained a commanding position after the Revolution.

John Singleton Copley's portrait of Dr. Gardiner, probably painted in 1772, shows a vigorous, powerful man for sixty-five. The doctor confidently straddles his chair, his hand thrust inside his vest, while a warm smile plays on his lips—but not in his eyes, which defiantly engage the viewer's. He has the determined air of one who has sought life's challenges and met them squarely, willing to risk any consequences. However, John Adams, later attorney for the Kennebeck Company, characterized Gardiner as having "a thin Grasshopper Voice, . . . an affected Squeak: a meager Visage, and an awkward, unnatural Complaisance . . . ."[8] In spite of these handicaps, the doctor was clearly a power to be reckoned with.[9]

Silvester Gardiner had been given a fine education which prepared him well for the commanding role he now took in Kennebeck Company planning. His father, William Gardiner, one of the noted Gardiner clan of Boston Neck, Narragansett, Rhode Island, called himself a cordwainer (shoemaker), but in reality he was a wealthy man. When he died in 1732, he left an estate which included sixteen hundred acres of land and bequests of £3000.[10] Silvester was his youngest child. The Reverend James MacSparran, Anglican minister at Narragansett and husband of one of the Gardiner daughters, suggested that the boy was bright but seemed sickly and unfit for a vigorous life and should prepare for the practice of medicine. Accordingly, his father decided to give young Silvester his share of the estate at this time.[11] The boy was sent first to elementary school in Boston and then to Europe for the finest medical training then available. After eight years of study, which took him first to London and then to Paris, the young man returned to New England as a general practitioner in medicine.

Young Dr. Gardiner set up practice and an apothecary shop in his home on Winter Street in Boston at the sign of the Unicorn and Mortar. He married Anne Gibbins, daughter of a well-established doctor, and soon earned high regard as a brilliant and innovative physician and surgeon.[12] In 1759, two of his successful operations for gallstones were publicized in the Boston newspapers.[13] Two years later, he led a movement during a smallpox epidemic to build an inoculation hospital. The town was not ready for such modern notions, however, and the movement failed.[14] Dr. Gardiner's income from the practice of medicine and from his apothecary shop steadily increased.

At that time, the average colonial doctor managed on an income approximating that of a clergyman—about £100 a year. But Dr. Gardiner soon counted an income of nearly £700, for he had begun to import wholesale medical supplies from London for resale to apothecaries and physicians throughout New England and to speculate in land. The scope of his drug wholesaling is indicated in an invoice for medical supplies received by the doctor dated April 23, 1773, from the London firm of Harrison and Ansley. The itemized list, an extensive one, includes Florence oil, olive oil, Turkey figs, prunes, cinnamon, mace, nutmeg, sulphur, India rhubarb, gum ammoniac, myrrh, opium, saffron, white sugar candy, and a gross of small pillboxes. These items, some bordering on the exotic, were shipped in case or barrel lots. The total charge was £233.19-.[15] Gardiner became a very rich man. The

SILVESTER GARDINER (1707-1786)
Portrait by John Singleton Copley. Private Collection.

extent of his wealth is clear from his list of real and personal property lost during the Revolution which he submitted to the British government on October 23, 1783, for compensation. His total losses, which included six houses in Boston and a drug stock valued at £2000, were in the neighborhood of £6300.[16]

In achieving financial success, Silvester Gardiner soon acquired the reputation of being a hard man, both as a Kennebeck proprietor and as a businessman. He gave mortgages to needy settlers in Maine and credit to apothecaries and fellow physicians. When they failed to pay, he commenced lawsuits that often led to foreclosures or other judgments favorable to him. He seemed far more adroit at collecting debts that did the average creditor, which was probably the reason for his unpopularity.[17] His irascible nature became proverbial in Boston. It is not surprising that he also antagonized some of the Kennebeck proprietors, who felt he claimed more land than his share allowed and who distrusted his Anglican background.[18] None could deny his efficiency and inventiveness, however, or displace him from his position as leader. At the meeting on December 6, 1751, there was yet no hint of the divisions that this man would create in Company affairs.

A close contender in leadership with Dr. Gardiner during the early days of Company operation was William Bowdoin (1713-1773). Bowdoin exuded an aura of wealth, influence, and important family allegiances. The founder of the family was Pierre Baudoin, a Huguenot refugee from the French city of Rochelle who was forced to flee after the revocation of the Edict of Nantes by Louis XIV. Upon arriving in New England via Ireland, he moved his family to Casco Bay near Fort Loyal, where he was a neighbor of the Tyngs until the two families were driven out by the Indians.[19] Undaunted by this misfortune, Baudoin relocated in Boston and became a modestly prosperous merchant trader.[20] His son, James Bowdoin I, became a very successful one. By 1734, he was a proprietor of the famous Long Wharf in Boston.[21] In the 1730s, he also speculated in wild lands on the Upper Housatonic in eastern Connecticut.[22] During his last years, he began to accumulate shares in the Kennebeck Purchase tract. When he died in 1747, James Bowdoin I left a fortune which was valued at over £80,000 and included Kennebeck shares. The estate was divided among his heirs on the basis of two-sevenths each for his sons, William and James; one-seventh each for James Pitts and Thomas Flucker, two Bowdoin sons-in-law; and the re-

maining one-seventh set aside in trust for the children of Mary
Bayard, a Bowdoin daughter. Thus, each of the sons received
over £23,000, and the family of each of the daughters over
£11,600. The division of such a vast estate, much of it tied up in
mortgages and money let out at interest, took nearly ten years.[23]
By the time the final accounting was made, the children of James
Bowdoin I, a largely self-made man, were firmly entrenched
among Boston's merchant aristocracy.

The Bowdoins had further strengthened their social, economic,
and political positions through a series of dynastic marriages. William, the elder son, married Phoebe Murdock, the daughter of a
wealthy Plymouth merchant.[24] William's brother, James Bowdoin
II (1726-1790), married Elizabeth Erving, the daughter of John
Erving, a rich Boston merchant. Other Erving children married
into the Shirley, Scott, Winslow, Waldo, and Royall families, all
leaders in Provincial society. Elizabeth Bowdoin, the sister of William and James, married James Pitts (1710-1776), another
well-to-do Boston merchant. As were Elizabeth's brothers, Pitts
was a Harvard graduate, and became a Kennebeck proprietor.
Pitts was also a business partner of James Bowdoin II.[25] Thomas
Flucker, a one-time apprentice to James Bowdoin I, married the
latter's daughter, Judith, and inherited her share of the Bowdoin
fortune after her death. He prospered financially and politically,
and eventually became Secretary of the Province. As his second
wife, he chose Hannah Waldo, so to him in time passed the
Waldo Patent in Maine. These lands were appropriated during
the American Revolution by his son-in-law, Henry Knox. Unlike
the rest of the family, Flucker did not inherit a share in the
Kennebeck Purchase and played no part in its management.
Balthazar Bayard (?-1778), still another brother-in-law of James
and William Bowdoin, occasionally represented his wife and children on the proprietary board. Bayard was one of the landown-
ing New York Bayards, who, like the Bowdoins, was of Huguenot ancestry. However, unlike the Bowdoins or other Bayards,
Balthazar did not succeed in business, and appears to have been
heavily in debt to his father-in-law's estate.[26] It is significant that
his children's share of their grandfather's property was placed in
the hands of a guardian. Bayard did not trouble himself to attend
the December 6 meeting, realizing that William Bowdoin would
protect the interests of his (Bayard's) children. With the exception
of the rather embarrassing Bayard, members of the Bowdoin clan

were as successful in politics as they were in business. James Bowdoin I, after serving earlier in the House, became a member of the Council under Governor Shirley's administration. Seats in this upper house were also eventually won by James Bowdoin II, James Pitts, Thomas Flucker, and John Erving. Bowdoins could justifiably boast of family alliances which controlled great fortunes and generated extensive political influence.

For all his glamour, William Bowdoin lacked the strength of the preceding generations of Bowdoins. In contrast to Dr. Gardiner, he did not have the background for Kennebeck Company leadership. He had struggled to succeed as a merchant and probably aspired to political heights and popularity, but he achieved only mediocrity. Scorning small successes, he avoided Boston's minor political offices during his early career; in 1738 he even paid a fine rather than serve as constable. He concentrated on business affairs, using his father's considerable influence when it proved convenient. In 1745, his father urged him to solicit orders from General William Pepperrell at Louisburg. A subsequent business trip to England led to no permanent advantage.[27] In 1749, the year the Kennebeck Company was reactivated, he again refused to be drawn into politics, this time declining to serve as tax collector for Boston.[28] After trifling success as a merchant in the port city, Bowdoin retired to rural Needham, a most unfashionable country seat. He then began to transfer his investments from trade to land speculation and money lending. In 1751, he and James Pitts represented the family interests at the important December meeting. It is surprising that this man had the initiative to be one of the leaders to propose the settlement of Frankfort on the Kennebec. Meanwhile, politically ambitious at last, he offered, if elected, to serve as Needham's representative to the House at his own expense. The proposal was too much for the thrifty inhabitants of Needham to resist; Bowdoin was elected representative in 1752.[29] For a number of years during his tenure as representative, he was in positions of authority in the Kennebeck Company, serving as moderator until 1764, when he gave way to Dr. Gardiner. William and his brother, James, named a part of their Maine holdings Bowdoinham (incorporated in 1762) and began to improve them. After 1765, however, William seldom appeared at Company meetings, probably because of failing health. Although he proved to be a more potent influence in Company planning than his background hinted he would be, he

never did develop the strength and influence that James was to
wield, in either Company or politics. In 1748, the noted Boston
artist Robert Feke painted William Bowdoin, then thirty-five. Although the portrait is one of Feke's best, the viewer is drawn to
the fine satins, velvets, and embroidery of the sitter's clothing
rather than to the man.

Two other weighty proprietors who were present and voting at
the December gathering were William Brattle and Jacob Wendell. Each had a tie to Thomas Brattle, one of the original proprietors of 1661. William Brattle (1702-1776) was the grandson of
Thomas Brattle and the son of William Brattle, a noted preacher.
His uncle was Thomas Brattle, a rich Boston merchant instrumental in the founding of the liberal Brattle Square Church in
1699. His grandmother was Elizabeth Tyng, and his first cousin
was David Jeffries, long-time Company clerk. Jacob Wendell
(1691-1761), a member of an old Dutch family of Albany, had
come to Boston as a young man and married a member of the important Oliver family. Their twelve children married into many
prominent Massachusetts and New Hampshire families: the
Hunts, Holmses, Wibirds, Sewalls, Coopers, Penhallows, and Phil-
lipses. Jacob Wendell's son, John Mico, married Katherine
Brattle. These names represented a substantial part of the social
circle of the two royal colonies.

The moderate financial and greater political achievements of
William Brattle and Jacob Wendell contributed to their social prominence. William Brattle, Harvard 1722, combined middling success as a doctor, minister, and lawyer with widespread land
speculation and a series of political triumphs. In addition to the
Kennebeck Company investment, he had holdings in Brattleboro,
Vermont, named for him.[30] He was highly active in Kennebeck
Company planning during its early days and served on the usual
committees: the Standing Committee, the Committee to Defend
the Title, and the Committee of Ten.[31] Apparently, he approved
of the proprietary decision to lay out the town of Frankfort, but
he seems to have become disillusioned two years later. He never
attended another meeting after the one of October 23, 1754, and
for some inexplicable reason, failed to pay Company assessments
and permitted 6/192nds of his full share to be sold at the 1757
auction.[32] Massachusetts political and military affairs replaced the
Kennebeck Company in his areas of concentration. By the early
1750s he had become a firm ally and personal friend of Governor

WILLIAM BOWDOIN (1713-1773)
Portrait by Robert Feke. Courtesy of the Bowdoin College Museum of Art.

Shirley.[33] Political influence must have had much to do with his subsequent rise in Provincial affairs. In 1755 he was elected to the House, and then to the Council in 1756. He became Adjutant General of Militia in 1758, Brigadier and Commissary in 1760, and Major General in 1773.[34] In politics, Brattle was a strong factional figure and something of a maverick. He remained a stalwart Whig during the turbulent years of colonial opposition to the Crown in the 1760s and then unaccountably turned Tory on the eve of the Revolution.[35] Ahead lay an exile's grave at Halifax. John Singleton Copley, the Boston artist, painted General Brattle in happier days. Resplendent in scarlet coat, he poses with a cocked hat under one arm, and a hand on his sword hilt—a fat, aging gentleman whose face reflects pride in position and family.

Jacob Wendell faithfully attended proprietary meetings for some years and served on several committees that were charged with raising money for Company expenses.[36] He was actively involved in the Frankfort scheme, but he seems to have lost interest when the Company decided to build a new fort in the Kennebec Valley late in 1754. As was true of William Brattle, he never attended another Company meeting after that of October 23, 1754. Like Brattle also, Wendell let part of his delinquent share (5/192nds) be sold at auction on November 9, 1757, and later forfeited the remaining 3/192nds.

The actions of William Brattle and Jacob Wendell may be accounted for in several ways. One reason for their defection may have been simply that the Company was not advancing as they expected. Thus they may have resolved to cut their losses by refusing to pay assessments, consequently severing all connections with the Company. This theory may be true, considering that the two abandoned the propriety at the inception of the French and Indian War, when the whole Kennebec Valley was in peril of Indian attack. Another possibility is that they lacked the money to keep up their obligations. It is true that many of the great merchants of the day had cash tied up in inventories and uncollectible debts and found it difficult to lay their hands on ready money. This may have been true of Brattle who, for all his prestige, had a modest income. Wendell's refusal to pay does not seem to have been due to a lack of money because, when he died in 1764, an inventory of his property listed several tenements and warehouses in Boston, a town house on Oliver Street valued at £733.6.8, a distillery house with equipment valued at

£1066.13.4, and lands in Pittsfield appraised at £1067.10-, a total estate of £4741.16.8.[37] Such an estate places Wendell in the ranks of the moderately rich. A better explanation for the defection of the two men is offered by the anonymous author (probably James Flagg) of *A Strange Account of the Rising and Breaking of a Great Bubble,* an anti-proprietary pamphlet printed in Boston in 1767 which reviewed the history of the Kennebeck Company, 1749-1767.[38] According to the *Strange Account,* in 1754 the leading proprietors were determining for the first time to press their claim to the Atlantic Ocean. This new boundary conflicted with the claims of the Pejepscot Company, and Clark and Lake. The pamphlet indicated that some unnamed proprietors, not willing to push matters that far, ". . . had a sense of virtue [and] declared, they would not be concerned in such a Piece of abominable Wickedness, and quitted their Interest as Partners altogether."[39] Such a high sense of virtue was rare among colonial land speculators. Many Bostonians believed the Kennebeck Company case to be a weak one.[40] Doubts about this newly raised issue could well have been the reason that William Brattle and Jacob Wendell dropped their Company affiliations. Some of their close connections, namely heirs of the Tyng-Fox families, though they did not dispose of their holdings, showed little interest in the Company after that time and seldom attended proprietary meetings. Of the proprietors in attendance at the December meeting, however, they seemed to be alone in these doubts.

Certainly these opinions were not shared by Samuel Goodwin (1716-1802), who enforced Company claims on the Kennebec. Goodwin, a housewright of Charlestown, had at first attended meetings with his father. Upon the old man's death in 1752, Samuel had become the spokesman for the family interests. In being appointed to the committee to survey what became the town of Frankfort, he had a leading role in frontier development from the start.[41] After his appointment as agent in Maine on January 24, 1753, Samuel Goodwin moved his family permanently to the Kennebec, and David Jeffries replaced him as Company clerk.[42] Goodwin not only moved to the region, he helped subdue it. In short, it became his whole life.

Indispensable at first, as time passed Goodwin became less and less satisfactory to the other proprietors. In 1757, they admonished him for selling a lot at Frankfort without their permission, apparently because they considered the purchaser an unde-

WILLIAM BRATTLE (1702-1776)
Portrait by John Singleton Copley. Private Collection.

sirable settler. They did not disclose the exact nature of his offense in the Company records. The accusation was made there that Goodwin had been "stock jobbing" and "prosecuting his own private Interest even to the Detriment of that of the propriety."[43] Two months later, Company officials notified him that they were "determined to commit no more of their Affairs to [his] Management untill first [he had] been with them face to face."[44] Their patience finally exhausted, the erring agent was dismissed on February 11, 1761.

Samuel Goodwin's ouster did not mean the end of his participation in Kennebeck Company affairs, however, for he was a full shareholder by 1761 and entitled to all the privileges of corporate membership. Furthermore, living as he did at Frankfort, the base for proprietary operations in the Kennebec Valley, he could be useful to the Company. For this reason, when Lincoln County was established in 1760, he was permitted to move with his family into the new courthouse and operate an inn and general store there. The Goodwins never moved out of the building, although the Company made several attempts to evict them. In the early 1770s, the proprietors pressured Goodwin to turn his old accounts over to them for settlement, but he seldom answered their correspondence.[45] A curious inertia seemed to grip the Standing Committee when attempting to deal with him. Regardless of threats, Goodwin did as he pleased, and little was done about it. Probably he knew so much about confidential Company affairs that he was immune from prosecution. He remained in his courthouse lodgings, but his financial situation gradually worsened over the years. He went less and less frequently to Boston and rarely dropped in on proprietary meetings.

At the December meeting kindly, officious David Jeffries (1714-1785) was in a prominent position. Although of modest means and only a half-share owner, Jeffries, Harvard 1732, could confidently take his place at the table as a member of one of Boston's oldest families. He could boast of his direct descent from Thomas Brattle. William Brattle was his first cousin. Jeffries was related to the Belcher, Usher, Noyes, and Winslow families, as well as the Jaffreys and Wentworths of New Hampshire[46] His first wife was his cousin, Sarah Jaffrey; his second, a daughter of Byfield Lyde, a Salem merchant; and his third, a member of the Winslow family. David Jeffries seems to have impressed the proprietors with his executive ability, for he held several offices generally pre-empted by the large shareholders. Perhaps they were influenced by his election to the position of town treasurer of Boston, a post he held from 1750 until he resigned it in 1782. He was appointed to a minor committee in the Company as early as February 13, 1749, and afterward to most of the key ones: the Standing Committee, the Committee to Defend the Title, the Auditing Committee, and the Committee of Ten. He became tax collector in February, 1754.[47] From 1753 to 1766, he filled the position of Company clerk. The salary was only £20 per year for this part-time work, which must have become increasingly time-consuming. Also, the salary was usually in arrears.[48] Pleading the pressures of business, he resigned as clerk and recommended Henry Allyne, a non-shareholder, as his successor. Jeffries continued to attend Company meetings regularly, however, and was one of the few old-time proprietors to maintain interest during the lean revolutionary years. His contributions to the Kennebeck propriety were significant.

The two remaining proprietors present at the eventful meeting of December 6, 1751, were far below the social plane of the other shareholders and had little influence in Company decision-making, yet they played an important part in developing the projected town of Frankfort. Nathaniel Thwing (1703-1768), a quarter shareholder, and John Tufts, owner of a half share, set an example for the other proprietors in moving to the new town, following in the footsteps of Samuel Goodwin. Probably their stations in Boston were so humble that they could only gain from the opportunities offered by the frontier.

Nathaniel Thwing, formerly a baker, became a justice of the peace in the new community.[49] He accumulated an estate and rose to colonel in the Massachusetts militia. His important contribution to the Kennebeck Company was made in the early 1750s, when he first served on the committee to encourage the settlement of immigrant Germans and then on a committee to govern the new town. In later life he returned to Boston, where he died of an apoplectic fit on April 18, 1768.[50] Befitting his improved position, he was honored by an impressive tombstone in King's Chapel burying ground.

John Tufts is not so well remembered. It is known that he was a descendant of the Peter Tufts who settled in Medford in the 1630s and built a fine brick mansion there which still stands. The

Tuftses who followed Peter were not so prominent, and left few records. There were several John Tufts in the Kennebeck proprietors' generation, none of whom was outstanding. The John Tufts who attended the December 6 meeting may have been any one of them. Company records attest to his regular attendance at meetings during the period 1750-1753, and to his emigration to the Kennebec River with Goodwin, Thwing, and others. As proprietors in residence, they were granted land for a sawmill at Frankfort on December 27, 1751.[51] The ambitious plan to utilize the timber assets of the town failed, but Tufts remained in the settlement. On July 23, 1753, he was granted four hundred acres in four lots at Frankfort.[52] Afterward he was seldom seen at proprietary meetings, and his last appearance was in 1759. Probably John Tufts was dead by 1763, for in February of that year, his heir, William Tufts, received a grant of 1600 acres near the mouth of Cobboseconte River.[53] At the time of the third proprietary land apportionment on November 14, 1764, William Vassall was in possession of the Tufts share.[54] Thus the Tufts influence in Company matters was slight.

Last on the roll, but probably not the least important person present at the gathering, was Thomas Marshall (1719-1800), serving as temporary proprietors' clerk. Marshall, a tailor in King Street, Boston, was never a shareholder in the Kennebeck Purchase, yet he moved freely in proprietary circles from 1749 through 1753. He first appeared at the meeting of December 19, 1749, the year of Company reorganization, as representative of the Boyes heirs. The Boyes quarter interest in the Company had been willed to Antipas and Samuel Marshall, near relatives of Thomas. These shares were at some later date dispersed to Charles Apthorp, Thomas Hancock, Silvester Gardiner, James Bowdoin, James Pitts, and Benjamin Hallowell. Marshall probably represented these men before they became active in the Company.[55] In this position of power, he served as Standing Committee member, collector, assessor, clerk *pro tem,* and clerk over a four-year period.[56] As the six proprietors he represented gradually assumed more and more control for themselves, Marshall's authority declined. On February 13, 1754, he was replaced as clerk by David Jeffries.[57] Marshall's attendance ceased, and he faded into the background, appearing again briefly in 1774. At that time he requested a Company grant, and was awarded four hundred acres of land at Winthrop "In full Consideration for all his services for this Propriety . . . ."[58] Even though Thomas Marshall was a man on his way out, he must have taken a keen interest in the proceedings on December 6, 1751.

Thomas Marshall's name completes the roster of the early proprietors who shaped and implemented policy during the formative years of the Kennebeck Purchase Company. Each shareholder played a vital part in corporate proceedings—from the gentlemen of position and influence who dictated procedures from their Boston base, to the middling and lesser sort who risked their lives and contributed their labor on the Maine frontier. There was, perhaps, a sense of unity in their efforts at that time which would never again typify Company actions.

The eleven shareholders present at the meeting of December 6, 1751, were not yet fully representative of what the propriety would become at its height. When they committed the Kennebeck Purchase Company to planting the town of Frankfort, factional disputes were only just beginning to intrude. Emerging leaders such as Dr. Gardiner and William Bowdoin would devise new Company plans and demand new loyalties. They would also add to the discord in proprietary ranks. To a large extent, the log village they proposed to erect beside the broad Kennebec would be the testing ground of their leadership.

NOTES

CHAPTER III

1 Resolutions, Dec. 6, 1751, K.P.P., Records, I, 102.

2 *Ibid.*, 103.

3 Edward Winslow would not attend another proprietary meeting after Feb. 12, 1752, and William Bowdoin took his place as moderator after the Dec. 6, 1751, session. Circumstances suggest that Winslow must have been overruled in his opposition to proprietary plans for expansion.

4 Shipton's *Sibley's Harvard Graduates*, X, 100.

5 *Ibid.*, 101-108.

6 John Temple to Kennebeck proprietors, July 6, 1780, K.P.P., Loose Papers, 1760-1790. Temple, a minor proprietor himself, as an heir of Captain Robert Temple, was attempting to recover lands he claimed the Company had first granted him and then rescinded some years later after heavy investment on his part.

7 Dr. Gardiner had earlier served as moderator under the Company's Fourth Warrant, Oct. 17, 1752-Sept. 20, 1753. He often presided as moderator *pro tem* in subsequent years.

8 John Adams, *The Adams Papers: Diary and Autobiography of John Adams,* ed., L.H. Butterfield (Cambridge, 1961), I, 151. Adams also commented that Gardiner was "fribble" (frivolous).

9 Dr. Gardiner still exerts a force upon his descendants. A present member of the Gardiner family recollects the effects which a childhood of eating three meals a day under the stern eyes of the old gentleman's portrait has had upon character building.

10 Henry W. Webster, *Silvester Gardiner, Gardiner, Maine, Historical Series,* Number Two (Gardiner, Me., 1913), 4.

11 Robert H. Gardiner, *Early Recollections* (privately printed, 1930), 14. This account of the Gardiner family, which includes many references to Dr. Gardiner, was written by the doctor's chief heir, who was four years old at the time of his grandfather's death. The work was written in R.H. Gardiner's old age and was not published by his family until many years after his death. His short account of the history of the Kennebeck Purchase Company was printed in *Me. Hist. Soc. Collections,* 1st Series, II (Portland, Me., 1847), and established Dr. Gardiner as a great benefactor of the people of the Kennebec Valley. This legend has been perpetuated by many later writers, including: North, *Augusta;* Hanson, *Gardiner;* Webster, *Silvester Gardiner;* Charles E. Nash, *The History of Augusta* (Augusta, Me., 1904); Allen, *Dresden;* and Evelyn L. Gilmore, *History of Christ Church, Gardiner, 1793-1962* (Gardiner, Me., 1962).

12 Shipton's *Sibley's Harvard Graduates,* XIII, 595. Among the

cherished possessions of Dr. Gardiner was the superb medical library collected by his father-in-law, Dr. John Gibbins.
This was confiscated during the American Revolution, along
with the rest of the Gardiner estate in Boston. The doctor's
son, John Gardiner, Harvard 1755, a Whig, petitioned for its
return, promising that he would donate it to the college. It
is still a part of the Harvard Medical School Library.

13 Carl Bridenbaugh, *Cities in Revolt: Urban Life in America,
1743-1776* (New York, 1955), 201.

14 *Ibid.*, 327.

15 "Invoice of Merchandise Ship'd by Harrison & Ansley - On
Account & risque of Mr. Silvester Gardiner," London, Feb.
25, 1773, Silvester Gardiner Papers, Me. H.S. Most of the
items listed are clearly medical supplies; others imply that
Gardiner, like most colonial storekeepers, dealt in a general
line rather than in strict apothecary needs.

16 "Dr. Gardiner's Lost Real Estate," Oct. 10, 1783, Gardiner,
Whipple, and Allen Papers, II, 15, M.H.S. Gardiner also
claimed that his Kennebeck estates had been damaged to the
value of £3000.

17 In 1771 Gardiner charged that Dr. William Jepson of Conn.
owed him £2923.1.2, after many years of a partnership begun
in 1757. *A True State of the Copartnership of Gardiner and
Jepson, taken from their Books and Settlements from Time
to Time under Jepson's Own Hand* (Boston, 1771). Printed
pamphlet of 4 pp. Silvester Gardiner Papers, Me. H.S. More
typical, perhaps, was the attachment of the goods of John
Metcalf, physician of Wrentham, Mass., to the value of £60
for a debt of £44.11.2, on June 7, 1774. Silvester Gardiner
Papers, Me. H.S.

18 The doctor's colorful language sometimes displayed an ironic
humor. On Aug. 20, 1768, an angry Gardiner stormed to the
Kennebeck proprietors about a Company settlement of a land
dispute and complained that ". . . as for the Diamond
[shaped] Lot there has been so much opposition to my having
it as if there was something Peculiar in its Mark . . . ."
Silvester Gardiner to Kennebeck proprietors, Aug. 20, 1768,
K.P.P., Loose Papers, 1760-1780.

19 Temple Prime, *Some Account of the Bowdoin Family* (New York, 1894), 4.

20 "Inventory of the Estate of Peter Bowdoin," Sept. 7, 1706, Bowdoin Family Papers, Hawthorne-Longfellow Library, Bowdoin College, Brunswick, Me. Pierre Baudoin left an estate of £1344, of which £725 was in cash.

21 Winsor, ed., *Memorial History of Boston,* II, xx. Bowdoin's name appeared on a petition to widen Long Wharf from 10 to 14 feet.

22 Grants of James Bowdoin I on the Upper Housatonic, Massachusetts Archives, CXIV, 161, 162, 169, 170, hereafter cited as M.A.

23 "Inventory of the Estate of the Late Hon. James Bowdoin Esqr. accounted to the Judge of Probate 31st May 1757," Waldo-Knox-Flucker Papers, Me. H.S. The total value of the estate was £82,875.15.1 and included extensive real estate, mortgages, household furnishings, wearing apparel, silver plate, slaves, and even a four-wheeled chaise.

24 Shipton's *Sibley's Harvard Graduates,* IX, 475. William Bowdoin was a member of the Harvard class of 1735.

25 Prime, *Some Account of the Bowdoin Family,* 4-5. James Pitts, Harvard 1731, received two-thirds of his father's large estate in 1729. He owned lands in Bedford, N.H., and in Rockingham, Vt., and maintained an extensive estate at Dunstable, Mass.

26 "Inventory of the Estate of the Late Hon. James Bowdoin Esqr." At the time of Bowdoin's death, his son-in-law owed him £6882.10.11, which was deducted from the Bayard share of the estate.

27 *Mass. Hist. Soc. Collections,* Series 6, X, 364-365.

28 Shipton's *Sibley's Harvard Graduates,* IX, 473.

29 *Ibid.*

30 *Ibid.*

31 Proprietary Records, K.P.P., Records, I, 6; II, 77.

32 "Shares and Proportions of the Proprietors in the Kennebeck Purchase . . . ." Thomas Marshall bid in Brattle's share, serving as intermediary for several of the proprietors.

33 John A. Schutz, *William Shirley: King's Governor of Massachusetts* (Chapel Hill, 1961), 180.

34 Shipton's *Sibley's Harvard Graduates*, VII, 16.

35 Edward D. Harris, *An Account of Some of the Descendants of Captain Thomas Brattle* (Boston, 1867), 39-40.

36 Proprietary Records, K.P.P., Records, I, 118-134. Wendell was a member of the following committees: Committee to borrow £200, Jan. 17, 1752; Committee to borrow £15, Mar. 4, 1752; Committee to borrow £400, May 5, 1752; Committee to borrow £300, July 20, 1752.

37 "Appraisal and Apportionment of Jacob Wendell's Estate," probated Jan. 6, 1764, Suffolk County Probate Records, LXII, 14-18. At that time any person with an estate valued at above £2000 was considered a rich man.

38 _____, *A Strange Account* . . ., 249-268.

39 *Ibid.*, 252.

40 See Samuel Fitch to Henry Lloyd, Jan. 18, 1755, *Papers of the Lloyd Family of Lloyd's Neck, New York*, II, 526. The Lloyds were minor shareholders in the Kennebeck Company.

41 Company Resolution, Dec. 19, 1749, K.P.P., Records, I, 6.

42 Company Resolution, Jan. 12, 1753, K.P.P., Records, I, 164.

43 Kennebeck proprietors to Samuel Goodwin, Sept. 8, 1757, K.P.P., Loose Papers, 1640-1759.

44 Kennebeck proprietors to Samuel Goodwin, Nov. 30, 1757, K.P.P., Loose Papers, 1640-1759; Company Resolution, Feb. 11, 1761, K.P.P., Records, II, 264.

45 Kennebeck proprietors to Samuel Goodwin, June 9, 1773, K.P.P., Loose Papers, 1760-1790; Report to the Kennebeck propriety on Samuel Goodwin Accounts, Mar. 24, 1774, K.P.P., Records, III, 100; Samuel Goodwin to Henry Allyne, Oct. 16, 1776, Goodwin Papers, 1753-1791, Pownalborough Court House Papers, Lincoln County Cultural and Historical Association, Wiscasset, Me., hereafter cited as P.C.H.P.

46 Shipton's *Sibley's Harvard Graduates*, IX, 171-173.

47 Company Resolutions, Nov. 28, 1750, K.P.P., Records, I, 50; Dec. 19, 1750, K.P.P., Records, I, 56; June 20, 1750, K.P.P.,

Records, II, 26; Nov. 7, 1753, K.P.P., Records, II, 46; Feb. 13, 1754, K.P.P., Records, II, 51.

48 Company Resolution, Oct. 4, 1758, K.P.P., Records, II, 185. On that date David Jeffries was voted £20 per year for his services as clerk for the five-year period which had commenced Sept. 20, 1753, and ended Sept. 20, 1758, or £100 in all. After that he was paid more regularly.

49 Allen, *Dresden,* 498.

50 Nash, *Augusta,* 78.

51 Company Resolution, Dec. 27, 1751, K.P.P., Records, I, 112-113.

52 Company Resolution, July 23, 1753, K.P.P., Records, II, 33.

53 Company Resolution, Feb. 9, 1763, K.P.P., Records, II, 316. William Tufts received 1/2 of Lot No. 12 on the east side of the Kennebec.

54 "Shares and Proportions . . . ," K.P.P., Records, II, 1-15.

55 *Ibid.*

56 Company Resolutions, Dec. 19, 1749-Sept. 20, 1753, K.P.P., Records, I; II, 1-41.

57 Company Resolution, Feb. 13, 1754, K.P.P., Records, II, 51.

58 Proprietary Grant to Thomas Marshall, May 11, 1774, K.P.P., Records, III, 101.

IV

"To Encourage Setlers Among Us"

Plans for the first Company town had been developing for a two-year period, and the proprietors' Third Warrant (July 6, 1751) outlined all of the steps they were about to take at their meeting on December 6, 1751.[1] The arrival of German immigrants in Boston late in 1751 was the catalyst which jolted the Company to immediate response.

The proprietors were agreed that a settlement on the Kennebec must be commenced without delay. As they well knew, land without settlers was valueless. A new town would enable them to begin to profit from their holdings, even though the expenses incurred would certainly be enormous. New inhabitants would clear the land, build farmsteads, and cultivate crops. They would serve as a labor force to cut the valuable timber and prepare it for shipment down the Kennebec, develop fisheries, and provide a market for the surplus goods of the merchant-proprietors. Rival land companies would be shown that the Kennebeck Purchase Company was determined to enforce its claims.

A speedy introduction of settlers into the region was imperative, everyone concurred, but the settlers themselves were wanting. In spite of the large natural increase in New England's population and the rising scarcity of land in Massachusetts, relatively few farmers were willing to migrate from settled towns to the Maine frontier. Continuing Indian raids and the absence of adequate protection from strategically placed Provincial forts in the valley combined to discourage all but the reckless from populating the region of the Kennebec. Furthermore, the terms on which the propriety offered land in its tract were no more attractive than those offered in more accessible areas. Discounting the possibilities of luring native New Englanders in any significant numbers, at least during the formative period of development, the proprietors seized upon the idea of importing foreigners to solve their problem.

In reaching this decision, as with so many others, the proprietors relied upon precedents set by earlier land companies instead of formulating original policies. Many examples existed in colonial America for the wholesale planting of colonies of the foreign-born. These included Count Zinzendorf's scheme to bring Moravians to Georgia in 1735[2] and the plan of the Massachusetts General Court to settle Germans on the Province's western frontier at the very moment when the Kennebeck proprietors were deciding to build their town.[3] But there were several precedents for taking such steps in Maine itself. Captain Robert Temple's venture to plant over one hundred Scotch-Irish families near present-day Bath, Maine, had failed because of Indian attacks, but the settlers were not all lost to the new country, for many had located permanently at Georgetown and Yarmouth.[4] Furthermore, Temple had proved that the plan itself was feasible, and the Company now had the benefit of his experience. Examples of two successful Maine attempts at transplanting immigrants were those of the Lincolnshire Company and the Waldo venture. The Lincolnshire Company brought some seventy Scotch-Irish families to live on the St. George River near Warren.[5] In 1740, Samuel Waldo, powerful proprietor of the Lincolnshire Company, persuaded more than fifty German families to settle at Waldoborough.[6] These two successes may have encouraged James Bowdoin in 1748 to present to the Massachusetts General Court, a proposal entitled "Some Thoughts on the Importation of Foreigners."[7] In this proposal, young Bowdoin advocated that his province follow the example of Pennsylvania and encourage foreign settlement on the frontier. While Bowdoin admitted that much of the vacant land in Massachusetts was in private (corporate) hands, he argued that these tracts had originally been granted "on Conditions that the Grantees should settle a certain number of Families, and make such Improvements as are set forth in the Conveyances."[8] These conditions had often been disregarded (as was true of the Kennebeck Purchase Patent). Presence of new foreign settlers would legitimize and safeguard continued possession of these lands. Continuing, Bowdoin hinted that "There are large Tracts of Land at the Eastward, which at present lye waste and uncultivated."[9] Surely he must have meant the Kennebeck Tract, a portion of which he had only the previous year inherited from his father's estate. Further, Bowdoin stressed the resources that companies like his own could expect to reap from their holdings:

> The woods [are] stored with Masts, Yards, Spars & a variety of other Timber suitable for the Ship-Builder & other Mechanics; & a great number of Pitch-Pine-Trees, which are that Source of Pitch Tar & Turpentine - The Rivers & adjacent Seas abound with Fish of most Sorts, particularly Salmon, Sturgeon, Alewives, Shad, Mackerel, & beyond all Codfish. - These are some of the natural Advantages we have.[10]

These were the riches that the Kennebeck proprietors were aching to grasp for themselves, and which could become theirs if the General Court saw fit ". . . to encourage Setlers among us . . . ."[11]

James Bowdoin's proposal fell upon receptive ears. During the absence of Governor William Shirley in England, Lt. Gov. Spencer Phips presided over the Provincial government. Phips had Maine roots, and was the nephew of former Governor Sir William Phips, the Maine-born fisherman who had risen to meteoric heights after salvaging a fabulous treasure from sunken Spanish galleons. The younger Phips was intrigued by the colonizing idea, and in his address to the General Court on November 23, 1749, advocated a policy of persuading "industrious and well-disposed Protestant Foreigners to settle among us."[12] His interest soon caught the attention of a German-born adventurer, Joseph Crellius. Crellius was a native of Franconia, who by 1740 was living in Pennsylvania, where he had earned some reputation by printing the second German newspaper in the colonies.[13] By the end of the decade, he had turned to the contract immigration business, and made several trips back to Germany to arrange the details. Somewhere along the way he met Frederick Curtius, a doctor who had accompanied Samuel Waldo's German immigrants to Broad Bay on the Maine coast in 1742.[14] Later Curtius had become a shipbroker in Rotterdam, who specialized in sending cargoes of immigrants to America. His reputation was generally unsavory.[15] Curtius informed Joseph Crellius that the Massachusetts General Court was then seeking German immigrants to be settled in four new townships, two in the west near Fort Massachusetts, and two in southwestern Maine near Berwick.[16] The legislature's intent clearly was to bolster its weak frontier, and it was willing to reward with a large land grant the agent who brought prospective settlers to the Province. Here was an opportunity to turn a quick profit. Crellius easily got himself appointed by Lt. Gov. Phips as commissioner to import German immigrants as settlers. He then made his way to his homeland to begin recruiting, arriving in the late summer of 1750.

Once on the continent, Joseph Crellius became a part of the highly organized immigrant brokerage trade. He played the role of the ill-reputed "Newlander," the flashily dressed veteran of settlement in America, with his gold watch and talk of unbelievable wages of one florin a day in America.[17] In addition to touring the cities and provinces himself and hiring recruiters who would be paid one florin per head for prospective immigrants, Crellius also had to make arrangements with shipping firms to transport his charges and to induce substantial German magistrates to guarantee his proposals. In Rotterdam, the chief port of exit, were four preeminent English companies that specialized in the shipping of human cargoes. John Stedman and Company consented to handle Crellius's immigrants.[18] The agent was fortunate enough to have a letter of introduction from Lt. Gov. Phips to Heinrich Ehrenfried Luther, a printer and aulic counsellor of the empire at Frankfort. This dignitary, impressed by the credentials presented by Crellius, was pleased to sponsor his mission. At this point, all paths had been smoothed, and the agent must have looked forward to a successful and remunerative voyage.

Poor management, dishonesty, and competition from other agents all helped to thwart Crellius's plans. His pamphlets and circulars stirred up a hornet's nest when his extravagant claims of opportunities awaiting immigrants in Massachusetts ran afoul of those of John Dick of Rotterdam, commissioner of a similar project for Nova Scotia.[19] Crellius was soon embroiled in a pamphlet war with Dick's agent, one Kohler. Charges and countercharges were made, to the credit of neither. Seeking to help Crellius, Henry Luther attempted to publicize the advantages of life in New England. Crellius reported in a letter sent to Boston that "Mr. Luther has thought fit to publish sundry advertisements in commendation of this Province [Massachusetts]. By the last [letter] of the 26th August, he endeavours to evince that the Province is not new, having a University founded a great many years ago."[20] Crellius must have known, if Luther did not, that the new recruits would soon find themselves settled far from Harvard College. Meanwhile, Crellius and Luther were having their differences. Crellius was interested in a quick, profitable, economical shipment. If packing the immigrants in like herring would increase his profit, well and good. Luther, his Frankfort reputation at stake, and a compassionate man in any case, was genuinely concerned with upgrading the recruiting and transportation of the German immigrants and acclimatizing them in America. With these views in mind, he made several unsuccessful attempts to persuade the Massachusetts legislature to adopt his truly worthwhile proposals for legislation regulating immigration. Hearing accounts of irregularities in the enlisting methods used by Crellius, Luther began to see the commissioner for the scoundrel he was. Naturally, he was appalled to learn that Frederick Curtius was handling the transportation arrangements.[21]

In spite of numerous difficulties, Joseph Crellius somehow got a cargo together. But it was a much smaller group than he had expected. Under close watch to make sure they would not be pirated by other commissioners, the immigrants were transported down the Rhine—a tedious, expensive journey of many weeks, during which some exhausted their savings. They landed at Rotterdam to await the longest part of their voyage. Here, John Stedman had provisioned the English ship *Priscilla*, out of Cowes on the Isle of Wight, with Captain John Brown as commander.[22] The vessel left port in late June, 1751. Although the average length of an Atlantic crossing was eight to ten weeks, the *Priscilla* was at sea over four months.[23] The sufferings of its passengers must have increased accordingly, but no records recount the horrors of that particular voyage. The passengers did complain upon landing, however, of the inhumane treatment they had received at the hands of Captain Brown.[24] Not until November 14, 1751, did the *Priscilla* arrive in Boston harbor. For a time, the immigrants remained aboard ship, subject perhaps to quarantine imposed by the port authorities. There they awaited their fate.

By the time of their arrival, the immigrants' prospects had changed for the worse. The surviving passengers, their number unknown, arrived penniless for the most part. They either had been forced to pay their own passage or were in debt for them. As immigrants to be granted one hundred acres of good Massachusetts land, their futures had earlier seemed bright. Only a short time before, the General Court had extended them a welcome. Now it seemed indifferent to their situation.

Thomas Hutchinson explained the reason for the legislature's change of heart in a letter written to Samuel Waldo on December 13, 1751. He commented that Crellius

> . . . finally brought but a part only of the passengers he expected, which in some measure defeats the intent of the Government in encouraging their importation hither . . . although it was not a condition of the Grant of the lands that there should be a sufficient number for a Township settled at the same time, yet it was imagined it would be so . . . .[25]

The General Court had little interest in sponsoring new colonists on the frontier whose numbers were too small to be self-sustaining, and could only be a burden on the Province. Also, many of the immigrants had ideas of their own as to their destination.

It seems remarkable that these strangers, set down in a foreign land, could have formulated plans for their future. It is more likely that some had already been approached by land speculators like the Kennebeck proprietors who were bidding for their services. As Thomas Hutchinson informed his friend Waldo, "The French that are among them by the Accounts they have received of the Western Frontier think that will be most agreeable to them, and some of their number are gone to view it, the Germans are sending some of their number to the Eastern parts and I am inform'd that there are some who are inclined to go upon Lands belonging to private persons."[26] The immigrants scattered in all directions. Some thirty-odd families finally received land near Fort Massachusetts, but only relatively useless ten-acre plots—not the hundred acres per family originally promised.[27] Others may have drifted to the Germantown district of Braintree to join the German glass blowers there. Some appear to have gone to Waldo's Broad Bay colony. Still others found their way to the new Kennebeck Purchase town on the Maine frontier. Quick action by the Kennebeck proprietors secured these prospective settlers for their own expansionist project.

As early as the meeting of December 6, 1751, a full week before Hutchinson wrote his letter, the proprietors had already engaged a group of the immigrants to go to the Kennebec. The committee composed of Dr. Gardiner, William Bowdoin, and Nathaniel Thwing, soon to be augmented by other proprietors, worked out the conditions for settlement. The immigrants would receive free water transportation from Boston, one hundred acres of land per family (the same amount originally voted by the General Court), and provisions advanced for one year, instead of the half year first promised—all provided they remained permanently on the Kennebec.[28] The bargain was as much as the strangers could expect, and they had little alternative but to accept. Those who chose to go to Fort Massachusetts received much less. The Maine frontier seemed to offer the most palatable escape from their dilemma. If they chose to remain in Boston, many would be sold as indentured servants to pay their debts; others would probably be warned out of town by local officials as transients liable to become public charges. Those who chose the Kennebec were required to give their bonds to proprietors to cover passage debts and the cost of a year's provisions in the new town. The number who did this is unclear, but John Pochard, for example, mortgaged forty acres of the land he had not yet received to William Bowdoin for £25.6.15 to cover his family's passage from Rotterdam to Boston. This sum was not paid in full until 1773.[29] The immigrants would begin their lives in the New World firmly saddled with debts.

Realizing how much was at stake, the proprietors had previously selected a town site overlooking the Kennebec possessed of the advantages of good soil, an extensive stand of timber, and excellent transportation afforded by a fortunate location at the juncture of the Kennebec and Eastern rivers. It was within two miles of Fort Richmond, where a garrison was maintained by the Province. There would also be the support offered by the towns of Woolwich, Georgetown, Walpole, Harrington, Townshend, Topsham, and Brunswick, all planted earlier farther downstream or along the nearby coast. The Kennebeck proprietors now met frequently in extra sessions, feverish to get their grand project underway. At their meeting on December 11, they voted that the proposed town should be called Frankfort.[30] It has been suggested that this was done less as a compliment to the origin of the new settlers than as a tribute to Heinrich Ehrenfried Luther, Chancellor of State at Frankfort in Germany, the worthy who had done so much to bring them to America.[31] At a meeting two days later, proprietors voted that when a total of twenty immigrants were ready to move to Frankfort, they should be supplied with transportation. On the same date it was announced that

Peter Wild, who had come on the *Priscilla* as interpreter, was about to return to Germany. The proprietors resolved that Wild should be commissioned to engage Protestant families in Holland and Germany to come to Frankfort on the same terms as the recent arrivals.[32] This plan seems to have aborted. On December 27, it was decided instead that Wild would go to Frankfort and receive an extra one-hundred-acre grant for his services.[33] But there is no evidence that Peter Wild ever went to Frankfort. A scoundrel in fit company with Crellius and Curtius, he probably thought it best to leave the country. Wild, although an assistant to Crellius, had formulated a scheme to send the immigrants aboard the *Priscilla* to a village of the Pemaquid proprietors instead of to the Western Massachusetts settlements. This scheme was divulged to Lt. Gov. Phips by Crellius on his arrival in Boston.[34] It is likely that Wild, his intrigue thwarted, had induced some of the *Priscilla's* passengers to go to Frankfort instead. After arranging their transportation, Peter Wild disappeared.

Matters went no better for Joseph Crellius. He did not make the expected profit or receive his reward of land from the General Court, nor did he remain long in Massachusetts. Instead, he abandoned his charges and returned to Germany to round up another cargo, this time as the three-fold agent for Massachusetts, Samuel Waldo, and the Kennebeck proprietors.[35] In the summer of 1752, he shipped his second and final load of immigrants to Boston, possibly delivering some passengers to Halifax while en route to Massachusetts. By that time the first Frankfort settlers were fully established on the Kennebec.

The proprietors had learned by late December, 1751, that the twenty expected settlers, mostly heads of families, were ready to move to Frankfort. Dr. Gardiner's committee had by that time further defined the requirements for householders' lots—requirements that were to provide a model for small land grants throughout the Kennebeck Purchase:

> . . . that Each Settler Respectively Clear five Acres of Land & Build a House of Twenty feet Long and Eighteen feet Wide on their respective Lotts in three years—
>
> That they shall not sell to any Inhabitant or any other Except to those that will settle on the Respective Lands till Fifty Familys be settled in said Township.[36]

The exact date when the first settlers reached their Frankfort destination is unknown, but it must have been quite early in the spring. At this unpromising time of the year, the settlers would be able to do little more than begin to clear the land. The hauling of logs, at least, could be done with least effort while snow still covered the ground.

Samuel Goodwin was already on the scene to welcome the immigrants. He was soon joined by Nathaniel Thwing, Samuel Fowle, and John Tufts. These four shareholders were to cooperate with the townspeople in the construction of a sawmill, to dispense provisions, and to supervise work on a palisade.[37] Major proprietors would also keep an eye on affairs. In January, 1752, Dr. Gardiner, William Bowdoin, and Gershom Flagg, already managing settlement details back in Boston, were appointed to form a committee "to Settle and Regulate the Town of Frankfort on Kennebeck River and to appoint one or more Persons under them for that purpose."[38] This group was later expanded into a "Committee of Ten," and included nearly all of the large shareholders. Of these, the indomitable Dr. Gardiner was to prove by far the strongest moving force.

The first task assigned the settlers was the erection of the previously voted Company fort at the proposed center of settlement overlooking the river. Although Fort Richmond was only two or three miles away, and could provide a haven for the newcomers in an emergency, it was located inconveniently on the opposite bank of the Kennebec, and was in almost ruinous condition. Under the circumstances, only the presence of additional defense could persuade other settlers to venture to the area in any numbers. Accordingly, the proprietors drew up plans for this "Defencable House" to shelter the settlers while their own homes were being constructed.[39] The structure as it was first built seemed to be merely a palisade for the protection of the first arrivals. It is likely, however, that at least one blockhouse was also erected at this time. Two years later, in 1754, the British again went to war with the French and their Indian allies, so additional protection was drastically needed at the fort. In this emergency the Committee voted "to build a House Sixty by thirty two Feet Within the Piquets of the Defencable House at Frankfort to be improved as Barracks, upon the best Terms in the Cheapest Manner they can."[40] For further protection they also bought one hundred pounds of bullets and five hundred flints.[41] The proprietors had meanwhile christened their outpost Fort Shirley to remind the royal governor of his friendship for the Company.

The Thomas Johnston Map of the Kennebec and Sagadahock rivers provides a valuable insert plan of the fort shortly before its name was changed from Fort Frankfort to Fort Shirley.[42] The map shows a palisade two hundred feet square, not the much larger dimensions originally voted by the proprietors. Two large blockhouses appear at opposite corners of the stockade, one mounted with six cannon and the other with seven. Three fair-sized buildings, probably barracks and storehouses, range around the fortified square. Company records mention the stockade, two hundred feet on a side, and the two blockhouses, but cite only one barracks building.[43] The only reference to weapons made in proprietary accounts was to eight carriage guns and one dozen small arms ordered for the fort in 1752.[44] These were armaments formidable enough to frighten nearby Indians, if not sufficient to ward off a full-scale attack.

Once the Frankfort settlement was launched, the "Forreign Protestants" began their struggle for survival. Life could not have been easy for them for the first few years, and in the beginning must have been intolerable, even for people fresh from the horrors of an immigrant ship. On their arrival they may have been housed at Fort Richmond, where Samuel Goodwin made his headquarters, or they may have been quartered in a blockhouse at the unfinished Fort Frankfort. Not until the fort was completed would they be allowed to begin clearing their own lots and start erecting log houses which would become their first homes in the wilderness. The building of Fort Frankfort must have taken longer than the proprietors had anticipated. On May 11, 1752, members of the Committee informed Paschal Nelson of their progress. There were then:

> . . . about fifty Men at Work, in building a Hous of Defence as is Customary in the Eastern Parts but in a Much Stronger Manner, & have sent Down Eight Carrig Guns & Amonision. We sent Down Fifty four Germans & have agread to Suply them with Provisions for Twelve Months . . . and we are in hope of having 150 or 200 Famileys of Germans in the Fall, as We Shall have a Good hous to Receive them, & hous that will be safe from the Indians.[45]

With all of the work at hand, it was clear that these fifty-four "Germans" would have no opportunity to plant crops that year, so their continued dependence upon Company-supplied provisions was a foregone conclusion.

The proprietors spoke of their charges as "Germans," and in-

deed they had left Germany to find a new homeland, but most
of the first contingent were really of Huguenot extraction. This is
certainly demonstrated by their names—Goud, Pouchard, Pechin,
Malbon, Rittal, Houdelette, and Bugnon.[46] In 1752, to the people
of British America, the word "Frenchmen" implied Romanism
and the enemy, and for this reason it was easier for all concerned
to think of the immigrants as "German." As Germans they con-
sistently appeared in Company records. Probably the confusion
arose because the Huguenots were soon joined by native Germans in their settlement. For the most part, the settlers were
more than simple peasants. Charles Etienne Houdelette was a
lace weaver, Francis Rittal a tailor, and Louis Cavalier a linen
weaver.[47] These were badly needed skills in the colonies, but not
of the sort that could be utilized immediately in the environment
of Frankfort. Because they had been reared in urban areas, the
immigrants were awkward and lacking in the skills of the frontier. Their adjustment was long and difficult, but their lives had
not been easy in the past. Most of the older generation had been
born in France, but were forced to flee to the Rhineland. The
move to Maine represented at least the second uprooting for
them. Furthermore, there was at first not even the stability of
family life. Apart from four or five men who brought their wives
and a very few children, the group was composed either of men
whose families were still back in Germany or of single men who
would have to find spouses as well as homes in the wilderness. A
previous generation of Huguenots had prospered in America, but
those earlier arrivals—Bowdoins, Faneuils, Manigaults, and
De Lanceys—had been merchants settled in coastal cities, not untrained husbandmen eking out a living on the frontier. Yet the
Frankfort contingent might at least ease the way for their kins-
men who would arrive later.

Other immigrants followed the first Huguenots to reach the
Kennebec, but not in the numbers the proprietors had expected.
Several letters written in September, 1752, by Huguenot leaders
at Frankfort pleaded for assistance for friends and relatives who
had been led astray. The abducted people had originally been
bound for Boston as members of Crellius's second shipment on
the *Priscilla*. They ended instead at Halifax through the deviousness of the immigrant broker.[48] Requests for help written to the
proprietors by the Frankfort settlers were in French, but were
translated by Peter Chardon, a wealthy Boston merchant who,

No.22 John Tufts   No.23 John Tufts
No.21 John Tufts   No.24 Charles Cushing
No.20 John Tufts   No.25 Jonathan Bowman
No.9 John Tufts   No.10 John Barker
No.8 Samuel Goodwin No.11 Thomas Low
No.7 Samuel Oldham No.12 Elias Cheney
No.6 Edmund Bridge No.13 Abner Marson
No.5 Samuel Goodwin No.14 Stephen Marson
No.4 Samuel Marson No.15 William Cushing
                    No.16 Samuel Goodwin Jr.
                    No.17 Peter Chardon
                    No.18 Peter Chardon
                    No.19 Jacob Bailey
                    No.20 Daniel Goodwin

KENNEBEC RIVER

EASTERN RIVER

Church Lot Episcopal

Mark Carney   No.24 Philip Fought No.25
James Cooper   John Henry Kil.
Samuel Turner   No.22 Zachariah Nardin
Adam Couch   No.21 Samuel Turner
John McGown   No.20 William Mitchell
Joseph McFarland No.18 Michel Stilfin   No.1-A
Benjamin Kendall No.18 Joseph McFarland
Uzziah Kendall   No.17 Charles Estienne Noisilette
James Goud   No.16 Abraham Pochard
George Pochard   John Pochard   No.2 - 400 Acres
David Joy No.14   John Goud?
William Storey No.13   Louis Cavalker
John Spevin No.12   Jacob Carlor   No.3 - 400 Acres
George Jacquiss No.11   John Stain
Abiathar Kendall No.10 Daniel Goud   No.4 - 400 Acres
John George Goud No.9   James Bushon
Roger Lucas No.8   John Henry Layor
Jonathan Bryant No.7   Wolf Rupert   B/ramd's Lot - 300 Acres
Frederick Peclin No.6   Amos Paris
John George Peclin No.5 Daniel Malbon
Denis Lines No.4   Philip Mayer   Pownall's Lot - 500 Acres
Gardiner to Charles Callman No.3 George Mayer
James Wyman No.2   John Ulrick Mayer
James Patterson No.1   Cassinte Mayer

B CALL

5 Miles

Lot No.18 - 3200 Acres

Lot No.19 - 3200 Acres

N S E W

This lot belongs to Col. Nath'l. Thwing
The South Line of Pownalboro which is the North Line of Woolwich
E.S.E. is 5 Miles and 54 poles to Mount Swag River

PLAN OF PART OF POWNALBOROUGH showing Plymouth Company grants to the present town of Dresden, drawn from old plans and records. From Charles E. Allen's *History of Dresden, Maine,* 1931.

like the Bowdoins, was of Huguenot stock. The people of Frankfort protested the injustice, and begged for a speedy reunion with their kinfolk. They were especially concerned with the fate of the wife and children of Daniel Malbon, and the sisters of Daniel Jacob, both Frankfort residents. They explained to the proprietors that these ". . . persones would be very necessary amongst us, some being Artist, and brought to Such Trades, as wee can't well do without."[49] The proprietors arranged for the passage of the separated immigrants, and the families were reunited.

The French settlers had been complemented from the beginning by a few German immigrants, including Wolf Rupert; Phillip, George, John, and Cassimir Mayer; and Phillip Fought. As none of these people gave bonds to William Bowdoin for passage money, it is reasonable to suppose that they had been living in Massachusetts for some time before moving to the Kennebec. Probably they came from the Germantown glass factory, in which the Bowdoins had an interest. When the venture failed, the business associates were faced with the problem of ridding themselves of their employees and some even more recently arrived Germans.[50] At this point the Kennebeck proprietors sent Thomas Marshall to Germantown to persuade some of the people there to relocate at Frankfort. The Mayers, Ruperts, and Foughts must have been among them.

During the summer of 1752, English settlers, mostly from the older settlements near the mouth of the Kennebec, began moving into the new town. These experienced colonists were now willing to take a chance at existence in the Frankfort outpost because a substantial fort had been constructed, the truce with the Indians still held, and the first arrivals had overcome the initial hardships of pioneering. For some, it meant a move of only a few miles. From the standpoint of the proprietors, these were more desirable settlers than were the French and the Germans, for they were hardy, self-sufficient, and accustomed to the ways of the frontier. They were also more quarrelsome and, as they had resided in the region for a long time, felt they had a prior claim to the lands of the Kennebec. Their coming to Frankfort caused immediate controversy, for the foreign elements complained of discrimination against them by the later arrivals. The Europeans had received forty acres of land per family, in two twenty-acre sections, as the first installment of their hundred-acre grants, but had still not received their deeds. The newcomers were given the same arrangements, but were not satisfied with them. The French and Germans were alarmed to witness "The English, Quit their first Lotts, and settle on the French Line, in such a manner as to Oblige Some of us, to take up with the other twenty Acres, at a great distance from the first, all tho we had most finish'd our Settlements."[51] The immigrants had already completed their homes, except for the roofs, and now would be obliged to start again with winter coming on. They did not hesitate to inform the proprietors of their plight, nor to remind the Company of its promises to supply them with a settled minister and a schoolmaster.[52] Again the proprietors intervened, and the Rhinelanders were confirmed in the possession of their original lots, but the pastor and the schoolmaster would not arrive for many years.

By the end of 1752, the Kennebeck proprietors had accomplished their initial goal of populating the town, although not on the scale they had anticipated. The problem of attracting settlers to their holdings on the Kennebec would continue to plague them until the conclusion of the French and Indian War. For the moment, they were faced with a situation that was entirely unproductive—a miserable village of log huts filled with fifty-odd people eating their heads off at Company expense, the land still lying undeveloped, and bills mounting every day. But the proprietors were equal to this challenge, as they would be in the future to even greater ones. Somehow they contrived to make the situation pay and exploited their proprietary town of Frankfort as the nucleus of a growing little empire on the Kennebec. The proprietors would not always be so successful, but the process of consolidating Company gains was at least now begun with the kind of careful planning, resourcefulness, and opportunism that would make future Company triumphs possible.

NOTES

CHAPTER IV

1 Third Warrant, July 6, 1751, K.P.P., Records, I, 83-88. The warrant provided for the election of officers, continued sur-

veying of Company lands, prosecution of claims against trespassers, the laying out of two towns, and the building of a fort to protect them.

2 William W. Sweet, *The Story of Religion in America* (New York, 1950), 106.

3 Erna Risch, "Joseph Crellius, Immigrant Broker," *New England Quarterly*, XII, 245-248.

4 Temple Prime, *Some Account of the Temple Family* (New York, 1894), 34.

5 Akagi, *Town Proprietors*, 258-268.

6 *Ibid.* In 1735-36 Waldo also brought over about 45 Irish families, who settled the town of Warren.

7 "Some Thoughts on the Importation of Foreigners," Bowdoin-Temple Papers, I, 12, M.H.S. Mss. of 3 pp., tentatively dated 1748. There is no indication that the manuscript was ever published. The Bowdoin family had a long history of interest in Maine lands, dating back to the settlement of Pierre Baudoin at Falmouth in the 1680s. James Bowdoin I was a full shareholder in the Lincolnshire Company in 1730, and shortly thereafter began to buy up shares in the Kennebeck Company.

8 *Ibid.*

9 *Ibid.*

10 *Ibid.*

11 *Ibid.*

12 *Massachusetts Court Records*, XIX, 62.

13 Risch, "Crellius," 246

14 *Ibid.*

15 *Ibid.*

16 *Ibid.* 247. Fort Massachusetts had been destroyed by the French and Indians in 1746, but was rebuilt by the Province, which now wished to encourage settlement in the area.

17 Abbott E. Smith, *Colonists in Bondage: White Servitude and Convict Labor in America: 1607-1776* (Chapel Hill, 1947), 61.

18 Risch, "Crellius," 241. The other firms were Isaac and

Zachary Hope, Dunlop and Company, and Harvard and Company.

19 *Ibid.* 250.

20 Allen, *Dresden,* 133. Joseph Crellius to member of Mass. government, probably Spencer Phips, 1751. Luther's letter was motivated by the attempt of his rivals in recruiting to discredit him with the people of Frankfort by printing articles relating to the slowness of Crellius's ships and the primitive conditions prevailing in Mass.

21 Risch, "Crellius," 251.

22 Allen, *Dresden,* 133.

23 Risch, "Crellius," 267. It is possible that the ship may have made some port calls before it reached Boston. The number of passengers aboard is unknown, but it must have been close to 300. Figures do exist for the *Priscilla's* second voyage. In a letter written to the Board of Trade on December 22, 1752, John Dick stated that one ship loaded with Germans had cleared Gosport for Boston during the previous year with 271 1/2 freights. Anyone over 14 years of age was classified as a full freight, children between 14 and 4 were called a half freight, and those under 4 were not counted. Thus it is impossible to know exactly how many passengers were aboard the *Priscilla* during its second voyage. Smith, *Colonists in Bondage,* 211; 315.

24 Allen, *Dresden,* 133-134.

25 Thomas Hutchinson to Samuel Waldo, Dec. 13, 1751, Thomas Hutchinson Letter Books, Mayo Copies, XXV, 5, M.H.S.

26 *Ibid.* Hutchinson also mentioned that some of the immigrants had found temporary work in the Boston area, and that a number had been taken in or supported by city residents.

27 Risch, "Crellius," 267.

28 Resolution, Dec. 6, 1751, K.P.P., Records, I, 103. In spite of proprietary promises, the settlers received an initial grant of only 40 acres each, hardly enough to support a family.

29 Allen, *Dresden,* 208. At least 11 others mortgaged themselves to Bowdoin for sums ranging from £3-11 to £28.5.3, the larger sums representing family groups.

30 Resolution, Dec. 11, 1751, K.P.P., Records, I, 104.

31 Allen, *Dresden,* 51. Allen and others have pointed out that the immigrants themselves did not come from Frankfort, but from the surrounding countryside.

32 Resolution, Dec. 11, 1751, K.P.P., Records, I, 107.

33 Resolution, December 27, 1751, K.P.P., Records, I, 111.

34 Risch, "Crellius," 251.

35 Smith, *Colonists in Bondage,* 207.

36 Resolution, Dec. 18, 1751, K.P.P., Records, I, 108. The requirement to build a house and clear land in order to gain title was already traditional in New England. Proprietary grants merely conformed to what might have been expected by settlers then moving to townships authorized by the Massachusetts General Court. For a detailed description of the planting and settling of such townships, see Charles E. Clark, *The Eastern Frontier: The Settlement of Northern New England, 1610-1763* (New York, 1970), 121-225.

37 Resolution, Dec. 18, 1751, K.P.P., Records, I, 108.

38 Resolution, Jan. 17, 1752, K.P.P., Records, I, 120. At this time Gershom Flagg was appointed to take the place of Nathaniel Thwing on the supervisory committee. As the best qualified builder in the group, he must have directed the construction of the Company fort.

39 Resolution, Dec. 6, 1751, K.P.P., Records, I, 102.

40 Resolution, Mar. 27, 1754, K.P.P., Records, II, 56.

41 *Ibid.*

42 Thomas Johnston, *A Plan of Kennebeck and Sagadahock Rivers, with the adjacent Coasts* (London, 1755). A copy of this rare engraved map is owned by the Me. H.S.

43 "A Brief State . . . ," K.P.P., Records, I, 65.

44 "An Account of Sundrys Wanted to Carry Down to Frankfort in Kennebeck River," Jan., 1752, K.P.P., Loose Papers, 1625-1759.

45 Kennebeck Committee to Paschal Nelson, May 11, 1752, K. P.P., Loose Papers, 1690-1753.

46 Allen, *Dresden,* 125-127. Allen showed indisuptably that most of the early settlers were Huguenot.

47 *Ibid.*, 140.

48 French settlers to Kennebeck proprietors, Sept. 13, 1752, K.P.P., Loose Papers, 1640-1759. In this letter the immigrants accused Crellius of diverting their friends' destination to Halifax.

49 *Ibid.*

50 Akagi, *Town Proprietors*, 266; Lucy F. Bittinger, *The Germans in Colonial Times* (Philadelphia, 1901), 135.

51 French settlers to Kennebeck proprietors, Nov. 2, 1752, K.P.P., Loose Papers, 1648-1759.

52 *Ibid.*

V

The Propriety:
Other Luminaries

The decision made by Dr. Gardiner, William Bowdoin, and others of their committee to implement settlement of their Kennebeck tract aroused keen interest among many shareholders who had previously been lukewarm in their attachment to the Company. As the town of Frankfort became a reality, new investors, lured by the prospect of profits inherent in an aggressive, enterprising company, were more than willing to join forces with the proprietary policy makers. Anticipating projected land divisions, they supported the continued development of the town in spite of mounting expenses, and approved even more ambitious plans for corporate expansion.

As the years passed, new leaders emerged from Company ranks and took their places as able companions to the resourceful Dr. Gardiner. In time, also, older proprietors faded away. Their contributions may have been soon forgotten or dimly remembered by the surviving membership but, in any event, their places were soon filled, and the propriety continued its planning on an unswerving course. Captain Robert Temple was an early source of inspiration to the reactivated Company.

On April 17, 1754, Henry Lloyd II wrote to his father, Henry Lloyd of Lloyd's Neck, New York, to inform him of the death of his uncle, Captain Robert Temple (1694-1754), four days before. Temple had been "dangerously ill of a Nervous Fever" for sever-

al weeks, but had rallied long enough to name young Henry as
an executor along with his son, Robert, Jr., and Colonel William
Brattle.[1] It was ironic that Captain Temple, a leading strategist of
the propriety, who had not been present for the fateful meeting
of December 6, 1751, should have died at a time when the Kennebeck Purchase Company was on the threshold of its greatest expansion. Certainly he would have approved of its new plans as
he had supported the decision to build Frankfort. His enthusiasm
and the prestige his name and fortune lent to the Company
would be sorely missed.

Captain Robert Temple had inherited an established social position from his uncle, Sir Thomas Temple, as well as the prospect
of the succession to a baronetcy. A friend of Charles II, Sir Thomas had retired to Boston after a stormy career as governor of
Nova Scotia.[2] By the time of his death, this unconventional Anglican royalist had been accepted in Puritan circles in Massachusetts. It was from Sir Thomas that Robert Temple had obtained
an interest in the Kennebeck Company. Temple had emigrated
from Ireland to Boston as a young man in search of a fortune and
had done well by marrying his cousin, Mehetable Nelson, the
daughter of John Nelson. Nelson, a wealthy merchant, had been
a leader in the rebellion against Governor Edmund Andros in
1689.[3] With his father-in-law's assistance, Temple prospered. Evi-
dences of his success are his purchases of Noddle's Island in Boston Harbor, where he built an imposing mansion, and of Ten Hill
Farm, the old Governor John Winthrop property in Charlestown.

Captain Temple enthusiastically supported the reorganization
of the Kennebeck Purchase Company during its early years, serving on the Standing Committee, the Committee to Defend the
Title, and the Committee of Ten.[4] He played an important part
in the planting of Frankfort and in the planning of Fort Western,
which he did not live to see erected. When the proprietors met
on April 17, 1754, first on the agenda was the motion to name
Thomas Hancock to replace the deceased Robert Temple in his
various committee assignments.[5] In later years, however,
Temple's sons, Robert, Jr., and John, would represent their father
on the proprietary board.

In the meantime, another connection of the Temples, Paschal
Nelson, kept family interest alive in the Kennebeck Purchase
Company. Paschal Nelson (?-1759), Temple's brother-in-law, had

graduated from Harvard in the class of 1721. A younger son with a reputation for carousing, he did not share in his father's estate. Paschal Nelson made a career for himself in America and England as a hanger-on of the great and influential. Well armed with letters of recommendation, he spent his time in anterooms, soliciting for public office.[6] While waiting for the big opportunity that never arrived, he occupied himself as a junior Army officer and attended to details of family business. By 1752, he was living on half pay in the Westminster Parish of London, where, in spite of frequent plans to return to Boston, he remained until his death. Nevertheless, a steady correspondence between London and America kept him informed of proprietary maneuverings, which he in turn passed on to his Temple, Nelson, and Lloyd relations. He himself assumed management of the family holdings during the interval between Captain Temple's death and his own. As agent for the proprietors living in London, he was helpful in ferreting out musty records there that pertained to the patent.[7] At his death on July 19, 1759, he left his Kennebeck lands to his various nephews, with John Nelson of Portsmouth, New Hampshire, and John Temple, then living in London, receiving the major portions.[8]

Charles Apthorp (1698-1758), who was related to both Robert Temple and Paschal Nelson, and Thomas Hancock (1703-1764), Apthorp's business partner and close friend, were two Johnny-come-lately shareholders who became indispensable members of the propriety.[9] Thomas Hancock was the son of the Reverend John Hancock of Lexington, a Congregational minister. Finances did not permit the young Hancock to attend Harvard, so his father apprenticed him to Samuel Gerrish, a Boston bookseller.[10] As soon as he completed the terms of the indenture, he opened a bookstore of his own, with the help of Daniel Henchman.[11] Finding it impossible to succeed by selling books alone, Hancock gradually shifted to a more general line of goods. As a merchant, he came into his own and acquired wealth. Much of his fortune was accumulated while in partnership with Charles Apthorp, who had grown up in England and received an upper-class education at Eton. In America he became a merchant, and Paymaster and Commissary of British land and naval forces stationed in Boston. The latter was a highly lucrative post, and a situation he was willing to share with Thomas Hancock, who also had important connections in England. A merger enabled them to exploit most of the available government contracts, and protected their individual interests. The formation of a partnership proved to be a wise business move for both of the men, who then used a part of their large profits to speculate in land on the Kennebec.

The two partners must have presented an interesting contrast at proprietors' meetings. Charles Apthorp was a gentleman born and bred; he was a handsome man, debonair and fashionably dressed—the curls of his elaborate wig in perfect order. Thomas Hancock, however, had achieved his position only after hard work; he was stocky and bulldog-like, with a pug nose and hair clubbed back simply. At times he might ride in a carriage emblazoned with his own (spurious) coat of arms, but if the occasion arose he could get down to the level of the dock worker in language and actions. Although the two men differed in their outward appearance, they were similar in their conspicuous style of living. The mansions and splendid furnishings of each were often copied by the lesser gentry. Apthorp was an Anglican and Hancock a Congregationalist, but they were in agreement concerning the prerogatives and obligations of the ruling class. In addition to his business success, Hancock had entered politics, and finally achieved that badge of prestige—a seat on the Council. Each man filled a vital role in the Kennebeck propriety.

Hancock and Apthorp were hard-working members of the Committee and attended proprietary meetings without fail. Both first became active in the Company in the winter of 1751-1752. They were frequently appointed to committees charged with raising money for important Company purposes, including the Committee to borrow £400 and the Committee to borrow £300 in 1752, the year of heavy proprietary investment at Frankfort.[12] Hancock was especially active in affairs leading to the town's founding and the later building of Fort Western. The firm of Hancock and Apthorp received its payment for government contracts in pounds sterling in an era when money was scarce and barter a common resort. Thus they became a valuable asset to the propriety, and furnished more than their share of the cash needed to develop Company holdings northward along the great river and to push the expensive lawsuits necessary to legalize proprietary claims to additional territory in the south.

Political influence contributed immensely to the succcess of the

THOMAS HANCOCK (1703-1764)
Portrait by John Singleton Copley.
Courtesy of the Fogg Art Museum, Harvard University.

partnership of Hancock and Apthorp. Hancock's chief connection leading to valuable contracts was Christopher Kilby, an old Boston friend. As Massachusetts agent in England, Kilby had helped engineer the appointment of William Shirley as governor. By 1756, Kilby had become Agent Victualler for the British Army at Boston.[13] His association with Sir William Baker (1705-1770), a London merchant with many trading contacts in America, probably led to Baker's purchase of a full share in the Kennebeck Company.[14] James Boutineau, the first cousin of William and James Bowdoin and an attorney, represented Baker in proprietary meetings. Charles Apthorp's military contracts came through business relationships with such London firms as the one owned by Chauncey Townshend, a member of the House of Commons. The Townshend concern held the contracts to supply British Army rations to Nova Scotia and Newfoundland.[15] Apthorp's son-in-law, Barlow Trecothick of London, later Lord Mayor and member of Parliament, handled the British end of the business. The American agents, 1744-1764, were Hancock and Apthorp. The Apthorp monopoly did not stop with the death of Charles in 1758, for his sons carried on the business. Thomas succeeded him as Paymaster in Boston and held that position until the British evacuation of the city in 1776.[16] Meanwhile, Charles Ward Apthorp, the oldest son and chief heir, married a daughter of James McEvers of New York City, and his sister, Elizabeth, married a McEvers son. James McEvers and his partner, John Watts, were agents in America for the British money contractors Fludyer and Drummond.[17] Charles Apthorp also shared in this contract. On his death, Charles Ward Apthorp succeeded to a half share of his portion of the money contract.[18] Charles, Sr., had built a lasting commercial dynasty which had helped to finance the Kennebeck Company, but family interest in the enterprise did not continue long after his death.

Charles Apthorp's large estate in New England was dispersed among fifteen surviving children. Real estate and personal property alone came to £13,600; government contracts and mercantile interests must have swelled the total value to much more.[19] As the eldest son, Charles Ward Apthorp received a double portion of the estate; this included the full Kennebeck Company share. His business interests were then centered in New York, so he was unable to supervise his Maine lands properly. On June 16, 1760, he gave to Silvester Gardiner power of attorney over his Kennebeck share, ". . . with full Power to appear for me at any Proprietary Meeting & there Vote Act & Transact for me in as full & ample Manner as if I was present . . . ."[20] After this, Apthorp family interests lessened in the Company, although assessments were paid regularly and land grants received periodically.

Thomas Hancock survived his business partner by six years. During this brief period, he invested heavily in the Kennebeck Company and became a double shareholder. But Hancock's heirs, like Apthorp's, did not continue his enthusiasm for the Company after his death in 1764. The merchant-capitalist left an enormous estate, the exact amount known only to his widow and nephew. After very substantial bequests (£10,000 sterling plus mansion, household furnishings, plate, chariot, and paintings to Lydia, his wife; £1000 to Harvard for a chair in Oriental Languages; £100 to the Brattle Square Church; and generous gifts to several nieces and nephews) designated initially, by far the largest part of his estate went to his nephew and adopted son, John Hancock.[21] Besides owning this property, the younger Hancock controlled the spending of his Aunt Lydia's money, and eventually inherited it at her death in 1778. This great fortune, together with the double share, made John Hancock one of the most important proprietors of the Kennebeck Company. His concerns, however, became increasingly political and, after 1765, he began to take less and less interest in the Company.[22] Perhaps his assistance was not needed. Younger members of other opulent families were already filling the void occasioned by the deaths of older proprietors. Chief among these was James Bowdoin.

James Bowdoin (1726-1790), who was to become second only to Silvester Gardiner in proprietary influence, was slow in assuming a prominent place in Company proceedings, perhaps preferring to let his older brother William take the lead. He attended meetings sporadically in 1750 and 1751, and held no offices or committee seats. He did not appear at the eventful meeting of December 6, 1751, but the decision to sponsor a Company town apparently captured his interest; from the beginning of 1752 until the start of the American Revolution, he was indisputably a leading light of the propriety.

Young Bowdoin, only twenty-six in 1752, soon rose to power. He was appointed a member of the various Company committees to raise money, and became treasurer and assessor in Sep-

tember of 1753 and a member of the Standing Committee in
October. He continued as treasurer for over twenty-five years.
James had the ambition of his older brother, and far more ability. Like William he gradually withdrew from mercantile pursuits
and invested in money lending, land speculation, and commercial
development. His industrial investments included shares in a paper mill at Milton and an iron works at Bridgewater, and also,
with his brother, an interest in a Braintree glass factory. James
Bowdoin appears to have been the eighteenth century colonial
embodiment of the Renaissance Man, for his interests spanned
business, politics, writing, and science. He fancied himself as a
poet; his prose was much better. As the author of proprietary
pamphlets contesting the claims of rival land companies, his literary talents proved valuable to the Company. For years Bowdoin
maintained a correspondence with Benjamin Franklin on such
subjects as the luminosity of sea water and electrical experimenta-
tion. His letters are crowded with details about the management
of his many properties; orders to British merchants reveal a love
of books, fine furnishings, jewelry, and clothing. Robert Feke
painted James Bowdoin's portrait in the same year that William
Bowdoin sat for him. James is dressed in elegant silks and satins
similar to those worn by his brother, and is standing in a romantic landscape. Perhaps the artist was drawn to the warmer personality of the tall, handsome, faintly smiling James and took
greater pains with his portrait; at any rate, it makes a better
impression on the viewer than does that of the colorless William.
It is not surprising that James Bowdoin soon eclipsed his brother
in proprietary and provincial politics.

Somehow, James Bowdoin, an aristocratic young man born
with every advantage, managed to make himself attractive to the
homespun Boston electorate. In 1752 he first stood for election as
one of the town's representatives in the House, and served there
for several terms.[23] In 1757 he advanced to the Council, reaching
a position never held by his brother. For much of his political career, James Bowdoin was a conservative in provincial politics,
but following the passage of the Stamp Act, he grew increasingly
radical. As the colonies moved toward an open break with England, he became an avowed Whig leader, operating from a
powerful base in the upper house.

Benjamin Hallowell's first appearance at a proprietary meeting,
on April 29, 1752, came not long after Dr. Gardiner and James

Bowdoin began to take an interest in the Company.[24] Like them, he seemed drawn by the promise of action. Hallowell (1699-1773), the son of Benjamin and Mary Stocker Hallowell of Boston, was a shipwright in early life. A self-made man like several of the other proprietors, he eventually became the owner of a shipyard, a ropewalk, a Boston mansion, and two Kennebeck shares.[25] In spite of his prominence, his personality does not stand out strongly against those of his more colorful associates. Three ambitious sons seemed much more in evidence than their father, and their actions during the decade of the 1760s did affect the fortunes of the propriety. Benjamin and Robert became customs collectors, whose decisions often influenced important Revolutionary issues. Briggs Hallowell, the youngest son and a sea captain, settled on the Kennebec River and alternately helped and opposed the proprietors in their designs. He was a thorn in the side of Dr. Gardiner for many years and played a dramatic role in an opening crisis of the Revolution in Massachusetts. Old Benjamin Hallowell, unlike his venturesome offspring, was a close friend and dependable ally of Dr. Gardiner in implementing Gardiner's ideas into Company policy.

Benjamin Hallowell was typical of several of the lesser known proprietors. Older men usually, they were content to do their duty and let other, quicker minds do the leading. William Tailer (?-1789) was a good example of the do-nothing shareholder; Jabez Fox (1705-1755) suffered from chronic ill health; Nathan Stone (1707-1781) and Habijah Weld (1702-1782) lacked interest; Edward Tyng (1683-1755) was afflicted with mental ailments; Florentius Vassall (?-1778) lived in England; and his cousin William Vassall (1715-1800) was largely preoccupied with his own business affairs.

William Tailer owned a full share in the Kennebeck Purchase. A merchant, he contributed nothing tangible to the Company except his consistent presence at proprietary gatherings. Tailer, like so many others in the Company, could well boast of his genteel background in Massachusetts. He was the son of Lt. Gov. William Tailer and the grandson of a third William Tailer, a rich Boston merchant who caused great scandal among the latter-day Puritans by committing suicide in 1682. He was also the grandson of William Stoughton, another early eighteenth century lieutenant governor of the Province, and was connected with the prominent Nelson, Danforth, and Cooper families of Boston. Tailer may

JAMES BOWDOIN II (1726-1790)
Portrait by Robert Feke. Courtesy of the Bowdoin College Museum of Art.

well have been influenced to begin accumulating fragments of proprietary shares by Captain Robert Temple, who had married Tailer's niece.[26] He began to attend Company meetings late in 1752, when the first proprietary town was a going enterprise.[27] He never held office. His single moment of proprietary leadership—if it was that—came at a poorly attended meeting on January 14, 1761, when he served as moderator *pro tem*.[28] Tailer, a Loyalist, was proscribed and banished in 1778, but he returned to Massachusetts after the Revolution and died at his Milton estate in 1789.

Jabez Fox was the half shareholder who had been forced by financial reverses to sell his portion to James Bowdoin.[29] His father was the Reverend John Fox of Woburn, and his mother was Mary Tyng, the daughter of an original Kennebeck tract purchaser. John Fox had the advantages of a Harvard education, but his family was land poor. At Falmouth, Maine, only a small frontier town when he reached it, Fox shone as a merchant, notary public, surveyor, and representative to the House. He was an important personage in Falmouth, living in a "mansion," and achieving election to the Council at the height of his career in 1752.[30] But his health suffered as his finances did. He died on April 6, 1755, leaving an encumbered estate to his widow.[31]

Edward Tyng, Jr., the brother of Mary Tyng and an uncle of Jabez Fox, was born in Maine during the Indian wars. Like Fox, he spent much time at Falmouth, where he lived the life of a colonial grandee. His second wife, Ann, was the sister of Samuel Waldo, developer of the Waldo Patent. Tyng was in partnership in Falmouth with Phineas Jones, and dispatched cargoes in his own ships. It was as commander of the snow *Prince of Orange* that he captured a French privateer, the *Vigilante*, a warship of sixty-four guns, in 1744.[32] At the siege of Louisburg the next year, he was appointed Commodore of the Provincial fleet and won further honors for bravery. During the next few years, his mind began to give way. He attended few proprietary meetings, and none after December 19, 1750.[33] He died in Boston on September 8, 1755, at the age of seventy-two. Because his children failed to pay their numerous assessments, the Tyng share was sold for taxes in 1758.[34]

The Tyng heirs did not forget their loss. In 1764, they petitioned the General Court for restoration of their father's share, claiming that Tyng had been deranged for some time before his death and unable to transact business. They further noted that their sister, Ann Tyng, who managed affairs after their father's death, died fourteen months later and that neither of them could assume the responsibility for the estate; William was a minor and Edward had been captured by the French at Oswego. The sons claimed that default of the Kennebeck Company share had been through no fault of their own and demanded the restoration of it.[35] The Tyng heirs failed to win support from the General Court, although some members sympathized with them. From a vantage point in Charlestown, Edward Goodwin wrote to his brother Samuel that the representatives ". . . to a man are of the opinion that the young men ought to have their Land again [after] paying the Charges . . . . They say it is barbarous to have two orphangs thus Ronged."[36] The treatment accorded the Tyng family ultimately proved very costly for the Kennebeck proprietors, for the notoriety of the case contributed to the reservoir of ill will then building against the Company.

The misfortunes of the Tyng family did not affect the resolution of other representatives of their extended family group to profit from their Kennebeck holdings. The Reverend Nathan Stone of Southborough and the Reverend Habijah Weld of Middleborough, two Congregational ministers, had each gained possession of a one-quarter share in the Kennebeck Purchase through marriage to sisters of Jabez Fox. Neither minister participated in the management or development of the Company, but each was considerably enriched from the land divisions. They or their heirs had each received 3,545 acres by 1795 and the promise of more to come.[37] Nathan Stone attended just four proprietary meetings—one in 1753, one in 1772, and two in 1774. The last three meetings were occasions for land divisions, indicating the direction of his interest. Habijah Weld never made an appearance. The two men held no offices, but they were careful to meet their assessments and remain in good standing.[38]

The ministers were not alone in this respect. Florentius Vassall and his cousin William Vassall also benefited as absentee landlords. Florentius Vassall of Wimpole Street, London, never saw his Maine estates, although he may have visited Boston briefly in 1775.[39] Florentius Vassall, like his cousin, lived luxuriously on the profits of his Jamaica plantations. He purchased his full Company share from William Brattle before June 6, 1753, because on that date he was voted agent for the proprietors in England, with full powers to ". . . prefer any Petitions or Commence any suit in Council or any other Courts of Law or Equity . . . ."[40] He continued as agent until the Revolution and actively assisted the proprietors in locating copies of old deeds as well as expediting an important lawsuit appealed to the King in Council. While Vassall enjoyed himself in London, Dr. Gardiner used his proxy in Company meetings.[41] When the war came, his Maine lands were confiscated by the Massachusetts revolutionary government. Vassall did not give up easily. Upon his death in 1778, his claim was passed on to his son Richard, from whom it descended to his granddaughter Elizabeth, Lady Holland. Her lengthy and involved lawsuit to recover the estate finally terminated unfavorably in 1851.[42]

William Vassall, the son of Leonard Vassall, chose to live in Boston. He was a member of the Harvard class of 1733 and took a master's degree there ten years later.[43] In addition to his Green Island River plantation in Jamaica, he owned several houses in Boston and a splendid mansion at Bristol, Rhode Island.[44] Although, according to the terms of his father's will, he had promised not to gamble more than twenty shillings in any game of chance, he did indulge himself in frequent lawsuits. Jermiah Gridley, John Adams, Benjamin Prat, and James Otis, Jr., often represented him—to their profit. It was said that going to court cost "Billy" Vassall £1000 per year.[45] Several of his lawsuits were noteworthy in New England. As he did not always win, he might have done better to stick to gambling. Vassall was a latecomer to the Kennebeck Company, having purchased his half share from John Tufts.[46] He attended proprietary meetings with interest, but served only on the Committee to Examine Accounts.[47] His main concern for his holding was clearly a quick profit. On March 22, 1775, less than one month before the battle of Lexington, Vassall bought a 1/48th share of 72,000 acres from the Company for £25, apparently unaware that the foundations of the Kennebeck Company were shaky because of the worsening political situation. He was joined in this purchase by Dr. Gardiner and several other proprietors.[48] Soon afterward, Company operations broke down and ceased for the duration of the American Revolution. Unlike his cousin Florentius, William Vassall, a Tory, did succeed in regaining his Maine property after the Revolution.[49]

The remaining proprietors of the Kennebeck Purchase Com-

pany present a study in contrasts. Gershom Flagg (1705-1771) and
Jonathan Reed (1718-1808) were both closely connected with the
founding of Frankfort, yet Flagg made a far more tangible contribution to the success of the Company than did Reed, who
merely emigrated to the new town. Gershom Flagg was only a
half-share owner, but his work for the proprietors entitled him to
the impressive title of master builder. Flagg was a housewright
by trade, born in Boston, where he received most of his contracting commissions. His professional reputation was excellent. He
shingled the tower of King's Chapel in 1762 and did some glazing
there the following year. At the time of Flagg's death, a large balance was still owing to him for work done on that Angilican structure.[50] Gershom Flagg was also the contractor for a project completed for John Hancock during 1768-1769. The total charge was
£38.18-, considerably more than he received for his renovations
at King's Chapel.[51] The contract may have involved repairs to the
old Hancock mansion, where John lived after his uncle's death.
Legends that Gershom Flagg constructed several imposing mansions in the Boston-Cambridge area have not yet been substantiat-
ed. There is no doubt that he built several major structures on the
Maine frontier. These included the Kennebeck Company's Fort
Western at present-day Augusta, work on the Province-financed
Fort Halifax at Winslow, and the Company's Pownalborough
Court House.[52] In 1759, Flagg accompanied Governor Thomas
Pownall on the Penobscot Expedition and erected the blockhouse
on that river. His share of the Kennebeck Purchase, which totaled
7,090 acres when he died in 1771, should have made him a wealthy man.[53] Robert Feke's portrait of Flagg, one of his best, shows
a clear-eyed, resolute man in the prime of life, with a round, pen-
sive face. He was a Baptist, and had know religious discrimination in Massachusetts Bay.[54] The letters he sent to the principal
proprietors show a certain obsequiousness, a ". . . hope, sir, you
will excuse my freedom in this . . ." approach which was an appropriate response by an artisan to his betters.[55] His son James,
however, was ready to defy Dr. Gardiner and lampoon the
whole   Kennebeck   Company   when   he   believed   himself
wronged.[56] Gershom's restraint may have been diplomacy, for he
had much to gain from his connection with the Company.[57]

In contrast to Flagg's labors for the Company, Jonathan Reed's
services made little impression on proprietary policy. Reed, a native of Woburn and a quarter-share holder, was present at many

Company meetings, 1750-1754, after which he moved to Frankfort. In 1757 he was granted four small lots in the town, approximately ninety acres, with the exception of the white pine trees
which were reserved for the Royal Navy.[58] In later allotments he
received 2,745 acres more. He appears again in Company records
when the Pownalborough Court House was renovated. In 1768
and 1769, he ". . . was employed to see it done."[59] From time to
time he made the long trip from the Kennebec to Boston, appearing for the last time at a proprietary assembly on September 11,
1771.[60] In his old age he moved from Frankfort to nearby Woolwich, where he died in 1808 at the remarkable age of ninety.[61]
He had outlasted nearly all of the original proprietors, and all of
the principal Company officials. His name completes the roll call
of proprietors of the Kennebeck Purchase, appropriately enough,
as he appears to have been the least of them. The lengthy roster
incorporates the names of the famous and the unknown, the rich
and the poor—almost a perfect cross section of colonial life. But
to Bostonians familiar with the Company and its dealings, it was
the "Seven or Eight good men"—the great proprietors—who really made up this speculative enterprise. So it seemed to John
Adams, a rising young lawyer in the early 1770s.

In addition to being employed privately by several of the proprietors, John Adams was a defense counsel in Company cases,
and had many opportunities to observe the proprietors in action.
Through his eyes, we see a side of the Company best known by
contemporaries. A keen judge of character, Adams soon detected
individual foibles, conceits, and factional tendencies. In 1771 he
wrote in his diary: "Going to Mr. Pitts's, to meet the Kennebeck
Company—Bowdoin, Gardiner, Hallowell, and Pitts. There I
shall hear Philosophy, and Politicks, in Perfection from H.—high
flying, high church, high state from G.—sedate, cool, Moderation
from B.—and warm, honest, frank Whiggism from P. I never
spent an Evening at Pitts's. What can I learn tonight."[62] His comment later than evening was anticlimactic: "Came home and can
now answer the Question. I learned nothing [although] the Company was agreeable enough."[63] Perhaps Adams had been misled
by the general reputation of these gentlemen. If he had been
asked to generalize about the Kennebeck proprietors, however,
John Adams could have made several assertions with certainty.
First, he could have commented that nearly all of the great proprietors, and many of the smaller ones, were educated men of

wealth with influence in the Province. Adams could also have pointed out well-known proprietors in the House and on the Governor's Council and have commented on the social prominence of the group.

One measure of social prestige in Boston during pre-Revolutionary years was the ownership of a carriage. In 1768 a French visitor noted twenty-two aristocrats of the town thus distinguished, among them: Governor Francis Bernard; Lt. Gov. Thomas Hutchinson; James Pitts, James Bowdoin; his father-in-law, John Erving; John Hancock; Silvester Gardiner; William Vassall; Thomas Flucker; James Boutineau; Grizzel Apthorp, Charles Apthorp's widow; John Apthorp, his son; and an Apthorp son-in-law, Dr. Thomas Bulfinch.[64] The Kennebeck proprietors on this list were obvious as individuals who had accumulated enough capital to afford the luxury of speculative investment. John Adams, the interested observer, watched the Kennebeck Company develop under the leadership of these men and finally break down in 1775.[65]

In 1752, however, the Kennebeck proprietors could not have foreseen the setbacks which still lay far in the future, for their minds naturally were occupied with the more pressing concerns of the moment. True, their frontier outpost had at last been established—a little cluster of log huts huddled beside the river. But its prospects appeared bleak. Only the truly visionary among the proprietors could imagine this place as the seat of a new inland empire. Frankfort's future would depend largely upon continued peaceful relations with the French and Indians, but proprietary labor there had only begun. The next few years would find Dr. Gardiner and his Standing Committee completing their planting efforts at Frankfort and looking ahead toward further exploitation of their valley.

NOTES

CHAPTER V

1 Henry Lloyd II to Henry Lloyd, Apr. 17, 1754, *Papers of the Lloyd Family*, II, 515-516.

2 Arthur H. Buffington, "Sir Thomas Temple in Boston, a Case of Benevolent Assimilation," *Publications of the Colonial Society of Massachusetts,* XXVII, *Transactions,* 308-319.

3 Winsor, ed., *Memorial History of Boston,* II, 14-15.

4 Company Resolutions, Nov. 28, 1750, K.P.P., Records, I, 52; Dec. 19, 1750, K.P.P., Records, I, 56; Nov. 7, 1753, K. P.P., Records, II, 46.

5 Company Resolution, Apr. 17, 1754, K.P.P., Records, II, 62.

6 Shipton's *Sibley's Harvard Graduates,* VI, 505.

7 Company Resolution, May 20, 1751, K.P.P., Records, I, 29. Nelson was directed to "get Copyes of the Grants or any Other Paper Relating this Proprietes."

8 Will of Paschal Nelson of London, July 19, 1759, *Papers of the Lloyd Family,* II, 569-570.

9 Apthorp's handsome wife, Grizzel Eastwicke, the granddaughter of a baronet, was a first cousin of Henry Lloyd I.

10 William T. Baxter, *The House of Hancock: Business in Boston, 1724-1775* (Cambridge, Mass., 1945), 5. Baxter provides valuable insight into the merchant activities of Thomas Hancock and his famous nephew, but sheds little light on their interest in land speculation.

11 Hancock later married Henchman's daughter, Lydia.

12 Company Resolution, May 5, 1752, K.P.P., Records, I, 127; July 20, 1752, K.P.P., Records, I, 134.

13 Henry W. Foote, ed., *Annals of King's Chapel* (Boston, 1882-1896), II, 92-93. Kilby and Hancock were so close that the former's daughter continued to live with the Hancock family after Kilby returned to England. Thomas Hancock later made the arrangements for her marriage in America.

14 John Shy, *Toward Lexington: The Role of the British Army in the Coming of the American Revolution* (Princeton, 1965), 333. At the second sale of delinquent proprietary lands in 1758, John Sweetser bid in several shares including that of Phineas Jones, which he later sold to the following proprietors: Thomas Hancock, James Pitts, Benjamin Hallowell, Silvester Gardiner, James Bowdoin and William Bowdoin. The Jones share must have been sold to Baker through the

good offices of Thomas Hancock. "Shares and Proportions
. . . ." Sir William Baker had important army contracts in
America and was, in addition, a political ally of James De-
lancey of New York as well as his commercial correspond-
ent. Stanley Katz, *Newcastle's New York: Anglo-American
Politics, 1732-1753* (Cambridge, 1968), 208. As M.P. for
London in the 1760s, Baker defended the American position
before Parliament at the time of the Stamp Act crisis.

15 Shy, *Toward Lexington*, 334-335.

16 James H. Stark, *Loyalists of Massachusetts* (Boston, 1910),
351-354.

17 Shy, *Toward Lexington*, 337.

18 Henry Lloyd II to Henry Lloyd, Feb. 21, 1759, *Papers of the
Lloyd Family*, II, 564. The letter explained that Apthorp had
offered William Smith, Lloyd's nephew, the superintendency
of the Halifax office of the money contract at £120 per year,
a handsome sum for that day and indicative of what the full
contract was worth.

19 Will of Charles Apthorp, probated May 25, 1759, Suffolk
County Probate Records, LVI, 68, No. 11871.

20 Charles Ward Apthorp to Silvester Gardiner, June 16, 1760,
Gardiner-Whipple Mss., II, 91, M.H.S.

21 Will of Thomas Hancock, Probated Aug. 10, 1764, Suffolk
County Probate Records, LXIII, 140-143. The lands in the
Kennebeck Purchase inherited by John Hancock did not include 17,800 acres there willed to other relatives and friends.
According to the elder Hancock's wishes, no inventory was
given to the Probate Court of the property willed to his nephew.

22 On the death of his uncle, John Hancock was elected to the
Standing Committee, May 15, 1765, K.P.P., Records, II, 390.
He attended several meetings during the period Aug. 15, 1765-
Feb. 10, 1767, nearly all of which were adjourned for lack of
a quorum. He did not appear again until Sept. 11, 1771.

23 Shipton's *Sibley's Harvard Graduates*, XI, 515.

24 Hallowell first attended a Kennebeck proprietors' meeting
on Apr. 29, 1752, and became a member of the Standing Committee in Oct. of that year. K.P.P., Records, I, 126; 149.

25 "Inventory of the Estate of Benjamin Hallowell late of Boston Esqr. dec'd," Mar., 1773, Suffolk County Probate Records, LXXII, 290-292. The inventory of the Hallowell estate is an unusually complete one. It includes a mansion house valued at £1100, and an itemized, room by room account of its furnishings. There were 213 ounces of silver plate appraised at £71, a modest amount for a wealthy man. Total value of Hallowell's Boston properties was £2275.14.6. No price was set on his Kennebeck shares. In his will, much Maine land was left to his sons and daughters, including a sawmill at Cathance River, which must have been a useful adjunct to his Boston shipyard. Will of Benjamin Hallowell, dated Jan. 25, 1773, Suffolk County Probate Records, LXXII, 177-179.

26 Winsor, *Memorial History of Boston*, II, xxiii.

27 Company Records, Nov. 29, 1752, K.P.P., Records, I, 154.

28 Company Resolution, Jan. 14, 1761, K.P.P., Records, II, 259.

29 See Chapter II.

30 Shipton's *Sibley's Harvard Graduates*, VIII, 134-135.

31 *Ibid.*, 135. Interestingly enough, Fox's second wife was the widow of Phineas Jones, who purchased Kennebeck shares in the early 1730s before the Company was reactivated. As a Falmouth merchant, Jabez Fox furnished supplies for Edward Tyng's *Prince of Orange*. Jabez Fox Account Book, 260, Me. H.S.

32 Gould, *Portland in the Past*, 249. For this exploit, the grateful merchants of Boston presented Tyng with a large covered standing cup, made by Jacob Hurd, which Tyng called his "Bishop." It was confiscated by Continental soldiers from the Loyalist Tyngs at the start of the Revolution but later restored by act of the Mass. Prov. Congress. It is now in the Garvan Collection, Yale University.

33 Company Records, Dec. 19, 1750, K.P.P., Records, I, 59.

34 "Shares and Proportions . . . ."

35 Tyng v. Kennebeck Purchase Company, May, 1764, M.A., XLI, 469.

36 Edward Goodwin to Samuel Goodwin, May 6, 1763, Goodwin Papers (1753-1791), P.C.H.P. Representatives of another

branch of the Tyng family sued the Kennebeck proprietors in 1753. Eleazer Tyng of Dunstable and his son John claimed that, as the descendants of Jonathan Tyng, son of Edward Tyng I, an original proprietor of 1661, they had been excluded from their share of the Kennebeck lands by Edward Tyng II, Jonathan's older brother. They lost the case at that time, but renewed it after the Revolution. On June 16, 1784, John Tyng and John Lowell, who had purchased a part of John's claim, were awarded their demands, a matter of 13,885 acres in the Kennebeck Purchase, and were admitted as members of the propriety. K.P.P., Loose Papers (1625-Oct., 1757); Nash, *Augusta*, 282-283.

37 "Memoranda of the lands granted to the Several Proprietors of the Kennebeck Purchase from the late Colony of New Plymouth from the 11th December 1754 to the 3rd June 1795 Inclusive," K.P.P., Loose Papers, c. 1795.

38 Habijah Weld's 1/4th share was sold at auction as delinquent on Nov. 9, 1757, but he later redeemed it. "Shares and Proportions . . . ." Of Weld, it has been written that the abundant ". . . hospitality of the parsonage was more than a ministerial salary could provide and it is to be explained by the fact that the Welds inherited large tracts in Maine from the Tyngs, Savages, and Foxes. The minister was a Kennebeck proprietor and owned lands in Pittston and neighboring Maine towns." Shipton's *Sibley's Harvard Graduates*, VII, 270. See also VII, 100. Stone tended toward Toryism and Weld favored the Whig side in politics, yet the two ministers had much in common. Each was the son of a minister. Stone's first and second wives were the daughters of ministers, and Weld's four daughters married ministers. Both men graduated from Harvard and had influential family connections. Habijah Weld was descended through his mother from the important Savage family of Boston. Nathan Stone was a grandson of Governor Hinckley of the Plymouth Colony.

39 Nash, *Augusta*, 79.

40 Company Resolution, June 6, 1753, K.P.P., Records, II, 24.

41 Vassall sent his power of attorney to Gardiner on two separate occasions, July 26, 1756, and Feb. 25, 1761. Gardiner-Whipple Mss., II, 91, M.H.S.

42 "The Vassalls of New England," *New England Historic and Genealogical Register,* XVII (Albany, 1863), 61.

43 Shipton's *Sibley's Harvard Graduates,* X, 351. Two other Vassall brothers also held Harvard degrees: Lewis (1728) and John (1732).

44 "The Vassalls of New England," 60-61.

45 Shipton's *Sibley's Harvard Graduates,* X, 351.

46 See Chapter III.

47 Company Resolution, Dec. 11, 1771, K.P.P., Records, III, 77.

48 Proprietary Records, Mar. 22, 1775, K.P.P., Records, III, 119. At this meeting, Dr. Gardiner bought 1/6th of the same tract for £200 and bought Florentius Vassall and Charles Ward Apthorp each a 1/24th share at £50.

49 See Chapter II.

50 Foote, *Annals of King's Chapel,* II, 225. Flagg's final bill was for £17.13.9.

51 Summary of work done by Gershom Flagg for John Hancock, payment rendered July 7, 1768—July 12, 1769, John Hancock Receipt Book, Sept. 11, 1764-Feb. 20, 1784, Baker Library, Harvard. At Gershom Flagg's death in 1771, there was a balance remaining of £3.2.3/4, which John Hancock paid to James Flagg, Gershom's son and executor.

52 Itemized accounts still exist in Company records for Fort Western and the Pownalborough Court House.

53 "Memoranda of the lands granted to the Several Proprietors . . . ," K.P.P., The list shows that Gershom Flagg had drawn 7,090 acres in Company divisions, had received 2,400 additional acres "for services or a valuable consideration," and that 3,070 acres were still owing to his heirs by the Company.

54 The Baptists of this era were deprived of their full civil and religious rights in Mass., and did not achieve them until after the Revolution. Gershom Flagg was a member of the First Baptist Church of Boston.

55 Gershom Flagg to Silvester Gardiner, May 29, 1759, K.P.P., Loose Papers, Nov. 1757—Apr. 1768.

56 While it cannot be conclusively proved that James Flagg

wrote "The Strange Account . . .," it would have been to his distinct advantage to do so. Pamphlets he printed and distributed during his protracted lawsuit with Dr. Gardiner, however, leave no doubt of his opinion of that gentleman. In *A Short Vindication of the Conduct of the Referees* [Edward Payne and Henderson Inches] *in the Case of Gardiner Versus Flagg, Against the Unjust Aspersions, Contained in Two Anonymous Pamphlets Lately Published and Handed About* (Boston, 1767), he referred to Gardiner as "more remarkable for the warmth of his head, than for the honesty of his heart . . . ."

57 In spite of his extensive land grants, Gershom Flagg was insolvent at his death. In 1772, Gershom Flagg, Jr., and James Flagg, his administrators, petitioned the Sup. Court of Jud. for permission to sell real estate valued at £347.3.5 1/2 to pay outstanding debts. Some of his property may have been distributed to his children before his death, for they owned extensive lands in the Kennebeck tract. Petition by James Flagg and Gershom Flagg, Jr., to the Sup. Court of Judicature, 1772, Records of the Supreme Judicial Court for Suffolk County.

58 Proprietary Grant to Jonathan Reed, Sept. 7, 1757, K.P.P., Records, II, 130-131.

59 "Sundry Accounts Dr. to James Bowdoin, Esqr.," May 29, 1768, K.P.P., Records, II, 130-131.

60 Proprietary Records, Sept. 11, 1771, K.P.P., Records, III, 73.

61 Allen, *Dresden*, 571.

62 John Adams, *The Adams Papers: Diary and Autobiography of John Adams*, II, 5-6.

63 *Ibid.*

64 "Names of Carriage Holders in Boston, 1768," *Massachusetts Historical Society Proceedings*, 2nd Series, I, 225.

65 Adams commented upon individual proprietors and their actions many times in his diary. See *The Adams Papers: Diary and Autobiography of John Adams* for revealing remarks concerning the following: Charles Apthorp, I, 82, 150; James Bowdoin, II, 5, 61-62, III, 324; Silvester Gardiner, I, 151, II, 61-62.

VI

Consolidating Company Gains

The continuing progress of Frankfort on the Kennebec was vital both to the proprietors and the settlers they had brought there. The proprietors needed to establish a strong base of operations from which to develop further their still almost untouched territory. During the 1750s, therefore, Kennebeck Company leaders carefully formulated and executed plans for the expansion of Frankfort and for projected new townships to the north. The immigrants were also dedicated to the future of their settlement, for in its success lay theirs. They began life on the Kennebec heavily dependent on the Company, and could become self-sufficient only by perseverance and hard work. Frankfort was thus a gamble to both groups. During the opening months of 1752, the Kennebeck proprietors faced the immediate problem of keeping their new tenants provisioned and reasonably contented. Other pressing issues involved supplying Frankfort with needed services, including local government; the continued surveying of proprietary lands; commencing additional towns; considering a first division of land to proprietors; and treating with the Indians to maintain peaceful relations. Most of these plans were enumerated in the Company warrant of July 6, 1751. The years 1752-1754, when a beginning was made to resolve these problems, were especially critical to the ultimate success of the proprietary investment.

The proprietors knew that swift, dependable transportation be-

tween Boston and the Kennebec was essential for the continued
existence of Frankfort and the development of its resources. A
ship had been hired to bring the immigrants to Frankfort, but its
regular use would be prohibitive, and a constant drain on the
Company. In 1752 the proprietors debated whether to "Purchas
or Hire one or more Sloops to apply to Frankfort."[1] Dr. Gardiner
now volunteered his services. With Company approval, he would
construct a sloop at his own expense and operate it for proprietary purposes. His proposal was accepted. Gardiner's sloop plied
the Kennebec for many years—in the summer months, when the
ship could anchor under the walls of Fort Frankfort, following a
regular Boston-Frankfort schedule; and in the winter, because of
ice on the river, traveling between Boston and the Sheepscot River, a nearby waterway which flowed into the Atlantic. For his ac-
commodation to the Company, Dr. Gardiner was tendered a special grant, described in his own words as "400 Acres of Land up
Sheepscut River . . . then not worth more than 2sh/Acre."[2] For
all of his deprecation of the emoluments received, Gardiner
made the shipping business pay. He charged the Company for
cargoes transported to Frankfort and accepted private shipments
at a premium. For years he controlled a monopoly on the fastest
passage to the Company town. The sloop was also convenient for
Gardiner's own annual summer inspection tour of his holdings,
and furnished easy transportation for other proprietors who occasionally visited the Kennebec.

Gardiner was strategically situated to handle Company shipments, for his Committee of Ten was entrusted with the management of supplies for the dependent settlers during their first year
on the river. For this purpose the proprietors proposed raising an
initial fund of £1800 (Old Tenor) and estimated costs for the next
six months at an additional £1200. The Committee of Ten dutifully gave its bond of £3000 in January, 1752, before actual settlement commenced.[3] The first list of supplies to be purchased by
the doctor was singularly complete, including foodstuffs of all
kinds, wearing apparel, firearms, farm utensils, construction
equipment and materials, such indispensable items as a doctor's
box and even two pairs of tooth drawers, a flag, two drums, and
padlocks for the front gate. The culinary talents of the inhabitants would be severely tried by such standard New England
fare as pork, Indian meal, peas, white beans, cheese, and molas-
ses—the salt, sugar, and spices provided might render them palat-

able. Dr. Gardiner drew up the grand shopping list, but it was understood from the beginning that the goods themselves would be procured from the stores and warehouses of Kennebeck proprietors.[4] The medicine chest itself, as might be expected, came from Dr. Gardiner's own apothecary shop. A study of the Company ledger reveals that most of the active proprietors regularly met corporate needs to their own profit. Nathaniel Thwing dealt mainly in foodstuffs: rum, bread, salmon, pork, Indian meal, rye meal, rice, and sugar.[5] Benjamin Hallowell traded, not surprisingly considering his shipyard and chandlery business, in twine, codlines, compasses, hinges, staples, belts, chains, and hooks.[6] Thomas Marshall, Jacob Wendell, Thomas Hancock, William Tailer, and Silvester Gardiner could provide almost anything on demand; bread, hoes, cooperage, tin kettles, blankets, paper, Osnaburg dress lengths, leather, and candles.[7] Their inventories exemplify the diverse nature of the stock of most New England merchants.

Some of the wealthy proprietors, notably Charles Apthorp and the two Bowdoins, provided mostly cash for the infant settlement's needs.[8] Apthorp had available good English sterling received from his army and navy contracts, and probably found it more convenient to pay his share in silver than in goods. The Bowdoins by this time had invested most of their recent inheritance in land and money at interest; they could not well supply Company needs in kind. This was not true of most of the other great proprietors, who as merchants received almost anything in trade. Many of these items, especially the less desirable ones, could now be palmed off on the Company as installment payments on the inevitable levies, thereby saving their always scarce cash for more pressing purposes.

The account of James Pitts, a double share holder, illustrates just how large a return a proprietor might realize through dealings with the Company. During 1753, a year of massive proprietary investment at Frankfort, Pitts supplied the Company with goods in quantity on easy terms. He traded mostly in foodstuffs and hardware—bread, beef, pork, flour, and rum by the barrel; potatoes, rye, corn, salt and wheat by the bushel; and axes, hoes, spoke shaves, pails, and tin kettles by the dozen. He also furnished blankets, woolen yard goods, cheese, pitch, coffee, sugar, yarn hose, lime, and candles upon occasion. His total charge for goods sent to the Kennebec between March and November,

1753, was £539.4.1/2. A similar account for April, 1756-September, 1764, a period when the Company was supplying Fort Western but was no longer burdened with the support of the settlers at Frankfort, added a total charge of £327.0.11.[9] Pitts had thus provided the Kennebeck propriety with goods and services totaling £866.6.3 1/2 during the years 1753-1764. In the same period, he had also paid his share of the frequent Company assessments levied upon the proprietors. His proportion of the £2800 tax voted on December 13, 1753, was £58.6.8. The tax of £1400 assessed May 5, 1756, cost Pitts £41.13.4. Further charges for an assessment of £700 voted on February 16, 1757, cost him an additional £20.16.8.[10] His assessments for the years 1753-1764, therefore, amounted to only £144.7.4, and he had during the same period received nearly £900 from the Company on his account. Of course, this was not all profit, but he must have made at least a 10% return on the provisions supplied, and probably 15%. He could not have expected a better return than he received. Natually, Pitts had considerable extra expense for the registering and surveying of the lands granted him by the Company, plus the cost of developing those lands and encouraging settlement upon them. In the twelve-year period he had received 8,800 acres from the Company in three divisions, and could look forward to future divisions totaling perhaps 12,000 acres more. Pitts had received his first Company share from the Bowdoin estate, and the price he paid for the second was minimal, under £200. James Pitts's investment in the Kennebeck Purchase had, according to the record, been of scant expense to him.

An examination of the accounts of other merchant-proprietors, such as Silvester Gardiner, Thomas Hancock, and Benjamin Hallowell, would tell a similar story. In addition, regular employees of the Company, like David Jeffries, Samuel Goodwin, Jabez Fox, and Gershom Flagg, earned a supplement to their incomes that partially covered their assessments. The Frankfort group—John Tufts, Samuel Fowle, Jonathan Reed, and Nathaniel Thwing—also worked for the Company occasionally. Least fortunate were small shareholders such as the Congregationalist ministers, Nathan Stone and Habijah Weld, who had to meet assessments with cash payments. Even they found the rewards of proprietorship far in excess of expenses.[11] One must conclude that for most members of the propriety, operation of the Kennebeck Purchase Company was remunerative as a going business concern apart from its primary rewards in land grants.

Once the necessities of life were hauled from Dr. Gardiner's sloop up the river bank to Fort Frankfort, they were distributed to individual families and credited to their accounts. In time, families fell into the habit of ordering specific commodities for their personal use. This practice was far more satisfactory than drawing from the fort's ill-stocked Company store. Their lists show something of individual preferences and a common desire for men's hats, onions, black pepper, and smoking tobacco. John Pochard, perhaps with more skill in carpentry than most, requested spoke shaves, chisels, a handsaw, gimblets and an axe. Several of his neighbors wanted coarse cloth and thread to sew their own clothes. John Bugnant's needs were more earthy. In addition to a small barrel of vinegar, he also ordered a barrel of rum. Another settler, probably the linen weaver Louis Cavalear, asked for "a Small Quantity of the best Flax for a piece or two of Linen."[12] The immigrants' needs were modest and few; no luxuries crowded their lists. They required only what they could not make themselves. Homes, furnishings, farm implements and, in the future, food, must all come from the labor of their own hands. While a few carried on their own trades in a modest way, they could not afford to specialize. The crushing level of debts, which most were saddled with, and the necessity of subsistence-level farming in the absence of a stable economy made it extremely unlikely that they would aspire to go into business for themselves. Furthermore, the proprietors had pre-empted any such opportunities.

It was soon apparent that the proprietors intended to dominate whatever economic opportunities existed in the town. They already monopolized the available transportation, and controlled the town's only retail store. Plans made by Nathaniel Thwing, Samuel Goodwin, Samuel Fowle, and John Tufts to build a sawmill in return for a one-square-mile grant had miscarried, so Goodwin now proposed to complete the undertaking alone. His ambitious plan called for receiving the 640-acre tract plus a small millstream and four hundred acres on the northern side of the first grant. All of this would be his provided he constructed the sawmill and gristmill within one year.[13] The task was a difficult one, as well as very expensive, and Goodwin failed to complete it. Reluctantly, he agreed to transfer his grant, complete with mill rights, to the ever-willing Dr. Gardiner for the nominal sum of ten shillings.[14] As usual, Gardiner succeeded where others failed. For many years his concession was the only one on the river, and settlers brought their grain to his gristmill from as far away as Fort Halifax, thirty miles up the Kennebec. The doctor built well, for his two mills remained in operation for nearly one hundred years.

While the process of bringing conveniences to the Frankfort inhabitants proceeded, the proprietors continued to advertise for useful additions to their colony. Apart from the stipulation that the applicants be of good character, the primary requirement was that they be Protestants in good standing. The standard one-hundred-acre grant to settlers was amended when necessary to attract persons possessing skills that were badly needed at Frankfort. The first settled minister at Frankfort would be given one hundred acres clear for himself and the use of an additional two hundred acres to be established as a perpetual parsonage lot.[15] The proprietors were also interested in attracting those skilled in the "mystery" of a trade to the town. Samuel Oldham received his Lot No. 7 provided that within one year he construct a brick kiln and produce one kiln full of bricks.[16] Daniel Goodwin of Frankfort was given his one-hundred-acre Lot No. 16 provided he follow the trade of blacksmith for ten years "if he lives so long."[17] The potter's craft was to be pursued by Elijah Phips for three years in return for Lot No. 6.[18] Sometimes the terms of a grant would be eased if the grantee was willing to provide payment in kind. Thus, in order to gain title to the one hundred acres of Lot No. 21, Thomas Parker had to "deliver 40 cords of wood at a landing place on the Eastern River within 8 months."[19] All of the foregoing were relieved of any of the usual requirements for landholding in view of their contributions to the new community.

Sometimes special restrictions were attached to a grant of land. Although a proprietor, Jonathan Reed was allowed five small lots in 1757 with the stipulation that "all the white pine Trees which are fit & suitable for Marks for the Royal Navy [are not to be] . . . cutt down on penalty of Ten Pounds Lawful money for every tree he shall cutt or cause to be cutt down."[20] The ownership of mast trees suitable for the Royal Navy was then held by the proprietors to be vested in the King. By May 3, 1758, however, they had changed their minds and decreed that, in the future, grantees would be allowed to retain the white pine for their own use.[21]

By 1753, the proprietors had developed a standard printed form for their individual settler's grants. The new form, used until 1760, listed the complete terms for taking up land. The old requirements of building a dwelling house of eighteen by twenty feet and clearing five acres within three years were retained, and a stipulation that the grantee must live on the land for seven years before obtaining a clear title was added. The proprietors made allowances for the prevailing uncertainties of frontier life. In the event that an Indian war interrupted a settler's labors, he or some member of his family, "within Six Months after the peace is made," could return, and subsequently "Repair and Dwell on said Premises, so as to compleat the Seven Years."[22] Even this provision failed to attract many settlers during the harsh period of the French and Indian War.

In addition to the requirements listed on the "Form for a Grant," the proprietors did not hesitate to impose other conditions on their grantees from time to time. These extra obligations must have caused frequent grumbling, and must have been difficult to enforce. On November 2, 1757, the Company decided that ". . . the Grantee or Some Person under him shall work three Days at least in making or repairing the High Ways in said plantation of Frankfort in every Year for ten years to come, and at such times in the Year when it shall be required by the Standing Committee or their Agents . . . .';[23] They further stipulated that settlers should also work for two days per year on a ministerial lot, meeting house, or parsonage.[24] The proprietors reserved the right to build highways where they wished, regardless of whose land they crossed. They also claimed the privilege of annexing landing places along the river wherever they chose, and even declared themselves entitled to ". . . one half of all the wood which shall be drawn to the waterside."[25] Some of these terms, reminiscent of those imposed upon serfs by medieval lords of the manor, were common enough in the regularly established towns of New England, but there they would have been voted in town meeting. Restrictions imposed by proprietary fiat could only breed resentment in the Frankfort residents and make future recruitment for that town and others more difficult, as the proprietors soon learned.

The propriety was committed to moving beyond Frankfort and setting up new townships. On a single day in October, 1752, the Kennebeck Company signed over three townships, each five miles square, to new proprietors in return for promises to supply settlers for the towns. These new settlements were to be located to the north of Frankfort. Number 4 went to Gershom Flagg, a member of the Committee of Ten; Number 2 was given to the Amsterdam merchant John Stedman; and Number 3 fell to Heinrich Luther of Frankfort, Germany. The latter two recipients were concerned in the shipment of immigrants to Boston earlier that year. The conditions were identical: "provided he will send 100 families of men of 21 years of age & upwards in the Space of three years to settle on said five Miles."[26] The Europeans failed to repeat their earlier success in providing settlers for the Kennebec. The peak year of the immigrant trade in Germany had been 1752. After that, public reaction was strong against the activities of the recruiting agents, and the rulers of many German states began to forbid the traffic.[27] However interested Stedman or Luther may have been, they could not meet the terms of the contract and may have even refused to accept it. As early as June, 1753, Florentius Vassall of London was offered "5 square miles of land on the Kennebeck, either No. 2 [if Mr. Stedman doesn't take it] or No. 3."[28] Since nothing more was heard of Stedman or Luther, grants No. 2 and No. 3 became available—grant No. 2, of course, now going to Vassall if he wanted it. But Vassall did nothing. Gershom Flagg's grant had also been dropped, so grant No. 4, too, became available to prospective proprietors. Flagg, an artisan of modest means, could not have hoped to marshal the resources necessary to support such an ambitious project. The situation was discouraging.

Undaunted, in 1753 the proprietors prepared a "Form for a Proprietor's Grant" at the same time they codified the grant for settlers. No proprietor ever actually fulfilled its conditions. As was true of the grants of the three abortive townships, the proprietor or proprietors had to settle one hundred families upon the assigned tract. Each family then had to abide by the conditions laid down for individual grantees of one hundred acres. In addition, the proprietor was directed to reserve one hundred acres for a school, twenty acres for a cemetery and, finally, lay out a perpetual common/training field for militia use.[29] These terms would have been difficult enough to fulfill in peacetime, but on the New England frontier of the 1750s they were practically impossible, as the proprietors of the Kennebeck Company later sadly observed:

> To 1755—the said Proprietors granted at different times to Certain Persons Six Townships [Exclusive of Frankfort] of Five Miles Square each on condition of their settling 100 Families in each in three years from their respective Grants—many Families had engaged to go, but the bad temper of the Indians for a Considerable Time before they Committed Hostilitys and the Consequent War prevented the Grantees fulfilling the Conditions of their Grants, by which means said Townships reverted to the Proprietors.[30]

The Indian troubles were real enough. Before any action could be taken in regard to planting the proposed towns, the French and Indian War had broken out. There were occasional raids in the valley during the period 1754-1760, in spite of new fortifications constructed there. Whether they were serious enough to discourage settlement is a matter for speculation. Settlers were pouring into other colonial frontiers during the same period. The fact remains that the Kennebeck proprietors, whether because of their reputation for harshness, their stringent land grants, or the French and Indian War, were simply unable to attract settlers to their holdings in any numbers.

In spite of the failure of Flagg, Stedman, Luther, and Vassall to plant settlements (since these men had even for a short time held grants), the proprietors had established the precedent that a Company shareholder or even an outsider might take up land in quantity. The exercising of this prerogative was soon formalized by Company edict, for the proprietors voted "that every Petitioner shall have a Grant of all such Lands by him petitioned for, as are of his or his Tenants actual Clearing and Subduing the same being now under their Improvement, and not before Petitioned for by any Other."[31] The foregoing resolution in effect gave each proprietor, great or small, a free hand in pre-empting as much land on the Kennebec as he could handle. After the failures of Gershom Flagg and Florentius Vassall to found proprietary towns, however, no other single shareholder attempted to establish such enclaves on the river.[32] For the time being, the proprietors had to be philosophical about their heavy expenditures, exercise patience, protect their interests, and wait for a more favorable climate for further development. After the war, settlers began to move into the region in large numbers, and there was no need

for any individual proprietor to venture all in advancing his own
fortunes and those of the Company. Instead, most shareholders
opted for smaller grants in a number of newly established towns
in an attempt to spread their risks.

Accordingly, during the critical years of the early 1750s the proprietors took up comparatively little land. Other than for relatively modest holdings allotted to Dr. Gardiner, Samuel Goodwin,
John Tufts, Samuel Fowle, and Nathaniel Thwing in return for
special services to the Company at Frankfort, the Kennebeck proprietors received not an acre. They had planned a general first division of Company lands as early as February 3, 1753, but this division was not enacted.[33] The proprietors did not actually vote
the land until January 7, 1756, when the Indian danger had largely abated and Company holdings were beginning to rise in value.
At that time, twenty-four 3200-acre lots were laid out, and each
full shareholder (8/192nds) received a full lot.[34] This first division
marked the inception of a land distribution policy that would
make small holders comfortably wealthy and great proprietors
rich.[35]

The proprietors began to see a small return on their investment
and the immigrant settlers were determined in their efforts to
wring a living from the land. Before they could become self-sufficient, however, the settlers would need to feel secure against attack. As they moved out toward the forest where they built their
farmsteads, there was always the fort at their backs, but they
lived in ever-present dread of the day when Indian wars cries
might ring out along the Kennebec.

The proprietors, too, feared the resumption of Indian attacks,
which might so easily put an end to their enterprise. They remembered tales of the burning of Brunswick in 1722, when more than
sixty houses were put to flames, and the more recent raids on
Swan Island in 1750. The Norridgewocks on the river were weak,
it was true, but in the event of another war with the French they
would be allied against the English. The Norridgewocks were
strongly opposed to any new settlements on the river, and existing treaties guaranteed them against further encroachments on
their territory. The building of Fort Frankfort and the founding
of the proprietors' village violated these treaties. As a highly vocal group with some skill at bargaining, the Indians lost no time
in protesting to the Massachusetts General Court. The immediate
result was the signing of the Treaty of 1753.

The Kennebeck proprietors had already attempted to make their own peace with the Indians of the region. After the Norridgewock protest to the General Court, the Company appointed Samuel Goodwin and Captain Lithgow of Fort Richmond to "treat with the Indians in order to quite [quiet] them."[36] Goodwin and Lithgow were directed to "give such satisfaction to the Indians as to make them easy, and allow of said proprietors going on with their settlements up said River."[37] They were also authorized to procure a quit claim deed from the Norridgewocks at a cost of not more than £50.[38] This quit claim would have been cheaply bought at many times the price, but there is no record that the proprietary action succeeded. Nevertheless, conciliation was the order of the day. In July, 1753, Samuel Goodwin received a barrel of rum from the proprietors and instructions to "treat the Indians that go to Frankfort, to make them easy."[39] Meanwhile, the proprietors continued their policy of placating the Indians while keeping to their original plan to settle the upper valley, a policy which seemed to have the support of the Massachusetts government. This duplicity goes far toward explaining the allegiance of the Norridgewocks to the French when war again erupted in 1754.

The Provincial government seemed disposed to assist the proprietors. Fort Richmond had served as the chief strong point on the Kennebec from the time of its building by the Pejepscot proprietors in 1719. In 1722, a year of troubles, its garrison climbed to fifty men, and in 1723 the fort had been enlarged at Provincial expense. The Province also constructed a truck house there in 1740 to facilitate trade with the Indians, and erected a smaller building nearby where native visitors could be lodged. Fort Richmond became a favorite gathering place for the tribes, and more than one conference had been held on the site. In September, 1753, perhaps at the instigation of the Kennebeck proprietors, Governor Shirley called the chieftains to Fort Richmond. Sir William Pepperrell represented the royal governor; his fellow commissioners were William Hubbard, John Winslow, Jacob Wendell, and James Bowdoin.[40] It appears more than coincidence that two Kennebeck proprietors were among the four commissioners present. On September 28, bargaining began.

The Norridgewocks had rehearsed their complaints well. They admitted that they were resigned to English settlement of "all the lands below Frankfort," but emphasized that "we hope you will not settle any further up the river. The Indians hunt on both sides of us: we have but a little space; we desire to live as brothers; but this country is necessary for our subsistence."[41] They had already witnessed the driving away of all game below Richmond Fort, and struggled to retain possession of what little was left. Pepperrell replied with a statement designed to allay their fears; Indian lands above the fort were safe from English encroachment, they were assured. The commissioners did not mention that the Kennebeck proprietors had already surveyed these lands, and were now preparing to carve out townships there.

Pepperrell and his fellow commissioners then presented the new Treaty of 1753 to the reluctant chiefs. Both sides agreed to abide by the terms of "the Articles of Peace made and entered into at Falmouth, in Casco bay, October the 16th, 1749, and Ratified and Confirmed on the twentieth day of October last at St. Georges . . . ."[42] Twelve members of the Norridgewocks were present to sign the treaty; among the witnesses for the British side were William Brattle, William Skinner, and Samuel Goodwin. Brattle was present not only as a Kennebeck proprietor but also as a senior officer of the Massachusetts militia; Skinner was a leading proprietor of the Pejepscot Company.

With Indian relations temporarily improving, the Kennebeck proprietors could turn more of their attention to their new enterprise. Some form of local government must be provided. Provisions must be made for future expansion, and additional house lots laid out. The town must be developed as a credit to the propriety and as an advertisement to ensure the future success of proprietary development.

The physical appearance of early Frankfort differed considerably from that of the traditional nucleated village found elsewhere in New England. Proprietors of townships customarily created a central common, to be used for grazing the sheep and cattle of the citizenry. This was usually surrounded by small house lots, with a large plot reserved for the meeting house. Beyond the settlers' homes stretched their fields, divided into narrow strips. From time to time, the original settlers would grant themselves additional acreage from the lands owned in common, at ever-increasing distances from the town center. For many years the townspeople would continue to plod out to work these new fields each day, returning to their homes at night. Not until the next generation would farmers divorce themselves from the

security of their village homes to dwell instead at their more economically important homesteads. This pattern was a common
one throughout Massachusetts and the Connecticut Valley.[43]

At frontier Frankfort the situation was different. While a large
common was set aside where a courthouse would eventually be
built within the walls of the fort, the church and parsonage lots
were located some distance apart. The first settlers did not farm
their lands together; instead they were assigned twenty-acre
house lots within the narrow peninsula bounded by the Kennebec
and Eastern rivers, but not adjacent to the common. Here they
constructed their first homes. As time passed, and these plots
proved insufficient to support the needs of their families, the settlers reached out to claim their large eighty-acre holdings which
were located across the Eastern River. Frankfort was decentral-
ized from the beginning, and would become more so.[44] Latecomers to Frankfort, like those in villages elsewhere in New England,
would find that the richest land had already been allotted. Because grants of land on the customary terms were no longer being given by the proprietors, new settlers were obliged to buy
their acreage at a premium price.[45]

Other significant differences separated the Frankfort experience from that of the conventionally established New England
towns. Nowhere is this more evident than in government. Elsewhere the town meeting system prevailed; and the landowners,
who were often resident proprietors, met at regular intervals to
transact the business of the town and elect their officials—select-
men, sealers of weights and measures, fence-viewers, hogreeves,
and many other positions.[46] As several historians have shown, in
colonial towns social democracy was often restricted, but there
was ample economic opportunity. While limited economic opportunity existed at Frankfort, there was little political democracy in
the town. Local government, all agreed, was necessary, but the
proprietors were determined to control it. The Standing Committee solved the problem by simply appointing a supervisory group
to supersede Nathaniel Thwing, who for a few months had exer-
cised sole control over the town's affairs. Thwing, John Tufts,
and Samuel Goodwin, all proprietors resident at Frankfort, plus
two others "to be Chose by the Inhabitants of Said District"
would now make all necessary decisions, deferring to the Committee on really important issues, according to a ruling made on
August 10, 1753.[47] Responsibility would be rotated, for it was de-

cided by the Committee that "Major Thwing [was] to be Chairman the first Weack, Samuel Goodwin the Second and John Tufftes the third Weack Till further Order."[48] Surviving records do not tell us which of the town's inhabitants were chosen to complete this unique governing committee. Their minority representation on the board was subject to veto by the proprietary group, but this system was better than nothing. Frankfort was governed directly by the proprietors in this manner until 1760, when the township was incorporated as Pownalborough, a move which paved the way for a town meeting system.

During their first years on the Kennebec, however, the immigrants struggled to survive. Notwithstanding the hardships they endured, these French and German settlers remained almost to a man at Frankfort, where their descendants, the Pushards (Pochards), Gouds, Stilphens, Rittals, Pechins, and Houdelettes still live. They began their tenure on the frontier deeply in debt, owing the proprietors for their passage money and the stores they consumed during their first year at Frankfort. For years afterward they were at the mercy of the proprietors, who controlled the principal sources of income except for manual labor. They did not receive the promised land grants until the summer of 1753, over a year after their arrival.[49] By then their stake in the township was well established. During the next few years the immigrants braved Indian raids, famine, and rising debts. Gradually they made progress, but to the newcomer, their lives appeared miserable. Looking back upon conditions at Frankfort as he remembered them at his arrival in 1760, Parson Jacob Bailey characterized the residents as:

> . . . thinly settled along the banks of rivers, in a country which afford a rugged and disagreeable prospect; . . . so poor, not to say, idle, that their families almost suffered for necessary food and clothing, and they lived in miserable huts, which scarce afforded them shelter from the inclemency of the weather in a vigorous climate. And their lodging were rather worse than food, clothing, or habitations. I might add many affecting instances of their extreme poverty—that multitudes of children were obliged to go barefoot through the whole winter, with hardly clothes to cover their nakedness,—that half of the houses were without chimneys—that many people had no other beds than a heap of straw,—and whole families had scarce anything to subsist upon, for months together, except potatoes, roasted in the ashes.[50]

During his own first years at Frankfort, Parson Bailey shared the hardships of frontier life with the settlers, and remained with them to watch the town grow and eventually prosper.

Frankfort stirred into activity during the decade of the 1760s. A major stimulus was the Massachusetts legislature's creation on July 24, 1760, of the new Lincoln County, with Frankfort as its seat. Proprietary influence in government had helped bring this about; proprietors also changed the town's name to Pownalborough in honor of the royal governor. Coincident with the birth of Lincoln County was the incorporation of the town of Pownalborough.[51] Now at last the inhabitants had home rule, but the area's boundaries had been stretched to include Wiscasset, a nearby village with a larger population than Frankfort's. The people of Wiscasset had not favored the merger, but when it was forced upon them they simply took over the government of the combined townships.[52] At the first town meeting, held on June 25, 1760, nearly all of the officials elected were from the Wiscasset section. Not a single French or German name appeared among the successful candidates for office. Wiscasset continued to dominate until the two sections were again divided into separate towns. For the time being, however, the new importance of Pownalborough created additional business and prosperity for all the inhabitants. Judges, lawyers, and clients flocked to the imposing Pownalborough Court House, constructed at proprietary expense. The population soared, and the town's future seemed assured.

The growth of Pownalborough paralleled that of Lincoln County and other Maine counties, as the 1764 census reveals. In that year, Maine contained 24,000 inhabitants, of whom 11,145 lived in York County, 8,196 in Cumberland County, and 4,347 in Lincoln County. The last included only six incorporated towns. Of these, Georgetown, a busy center of the mast trade, was largest with 1,329 inhabitants. Pownalborough, which included Wiscasset, trailed with 899 persons. The other towns were much smaller. Bowdoinham had only 200 inhabitants; Woolwich, Topsham, and Newcastle reported populations of 415, 327, and 454, respectively.[53] Only Pownalborough and Bowdoinham were wholly within the Kennebeck Purchase. On June 9, 1766, the Massachusetts General Court ordered that provincial towns take a careful census of the number of inhabitants and houses located within their borders. The Pownalborough census was taken painstakingly, and the details tell much about the lives of its people. The west side of Pownalborough (not including Wiscasset) then contained:

   69 familes
   17 inhabited frame houses
   45 inhabited log houses
   54 one-story houses
    8 two-story houses
    1 three-story house (the Court House)
  111 rooms with fireplaces
   34 brick chimneys
   19 stoned cellars
 3852 lights of glass[54]

In Pownalborough, most families lived in separate houses. Nearly all of them were still occupying the crude log dwelling houses they had constructed upon first arriving in the settlement. Finished cellars and brick chimneys were by no means common to all, as Parson Bailey also indicated. It is impossible to determine whether all homes had some glass windows; probably they did not, for a building like the Court House would require nearly nine hundred lights alone. Substantial two-story houses were still a rarity; by far the most elaborate was the riverside mansion of Judge Jonathan Bowman, cousin of John Hancock. His house boasted fireplaces in each of its eight rooms, several of them fully paneled, and a handsome carved staircase. In spite of such rare refinements, the Pownalborough of 1766 was still not far removed from the frontier stage, although the lot of its people was somewhat more comfortable than it had been a decade earlier.

By the middle 1760s, the town's French and German settlers were becoming acclimatized to life on the frontier. They were erecting more substantial houses, gradually paying off their indebtedness to the Company, and learning English customs and the language. Their children were growing up, receiving land grants of their own, and sometimes marrying into the families of Yankee settlers. They were beginning to think of themselves as Americans.

Like men of varying interests and abilities everywhere, the immigrant settlers of Pownalborough prospered in different degrees, but their general level of achievement testifies to the relative poverty of the town as compared to the more settled regions of Massachusetts—Andover, for example, which contained four generations of inhabitants by the 1760s. Its records have recently been carefully studied, making it useful for purposes of comparison.[55] By the late 1760s, Pownalborough inhabitants had not begun to approach the older town's general prosperity. One of the most successful immigrants in the Maine town was Jacques Bugnon, whose estate was inventoried on June 3, 1769.[56] Although Bugnon's assessors did not set values on individual items, they estimated his total net worth at £251.0.5. This was a sizable property for a Pownalborough immigrant-farmer of the first generation to accumulate, but by Andover standards, it suggested less than middling success.[57] John Cavalear, who died in 1768, left property appraised at £100.13.4, property which in Andover would have placed him in the lower 20% of the population.[58] Cavalear, however, may have divided some of his assets among his children during his last years, a fairly common practice in New England.[59] Most interesting is the estate of John Ulerick Mayer, which was appraised on January 9, 1764. His farm of one hundred acres, with improvements, was estimated to be worth £57.6.8; a cow and two heifers were valued at £8.5.4, and two silver watches at £6. The large quantity of linen goods in the estate, including numerous napkins, tablecloths, and twenty-four yards of material, suggest Mayer's trade of linen weaver. He also possessed some of the finer things of life, such as silk stockings, lace, books, a complete set of clock works, and three silver spoons. The total estate was valued at £138.0.12.[60] John Mayer, John Cavalear, and Jacques Bugnon were representative of the Rhinelanders who had emigrated to frontier Frankfort in 1752. It could not have been expected that in their lifetimes they would match the achievements of third and fourth generation Americans. Nevertheless, the evidence shows that by the outbreak of the American Revolution these immigrants were overtaking their neighbors of native stock and were increasingly being accepted on an equal footing with them.

Even as early as 1764, Parson Bailey could paint a more optimistic picture of life at Pownalborough than he had drawn upon his arrival four years before. Bailey reported that:

> . . . the banks of Kennebec, which five years ago were covered with impenetrable forests and almost destitute of inhabitants, are now adorned with pleasant fields, some stately buildings, and a multitude of people. Shipbuilding multiplies apace, navigation increases, and we have had several vessels loaded in the river this summer for Europe.[61]

By that census year some diversification of occupations had already appeared. Flax was successfully grown and processed by the linen weavers. Several brickyards were in operation. The farmers produced potatoes, corn, peas, and winter and summer wheat. Fruit trees were bearing, and dairy herds were increasing. Yet external appearances were deceiving. In spite of the flurry of activity reported by Parson Bailey, who tended to view improvement through a roseate haze, farmers at Pownalborough remained largely at the subsistence level. At times, notably during the American Revolution, even the production of the staple food crops declined. The community was often on the verge of starvation in winter, and dependent upon foodstuffs shipped in from Boston. Most of the settlers' energies were occupied in lumbering, legally or otherwise, neglecting their planting for the quick profit and the town's economy remained lopsided and unstable.

Until 1760, the people of Pownalborough did not have the stability and self-direction which a town-meeting form of government would have afforded. Instead, they were subject to the whims and vested interests of a proprietary committee. More important, the population was sadly lacking in the homogeneity of the typical New England village, as it was made up of a motley blending of Huguenots, Germans, and native Americans whose religious differences further complicated matters. Pownalborough was unique; as it grew, it came even to look different from other New England towns. Absent was the familiar village green, dominated by Congregational meeting house and courthouse. As soon as they were able, farmers moved away from the vicinity of the fort and erected crude houses scattered along the banks of the Kennebec and Eastern rivers. Pownalborough remained small, poor, and straggling.

By the outbreak of the American Revolution, the potentialities of the town as a base for Company operations had been fully explored, and its limitations painfully recognized. Its diverse population had attained modest independence but had not fulfilled the expectations of Company leaders. Proprietary dreams of creating a metropolis here were never realized. The place remained a backwater village—too far from the ocean for importance as a port, too far up the Kennebec to become a marketing center, and too unrewarding to attract the ambitious. Yet Pownalborough was a success in that it survived.

NOTES

CHAPTER VI

1 Fourth Warrant, Aug. 31, 1752, K.P.P., Records, I, 135-145.

2 "An Account of Dr. S. Gardiner's Holdings . . . ."

3 "An Account of Sundrys Wanted to Carry Down to Frankfort in Kennebeck River," Jan., 1752, K.P.P., Loose Papers, 1625-1759. The Committee of Ten then included Gardiner, Jacob Wendell, William Brattle, Robert Temple, Charles Apthorp, Thomas Hancock, James Bowdoin, William Bowdoin, James Pitts, and Jabez Fox.

4 *Ibid.*

5 "Account of Nathaniel Thwing," K.P.P., Ledger, 1754-1800, 41.

6 "Account of Benjamin Hallowell," *ibid.*, 43-44.

7 "Accounts of Thomas Marshall, Jacob Wendell, Thomas Hancock, William Tailer, and Silvester Gardiner," *ibid.*, 25-48.

8 "Accounts of James Bowdoin, William Bowdoin, and Charles Apthorp," *ibid.*, 29-46.

9 "Account of James Pitts," K.P.P., Day Book, May, 1754-1800, 25-29; Ledger, 1754-1800, 9-10. During the same period Dr. Gardiner's account totaled £1371.6 1/2; William Bowdoin's was £423.4.8; James Bowdoin's was £666.4.10; Benjamin Hallowell's was £381.1.4 1/2; and Gershom Flagg's was £735-. Of these, the first four did make substantial disbursements from private funds to meet Company expenses. Flagg's account stemmed mainly from his building activities for the Company.

10 "Sundry Accounts Dr to Kennebeck Purchase for an Assessment of £2800," K.P.P., Day Book, 1754-1800, 38-39; "Sundry Accounts Dr. to Kennebeck Purchase for an Assessment of £1400," *ibid.*, 60-61; "Sundry Accounts Dr. to Kennebeck Purchase for an Assessment or tax of £700," *ibid.*, 62-63.

11 By 1795 the estates of Habijah Weld and Nathan Stone had receved 2595 acres each on total assessments of only

£58.6.8. Even at the low valuation of 8 sh/acre, their lands must have been worth £880 in 1762.

12 French settlers to Peter Chardon, Sept. 13, 1752, K.P.P., Loose Papers, 1640-1759.

13 Grant to Samuel Goodwin, Feb. 9, 1754, K.P.P., Records, II, 9.

14 Allen, *Dresden,* 200. Dr. Gardiner completed his undertaking at great expense by contracting with Aaron and Simon Willard of Concord, Mass., to build a garrison house, sawmill, and gristmill in Aug., 1754.

15 Resolution, Dec. 11, 1754, K.P.P., Records, II, 81.

16 Grant to Samuel Oldham, Feb. 1, 1758, K.P.P., Records, II, 142-143. Oldham, a stonemason, worked on the foundations of Fort Western and later constructed the foundations and chimneys of the Pownalborough Court House.

17 *Ibid.,* Grant to Daniel Goodwin.

18 *Ibid.,* Grant to Elijah Phips.

19 *Ibid.,* Grant to Thomas Parker.

20 Grant to Jonathan Reed, Sept. 7, 1757, K.P.P., Records, III, 162-165.

21 Resolution, May 3, 1758, K.P.P., Records, II, 159. As purchasers of the original grant from the Council of Plymouth, the proprietors took the position that the pine trees were their inviolate property, to be disposed of when and as they saw fit.

22 "Plymouth Company Form for a Grant," Jan. 24, 1753, K.P.P., Records, II, 172-182.

23 Resolution, Nov. 2, 1757, K.P.P., Records, II, 132.

24 *Ibid.* These provisions were probably never put into effect, for the ministerial lot was not granted until 1769, and the Anglican church, not a "meeting house," not erected until the next year. Congregationalist proprietors would not have approved of general forced labor on such a structure.

25 Resolutions, Nov. 2, 1757, K.P.P., Records, II, 132; June 5, 1751, K.P.P., Records, I, 70; and June 20, 1753, K.P.P., Records, II, 49.

26 Grants to Gershom Flagg, John Stedman, and Heinrich Luther, Oct. 27, 1752, K.P.P., Records, I, 152.

27 Risch, "Crellius," 265-266.

28 Grant to Florentius Vassall, June 6, 1753, K.P.P., Records, II, 24-25. No. 3 had previously been granted to Heinrich Luther.

29 "Form for a Proprietor's Grant," Jan. 31, 1753, K.P.P., Records, II, 5.

30 "A Brief State . . . ," K.P.P., Letter Book I, 66-67. One wonders whether the Company's conditions were so stringent that potential proprietors feared that their profit would not be large enough. Of a 5-mile-square, 16,000-acre grant, approximately 10,240 acres would be granted to settlers, leaving little more than 5,000 acres to the proprietor after all his expense. On the other hand, grants of less than 100 acres to each settler would not have found any takers. The other two grants mentioned were to Ephraim Jones, Eleazer Melvin, and Joseph Fry of Concord, Mass., for "21,000 acres of land near Swan Island" on Feb. 14, 1753, K.P.P., Records, II, 11-18; and to James Otis, Jr., John Winslow, Gamaliel Bradford, Samuel White, and William Tailer of "Plantation No. 3" on Feb. 14, 1753, K.P.P., Loose Papers, Nov. 1757—Apr. 1768. The Otis group renewed its grant in 1761 and was finally confirmed in it in 1773 after fulfilling the terms of settlement.

31 Resolution, Jan. 24, 1755, K.P.P., Records, II, 2.

32 William Tailer was one of several proprietors of the town of Winslow. See Note No. 30. Such later-established towns as Gardiner, Bowdoinham, Vassallborough, and Hallowell were named for proprietors having important interests there even though they were not town founders.

33 "Shares and Proportions . . . ," 6.

34 Ibid. In practice, not every proprietor received land, even if his assessments were paid. One feels that unless a proprietor took an active interest in the Company, and spoke up forcefully, he was likely to be passed over in the land divisions. Eventually, however, the leading proprietors were compelled by court actions, or the threat of them, to make compensation to those who had been slighted.

35 See Chapter II. By 1795 those proprietors owning double shares had received 20,360 acres each. Grants to smaller holders were in proportion.

36 "A Brief State . . .," K.P.P., I, 62.

37 Resolution, June 20, 1753, K.P.P., Records, I, 26.

38 Resolution, Nov. 7, 1753, K.P.P., Records, II, 47.

39 Resolution, July 30, 1753, K.P.P., Records, II, 35.

40 Allen, *Dresden*, 78-82.

41 *Ibid.*, 36.

42 *Ibid.*, 87-88.

43 Akagi, *Town Proprietors*, 103-114. For more detailed examples, see: Grant, *Democracy in the Connecticut Frontier Town of Kent*, 1-29; Kenneth Lockridge, *A New England Town: The First Hundred Years* (New York, 1970), 12-13; and Philip Greven, Jr., *Four Generations: Population, Land, and Family in Colonial Andover, Massachusetts* (Ithaca, N.Y., 1970), 41-71. In most cases, the impulse to move beyond village limits was opposed by the town fathers, who feared the dilution of their authority. The movement also frequently resulted in areas isolated from the main center of population being set off as separate towns.

44 See "Plan of Part of Pownalborough [Frankfort]" showing Kennebeck Company grants in the present town of Dresden; Allen, *Dresden*, 197. Today the original center of the town is almost depopulated.

45 As an example, when Captain Charles Callahan of the British Navy received 100 acres at Pownalborough in 1768, he paid a price of 8 sh/acre, or £40 for the land. Grant to Charles Callahan, Dec. 21, 1768, K.P.P., Records, III, 5.

46 For examples, see Michael Zuckerman, *Peaceable Kingdoms: New England Towns in the Eighteenth Century* (New York, 1970), 154-186; Grant, *Democracy in the Connecticut Frontier Town of Kent*, 128-140; Richard Bushman, *From Puritan to Yankee; Character and the Social Order in Connecticut, 1690-1765* (New York, 1967), 22-41; and John Demos, *A Little Commonwealth; Family Life in Plymouth Colony* (New York, 1970), 7-8.

47 Committee Resolution, Aug. 10, 1753, K.P.P., Loose Papers, 1690-1753.

48 *Ibid.*

49 The immigrants finally received their 100 acres "in 3 Spotts." On July 11, 1753, Charles Hudlet [Houdelette], Michael Stilphen, and Daniel Malbon were issued grants, K.P.P., Records, II, 29; and on July 16, the Company granted 100 acres each to James Frederick Jaquin, Adam Couch, John Henry Thiaz, Wolf Rupert, John Henry Layor, Abraham Pochard, Daniel Gowe, John Stain, Jacob Carloy, Louis Cavalear, and John Pochard, K.P.P., Records, II, 29-31.

50 William S. Bartlett, *The Frontier Missionary: A Memoir of the Life of the Rev. Jacob Bailey* (Boston, 1853), 88.

51 The town of Pownalborough was incorporated by act of the General Court on Feb. 12, 1760.

52 For details of the Company's quarrel with the Wiscasset Company, see Chapter VIII.

53 Evarts B. Green and Virginia D. Harrington, *American Population Before the Federal Census of 1790* (New York, 1932), 27.

54 Allen, *Dresden*, 273.

55 See Greven, *Four Generations*, 222-258.

56 William D. Patterson, comp., *The Probate Records of Lincoln County, Maine, 1760-1800* (Portland, Me., 1895), 49.

57 Greven, *Four Generations*, 222-258. Greven found that in the Andover of the fourth generation (shortly before the Amer. Rev.) 22.6% of the estates were valued at less than £200, and only 19.3% of estates were appraised at more than £1000.

58 *Ibid.*, 225, Allen, *Dresden*, 152. Louis Cavalear, the brother of John, and like him a linen weaver, left property worth only £48.9.1 in 1761.

59 Patterson, *Probate Records of Lincoln County*, 49-50. In his *Four Generations*, Greven has shown that the division of a father's estate among his children was a common practice in pre-revolutionary Andover, Mass.

60 Allen, *Dresden*, 158-159.

61 *Ibid.*, 739.

VII

Protecting The Valley

Indian attacks upon the Maine frontier in the early 1750s threatened all that the Kennebeck proprietors had hoped to accomplish in their valley. Their one successful planting venture at Frankfort was endangered, but more significant, fears of a full-scale war with the French and their Indian allies intimidated prospective settlers and prevented the founding of new towns along the river. The considerable resources of the proprietors were inadequate to defend the Kennebec in the event of a general war. However, the proprietors emphatically believed that the Province had a direct responsibility to protect the borderlands of its isolated York County. It is not surprising, then, that the proprietors reconsidered a resolution the Company had passed in 1750 to petition the General Court to rebuild Fort Richmond at public expense farther up the Kennebec River.[1] There, it would provide more effective defense of the frontier, and the Company would be free of the cost. The petition had failed then but in 1754 the situation was more critical.

Fortunately for the proprietors, their fears coincided with those of William Shirley, royal Governor of Massachusetts, whose responsibility as military commander and civil administrator of the Bay Colony included the defense of the northern frontier. Although lacking in field experience, Shirley already enjoyed a certain reputation for the brilliant attack he had planned on the French fortress at Louisbourg in 1745. A similar victory would freshen his waning prestige. Thus motivated, the governor took steps to defend the region by collaborating with the land company. In doing so, Shirley set a pattern that his successor as governor, Thomas Pownall, would find irresistible.

In 1754 the situation in central Maine demanded attention. The local Norridgewock Indians, although weak, never ceased to complain about the continuing invasion of their lands by the English, and grew increasingly hostile. As the upper Kennebec River valley has a network of waterways providing passage from Quebec, Company officials feared that the French and Canadian Indians would enlist the aid of the Norridgewocks in a united assault on the Maine settlements. In that event, few defenses existed to oppose them. Fort Frankfort was only a supply point, manned largely by recent immigrants untrained in frontier warefare. Fort Richmond, located nearby, and Fort Georges, some miles below at Brunswick, were in ruinous condition. It was clear that little could be expected of these outposts unless they were strengthened.

The proprietors' first duty was to protect Frankfort. Their anxieties were nevertheless tempered with prudence, and expense was always an important consideration. After the signing of the Treaty of Richmond in 1753, they decided that a policy of gift-giving to the Indians and constant alert might prove effective on a short-term basis if the charitable aspects were not overdone. Consequently, the proprietors warned Samuel Goodwin at Frankfort: "We approve of the Civilities you shewed to them [the Indians] but we would not have you too generous; for we think [if] you were to bestow all the provisions received belonging to the Company in Entertaining them they would upon the first Occasion cut the Throats of those who have heretofore treated them with the greatest kindness."[2] Then, as the situation worsened early in 1754, the proprietors took further steps to insure the safety of their people at Frankfort. Company officials ordered the settlers to enclose with pickets a nearby spring and to construct an extra barracks to house expected troops. They decided against providing the settlers with new weapons because ". . . in case [the inhabitants] be drove into Garrison they will doubtless bring their small arms into Garrison with them."[3] They were tempting Providence, however, for the settlers might well be taken by surprise outside the fort. Shortly afterwards, the proprietors resolved that Dr. Gardiner should buy nine additional small arms for the garrison at ". . . not more than 20 shillings each,"[4] and one hundred pounds of lead bullets, and that a proposed new barracks with dimensions of sixty by thirty-two feet should be erected within the fort.[5] Here the proprietors called a halt to their preparations, feeling that they had done enough. They had built a fort for the townspeople and provided it with cannon, rifles, powder, and shot. They had gone as far as proprietors of a speculative land company could be expected to go in the defense of Frankfort. The protection of the frontier was, after all, the responsibility of the Provincial government. Other than for a few lesser shareholders who had moved with their families to Frankfort, proprietors' lives were not endangered. They could easily select a point for curtailing their responsibility and turning it over to Governor Shirley.

William Shirley had by this time thoroughly demonstrated his ability to visualize the broad defense needs of a region, and he commanded the resources to protect the Kennebec valley in the current crisis. Following the success of his Louisbourg venture under the joint command of General William Pepperrell and Admiral Peter Warren, Shirley had spent several years in Europe, serving as a peace commissioner at the conference which produced the Treaty of Aix-la-Chapelle. From this vantage point, he soon recognized the need for defense planning on an intercolonial rather than on a provincial basis. When he returned to Boston in 1753, the people hailed him as their sure deliverer from future French invasion.[6] They recalled and magnified his Louisbourg undertaking in countless tavern harangues. Shirley discharged public expectations by encouraging frontier defense, bolstering crumbling fortifications, and reinforcing under-strength garrisons in the fall of 1753.[7] In these actions, he failed to receive widespread cooperation either from other New England governments or from his own until the situation became more critical. Massachusetts legislative committees opposed his plans to buttress such strategic points as Fort Dummer and Number 4 in New Hampshire territory because they were not the narrow responsibility of the Province; Shirley persisted in his view that protection of all New England was necessary. He even recommended to the Board of Trade that a union of colonies be attempted—a move that led to the precedent-making Albany Conference of 1754.[8] It was only logical that in the present emergency the Governor would move to defend the Maine frontier—a primary responsibility in any case. Certainly his deputy, Lt. Gov. Spencer Phips, had kept him abreast of the worsening situation there during his absence in Europe. During the early years of the 1750s Phips had received a steady stream of accounts of Indian raids, or threats of them, from Captain William Lithgow, commander of Fort Richmond on the Kennebec.

Lithgow, rotund and ambitious, was a professional soldier who fretted when there was no work to be done. He had come to Maine in the 1720s as a member of Captain Robert Temple's ill-fated Irish colony and later had been commissioned by the Province. He maintained his friendship with his patron and during the 1750s cooperated on many occasions with the Kennebeck proprietors. They paid him well for his faithful service by granting him land and recommending him for promotion. Lithgow was thus largely a creature of the Kennebeck Company. His military position made him a valuable link with the Massachusetts government in the Company's strategy to build a new fort on the river.

Lithgow's Indian alarms supported Company demands for Provincial assistance on the Kennebec. He reported in the spring of 1752 that the local Norridgewocks were willing to attend a conference at his fort if their promised gifts were forthcoming from the Province. He hesitated to approve such a conference with the Indians, he said, for they "have the last Summer Committed several acts of Hostility against us."[9] The results of the conference, which was nevertheless held at Fort Richmond, bore out his judgment on the faithlessness of the Indians of the valley. The Treaty of 1753 only temporarily eased tensions.[10] Within a few months the Norridgewocks were as much a threat as ever. During the winter of 1753 an atrocity committed against the Indians menaced the peace of the valley again. This time a report from the Kennebec that two Indians had been murdered by white men at Matinicus Island alarmed Dr. Gardiner. Because the murderers had escaped justice, he feared that the whole frontier would erupt in retaliation. Gardiner urged his fellow proprietors to warn the Provincial government, which he hoped would take appropriate measures.[11] But only a major threat would arouse the Massachusetts legislature to action. It was not long in coming.

Early in 1754 Captain Lithgow informed Lt. Gov. Phips that the French, according to reports, had constructed a new fort at the head of the Kennebec River near the Great Carrying Place, which afforded connections with the Chaudiere River.[12] The Chaudiere, in turn, provided easy water transportation from Quebec. New England must recognize and challenge this immediate danger, if it was a real one. Phips forwarded the Lithgow note to Governor Shirley on February 8. Shirley immediately ordered John North, a surveyor employed by the Kennebeck Company, to locate the fort and order the interlopers to leave the valley.[13] By the end of the first week in March, Shirley had decided upon a course of action, even though by then North could hardly have confirmed the report of a French fort near the Kennebec.

The Governor first alerted Maine militia companies of an impending action, and sought support from Governor Benning Wentworth of New Hampshire for an expedition to begin "as soon as the Rivers are clear of Ice."[14] Finally, he approached the combined houses of the Massachusetts legislature. On March 28, Shirley appeared before a joint assemblage of the House and Council and, in a stirring address, described his plans. He announced that, since the Lithgow report of January 23, he had "received further Intelligence that the French are settled very thick for 12 Miles on each Side . . . of the River Chaudiere at about 30 Miles Distance above the Mouth of it, and in the Midway between the River St. Lawrence and the . . .[Great] Carrying Place."[15] He was vague in reference to the construction of a French stronghold there—construction he had positively described to Governor Wentworth only ten days before.[16] If he had in the meantime learned that the report was false, the intelligence produced no change of plan. Continuing with his speech, the Governor resurrected the familiar specter of Father Rasle, who back in 1724 had incited the Norridgewocks to attacks on the frontier.[17] In that instance the Provincial government had waited too long before taking action. This time, Shirley proposed a *preventative* expedition. He advocated not only driving the French away from the Great Carrying Place, if this proved necessary, but also "build[ing] a strong Fort near the Head of the River Kennebeck, above the Settlements of the Norridgewalk Indians . . . ."[18] Shirley had not previously unveiled the proposal to build a Province fort in the wilderness, but the General Court approved of the plan.

Still the legislature hesitated to vote the funds necessary to make the expedition possible. Before doing so, the House voted to send James Bean of York and two companions on a reconnaissance of the upper Kennebec and Chaudiere rivers.[19] Only eight days later, the House endorsed the Governor's proposal, and the Council followed soon after. The House fact-finding mission could not possibly have returned with information in time to have influenced these endorsements, so the legislators must have accepted the Governor's version on faith.[20] The legislature decided that an army of five hundred officers and men would join the three hundred militiamen already alerted in Maine, and voted £5,300 to finance the Kennebec expedition and send several Massachusetts commissioners to the Albany Conference later in the summer. William Shirley's arguments and an unwillingness to leave the northern frontier unprepared in the likely event of a French and Indian attack stimulated the legislature to immediate action. Its prompt response must have been gratifying to the Kennebeck proprietors, who were already making their own preparations for cooperation with the projected expedition.

Proceedings at the meeting of April 3, 1754, showed that the proprietors had known about the Governor's plans long before the legislature did. The proprietors voted that, if the General Court decided to build a fort on the upper Kennebec, they would construct a fort at Cushnoc according to specifications already provided them by the Governor. They even named a building committee: Captain Robert Temple, Silvester Gardiner, James Bowdoin, William Bowdoin, and Benjamin Hallowell.[21] Temple soon died, and was replaced by Thomas Hancock. By April 10, Shirley's proposal had been approved by the legislature. Seven days later the Kennebeck proprietors formally voted to build their fort at Cushnoc.

The site Governor Shirley selected for the new Province fort was at the falls at Teconnett.[22] An even more strategic location would have been at the Great Carrying Place, but a fort here would have been almost impossible to supply. The proprietors would probably have preferred the site of Father Rasle's old mission at Norridgewock, close to the northern boundary of Company territory.[23] They could not have been too disappointed with the Teconnett site, however, which was located at the junction of the Kennebec and Sebasticook rivers in the upper part of the Kennebeck Purchase.[24] To further mollify the proprietors, Governor Shirley announced that he would later build another fortress even higher up the river than Teconnett.

Shirley selected the Cushnoc site for the proprietors' fort, some sixteen miles below Teconnett, for highly practical reasons.[25] In insisting upon this location, he explained that "the Depth of Water in the [Kennebec] River will not admit provisions & Stores to be transported in a Sloop higher than Cushnoc; so that it is necessary in Case a Fort shall be erected at Teconnett Falls, that a strong defensible Magazine should be built at Cushnoc for the Reception of the Governor's Stores and provisions."[26] The Kennebeck Company's fort would provide the magazine. The proprietors chose the title Fort Western in compliment to Governor Shirley, who had family connections in England named Western. Carrying the flattery a little further, they renamed their older Company fort downriver Fort Shirley. They also took immediate steps to comply with the Governor's building specifications.

According to Shirley's orders, Fort Western would consist of a two-story structure one hundred feet by thirty-two feet, built of timbers not less than ten inches thick, forming a combined barracks and storehouse protected by two twenty-four foot square blockhouses at alternate corners. Two small "watch boxes" twelve feet square would be constructed at the other corners. Shirley directed that a palisade be erected connecting the four strong points and enclosing the barracks. The proprietors were to supply four cannons, all four-pounders, for further protection. Governor Shirley agreed to furnish a guard for workmen during the construction period, and afterward a garrison for the structure.[27]

The members of the committee in charge of building Fort Western were experienced, for they constituted the committee that had raised Fort Shirley (Frankfort) two years before. Gershom Flagg was the master builder hired by the committee. His articles of agreement, signed on May 7, 1754, provided that he would receive five shillings per day until the work was completed and that he could hire carpenters, let out subcontracts for some of the construction, and occasionally leave the site during the building period to supervise the erection of the Province fort farther up the river.[28]

While these arrangements were being made, Governor Shirley was hurriedly making final preparations for his summer campaign. He proposed to hold a series of Indian conferences at Falmouth on the southern coast to make treaties and thus wean the local tribes from the French before he ventured up the Kennebec. Provincial forces under the able General John Winslow, descendant of one of the four original proprietors, would then push up the river and destroy the French fortifications at the Great Carrying Place. A part of Winslow's army would remain at Teconnett to raise the Province fort. As the Kennebeck proprietors would have begun building Fort Western while the Indian conferences were in progress, that construction would be well enough advanced to be of use when Winslow's army passed up the Kennebec. Timing his departure from Boston with the end of the Indian hunting season, Shirley expected to leave Castle William in Boston Harbor around the eighth of June.[29] It was not until June 22, however, that he finally embarked for the voyage to Maine, accompanied by General Winslow's troops, a quorum of the Council, and key members of the House. Delayed by storms, the little fleet did not reach Falmouth town until four days later. Shirley hastily established a temporary provincial capital in the mansion house of the severely ill Jabez Fox, a Kennebeck proprietor.[30] There the royal Governor prepared the details of his conference with the Indians.

Shirley planned to hold separate conferences with three Indian tribes at Falmouth: the Maine Norridgewocks and Penobscots and the "French" Canadian Arssegunticooks. The Norridgewock tribe was the smallest of the three, and considered the least threat. The Penobscot tribe, named for the river that ran through its hunting grounds, was a large and formidable group. The Governor considered cooperation with the Penobscots important because the Penobscot River, in the eyes of the English, marked the boundary between French and British territory in Maine.[31] Shirley knew little about the Arssegunticooks and awated their arrival with foreboding. The Norridgewocks and Penobscots sent delegates, but the Arssegunticooks never appeared.

The Norridgewocks and Penobscots did not present the opposition that Shirley may have anticipated. At the Norridgewock meeting, he took a forceful approach to Indian objections to the building of the new forts:

> . . . I told them that I did not ask their consent to the building the new fort, or extending the English Settlements upon the River Kennebeck, but only appriz'd them of our intentions, that they might not conceive false Alarm at our proceedings . . . I re-

minded them of the Calamities, which going to War with the English had brought upon them.[32]

Shirley compelled the Norridgewock chieftains to acknowledge
the reoccupation of the upper Kennebec on the basis of English
settlement there over one hundred years before. The Indian dele-
gation signed his peace treaty and departed. The Governor had
even less trouble in reaching agreement with the Penobscots,
probably because he was, as he observed, "sensible that they had
no property in that [Kennebec] River.[33] The Penobscots were
mainly concerned about possible British settlement on St.
George's River. As the Governor had no designs on that territory,
he readily agreed to limit his activities there, and signed a peace
treaty with the Penobscot leaders. On the whole, Shirley was well
satisfied with the results of his treaty-making. He not only had
made peace with the Norridgewocks and Penobscots, but had
persuaded them to restrain the Arssegunticooks and inform the
British of any warlike plans the Canadian Indians proposed. The
way was now cleared for the expedition up the Kennebec.

General Winslow's army, which started its journey on July 4,
proceeded very slowly up the river. After pausing at Fort Richmond to rest for a few days, the men continued to Fort Western.
Extracts from a private's diary shows their progress:

> 8 July. Sailed from Richmond fort When the Raft of Timber for
> the first fort [Fort Western] Come up the river With above three
> hundred tuns in it.

> 12 July. Landed att [sic] Cooshenauk Where the English had
> built a fort formerly.

> 25 July. Major General Winslow sett out upon the March from
> fort Western with ten Companys Was saluted with the Discharge
> of five Great Guns. We had two Gundalows in the river ten Whale
> Boats and Eighteen Battoes with Stores.[34]

While General Winslow's main army prepared for the march
from Fort Western, other units assisted Gershom Flagg's team of
carpenters in completing the structure.

Fort Western's principal building was a long, shingled,
two-story affair, with the outward appearance of three colonial
row houses. Three symmetrically placed doorways were bal-
anced by windows on the first- and second-floor levels. The inside was bare of ornamentation, though the officers' quarters had
built-in window seats and rudimentary Georgian moldings
around the fireplaces. The section reserved for the garrison was

Spartan in its simplicity—tongue-in-groove paneled walls, and cavernous fireplaces. This structure, an ambitious building for the Maine frontier, was the most costly undertaking the Kennebeck proprietors had yet attempted. Even before the four cannons and interior fittings had been added, bills totaled £662.1. 3/4. Gershom Flagg's charge for the main house, blockhouses, flankers, palisade, main gate, doors, shutters, and dormers was £215.14.3.[35] Equipment, provisions (including the ever-present ration of rum for the workmen), and the labor of carpenters, headed by Gershom Flagg, Jr., came to £74.16.9 1/4.[36] Young Flagg's own bill for the construction of doors, dormers, and "Dresser & Shelves & Sink" for the garrison kitchen and other carpentry work totaled £179.17.6 1/2.[37] Samuel Oldham, the mason, presented a bill for £192.2.6.[38] He did not complete his contract for the foundation walls, chimneys, and plastering until June, 1755. The total cost of Fort Western would have been much higher if its timbers had not been cut upon Kennebeck Company lands.[39] This new fort, operative during most of the construction period, supported Winslow's army while it was erecting the Province fort at Teconnett.

Late in July, General Winslow left Fort Western and proceeded upriver to Teconnett Point. He immediately began to direct the construction of the Provincial outpost, which Governor Shirley named Fort Halifax in honor of the President of the Board of Trade. Plans for the fortress included a large, two-story blockhouse overlooking the Kennebec and Sebasticook rivers and several smaller barracks and storehouses grouped around two sides of a square.[40] A stockade would surround the buildings. Twelve carpenters led by Captain Isaac Illsley of Falmouth, assisted by soldiers from Winslow's force, undertook the construction. Gershom Flagg provided occasional supervision as the work proceeded. Although the site chosen commanded the junction of two rivers, it was not the most strategic situation available; a better location on a nearby hillside had been rejected because of a lack of foundation stone in the immediate area. This decision to build on the river caused endless trouble later when the fort's commander found it was necessary to fortify the promontory or risk its use against the garrison.

On August 8, once the fort was well under construction and in a position to guard his advance, General Winslow decided to push northward with five hundred militia on a quest for the rumored French citadel. After two days he became ill and returned to Fort Halifax. Colonel Jedidiah Preble, second in command, plodded on, and by August 13 had reached the old Indian town of Norridgewock, only twenty-two land miles above Fort Halifax. He had seen few Indians along the line of march. When the troops finally reached the Great Carrying Place, they found no trace of a French fort, of enemy soldiers, or even of large groups of Indians. If there had been any warriors in the area, the Provincial army's unbelievably slow progress would have guaranteed their escape. After two weeks of tramping around the wilderness, Preble's forces returned to their base at Fort Halifax.

Governor Shirley no longer could maintain the fiction that the French were building a fort at the Great Carrying Place, but he was resolved to make as much capital out of the affair as he could. He could re-create some of the drama of Louisbourg by visiting the scene of operations as he had done then. Unfortunately, there was no captured enemy to inspect this time, and no conquered stronghold. Nevertheless, he could lend an aura of victory to the occasion by making a hasty state visit to the two new forts on the Kennebec, to be followed by a triumphal return to Boston. The publicity would be well worth any minor risks involved in the journey up the Kennebec.

Accompanied by members of his Council, Shirley sailed up the river on the sloop *Massachusetts* as far as Fort Western, where he made a quick inspection on August 30. The party, protected by a substantial guard trailing along the river bank, moved by whaleboat to Fort Halifax after spending the night on the *Massachusetts*. As the Governor's entourage neared the Provincial fort, it was "met by General Winslow on the River, with a detachment of 200 Men, whom the General had ordered to march to Cushnock to escourt him from thence."[41] Shirley paused in his inspection to lay the cornerstone of Fort Halifax.[42] His leavetaking of the new outpost was as hurried as his arrival.

Leaving behind one hundred men to garrison Fort Halifax, and another twenty at Fort Western, Governor Shirley began his return to Boston the next morning. He dined at Fort Western, slept at Fort Richmond, and returned to Falmouth late the next night, September 3. Five days later he was back in Boston after an absence of more than two months.[43] William Shirley's reappearance at his capital was the occasion for pageantry and showmanship. After spending the night at Castle William, the royal Governor approached the city the next morning in a state barge, welcomed by the booming of cannon. A crowd of admiring councillors and representatives escorted him to the Province House. It was "the greatest Concorse and Acclaim of the People that was ever known in Boston."[44] On Friday, October 18, the Governor presented his official version of the expedition at a joint meeting of the House and Council.

Considering the results of his foray into the Maine wilderness, Shirley did well to re-emphasize the preventative aspects of the expedition. He commented that:

> Though the Troops, Gentlemen, found no French Settlements to be removed, yet by their late march on both Sides the River Kennebeck to the Head of it, and the first Pond on the Carrying Place, you have probably prevented them from Attempts to make one there . . . there was not the least Probability that any other Expedients could have prevented the Miseries, and much greater Expence of a general War with the Eastern Indians from the beginning of the Summer than that which we have put into Practice.[45]

The Governor's speech met with the wholehearted approval of the Provincial government. The combined houses replied with a respectful address on October 30, stressing the accomplishments of building the new forts and placating the Indians at Falmouth. The Boston press echoed their endorsement, publishing at least two odes written in praise of Shirley. The first, addressed to the "Great Leader of our martial band," like the Assembly's address, emphasized the Governor's treaty-making and fort construction, and was the work of one *Philo*.[46] The other work, more ambitious, was written by John Beveridge, and appeared in Latin accompanied by a parallel English translation. Beveridge saluted the Governor as "the sure Palladium of our Land,"[47] who "we behold transform'd Norridgewalk's fierce Inhabitants, who now (Their Rage subdu'd) with Looks serene invite New England to erect, at Will, her Towers."[48] Shirley was no less than a messenger from Heaven, who had charmed the Indians by the "sweet Persuasion of [his] Tongue."[49] These plaudits must have brightened William Shirley's spirits immeasurably, yet such extravagant praise for a routine accomplishment could not stifle the mounting criticism which arose after a more careful consideration of Shirley's motives and actions.

As early as October, 1754, Governor Thomas Fitch of Connecticut, defending his own failure to support the expedition, commented that he had learned the alarm had been a complete mistake and that the French were not building any such fort.[50] To the Connecticut governor, the whole mission had been a needless and costly maneuver. In his *History*, written a few years later, Thomas Hutchinson heartily agreed with Governor Fitch. Hutchinson, himself a member of Shirley's government, suspected him of trying to provoke a war in hopes of receiving a regiment and being made a field officer.[51] Hutchinson dismissed the report of the French fort as a mere rumor. But, he admitted, "a rumor sometimes obtains credit, because the subject, from the nature of it, is probable."[52] Hutchinson implied that the building of Fort Halifax was unnecessary because it was never attacked. The charge persisted. During William Shirley's later years, he was even lampooned in the pamphlet that attacked Kennebeck Company politics.[53] The author of *The Strange Account of the Rising and Breaking of a Great Bubble* questioned Shirley's wisdom in directing the Kennebeck proprietors to build Fort Western fifteen miles above the center of Kennebec population (then at Frankfort), and the Province to construct Fort Halifax seventeen miles above that. This decision seemed poorly calculated to protect the people of the valley, but worse, he said, "I think it is plain to every Reader that 80 men in these Forts, during a Six Years' War, doing no Duty, eating the Province Provision, receiving Province Pay, was not to serve the Province but the Plymouth [Kennebeck] Company."[54] As contemporary witnesses, Governor Fitch, Thomas Hutchinson, and the *Strange Account* pamphleteer all took the same stand based upon hindsight: they criticized William Shirley's grand scheme because he failed to locate a French stronghold, and because his forts, once constructed, were not attacked. They misread, perhaps deliberately, his widely heralded preventive policy. They could not have predicted French strategy if Shirley's plans had not been executed. Nevertheless, there was no denying what many said at the time: that the Kennebeck proprietors were the immediate beneficiaries of Provincial military operations. Furthermore, there were indications that Shirley had profited personally from his maneuvers.

Surviving evidence strongly suggests that the Kennebeck proprietors made it worth Governor Shirley's while to locate Fort Halifax at Teconnett Falls and to built it at Province expense.[55] Several months after building the fort, Shirley received a full share in the Company from its proprietors. It is also a matter of record that proprietor Robert Temple's son married the Governor's daughter Harriet one month after the Massachusetts General Court voted approval of Shirley's expedition to the Kennebec—an arrangement that, as Shirley's biographer, John Schutz, has suggested, could have been made for services rendered.[56] But dynastic marriages were almost the rule among aristocratic Boston families, and were repeatedly indulged in to advantage by the Kennebeck proprietors.[57] Dr. Silvester Gardiner, the donor of the land, and the records of the Kennebeck Purchase Company, however, attest to Governor Shirley's receipt of a Company share. His land transfer, which was never transcribed in county records, took place on December 3, 1754,[58] eight months after Shirley's decision to build the fort at Teconnett. A week later at their regular meeting, the Kennebeck proprietors voted to grant to Dr. Gardiner in compensation for his loss of a full share, two large tracts of land from undivided Company territory. No other proprietor received land at that time. That the Company share was given to Shirley is evident from Gardiner's reimbursement by the other proprietors.[59] On February 5, 1755, the proprietors met again and amended their earlier vote to include the stipulation that Gardiner would also be exempt from the usual provision of settling two families upon his new grant within three years.[60] The doctor himself recounted the whole transaction to the Kennebeck proprietors some years later when he was called upon to justify the possession of lands he had received from the Company.

Gardiner explained that he had procured his initial Company share by purchase from the widow of Antipas Marshall and had augmented it by some smaller purchases to a one-sixteenth interest. He related, however, that:

> Some time after the Company thou't it for their Interest, that Governour Shirley should be interested in their patent, but if it could not be effected any other way then for one of the partners to grant him 1/24 [a full share], and in lieu thereof take such a Grant from the Company as should be agreed on. The thing labour'd as no one of the Company could be found willing to part with a twenty-fourth for so trifling a quantity of Land as the Company offered . . . but to save the Company, not the Doctor, he conveyed the remaining part of the 1/24 he bought of Col. Brattle with a £1000 Old Tenor Tax he had paid upon it, to Governour Shirley.[61]

Gardiner received in return the two large unimproved lots previously mentioned, about 11,200 acres in all, from the Company.

Historians have concluded that William Shirley accepted the valuable grant in return for building Fort Halifax within Company territory. Certainly Shirley's contemporaries thought so.[62] But the timing of the grant suggests otherwise: payment in December for services contracted for in April seems unlikely. It is true that during the colonial period debtors often let their accounts ride for years before coming to terms with their creditors, but this was a paper transaction not involving actual payment. The proprietors could have speedily enacted a deed of conveyance, as Shirley would probably have demanded. Furthermore, we can realistically interpret the construction of the Provincial Fort Halifax and proprietary Fort Western as a symbiotic relationship where both parties benefited equally. Massachusetts discharged its obligations to the Crown and to Maine settlers while the Kennebeck proprietors, their own needs met, paid a portion of the expense. Kennebeck Company leaders may have granted the share for another purpose altogether. In December, 1754, the proprietors were facing an urgent problem that required the Governor's immediate assistance. They could expect this aid only if Shirley had a substantial interest in the Company.

The Kennebeck proprietors had for several years been gravely concerned about the validity of their patent.[63] Regardless of what they professed publicly about the dimensions of their holding, they were well aware that their claim to lands stretching from Wesserunset to the sea would be extremely difficult to substantiate in Massachusetts courts, and even more difficult to enforce among the inhabitants of the hotly disputed coastal region. If they could induce the King to grant a new explanatory charter favorable to their interpretation, they would win the battle over land rights. Governor Shirley, secure in his latest triumph, might possess the influence to implement their wishes. The contents of a letter that he secretly wrote to the Lords of Trade on December 31, 1754, may explain the real reason for his receipt of a Company share several weeks before.

William Shirley's letter presented a forceful case for a new Company charter. He began by emphasizing the importance of the Kennebec River, the shortest route to Quebec, in the defense of the British colonies in America. The strategic importance of the river had prompted his expedition during the previous summer and led to the erection of two new forts along its banks. Shirley now proceeded to a favorite theme: the encouragement of settlement in close proximity to these forts. The inhabitants would supply provisions and garrisons for them. The Governor was convinced that the Kennebeck Purchase Company, a group which had already demonstrated its patriotism by the construction of Fort Western at great cost, could promote this beneficial settlement. He himself had examined the Company charter, had found it to be a good one, and was therefore willing to sponsor its cause.[64] The Kennebeck proprietors were now prepared to settle one thousand families in the area at their own expense. Development of the upper Kennebec could proceed rapidly,

> . . . provided their title to the land they claim here shall be confirmed to them by a New or Explanatory Patent from the Crown or in any manner so as to putt an end to the continual Interruption they meet with in their present Settlements . . . . If a new Patent can be Granted to this Company upon those conditions consistent with Justice to such as sett up Pretentions to the Lands claimed by them it seems evident my Lords that it would be a most happy circumstance for his Majesty's Service . . . it would absolutely secure to the Crown the possession of the most important River in New England for stopping the Encroachments of the French on that side, and gaining at the same time the principal pass into their Country . . .[65]

Shirley respectfully suggested that the King issue a new charter to the Kennebeck Company, legitimizing its claims, because older inhabitants of the coastal regions were "giving occasion to the New Settlers under them being harassed with little actions of Trespass which are Tryed in a County where the Judges Juries and Witnesses are generally more or less [personally] interested as they [the proprietors] represent to me in the claims made against them."[66] Under the new patent, persons already settled in disputed areas might be compensated for possible losses with a few hundred acres. Thus, no one would lose, and the Crown would gain much. The Governor observed that his son-in-law, William Bollan, Agent for Massachusetts, and Florentius Vassall, a proprietor living in London, were ready to help expedite matters in England.

In the context of this letter, Dr. Gardiner's statement that ". . . the Company thou't it for their interest, that Governour Shirley should be interested in their *patent* . . . ," takes on new meaning. Only he had the influence to procure a new patent, and a personal interest in the Company would help bring about his intercession. By his letter, William Shirley had done everything that was within his power to obtain a more advantageous patent for the Kennebeck proprietors. In doing so, he had jeopardized his own reputation. His petition to the Board of Trade on behalf of the Company without revealing that he was himself an interested party in the proceedings could have been grounds for his removal as governor, even in those free and easy times. Nor was he successful in his mediation. Surviving evidence indicates that the Board of Trade never presented Shirley's letter to George II, although it did offer the useful suggestion that the Company appeal its case to the King in Council.[67]

The Governor soon became occupied with much more important concerns: in 1755 he was named second in command of British forces in America by General Braddock. His long-coveted position as general involved duties that transcended personal and even provincial obligations. In his new responsibility, however, Shirley was charged with so flagrant a mismanagement of the Niagara campaign that he was forced to return to England in October, 1756, to defend himself against charges of incompetence.[68] Up until that time he had never attended a single proprietary meeting, and more important than that, he had failed to pay the assessments levied for the Company's operations. It was not surprising, then, that proprietary leaders decided that Shirley could no longer be of service to them.

After numerous warnings and public notices, the proprietors auctioned William Shirley's delinquent share, with others, on May 10, 1758.[69] They held the first auction in the series leading to the sale of Shirley's share on November 9, 1757. It appears reasonable, therefore, that if he really valued his share, he had been given sufficient time to redeem it, whether in England or not. He may have expected that the other proprietors would exempt him from the auction proceedings. Perhaps his share had become an embarrassment to him, and he was glad to forfeit it. In any case, when the auction was held, Shirley's son-in-law, Robert Temple, Jr., bought in one-half of his share, keeping this part in the family.[70] The rest fell to division by the leading proprietors. Thus William Shirley, King's Governor and friend of proprietors, passed from influence in the Company. The Kennebeck Company had shown that it could be as ruthless with former allies, once they had served their purpose, as it was in dealing with rival land companies and settlers who opposed it in the Kennebec Valley. Dr. Gardiner and his Standing Committee, temporarily without a friend at court, continued to promote the settlement of their tract, but with little results.

The forts William Shirley had planned contributed enormously to the defense of the Kennebec, and the continued maintenance of these forts meant that at least the settlers already in residence survived. Nevertheless rumors of full-scale invasions intermittently reached Boston from the Kennebec. Garrisons were reinforced, and extra supplies sent when needed, but the fears of impending attack effectively discouraged new settlers from entering the valley. The Kennebeck proprietors were no better off than they had been early in 1754.

A major problem in the defense of the upper valley was that presented by Fort Halifax itself. It was impossible to reach during harsh winter weather, so in the absence of local settlers who might have kept it supplied, it was necessary to accumulate provisions there to last for the entire season. The garrison was often on the verge of starvation. Also, because of the comanding hill behind the structure, it was almost indefensible. In 1755 William Lithgow, now a colonel, was appointed to command the fort and also rebuild it. He confessed that Fort Halifax as he found it was "one of the most extraordinary fortresses for ordinaryness I have ever seen or heard of."[71] Nor did he hold much hope for the fort after the renovations, for "After it is done, it will be as irregular ill formed assemblage of buildings as was ever huddled together to be called a fort, and it will be hard to defend these, on account of their irregularity, and the large circumference of the picket work."[72] The stronghold's defenses were corrected by connecting blockhouses on the hillside to the main fort by a palisade, but successive reductions in the size of Fort Halifax's garrison and that of Fort Western weakened the overall defenses of the valley. The soldiers of the two forts were barely able to maintain themselves behind their ramparts, let alone come to the rescue of embattled farmers in the region. It is not surprising that the proprietors now turned for aid to Shirley's successor, Thomas Pownall.

Governor Pownall proved nearly as amenable to proprietary suggestions as his predecessor had been. He counted among his personal friends Thomas Hancock, Benjamin Hallowell, and James Bowdoin, proprietors who had previously been on similar intimate terms with William Shirley.[73] Their relationship followed

a now-familiar pattern. Thomas Pownall was accused by contemporaries of over-hasty approval of a Kennebeck Company
proposal in March, 1758.[74] Ingenious members of the Standing
Committee reasoned that if the Province would enlist prospective
settlers of the Fort Halifax area as part-time soldiers, it would
both augment their slender incomes and further encourage settlement at its own cost. Eight proprietors of the Kennebeck Purchase Company, supported by three of their rivals from the Pejepscot Company, accordingly petitioned the Governor for the
creation of ranging companies on the Maine frontier. As "sundry
persons who have Expended large sums of Money in Advancing
the Settlements of the Eastern part of this Province,"[75] the petitioners proposed that one hundred fifty man companies be raised
in each of eleven frontier towns to guard the borders and maintain security. By these means "the Death of many valuable Subjects, and the total Despersions of the Inhabitants and breaking
up of the Eastern Settlements, both to the entire ruin of many
Men and Famileys"[76] could be prevented when an expected
French and Indian attack occurred the next summer.

Frankfort, the northernmost town and the only one of the elev-
en located in the Kennebec Valley, was in a prime position to
benefit from the ranging companies proposal. The Governor
granted the proprietary petition, for it was not only sensible and
workable, but also economical. The ranging companies composed of local settlers subsidized by the Province complemented
fort garrisons on the Kennebec frontier until the final defeat of
the French.

The efforts of the ranging companies did not prevent occasional new attacks. In August, 1758, Canadian tribes assaulted
farmsteads in the Kennebec Valley. The settlers fled before them.
Though the Indians did not kill any of the inhabitants, they did
considerable damage to unprotected homes. Governor Pownall
immediately made a hurried visit to the region to personally inspect defenses and survey the area of destruction. Learning that
British forces to the north had successfully subdued the enemy
and assumed control of the St. John's River in present-day New
Brunswick, Pownall decided to take similar action in Maine's
Penobscot Valley. An offensive in this area not only would violate the treaty Shirley had made with the Penobscots in 1754, but
would be tantamount to invading Canada, because the British

had recognized the Penobscot River as the boundary between their holdings and those of the French.

The heart of Pownall's plan was to build a fort on the lower Penobscot River. His expedition of three hundred men sailed from Boston to Falmouth to make preparations for the advance, much the same as Shirley's army had done five years before. A flotilla commanded by the Governor left Falmouth for the Penobscot on May 8, 1759. Soon to follow on another ship were the prefabricated parts of the blockhouse that would become the citadel of the new fort. An important passenger on this vessel was Gershom Flagg, the Kennebeck proprietor-builder who earlier had constructed Fort Western and supervised the building of Fort Halifax. Flagg went to work immediately upon arrival, and by the end of May the fort was well on its way to completion.[77] Governor Pownall then prepared to return to Boston. He remained on the site long enough to see the cellar and the first story of the forty-foot-square blockhouse completed and to name the fort for himself. General Preble, his second in command, who had accompanied Winslow on the Kennebec expedition, supervised the remainder of the work on the fort, a palisaded square, 360 feet on a side, with diamond-shaped flankers at each corner, surrounding the blockhouse.[78] Fort Pownall remained garrisoned by the Province until the beginning of the American Revolution, but it was never tried. The Governor's prompt action had cut the French off from further access to the sea, had helped protect northern Maine from possible attack, and was a contributing factor in the capture of Quebec later that year.[79] It further stabilized the position of the Kennebec settlements by making them a rear area. The French and Indian War soon ended, but Governor Pownall, a friend in time of war, would continue to serve the Kennebeck proprietors in civil affairs until he returned to England.[80]

The building of Fort Pownall symbolized the end of an era of conflict on the Maine frontier. Once the structure was operational, the Massachusetts legislature was besieged with prospective settlers who wanted to take up land on the Penobscot. Kennebec lands also increased in demand. The long-awaited capture of Quebec on September 13, 1759, several months after the completion of Fort Pownall, made the latter's very existence unnecessary. The "glorious year," 1759, put an end to the fear of the

French in British North America and, in New England, to the fear of their Indian allies as well.

The Kennebeck proprietors spent the later years of the 1750s in a holding action—in defending what they had. What was worse, circumstances compelled them to spend an additional £1400 to maintain their investments in the valley. They spent at least half of this sum to construct and support Fort Western. Standing Committee members grumbled that, although they had granted six townships to groups or individuals during this period, because of the "bad temper of the Indians for a Considerable Time before they Committed Hostilitys and the Consequent War,"[81] only Frankfort remained. For all of their outlay and influence with royal governors, the Kennebeck proprietors emerged from the French and Indian War with no more to show for their efforts than they had possessed in 1754. However, the decade of the 1760s would be different. Townships would multiply as the Kennebeck Company opened to development the territory between Fort Shirley and Fort Halifax. Proprietary lands would rise in value, but the immediate issue confronting the Standing Committee was a new sort of conflict. The disagreements with rival land companies which originated in the early 1750s would reach a culmination in the next decade, when proprietors would stake all on a drive to win mastery of the Kennebec River from Wesserunset to the sea. This greatest of all battles would be fought in the law courts of Massachusetts and Great Britain.

NOTES

CHAPTER VII

1 Resolution, Oct. 31, 1750, K.P.P., Records, I, 50.

2 Kennebeck proprietors to Samuel Goodwin, Feb. 27, 1754, K.P.P., Loose Papers (1625-Oct., 1757).

3 *Ibid.*

4 Resolution, Mar. 20, 1754, K.P.P., Records, II, 54-55.

5 Resolutions, Mar. 27, 1754, K.P.P., Records, II, 56.

6 Schutz, *William Shirley,* 168-169.

7 *Ibid.,* 169-171.

8 *Ibid.*

9 William Lithgow to Spencer Phips, Mar. 9, 1752, M.A., LIV, 260.

10 See Chapter VI.

11 Samuel Goodwin to Silvester Gardiner, Dec. 26, 1753, M.A., LIV, 269. It was later learned that the report was false.

12 William Lithgow to Spencer Phips, Jan. 23, 1754, M.A., II, 327.

13 North's mission was remarkably similar to that of the young George Washington in the Ohio Valley. It is not known whether North completed his mission.

14 William Shirley to Company Commanders, Mar. 18, 1754, M.A., LIV, 285. William Shirley to Benning Wentworth, Mar. 18, 1754, *New Hampshire Provincial Papers,* VI, 278-279.

15 William Shirley to the Council and House of Representatives, Mar. 28, 1754. William Shirley, *The Correspondence of William Shirley,* ed. Charles H. Lincoln (New York, 1912), II, 33-34.

16 William Shirley to Benning Wentworth, Mar. 18, 1754, *New Hampshire Provincial Papers,* VI, 278-279.

17 William Shirley to the Council and House of Representatives, Mar. 28, 1754. Shirley, *Correspondence of William Shirley,* II, 33-34.

18 *Ibid.,* 38.

19 Massachusetts House Resolution, Apr. 2, 1754, M.A., LIV, 174. Bean was perhaps the same Lieutenant Bean who had commanded one of the four companies sent by Massachusetts to destroy Father Rasle's Indian village of Norridgewock in 1724. Francis Parkman, *A Half-Century of Conflict* (New York, 1966), 174.

20 Perhaps the House decided that the threat of Indian attacks was certain enough to justify the expedition on preventive grounds alone. Also, the expenses voted were small in comparison with the cost of the Louisbourg expedition of 1745.

21 Resolution, Apr. 3, 1754, K.P.P., Records, II, 57-58.

22 Resolution, Apr. 17, 1754, K.P.P., Records, II, 63. The proprietary resolution incorporated the exact wording of Shirley's proposal to the Company.

23 Present-day Skowhegan.

24 See Thomas Johnston Map of 1755.

25 This was also the site of the old Pilgrim trading post. See Chapter I.

26 William Shirley to Kennebeck proprietors, Apr. 16, 1754, K.P.P., Records, II, 63.

27 *Ibid.*

28 Articles of Agreement between Gershom Flagg and the Kennebeck proprietors, May 7, 1754, K.P.P., Loose Papers (1625-Oct., 1757).

29 William Shirley to Benning Wentworth, Apr. 22, 1754. *New Hampshire Provincial Papers*, VI, 277-278.

30 Proprietor Jabez Fox died the year following Shirley's stay at Falmouth. His house was probably chosen as Shirley's headquarters because it was the most elaborate in Falmouth, and he himself was a member of the Council.

31 At this point the French still insisted that the boundary line was the Kennebec River.

32 William Shirley to Thomas Robinson, Aug. 19, 1754, *Correspondence of William Shirley*, II, 77.

33 *Ibid.*

34 "John Barber's Journal of the Kennebec Expedition, May 30-Aug. 17, 1754," *New England Historical and Genealogical Register*, XXVII, 281-285.

35 Gershom Flagg's Account "For Work done on the East. River framing Blockhouses & for Cushnoc for the Plymouth Company," July 22, 1754, K.P.P., Loose Papers (1625-Oct., 1757).

36 *Ibid.*

37 *Ibid.*

38 Samuel Oldham's Account, K.P.P., Loose Papers (1625-Oct., 1757).

39 Much of the timber was cut in the vicinity of Frankfort and floated upriver. Fort Western, carefully restored early in the twentieth century, still looks much as it did in the eighteenth.

40 The blockhouse still stands by the river in the present town of Winslow.

41 *The Boston Weekly News-Letter,* Sept. 12, 1754. This account of Shirley's visit, more complete than his own official version, was printed as an "Extract of a Letter from a Gentleman at Falmouth."

42 *The Boston Weekly News-Letter,* Sept. 26, 1754.

43 General Winslow must have returned at about the same time, as his expense account, for a total of £56.12.1 1/2. shows him back at Fort Richmond on Sept. 2. General Winslow's Expenses for the Kennebec Expedition, June 30-Sept. 30, 1754, Winslow Letter Book, M.H.S.

44 *The Boston Weekly News-Letter,* Sept. 12, 1754.

45 *Ibid.,* Nov. 7, 1754.

46 *Ibid.,* Sept. 26, 1754.

47 *Ibid.,* Oct. 3, 1754.

48 *Ibid.*

49 *Ibid.*

50 Thomas Fitch to Thomas Robinson, Oct. 30, 1754, Parkman Papers, XL, 31, M.H.S.

51 Hutchinson, *History,* III, 14.

52 *Ibid.,* 18.

53 A *Strange Account . . . ."* See Chapter III for the origin of this pamphlet, probably written by James Flagg.

54 *Ibid.,* 254.

55 George Dow, *Fort Western on the Kennebec* (Augusta, Me., 1922), 20-21.

56 Schutz, *William Shirley,* 179.

57 See Chapter III for the involved alliances of the Shirley, Temple, Waldo, Erving, and Bowdoin families.

58 "Shares and Proportions of the Proprietors in the Kennebeck Purchase . . . ," K.P.P., Records, III, 1-15.

59 Resolution, Dec. 11, 1754, K.P.P., Records, II, 81.

60 Resolution, Feb. 5, 1755, K.P.P., Records, II, 83.

61 "An Account of Dr. Gardiner's Holding in the Kennebeck Purchase to Feb. 22, 1768," K.P.P., Loose Papers (1760-1790).

62 See, for example, *A Strange Account . . .*, 255. Here the pamphleteer baldly states that Shirley "said he had got Fort Western and Fort Halifax built by the Province, on purpose to serve their [the proprietors'] Scheme."

63 See Chapters VIII and IX for details of the lawsuits they commenced to defend their patent.

64 William Shirley to Lords of Trade, Dec. 31, 1754, Colonial Office Papers, CO 5/887, Public Record Office. The complete text of this letter is reproduced in *Appendix* III.

65 *Ibid.*

66 *Ibid.* Shirley's letter was intended only for the eyes of the Board of Trade, and was kept a secret in New England. However, the Kennebeck proprietors were able to obtain a copy through means of their own, and sent the original version of this copy to Florentius Vassall, proprietor in London, who was in a position to help their cause. William Shirley to Lords of Trade, Dec. 31, 1754, Vassall Correspondence, Letters, papers, and maps relating to the Kennebeck Company *circa* 1754-1756, Maine Papers, Manuscript Division, New York Public Library. The cover sheet to this letter bears the notation: "Copy of Governr Shirleys Letter to the Lords of Trade recommending the case of the Kennebeck Co in regard to a new Patent. NB this is *not to be* shown by Mr Sharpe *to any* one." The letter itself appears to have been copied in at least four hands, suggesting that it was reproduced from Shirley's original by several very hurried proprietors, perhaps while the Governor was absent from his office. The letter bears the further note that "we had no time to correct it." On April 2, 1755, Florentius Vassall informed Mr. Sharpe, Company lawyer in London, that "I now send you all the papers I have or are necessary to Let you into the Kennebeck Companys dispute. The copy of Governr Shirleys late letter to the board of trade must be a secret with you, as it may not [be] agreable to know

that I have it (& how), but it may be useful to you in making a proper state of their case." Vassall Correspondence, New York Public Library. The proprietors had voted on Oct. 23, 1754, to appoint a committee to "prosecute and defend," consisting of Silvester Gardiner, James Bowdoin, William Bowdoin, Benjamin Hallowell, Thomas Hancock, Charles Apthorp, James Pitts, and William Brattle, with powers to institute any necessary legal actions in New England and Great Britain. A copy of the minutes of this meeting accompanied Shirley's letter to the Board of Trade. With it also went a lengthy, highly detailed petition which the proprietors had sent to the governor on Oct. 30, 1754. Public Record Office, Colonial Office Papers, C.O. 5, 887, 975. It seems significant that Shirley did not act immediately on the proprietary petition. Instead, he waited until after the receipt of his Company share before writing to the Board of Trade. This letter drew heavily upon material supplied in the petition.

67 The Board of Trade replied to Shirley's request on August 6, 1755. It did not encourage the Company's aspirations, stating that "the Difficulties, which the Proprietors alledge they are under from the Claims and Pretensions of others, who have settled within the Limits of their Grant, and which is the principle Reason assign'd by them for applying for a new Grant, may when the matter comes to be particularly discuss'd, operate as a Reason against it, or at least may render such new Grant ineffectual for the purposes for which it is desired, because it cannot set aside any Right or Interest, which the Province of the Massachusetts, by their Charter, or any Persons, by particular Grants, may have in the said Lands . . . ." The Board therefore suggested that the proprietors institute an action of ejectment against an opposing party which might be appealed to the King in Council as the best means of securing an explanatory charter which would guarantee their rights to the seacoast areas of the Kennebec River. This is the precise course of action which the proprietors followed some years later. See Chap. IX. Colonial Office Records, CO.5/918. The full text of the Board of Trade's letter is reprinted in Appendix IV. The proprietors mentioned this letter in a note sent to Thomas Goosetrey of London, Company lawyer, on Dec. 19, 1767. K.P.P., Letter Book I, 8,

and quoted from it in a letter written to Sir William Baker of London on Dec. 28, 1767. K.P.P., Letter Book I, 10.

68 Schutz, *William Shirley*, 242.

69 "Shares and Proportions . . . ," K.P.P., Records, I, 1-15.

70 The recording of the Shirley share is itself a puzzle. As entered in Lincoln County Deeds, III, 246-247, County Court House, Wiscasset, Me., on Dec. 3, 1754, Silvester Gardiner sold the 1/24th share to William Shirley for £400. As has been shown, this is untrue. The figure is also much higher than the going rate for Company shares at that time. Furthermore, the deed was not transcribed in the Suffolk County Records then or later. The transaction was finally recorded in Lincoln County Deeds as above on June 13, 1764, seven years after Shirley's share was auctioned off by the Kennebeck proprietors. At the time of the auction, Robert Temple, Jr., Shirley's son-in-law, bid in one-half of the share. On October 27, 1761, Shirley's conveying of the half share to Robert Temple, Jr., was entered in Lincoln County Deeds, IV, 12A-13. Here the transaction is spoken of as a gift, although Temple had purchased the half share at auction. These deeds seem to emphasize the fact that Shirley received the share from the Company, was embarrassed by the gift, and for this reason failed to register it in Suffolk County Deeds. By 1761, however, his son-in-law wanted some legal evidence of his own ownership of the half share. The parties involved then resorted to a coverup. Gardiner made out a deed acknowledging his sale of the share to Shirley, and Shirley in turn recorded the sale of one-half of the grant to Temple. No mention was made of the auction proceedings.

71 William Lithgow to William Shirley, Mar. 22, 1755, M.A., LIV, 394.

72 William Lithgow to William Shirley, Feb. 27, 1755, M.A., LIV, 360.

73 John A. Schutz, *Thomas Pownall* (Glendale, Cal., 1951), 87; 243.

74 *A Strange Account* . . . , 253-254. The pamphlet's author complained that "two Foot Companies . . . were paid by the Province, to range and guard the Inhabitants, [but] did very

little Duty besides carrying Provisions to the Forts, being under the Direction of Don Quixot [Dr. Gardiner]."

75 Petition of Charles Apthorp *et al.* to Thomas Pownall, Mar. 24, 1758, M.A., CSVII, 387-390.

76 *Ibid.*

77 Gershom Flagg to Silvester Gardiner, May 29, 1759, K.P.P., Loose Papers (Nov., 1757-Apr., 1768). In his letter, Flagg stated that he had completed work on the timbers for Fort Pownall, and would embark the next day for the Penobscot.

78 William D. Williamson, *History of the State of Maine, 1602-1820* (Hallowell, Me., 1832), II, 335.

79 *Ibid.*

80 The Kennebeck proprietors presented 500 acres of land at Pownalborough to the governor when he returned to England in June, 1760. Whether this was in return for past or future favors is difficult to determine. See Chapter VIII.

81 "A Brief State . . . ,," K.P.P., Letter Book I, 66.

VIII

Defending The Title

On November 16, 1761, Samuel Goodwin, resident agent of the proprietors on the Kennebec, committed his latest fears to paper. He confided to David Jeffries, Company clerk, that "I am worried day and night with the unruly People on Sheepscut River &c for they oppose the Company in all Shapes & Joyns in Purse as well as Every other way so I must se the Company soon if I can gett the business don which Doctor Gardiner hath assigned me . . . ."[1] Samuel Goodwin was not a man who was easily alarmed. He had been living on the river for at least ten years, and had many previous encounters with the hostile residents of the Kennebeck Purchase. These settlers, whose arrival in the area often predated reactivation of the Kennebeck Company, either purchased their own lands, or held grants under the Pejepscot or the Clark and Lake companies. In very few instances were they willing to accept the claims of the Kennebeck proprietors. Resistance centered in the coastal towns of Brunswick, Wiscasset, Woolwich, and Georgetown, where the settlers, encouraged as they were by the rival land companies, refused Kennebeck suzerainty. During the years 1750-1773, the proprietors fought a rising tide of ill will, which eventually spread among their own tenants and grantees. By 1773, the propriety earned the reputation of being a litigious and grasping group.

The Kennebeck proprietors, aware of the opposition they would encounter as early as 1749, the year their claims were revived, were quick to advertise their tract's boundaries. These, they claimed, quoting from the old Plymouth patent where convenient, extended "from the utmost limits of Cobbisconte, including Fifteen Miles in Breadth on each side of the River Kennebeck, and the said River to the Western Ocean, including the islands adjacent."[2] The upper boundary was uncontested and remained unsettled until after the American Revolution. But claiming the very shores of the Atlantic for the lower limits clashed with the boundaries of Brunswick, Woolwich, Georgetown, and other coastal settlements established by the Pejepscot and the Clark and Lake proprietors.[3] Nevertheless, the Kennebeck Company first attempted to win the support of these settlers by a combination of threats and promises of rewards. They were not very successful, for the inhabitants were content enough under their present landlords.

Brunswick, settled in 1715 and incorporated in 1738, and Topsham, founded in 1717 across the Androscoggin Bay but not incorporated until 1764, were strongholds of the Pejepscot Company.[4] In these places, Adam Winthrop and his associates had done their work well. They granted lands generously, spent money freely, and committed themselves to settle a minister and a schoolmaster in these towns. Their influence with the General Court made possible the building of a fine stone fort, Fort Georges, at Brunswick, to which the Province had contributed £400 and also the grant of a five-year tax exemption to the town to help speed development.[5] Fort Georges, reinforced by Massachusetts militia, significantly encouraged settlement in the region and safeguarded the frontier.

Concurrent with the founding of Brunswick and Topsham, Edward Hutchinson and his twenty-three associates of the Clark and Lake Company established the town of Georgetown nearby on the coast at the mouth of the Kennebec. Because it was to the advantage of Massachusetts to sponsor and maintain an outpost in the area, the Province provided a garrison to guard the little settlement of fifteen families for six months. Georgetown was officially incorporated on June 13, 1716,[6] grew rapidly, and encompassed within its limits the future towns of Bath, Woolwich, and Phipsburg. By 1764, Georgetown was the largest town in the Kennebec region and boasted a population of 1,319 people.[7] It was also the easternmost center of the mast industry in New England.

Opportunities for development of the mast trade also influenced the establishment of other settlements in the area. The townships of Harrington (Bristol), Townshend (Boothbay), and Walpole (Nobleboro) were founded in 1729. They owed their existence to the ambitious plans of David Dunbar, Surveyor of the King's Woods in America. Dunbar promoted his position as protector of the royal masts to control, temporarily at least, the entire Province of Sagadahock in eastern Maine. Here he hoped to create what he fondly called the Province of Georgia. It was not to be. Nevertheless, Dunbar moved to Maine and laid out the three towns between the Sheepscot and Muscongus rivers.[8] The settlements remained small, but the Kennebeck proprietors could not overlook their existence. Their opposition to Company schemes proved out of all proportion to their size.

By 1749, when the Kennebeck proprietors first began to consider developing their long-neglected tract, the six settlements established earlier were growing, with Brunswick and Georgetown well in the lead. It was difficult for their inhabitants, comfortable after several decades on the frontier, to accept Kennebeck Company pretensions to their lands merely on the strength of an ancient patent, and a doubtful one at that. They decided to resist, trusting to the law courts and the Massachusetts General Court for justice.

To Samuel Goodwin, proprietors' clerk resident on the Kennebec, fell most of the burden of enforcing Company claims and preventing trespassing on their holdings. Proprietors defined as "trespassers" anyone living within their territory who did not hold land under their grants. The direct approach of prosecuting individual trespassers would have been costly, and adverse court decisions fatal to their claims. The much simpler way was to grant land freely in the disputed areas to those settlers who recognized the Kennebeck proprietors as rightful authorities. Thus, as early as 1753, the proprietors voted not to "Molest or Disturb any Person or Persons of Such Houses and Land as Was by Them or their Predecessors with Great Cost and Labour Cleared and Subdued," provided that the settlers apply to them for new deeds.[9] The proprietors also offered the bait of promoting the speedy incorporation of those settlements that were still unorganized.[10] In addition, they proposed that in Harrington, Walpole, Townshend, New Castle, Wiscasset, Brunswick, Topsham, and Georgetown, "Six Acres . . . be Laid out for a Meeting house to stand upon for a Training Plain and to Lay out a Perpetual Common for that use and also Two Acres in Each of the Districts [to be] laid out in such Places as Shall be agreeable to the Inhabitants as a Burying Place and Lay for that use."[11] The people in these settlements must have wondered whose land was being granted to whom, as the Kennebeck Company had not established a legal right to the territory in question. Obviously the proprietors hoped that sheer bluster and promise of action in the procurement of ministers and the founding of churches and schools would carry the day for them. And so Samuel Goodwin plodded from one settlement to another, cajoling, and intimidating on behalf of his Company. Protests were not long in coming.

On October 17, 1754, the inhabitants of Wiscasset on the Sheepscot petitioned the Massachusetts government for relief from Goodwin's importuning. Thirty-six residents of the town complained that:

> . . . as of Late a number of Gentlemen calling themselves by the Name of the Proprietors of the Plymouth Purchase, have claimed our lands & by their Agent Samuel Goodwin Partly by Promises & Partly by Thretnings have Prevailed on a Considerable Number of the Inhabitants (without the least Pretence of Right as we Conceive) to take up under Them. So that we are thrown into great Confusion and Disorder . . . .[12]

Goodwin was then attempting to persuade the Wiscasset residents to combine with the Kennebeck Company town of Frankfort.[13] His efforts, however, only created resentment among the settlers he was seeking to annex. Although the Company later boasted that all but fifteen of the inhabitants of Wiscasset and the disputed towns nearby acknowledged the new claims, the Kennebec records themselves do not bear this out.[14] There is no trace of deeds from the settlers in the controversial region, and they continued to defy the Company until court decisions forced them to come to terms.

Between 1758 and 1761, at least thirty settlers, all from the Georgetown area, received grants from the Kennebeck proprietors confirming their possession of lands previously held under Clark and Lake. In every case the grantees paid for the cost of their new deeds, plus an amount varying from £6 to £100 according to the size of the tract involved. Typical was the situation of Shubael Hinckley of Georgetown, who on October 10, 1759, was confirmed in possession of Lot No. 27, 317 acres, pro-

vided that he pay £63.8 within twelve months as well as the cost
of the deed.[15] In a different category were thirty-eight other
Georgetown landholders who, in April, 1760, received clear titles
to their tracts without additional payment.[16] In these cases the
proprietors were probably so pleased to receive outward compli-
ance that they exacted no tribute. But Joseph Berry's position was
perhaps unique. His confirmation of Lot No. 25, 571 acres at
Georgetown, was apparently granted because, as owner of a sawmill, he was a decided asset to the proprietors.[17] The rush of settlers to accede to Company edict during this period was clearly
dictated by a recent proprietary settlement with the Clark and
Lake Company.

Clark and Lake proprietors had long claimed territory extending from the mouth of the Kennebec River up to Cobboseconte
Falls, well within "Kennebeck country," as well as lands above
the Kennebeck Purchase beginning at Negumkike. Almost immediately after Company reactivation, the Kennebeck proprietors began to oppose Clark and Lake boundaries, with Samuel
Goodwin leading the fray. Leaders of Clark and Lake in the
1750s included: Cadwallader Ford, clerk, treasurer, and strategist;
William Skinner; Edward Hutchinson, the uncle of Thomas
Hutchinson, who would figure in the struggle; and the Congregationalist minister, Samuel Webster. Clark and Lake representatives rapidly came to be the most intractable of the Kennebeck
Company opponents.

As early as March 27, 1751, the Clark and Lake group announced in a printed broadside widely circulated in the Boston
area that it would "prosecute all Persons in the Law who have
made Encroachments upon, or shall hereafter make any Encroachments upon, strip, waste, or Spoil any Land belonging to
or claimed by them."[18] This was but the first of its public an-
nouncements directed toward beating the Kennebeck proprietors
at their own game.

Each side pressed its claim to the disputed area. In 1754 the
Clark and Lake proprietors inserted an advertisement in the Boston newspapers decrying the Kennebeck Company. Cadwallader
Ford, spokesman for the Clark and Lake interest, emphasized the
validity of his company's Indian deeds, the one-hundred-year-old
ownership of the tract, and the £20,000 expended for improvements during that period. He also pointed out that his Company's
claim had been confirmed in 1743 by a decree of the King in

Council. To further embellish his case, Ford gleefully commented that Clark and Lake had already defeated the Kennebeck proprietors in an action for trespass at the Superior Court meeting at
York.[19] But, in the eyes of the Kennebeck proprietors, one battle
did not win a war.

The propriety was quick to respond. In its own advertisement,
dated May 29, 1754, the Kennebeck spokesman wrote off the
Clark and Lake deeds as illegal under Massachusetts law, said the
expenditures of its rival were merely claims for losses suffered in
Indian attacks, and dared Cadwallader Ford to produce the King
in Council decree. Finally, the author of the piece intimated that
the Kennebeck proprietors' loss of the court suit at York was
merely the opening round of a series of encounters that it would
not lose.[20]

By 1756, the protagonists were engaged in a major lawsuit. In
their "Plaintiffs State of the Case," the Clark and Lake proprietors insisted that Kennebeck holdings began at Cobboseconte and
ran upwards from there, leaving the Clark and Lake Company in
firm control of the river mouth and adjacent areas. They de-
plored the extralegal methods used by the Kennebeck proprietors
to persuade reluctant settlers, and accused them of having "used
actual Force in Taking and retaining some Possessions, and destroy[ing] the finest Part of the Timber."[21] To bolster their case,
the Clark and Lake interests printed an impressive array of Indian deeds dating back to the early 1600s, described company improvements both before and after the Indian wars, and ended by
casting doubts upon the rival claim. They resurrected the Hocking story[22] and used it to their own advantage. The point turned
on whether Hocking had been shot either on, above, or below
the Plymouth grant. From it, they concluded that the Pilgrims
had not controlled the lower reaches of the Kennebec River, stating: "(1) That their Limits were not the whole River. (2) That
their Trading-House which was at Cushnoc, was within their Limits. (3) That the Falls of the River which was one of their
Bounds, was above the said Trading-House."[23] Clark and Lake
proprietors logically insisted that, in any event, only a trading
post located near the falls of the Kennebec, as close to the center
of the fur trade as possible, would have been of value to the Pilgrims. The Clark and Lake State of the Case was a convincing
one, and was probably much closer to the truth than the Kennebeck claim to the whole river. Under the circumstances, the Ken-

nebeck propriety decided that a judicial decision would be against its best interests. Instead of pursuing the case in the courts, the Standing Committee suggested a more desirable alternative, to which even the Clark and Lake leaders agreed.

In June, 1756, both parties agreed to submit their boundary dispute to a committee of referees.[24] The formal agreement was to submit:

> all Controversies & Demands subsisting between the Two Companys to a Rule of Court to be intered into at the Superior Court now sitting at Boston & mutually to release to each other such part of the Lands which shall be awarded to them as may be necessary to transfer all the strength possible to each other's title in their several respective Lands, & mutually to confirm one another in the Title & possession of Lands as assigned & ceded.[25]

The adversaries next agreed on the mechanics of the referee action.

Five lawyers were to act as referees. Each side had the privilege of selecting one of these. If the two companies could not agree upon the other three, they were to be chosen by the Superior Court for Suffolk County.[26] The five worthies selected were Oliver Wolcott, chairman; Jeremiah Gridley; Benjamin Prat, Josephy Hawley; and Colonel John Worthington. It seems fairly certain that Prat was the lawyer chosen to represent the Kennebeck proprietors; he not only was outstanding in his field but had done extensive legal work for them earlier. Oliver Wolcott of Connecticut was a great-grandson of Thomas Clark of the original firm of Clark and Lake; probably he spoke for that firm. Worthington and Hawley, important political figures in western Massachusetts, may have been chosen in an attempt to include some referees from outside the vested interests of the Boston community. The two land companies agreed to share equally all expenses incurred by the referees, as well as their fees. Each company was entitled to legal counsel in addition to the privilege of choosing a lawyer among the referees.

Characteristically, the Kennebeck proprietors hired the best lawyers available. Company records show that James Otis, Jr., and Robert Auchmuty each received £24 for "pleading the case lately before the Referees."[27] Other accounts reveal that Wolcott, Worthington, and Hawley, all out-of-towners, boarded at the prestigious tavern operated by Benjamin Bagnall in Boston, the first two for twenty-two days and the third for twenty days in

December. Jeremy Gridley also occasionally dined at Bagnall's. The whole bill, including servants' accommodations, stabling for two horses, and such extra expenses as candles, tobacco, barber fees, rum, madeira, white wine, limes, sugar, and other makings of punch, came to £34.8.9 1/2.[28] Each referee was paid £30, or £150 in all, in addition to expenses.

While the referees were deciding upon the merits of the case, they were surprised by the appearance of an unexpected witness. As Cadwallader Ford later recalled, "The Honourable Thomas Hutchinson, Esqr. brought in a Paper, and said to the Referees, Gentlemen, I do not know but I have found a Paper that may shorten your Work."[29] The paper contained an agreement between Clark and Lake and the Plymouth Colony "and mentioned Cobbecyconte at the lowermost Bounds between the said Colony's Land and the said Clark and Lake's Land; and the said Agreement and Settlement was signed by Commissioners or a Committee from the said Colony, as he understood it, and the Name of one of the Signers was Prince . . . and Clark and Lake signed on the other Side; that the Paper was dated 1654, if he remembered right."[30] The Reverend Samuel Webster of Clark and Lake recollected the document to be an agreement on the part of the Plymouth leaders to throw their holdings together with those of the two partners for trading purposes. As Webster described the scene, "all examined it [the document] one by one, both Referees and Parties; and the Plymouth Gentlemen, the Most sanguine of them, appeared more and more confounded the more they viewed it, so that [I] expected they would easily have given up the case."[31] Thomas Hutchinson's later testimony on the matter added little explanation. The paper had belonged to his grandfather, Elisha Hutchinson, and was a plan or map setting a line of property between Clark and Lake and the Plymouth Colony representatives. Unfortunately he had forgotten the details, except that he knew the paper had affected the controversy.[32] This document undoubtedly marked the turning point of the referees' verdict, for the Kennebeck proprietors grudgingly accepted what was for them an unfavorable decision. Hutchinson's mysterious paper was never seen again. Cadwallader Ford later testified it soon after disappeared from the files he had assembled on the case. Only the Kennebeck proprietors would have profited from its loss.

The apprehensive Kennebeck proprietors learned the results of the referees' decision shortly after the close of the hearings on December 28, 1756. The report did not become public, however, until the August term of the Superior Court of Judicature at Boston in 1757. The referees awarded the town of Woolwich, directly to the south of the Company town of Frankfort, all of Arrowsick Island, and 450 acres on Parker's Island to Clark and Lake. This left a part of Parker's Island, including sections of Georgetown, a few smaller islands, and some land south of Frankfort to the Kennebeck proprietors.[33] This was far less than they had expected. Dr. Gardiner and his Standing Committee were furious with Hutchinson, and would never foget the role he played in their defeat.

Although they had agreed in advance to abide by the referees' decision and had been trounced in its terms, upon reconsideration Dr. Gardiner and his associates decided to hold out for more favorable results. They laid careful plans to contest the decision even before it was officially announced, searching desperately for an acceptable retreat. Finally, the Company's lawyers reported that there was "an uncertainty in the Boundary Line in the Awards given in the Superior Court" by the referees. The only remedy for this "uncertainty" would be for surveyors chosen by the two companies to search the boundaries.[34] Perhaps in this way the Kennebeck proprietors would salvage a larger share of the award. The proprietors also had other plans afoot.

Cadwallader Ford, representing the holders under Clark and Lake, later reported another maneuver attempted by his opponents. Supplying testimony in a subsequent legal test, he affirmed that after the referees' conference, "the said Proprietors of the Kennebeck purchase opposed said Reports [of the referees] being accepted and made a Motion to the Court to order said Report to be recommitted to said Referees and a New hearing of the case, which order of Court they obtained."[35] Rather than return the case to referees, however, the two companies agreed upon a settlement. For a price of £450, Clark and Lake released to the Kennebeck Company all of the coveted lands north of Woolwich.[36] The price seemed a heavy one for the proprietors to have paid for the outward appearance of having won their point. Furthermore, the territory they had acquired in their tilt with Clark and Lake was still woefully short of their goal of controlling the seacoast regions of the Kennebec. Nevertheless, during the next three years, settlers of Georgetown living in the areas awarded to the Kennebeck proprietors were compelled to come to terms with their new masters. Meanwhile the Standing Committee was reaching final agreement with another important adversary, the Pejepscot Company.

Proprietors of the Pejepscot Company and its subsidiary, the Brunswick Company, were as quick to oppose Kennebeck claims as were their neighbors. As early as March, 1750, they complained that Samuel Goodwin was pressuring their landholders to accept the Company's deeds. To add insult to injury, the Kennebeck proprietors had offered to defend any of their shareholders or grantees against the lawsuits of rival companies, had insolently described the bounds of their trumped-up claim, and had held out enticing terms to likely settlers.[37] The aggressive Kennebeck Company campaign was beginning to succeed. Brunswick proprietors, long entrenched in the region, were shocked to learn that "many of the People in Brunswick and Topsham . . . in a vile Treacherous Manner [had] Submitted themselves to their pretended claims."[38] The Brunswick group immediately launched a broadside of their own against their adversaries, announcing their intention not only of defending any inhabitants holding land under them who were prosecuted by Goodwin and Company, but of suing "anyone that shall be so imprudent as to take up under any other title."[39] The pamphlet battle was on![40]

In opposing the Brunswick proprietors, the Kennebeck shareholders were challenging a group well known for its colonizing activities in Maine after the turn of the eighteenth century.[41] Since the 1720s, these Pejepscot and Brunswick proprietors had been developing their lands leisurely, granting farmsteads to settlers, and complacently watching the slow rise in real estate values.

By 1750, the second generation of Pejepscot proprietors had lost interest in their Maine holdings. The older, ambitious leaders were dead, and their successors, men such as Benning Wentworth and Isaac Royall, were more concerned with their political careers, merchant affairs, or land speculations in other areas than with their Pejepscot shares. Proprietors' meetings were seldom held. Under the threat of Kennebeck Company encroachments, however, a few Pejepscot investors roused themselves to activity. Belcher Noyes, Company clerk, wrote ominous letters to fellow shareholders. William Skinner, a lawyer, contributed legal advice.

Few other proprietors rallied to the cause in spite of the alarms raised by Noyes and Skinner.

At first the two rivals confined themselves to a spirited pamphlet warfare. In a volley of May 15, 1751, the Pejepscot group emphasized its duty to "open the Eyes of People, and to undeceive those Persons that have been unwarily led to take up under the Plymouth [Kennebeck] Company's Claim."[42] In an impressive sampling of extracts from Indian deeds, they proved to their own satisfaction a prior claim to lands now contested by the Kennebeck proprietors. Noyes and his friends contended that "the Claim of the Plymouth Company begins at Cobbaseconte, and goes up the River of Kennebeck, and cannot extend below said Cobbaseconte, which is their lowermost Bounds toward the Western Ocean."[43] Outraged at these limitations on their holding, the Kennebeck proprietors responded with an eight-page "Remarks" in which they revealed documents from their own files and even from those of the Clark and Lake Company.[44] In the "Remarks," they commented that a recently published Pejepscot "Plan," a map engraved by Thomas Johnston of Boston in 1753, was invalid, and rejected the boundary limits outlined in their foe's earlier pamphlet. They concluded that the purpose of the Pejepscot proprietors had been to "blind the Eyes of the People, and to delude the ignorant, and so render ineffectual . . . the Endeavour of the Plymouth Company to settle the Eastern Lands [which would be] a great Advantage to the Province in general."[45]

The controversy continued, and by 1755 the Kennebeck proprietors had printed their own map showing their claims as opposed to those of both the Pejepscot-Brunswick proprietors and the Clark and Lake Company. Surprisingly, Thomas Johnston engraved this map as well, altering the boundaries shown on the earlier map to please his new customers. It was an impressive production, complete with a decorative cartouche and dedicated to Governor Shirley, but it did nothing to clarify the issue.[46] The conflicting company maps then circulating in Boston each had its own defenders. At that point the Kennebeck proprietors must have decided that this quarrel, like the one recently settled with Clark and Lake, could best be resolved by mutual agreement rather than by resorting to court action. By March, 1757, the rivals had drawn up their respective proposals for settling the disagreement, and by June 29 they had reached a consensus, basically setting the line of demarcation between company territories at the Cathance River where it flows into Merrymeeting Bay on the lower Kennebec near Topsham. In arriving at this agreement, it was necessary for each side to release some lands and, in disputed areas, to compensate landholders. On June 29, 1757, representatives of each group set their signatures to the final agreement.[47]

But the compromise did not end intercompany bickering for long. By 1759, Belcher Noyes was threatening the Kennebeck propriety with a court action because one of its tenants, Captain James McCobb, had refused to release his lands to the Pejepscot Company as the agreement had provided.[48] Kennebeck proprietors straightened the matter out. In the 1760s contention again surfaced, for the Kennebeck proprietors, claiming lands the Pejepscot people insisted were part of Topsham, proceeded with plans to incorporate a town to the northward to be called Bowdoinham. The Act for Bowdoinham came before the Massachusetts Council in 1762. Earlier the Pejepscot proprietors had enjoyed their own share of influence in the Council, and they may have expected to triumph again. This time, Belcher Noyes marshaled his forces in vain. Because he could not spur prominent investors such as Royall and Wentworth to action, the Brunswick proprietors were unable to prevent the incorporation of Bowdoinham on the basis of the Kennebeck Company's survey, and had to accept a reduction in the size of Topsham. In a letter to another proprietor, Noyes afterwards complained that the move "was objected to by Lieut-Govr [Thomas Hutchinson] on our Behalf but Mr. [James] Bowdoin stood up and imposed on the Board; Coll [Isaac] Royall said nothing."[49] Royall's inaction was lamentable; he was himself a member of the Council and not without weight there. Noyes and his friends could only bemoan the fact that they had not bothered to incorporate Topsham when the opportunity had arisen years before.[50] Members of the Standing Committee must have been equally disgruntled at this second intervention by Thomas Hutchinson, even though this time it had not succeeded. Again, his family interest in a rival land company, as well as a sense of justice, must have dictated his interference.

Animosities that had built up during nearly two decades of struggle between the two companies continued to fester. Pejepscot proprietors went on accumulating evidence to prove their adversary's claim worthless, and contested Kennebeck Company failure to honor the terms of the agreement of 1757. In 1766, they

forced their rival to cede four hundred acres of land on Cobboseconte Pond in return for final recognition of the Cathance River
as the dividing line between Topsham and Bowdoinham.[51] Four
years later, Belcher Noyes at a proprietors' meeting produced an
old Clark and Lake document which he believed proved conclusively that Kennebeck claims did not extend to the sea. Although
he apparently never used this document in a court action, feelings continued intense. When, soon after, an unusually high tide
destroyed much of Dr. Gardiner's river property, Noyes saw in
the incident a case of divine retribution for so grasping a group.
He observed to a correspondent that the claims of the Kennebeck
Company "would never prosper, and so it has turned out in providence for the said Company have mett with many frowns."[52]

Thus the Cathance River came to be the southern boundary of
the Kennebeck propriety on the western side of the Kennebec as
Woolwich was on the eastern side, except for scattered holdings
farther south in Georgetown and the islands. For the time being,
the Kennebeck proprietors acknowledged defeat in their drive to
the sea. But they would raise this issue again, in spite of the fact
that the Company had ostensibly come to terms with its rivals.
Dr. Gardiner and his Standing Committee were willing to wait.
Meanwhile, they were equally concerned with other issues affecting the development of their controversial grant, and one of the
most important involved their difficulties with the courts.

The Kennebeck proprietors were already convinced that they
were being deprived of justice in the local courts. Certainly the
Standing Committee were painfully aware that cases tried in the
York County courts usually went against them, although they
sometimes were able to have decisions reversed on appeal. There
was a general feeling among the proprietors that the north country itself, with its squatters and lumber pirates, was hostile to
them. Other great landholders agreed with them. As early as
1754, the Kennebeck propriety received a message from a Mr.
Timothy Prout of Black Point, Scarboro, near Falmouth, which
reinforced their own impressions. Prout understood the Company's situation concerning lawsuits, for he and his father experienced the same treatment from Maine settlers. The Prouts had
even considered appealing one of their own cases to the Privy
Council, and dropped the idea only because of the ruinous expense involved.

The primary legal problem in York County,[53] Prout explained, was that the people chosen for jury duty were so jealous of large property owners that they would be sure to find against them. He warned, "I dare venture to say to you as the Clerk of the Inferior Court said to me *you will never get a verdict of a Jury in this County,* all the Causes brought into the Court are first tryed in the Tavern and judgement passed there before its Tryed in a Court of Justice."[54] Prout related several instances of this kind of justice, one involving the Kennebeck Purchase. The local tavern keeper at York had informed Prout that "upon the Tryall of your [the Kennebeck Company's] causes, that you had lost all yr Causes, that you had lost one Cause even for land above Richmond Fort, that you stood no Chance for any Land there, that you had only the Liberty of Trading & Fishing &c upon the Lands."[55] In Prout's opinion, the only solution was to petition for the creation of a separate legal entity, well removed from the injustices of York County.

The idea of a separate county on the Kennebec River must have had instant appeal. The proprietors might have much to do with the selection of judges of an inferior court there, and juries would undoubtedly comprise settlers holding land under the Kennebeck Company. Subtle pressures could always be brought to bear upon such jurors. Prout's suggestion was a useful one, but the proprietors had already tried it. In 1752, they had been successful in leading the inhabitants of Frankfort in a petition to create a county on the Kennebec River. But the General Court, unfortunately, dismissed that petition on the grounds that the region's population was too small.[56]

The proprietors were not so discouraged that they would not try again, and selected the crisis of the French and Indian War as the ideal time for a new attempt. On April 22, 1755, two petitions, signed by the same inhabitants, were forwarded to the Massachusetts General Court. One requested the setting off of a new county; the other asked for additional military protection in view of the perilous times. More than five hundred signatures of "inhabitants" appear on the petition, many recognizable as names of early settlers in the area. The list also includes the names of at least twenty nonresident Kennebeck proprietors, great and small, While the shareholders had a vested interest in affairs of the region, to call them "Inhabitants of Kennebeck River" seems to stretch a point.[57] The Massachusetts General Court was still unimpressed with Company arguments, and did not enact the new petition. The proposal to create a new Maine county languished for several years, its passage perhaps delayed rather than hastened by the continuing French and Indian War.

Unexpectedly, on July 21, 1760, the General Court rushed through a bill to establish two new counties in Maine. The Falmouth area in southern Maine became Cumberland County, while the Kennebec River valley was set off as Lincoln County, with the county seat at Frankfort. Local settlers darkly hinted that undue influence with the General Court had brought this about.[58] Proprietors had already renamed Frankfort "Pownalborough" in honor of the Governor, who had left for England on June 3. Flattered though he may have been by this gesture, he had already received more tangible appreciation of his services. On May 14, nearly two months before the establishment of the new counties, the Company granted him five hundred acres of land in Frankfort.[59] Pownall had been accommodating to the proprietors during his years in Massachusetts, and they hoped to utilize his services in the future in the mother country. He would prove to be a faithful friend.

The Kennebeck proprietors were so eager to capture the new county seat that they volunteered to build the Pownalborough Court House at their on expense—an offer that may have had something to do with the General Court's decision. As was to be expected, Gershom Flagg received the building contract.[60] His agreement with the Company called for a structure forty-five by forty-four feet, three stories tall. Located as it would be on the bank of the Kennebec, the building would serve as a beacon, visible for miles around. It would stand not only as a symbol of the authority of the Province, but also as a special mark of the power of the Kennebeck Company over the river. Beyond its symbolism, the Pownalborough Court House would fulfill several useful functions in the town. Primarily, a large courtroom the width of the building would occupy half of the second floor. Much of the ground floor would be used as a tavern, convenient for townspeople and circuit riders alike. Samuel Goodwin was assigned tavern privileges here, as well as permission to operate a general store. He and his family would occupy rooms on the second and third floors. In an emergency, the courthouse could also serve as a garrison house, for it stood in the center of the rapidly deteriorating Fort Shirley. The simple yet imposing Georgian structure was much admired by the people of the Kennebec and was a credit to its builder.

Gershom Flagg's bill to the Kennebeck proprietors totaled £546.8.11 lawful money,[61] a large sum for this period, and only for a mere shell of a building at that. One huge chimney, several fireplaces, and the plastering of a few rooms had been completed, but much remained to be done. A second chimney and the rest of the interior work was finished by Samuel Oldham under the direction of Jonathan Reed, resident proprietor, in 1769.[62] These improvements added up to £101.2.4[63] Of this sum, £33 went to Oldham, the mason.[64]

The Pownalborough Court House was pressed into service as soon as its roof was in place. On September 12, 1761, Gershom Flagg informed David Jeffries that on the ninth of that month he "had the House well Covered and Shingled on the top and Covered over the lower floor with one Ruff Board putt up Seats table etc. proper to receive the Court which Enter'd the Same in procession."[65] He was pleased to inform Jeffries that the "Chief Judge with the Rest of the Gentry Drank the Company's health and wish'd all well."[66] In this fashion, with a degree of pomp and ceremony, justice came officially to the Kennebec.

It was not a difficult task to find young, ambitious lawyers who would settle on an expanding frontier. Charles and William Cushing, brothers and members of a powerful political family in Massachusetts, scenting the spoils of office, moved eagerly to Pownalborough. William was appointed Judge of the Peace and Quorum and Judge of Probate for Lincoln County,[67] and Charles, Sheriff.[68] Both did legal work for the Kennebeck proprietors and were rewarded with generous land grants. Jonathan Bowman, one of Charles's classmates at Harvard, did even better. It is said that it was through Uncle Thomas Hancock's influence with the General Court that Bowman became Collector of the Excise, Register of Probate, Register of Deeds, Clerk of the Court of Sessions and the Court of Common Pleas, and Justice of the Peace for Lincoln County.[69] He soon became the leading figure in the community, living in an imposing mansion by the river, and making his mark in local politics. Judge Bowman came also to be a valuable support to the proprietors at Pownalborough, faithfully serving his patrons' interests. But not even he and the Cushings could ensure proprietary victory in lawsuits tried in Lincoln County.

Because most of the Kennebeck Company's cases originated in Lincoln County, the judges, as interested parties, often had to disqualify themselves from sitting. Thus, as judges, Bowman's and William Cushing's activities had to be limited, and in this sense they were liabilities on the bench. The proprietors' high hopes for agreeable verdicts from Lincoln County jurors were also dashed. Jurors chosen from the Sheepscot area, Wiscasset, Georgetown, Topsham, and Brunswick were uniformly hostile. Pownalborough inhabtants, browbeaten and often sued themselves by proprietors, also showed their antagonism in the jury box. In the light of unfavorable decisions, the Company increasingly appealed more cases from Pownalborough to the superior court at Falmouth. This maneuver was time-consuming and costly, however, and the Standing Committee decided to seek a more practical solution.

Changing their strategy, the Kennebeck proprietors in 1763 petitioned the General Court to allow several court actions then pending, as well as future cases, to be removed for trial to the inferior courts of Middlesex, Essex, Suffolk, or Worcester counties in Massachusetts. They complained that in many cases the local judges "declined trying the Same, because they were interested in the Land lying within the Plymouth Patent."[70] Furthermore, they argued that, in the two counties recently carved out of the old York County, "great Numbers of persons . . . are Some way or other concerned in the Event of them [the cases]," so that "it is very difficult, if not impossible that your Petitioners should have impartial Juries in either of these countys."[71] All of this was true. In Massachusetts, on the other hand, the proprietors had many friends and far-reaching influence.

When the Council considered the petition on January 14, 1764, it decided, as had the House several days earlier, to hear from "Adverse Parties" before passing judgment. Nathaniel Donnell, Joseph Sergeant, Benjamin Woodbridge, and James Cargill, all of whom had cases then pending against the Company or individual proprietors, were notified and asked to show cause why the petition should not be granted.[72] Donnell and Cargill responded, as did the inhabitants of the towns of Woolwich, Walpole, Freetown, New Castle, Georgetown, and Pownalborough.[73] All vehemently opposed the petition.

The counter-petitions displayed an impressive amount of unanimity in their arguments. Nathaniel Donnell spoke for many when he charged that if the petition succeeded, it would "have a direct Tendency to Enable the largest Purse and not the Justest cause to prevail," for in the counties of Suffolk, Middlesex, Essex, and Worcester "the said Proprietors [are] Rich Numerous and [have] large connections."[74] The people of Freetown observed that they would be ruined if they had to attend courts at such a great distance. James Cargill's rejoinder was especially cutting. Scanning the list of signers of the proprietary petition, he noted that "some interested [parties] have artfully concealed their Names. It's well known by whose Interest and Influence these . . . Countys were planned and formed, & something like it was attempted some years ago, but could not be accomplished.[75] It is significant that the names of Thomas Hancock, James Pitts, James Bowdoin, and William Bowdoin were not on the list of petitioners. Of these, the first three were then members of the Council, and the last was a representative. They may have withheld their names from the petition, but they could not conceal their influence in Massachusetts government. Several years later, the author of the Great Bubble pamphlet also noted that the proprietors had earlier tried a similar ploy, and openly accused them of having bribed Governor Pownall with a land grant.[76] Whether or not this was true, it was believed in Boston. In any event, the General Court had little choice of action in the face of the many counter-petitions. The public outcry from nearly every inhabited place on Kennebec River, including the Company stronghold of Pownalborough, was too loud to be ignored. On June 8, 1764, both the House and the Council agreed to dismiss the proprietary petition. The action of the General Court was undoubtedly correct; to follow the Company's wishes would have been merely to replace a questionable form of injustice with an even greater one. Besides, the precedent set would have had far-reaching implications.

On the whole, proprietary attempts to extend their sway over the coastal regions of the Kennebec during the period 1750-1764 had been little short of disastrous. The Kennebeck proprietors' private settlements with the Pejepscot proprietors and with the Clark and Lake Company had left them far short of their goal. The new county court system had not operated as planned, and the proprietors had failed to obtain a change of venue from these new courts, which they regarded as prejudiced. They felt the Massachusetts Supreme Judicial Court to be unreliable; their enemy, Thomas Hutchinson, presided there. But as Timothy Prout suggested back in 1754, there was always the ultimate appeal to the King in Council. Such appeals cost small fortunes, but if their case was a strong one and resulted in the Privy Council's setting aside the "inferior" Indian deeds of their rivals, the expense would be worthwhile. This drive to the seacost, renewed in 1762, would occupy proprietary energies until almost the start of the American Revolution.

NOTES

CHAPTER VIII

1 Samuel Goodwin to David Jeffries, Nov. 16, 1761, Jeffries Manuscripts, Vol. 13, 142, M.H.S.

2 Resolution, Feb. 13, 1749, K.P.P., Records, I, II.

3 At one point in the patent, the original Plymouth grantees received "all Lands, Grounds, Sails, Rivers, Tradings, Fishings, Hereditaments and Profits whatsoever, lying or being within said Limits and Bounds *together with free Ingress, Egress and Regress,* with Ships, Boats, Shallops or other Vessels from the Sea commonly called the Western Ocean, to the said River called Kennebeck, and from the said River to the said Western Ocean." The upper and lower limits of the patent were described only by Indian place names, and by the mid-eighteenth century these limits could only be guessed at. The proprietors claimed all of the lower river including the coastal islands, but the italicized passage above seems to indicate that the grant was only along a *part* of the river, with free access to it. The later proprietors realized this weakness in their patent, and tried to underplay its significance. The Brunswick proprietors, on the other hand, exploited this point in pamphlets opposing the Kennebeck Company.

4 Rival land companies included the Pejepscot Company, its subsidiary, the Brunswick proprietors, Clark and Lake Company, the Pemaquid proprietors, and the Wiscasset proprietors. In the last years before the Revolution, the heirs of

Lord Edgecomb also contested Company claims, but without success.

5 Williamson, *History of the State of Maine*, II, 87-88.

6 *Ibid.*, II, 89.

7 Allen, *History of Dresden*, 267.

8 Williamson, *History of the State of Maine*, II, 166-167.

9 Resolution, Jan. 12, 1753, K.P.P., Records, I, 163-164. The settlers were given nine months to comply with the Company directive or face the consequences.

10 Third Warrant, July 6, 1751, K.P.P., Records, I, 83-88. The proprietors promised that if the inhabitants of New Castle, Wiscasset, Townshend, Harrington, Topsham, Brunswick, and Georgetown would allow Company agents to survey their lands (originally surveyed by other agencies many years before), the Company would petition the General Court for incorporation.

11 Resolution, May 8, 1751, K.P.P., Records, I, 66. These benefits were usual in townships established in New England.

12 Wiscasset inhabitants to Governor William Shirley, the House, and the Council, Oct. 17, 1754, *Maine Historical Society Collections, Documentary History*, 2nd Series, XII, 317-320.

13 The proprietors finally pressured the residents of Wiscasset into combining with Frankfort to form the new town of Pownalborough in 1760, when Lincoln County was created. The additional population represented by Wiscasset reinforced their argument that Frankfort should be made a county seat.

14 "A Brief State . . .," K.P.P., Letter Book I, 64.

15 Deed to Shubael Hinckley, Oct. 10, 1759, K.P.P., Records, II, 210-211.

16 Deeds to James Drummond *et al.* of Georgetown, Apr. 1-9, 1760, K.P.P., Records, II, 229-232, 236-244.

17 Deed to Joseph Berry of Georgetown, May 9, 1759, K.P.P., Records, II, 199-200. The proprietors had customarily made special concessions to settlers skilled in a trade in their early grants at Frankfort.

18 Printed advertisement, Mar. 27, 1751, P.P., IV, 349.

19 North, *History of Augusta*, 50.

20 Resolution to print an answer to Clark and Lake (with full text), May 29, 1754, K.P.P., Records, II, 70-73. North says this pamphlet was written by James Bowdoin.

21 *Plaintiff's State of the Case; the Proprietors holding under Lake & Clark, Plaintiffs, against Proprietors from Plymouth Colony, Defendants.* K.P.P., Printed Papers, 1-7. 7 pp., undated, but probably Dec., 1756.

22 See Chapter I.

23 *Plaintiff's State of the Case . . .,* 6.

24 "Act of Agreement between Kennebeck Company and Clark and Lake Company at York, June 17, 1756." Mss. in Chamberlain Collection, Boston Public Library.

25 Agreement between Kennebeck Company and Clark and Lake Company, Aug. 19, 1756, K.P.P., Loose Papers (1640-1759).

26 *Ibid.*

27 Lawyers' accounts, paid Apr. 25, 1757, K.P.P., Day Book, 64.

28 Account of the Plymouth [Kennebeck] Company with Benjamin Bagnall, Dec. 28, 1756, K.P.P., Records, Bills, and Receipts (1752-1804).

29 Testimony of Cadwallader Ford, June 8, 1765, "Appendix to the Appellants' Case," 14-15.

30 *Ibid.*

31 Testimony of the Rev. Samuel Webster, Oct. 29, 1765, *ibid.,* 15-16.

32 Testimony of Thomas Hutchinson, Nov. 12, 1764, *ibid.,* 15.

33 *The Award and Final Determination of the Referees respecting the Claims of the Proprietors of the Kennebeck Purchase from the late Colony of New-Plymouth, and the Company holding under Clark and Lake, relative to the Lands on each Side Kennebeck River,* Aug., 1757, P.P., Printed Papers. See also a shorter *Award,* K.P.P., Loose Papers (1640-1759).

34 Kennebeck proprietors to Cadwallader Ford, Mar. 16, 1757, K.P.P., Records, II, 121-122.

35 Testimony of Cadwallader Ford, Apr. 13, 1762, in Gardiner

v. Cargill, Court Files Cumberland and Lincoln Cos., 139167-139344, Suffolk County Court Records.

36 *Ibid.,*

37 Broadside, Jan. 24, 1750, K.P.P., Printed Papers.

38 Proprietary report, Mar. 18, 1750, P.P., X, 179.

39 Proprietary resolution, July 9, 1750, P.P., X, 179.

40 For a full account of the pamphlet warfare between the Kennebeck Company and the Brunswick proprietors, as well as the background of the Thomas Johnston maps of 1753 and 1755, see Lawrence C. Wroth, "The Thomas Johnston Maps of the Kennebeck Purchase," *In Tribute to Fred Anthoensen, Master Printer* (Portland, Me., 1952). 77-107.

41 See Chapter I.

42 Pejepscot Company broadside, May 15, 1751, P.P.

43 *Ibid.*

44 *Remarks on the Plan and Extracts of Deeds lately published by the Proprietors of the township of Brunswick (as they term themselves) agreeable to their Vote of January 27th 1753.* K.P.P., Printed Papers. Eight-page pamphlet probably the work of James Bowdoin, dated Jan. 31, 1753.

45 *Ibid.*

46 Thomas Johnston Map of 1755, Boston, 1755. A copy of this map is owned by the M.H.S. Johnston also printed another map of the Kennebec region in 1754. Stressing military considerations, it shows the location of forts along the river; contains insert plans of Forts Frankfort, Halifax, and Crown Point; and presents a detailed map of the region of the Great Carrying Place.

47 "Vote of Agreement & Final Issue of all Claims & Disputes between this proprietie & the Pejepscot Company," June 29, 1757, K.P.P., Records, II, 110-115.

48 Belcher Noyes to Kennebeck proprietors, Mar. 14, 1759, K.P.P., Loose Papers (1640-1759).

49 Belcher Noyes to Enoch Freeman, Nov. 8, 1762, P.P., V, 25.

50 Belcher Noyes to Enoch Freeman, June 22, 1763, P.P., V, 53.

51 "Vote of Pejepscot Proprietors June 11, 1766," K.P.P., Loose Papers (1760-1790).

52 Belcher Noyes to Pejepscot proprietors, Feb. 12, 1770, P.P., V, 25.

53 Unitl 1760, York County was the only county existing in that section of Massachusetts called Maine.

54 Timothy Prout to Kennebeck proprietors, Dec. 17, 1754, Vassall Correspondence, New York Public Library.

55 *Ibid.*

56 "A Brief State . . .," K.P.P., Letter Book I, 64. Failure of the petition for a new county is also mentioned in the explanatory text of the *Thomas Johnston Map of 1755.*

57 Petition of the Inhabitants of Kennebeck River for Protection. Accompanying petition is for the creation of a new county. M. A., CXXXVI, 270-280.

58 During the hearing of the Jeffries-Donnell case (see Chapter IX), Donnell claimed that undue haste had been observed by the Mass. House in rushing through the bills for the incorporation of Lincoln and Cumberland counties without a second reading, within two days, all at the urging of the Kennebeck proprietors. "Answer of Nathaniel Donnell, June 6, 1764," *Maine Historical Society Collections, Documentary History,* 2nd Series, XIII, 347-350.

59 Proprietary grant to Thomas Pownall of Lot No. 20 at Frankfort (Pownalborough), May 14, 1760, K.P.P., Records, II, 247. Pownall kept the land for many years, and after the American Revolution donated it to Harvard College to establish a chair of law.

60 Flagg had already constructed Fort Western for the Company in 1754, had supervised the building of Fort Halifax for the Province in the same year, and in 1759 erected Fort Pownall for Gov. Pownall near the mouth of the Penobscot River. See Chapter VII. Pownalborough Court House still stands by the Kennebec. It presents an austere appearance, and, apart from its dimensions, shows little of the grace of Georgian houses then being erected elsewhere in New England. The opposite sides of the house, one over-looking the Kennebec and the other what is now a vacant field, are identical. Each facade

originally featured a central doorway topped by a narrow window sash, surrounded by Georgian moldings and flanked by pairs of balancing windows. The doorways were replaced in the early 1800s. Five identical windows lend symmetry to the second floor, and the arrangement is repeated in the attic story. The heavy timbers of the structure, now clapboarded, were originally concealed with shingles left to weather, but the two great paneled doors and the many window frames were painted by Flagg's workmen. The broad hipped roof above is broken by a scuttle, or lookout, affording a magnificent view of the river which was the lifeblood of the region. The interior of the Pownalborough Court House recalls the simplicity of the quarters at Fort Western. Unpainted woodwork, plain plastered walls, and simple vertical pine paneling are characteristic, even in the courtroom, where one might expect further refining details. A ceiling beam in a ground-floor parlor displays the initials J.F., branded there for all time by James Flagg, son of the Company builder.

61 "Kennebeck Purchase Dr. to Gershom Flagg for time labour & expence in building a House at Pownalborough," K.P.P., Records, III, 134-138.

62 "Kennebeck Purchase Dr. to John Read for Sundry Tradesmens Bills &c for repairs done to the Court House in Pownalborough," Oct. 14, 1769, K.P.P., Records, III, 124.

63 *Ibid.*

64 *Ibid.*

65 Gershom Flagg to David Jeffries, Sept. 12, 1761, Jeffries Papers, XIV, M.H.S.

66 *Ibid.*

67 Shipton's *Sibley's Harvard Graduates*, XIII, 27; William Willis, *A History of the Law, the Courts, and the Lawyers of Maine From its First Colonization in the Early Part of the Present Century* (Boston, 1863), 689.

68 Shipton's *Sibley's Harvard Graduates*, XIII, 564.

69 *Ibid.*, 545-546; Willis, *Maine Lawyers*, 659.

70 "Petition to Governor Bernard from Kennebeck Proprietors (Praying to have its cases tried in Middlesex and other Mass.

county courts)," Dec., 1763, M.A., VI, 534-535. Counter-
petitions accompany this petition.

71 *Ibid.*

72 *Ibid.*

73 *Ibid.*

74 *Ibid.*

75 *Ibid.*

76 *A Strange Account* . . ., 253.

IX

Appeal to the King in Council:
The Company's Day in Court

The Kennebeck proprietors had long believed that their claim superseded those of rival land companies, and they yearned for a decisive court ruling that would substantiate that belief. Precious time and money had already been spent in disagreements with rivals, to little purpose. By 1765, the Company's Standing Committee was deeply involved in a new land dispute. Proprietary feuds with the Pejepscot Company and the heirs of Clark and Lake had ended in a stand-off but although these cases had ostensibly been settled, the decisions were not perforce forever binding. The Standing Committee had been careful to avoid entangling court decisions, preferring agreements with its opponents that might later be set aside. In the minds of the Kennebeck proprietors, the claims of the Pejepscot Company and of Clark and Lake were, after all, based merely on Indian deeds—deeds that the governments of both early Plymouth and Massachusetts had invalidated.[1] While the Kennebeck Company lands also included some Indian purchases, the Plymouth Colony patent had originally been granted by King James I to the Council of Plymouth, which in turn had made its own grants. If the courts could be induced to set aside the deeds of their rivals, the proprietors could attain their ultimate goal—the extension of the Kennebeck tract to the Atlantic Ocean. To achieve this objective, they fell back upon the suggestion first made by Timothy Prout in his letter of 1754, and reiterated by the Board of Trade in its reply to Governor Shirley in 1755.[2] The proprietors determined to institute a new case which they would appeal all the way to the King in Council.

An appeal to the highest court in the British Empire would not be without problems, however, for the proprietors realized that in the past the Massachusetts Superior Court had been inclined to favor appeals to the King in Council only in a few cases of personal actions. Furthermore, the Company feared the influence of Thomas Hutchinson, its proven enemy in previous legal actions. In his position as Chief Justice, he undoubtedly could sway the opinions of other justices to deny an appeal. Nevertheless, the proprietors were convinced that the right to appeal was inalienable and that certain precedents existed, favorable to their cause.

An appeal to the King in Council was by no means without precedent in colonial America.[3] In a Massachusetts example as recent as 1754, Vassall v. Fletcher, a defamation action, the King in Council reversed a Superior Court verdict and directed that William Vassall receive £2000 and court costs. The Superior Court of Judicature was unwilling to execute this order, and did so only after skillful maneuvering by Vassall's counsel, Jeremiah Gridley.[4] William Vassall could advise the other proprietors of the hazards of an appeal from a position of experience. A more pertinent case, which the town proprietors of Bow, New Hampshire, had appealed to England, even offered suggestions for an operating procedure. In 1749 the Bow proprietors, friends and family connections of Governor Benning Wentworth and holders of an extremely dubious title, filed a suit of ejectment against John Merrill, a settler holding land under the earlier and more enterprising Rumford proprietors. The plaintiffs lost in the court of common pleas, but appealed to the New Hampshire superior court and finally won the case in 1752. Merrill, backed by the Rumford proprietors, then appealed to the King in Council. The Council finally heard his suit, although the New Hampshire courts had denied his right to appeal. In June, 1755, Merrill triumphed. The Bow proprietors, not to be outdone, appealed to the King in Council in their turn, but were defeated in 1762 when that tribunal sustained Merrill and the Rumford proprietors.[5]

The Bow controversy and appeal to the King in Council seemed tailor-made for the purposes of the Kennebeck proprietors. They even took the precaution of consulting with the legal authority who had handled the Bow case. William Murray, later Lord Mansfield, had assisted British representatives of Merrill and the Rumford proprietors in gaining a hearing before the king. Shortly afterward, he resigned from the case upon his appointment as Chief Justice of the King's Bench.[6] Murray was renowned as a specialist in cases of appeal to the Privy Council.[7]

It was to Lord Mansfield that the Kennebeck proprietors wrote, probably in the fall of 1755, for an opinion on the validity of their own land claim.[8] They forwarded him a complete state of the case describing the history of the early Plymouth Colony grant on the Kennebec, its purchase by Antipas Boyes *et al.*, recognition of the patent by Massachusetts according to the Charter of 1691, services performed by the Company for the empire in settling the tract, and copies of the "inferior" Indian-purchase-based titles of their rivals.

Given this somewhat one-sided background of the situation, Lord Mansfield was asked to base an opinion on four general questions, answers to which would be vital to the future of the Kennebeck Purchase:

> 1. Are the heirs of the Boyes associates entitled to the Kennebeck tract granted by the Council of Plymouth to the Plymouth Colony's leaders in 1629?
> 2. Should the Kennebeck proprietors apply to the King for an explanatory and confirmatory grant to them, and might the Crown legally make such a grant?
> 3. Did the original grant extend to the sea, as well as conform to other lesser controversial boundaries?
> 4. In actions of ejectment, should not the Massachusetts courts permit appeals to the King in Council, especially in the case of a boundary question?[9]

Lord Mansfield's reply dashed some hopes of the Company and raised others.

In answering the first question, Mansfield stated that the proprietors had not supplied sufficient proof of their long tenure on the river, but that he supposed them to be a properly organized corporation. He emphasized that the question of present ownership might depend on what the proprietors had done to develop the tract and that "here it don't appear that any thing was done before 1748."[10] This was a weakness indeed. The King in Council might well wonder why the tract had lain idle when more aggressive land companies had started settlements near the coast. In answering the second question, Mansfield suggested that since Kennebeck territory was already under the legal control of Massachusetts, a royal colony, there would be no advantage to the Crown in making a new grant. Mansfield stressed the point that cases affecting boundaries must be tried in the Province before being appealed to the Privy Council. His opinion on the third question could be tested only in a court of law, but it must have gladdened the proprietors: "The Grant is very obscurely & unintelligibly penned; but I think the most probable Construction of the Limits is according to the . . . Description in the Question."[11] In other words, Lord Mansfield did suggest the possibility that the grant might be interpreted to extend to the ocean despite its vagueness. Regarding the issue of appeals to the King in Council in cases of ejectment, raised in the fourth question, he concluded that such appeals would be difficult to deny. This the proprietors had suspected all along. Because Mansfield's answers suggested that the proprietors had a fairly clear title as well as the right to appeal, they had little to lose in such an action. Indeed, if the King in Council favored the Company's case in a bill of ejectment against holders of lands secured by Indian deeds, it would appear that the proprietors' long-coveted claim to the seacoast would be assured.

The proprietors decided upon their future course of action late in 1755, but it was not an auspicious time to begin such an important lawsuit. French and Indian attacks on the frontier would keep the countryside in a turmoil for the next five years. In the meantime the Standing Committee could consolidate the Company position in other ways: defending the valley, encouraging settlement, and intriguing for the establishment of a separate county. They also searched diligently for a legal case that would meet their exact requirements.

The right moment finally arrived in 1762. The land selected for the test case lay in Georgetown and comprised a full 12,000 acres which Silvester Gardiner had received as his share in a previous land division. On April 1, 1762, Gardiner leased the enormous tract to David Jeffries, Company Clerk, to be occupied as farmland for a term of fifteen years.[12] Gardiner and the Standing Committee were well-aware that some of the land was already occupied by Joseph Sergeant, a tenant of Nathaniel Donnell, formerly of York, Maine. Donnell bought the tract from the heirs of Robert Gutch (Gooch), who in turn had purchased it from local Indians. If the proprietors could prove Donnell's claim invalid because it was derived from Indian deeds, an important precedent would be set. Because the creation of the Lincoln County courts had not brought the proprietors the favorable legal climate they had hoped for, they expected to lose their original lawsuit in Pownalborough inferior court and then to appeal it to the Massachusetts Superior Court meeting at Falmouth. On losing their appeal in that court, they would submit their case to the King in Council, where, encouraged by the Lord Mansfield opinion, they expected to win.

Everything worked according to plan. Jeffries's legal counsel, Robert Auchmuty, instituted a plea of ejectment, stating that the proprietor "entered into the . . . parcel of land and its appurtenances and was there possessed; and . . . being so there possessed, the said Joseph afterwards . . . on the second day of April next then with force and arms entered into the same parcel of land and its appurtenances, ejected the same David Jeffries therefrom and still unjustly holds him out of the same."[13] Nathaniel Donnell decided to stand himself "in the room of" Sergeant, claiming ownership of four hundred of the acres involved. He was represented by young David Sewall, like himself a native of York, The case was heard at the Pownalborough Court House during the September, 1764, session. As the Kennebeck proprietors fully expected, Jeffries lost the case. They were not discouraged. Following Lord Mansfield's suggestions, they then appealed the case to the Superior Court meeting at Falmouth, which heard the evidence on June 25, 1765. Predictably, the jury also found for Donnell and ordered Jeffries to pay the court costs of £12.18.6.[14] His counsel immediately responded with an appeal for review, which was granted.

At this critical stage in the case, the Kennebeck proprietors, acting with a new counsel, James Otis, Jr., methodically reassembled their evidence and searched for new support. Although they expected to lose the appeal, they were determined to muster as much strength as possible. Any new evidence would be useful when the suit finally reached the King in Council. Their lawyer combined depositions that had been taken in earlier lawsuits, some dating back to the 1720s, with those collected in preparation for the Falmouth hearing. He added court records and provincial laws to the brief. Suspense mounted as the time for the September appeal in review approached.

The impending appeal generated very real concern among the inhabitants of Boston. If the highest court in Massachusetts were to rule that Indian deeds were invalid in Maine, speculative land-holders all over the province who had investments east of the Piscataqua River would stand to lose heavily. In addition, hundreds of persons in Maine who had been occupying property under Indian deeds would be subject to eviction. Landowners awaited the decision of the Superior Court with foreboding. Even the General Court was alarmed.[15] The Kennebeck propriety must have especially feared the role that Thomas Hutchinson might play in the coming hearing. In his positions as Lieutenant Governor and Chief Justice, he undoubtedly could sway the opinions of other judges. Under his influence the Superior Court might well decide to deny an appeal to the King in Council. The proprietors were already convinced that such a denial could be overcome, but the delay would be costly and time-consuming. The vested interests of the Hutchinson clan in lands secured by Indian deeds made his position predictable. What musty documents would he now pluck from his files to confound the proprietors?

The implications of the coming court hearing may have disturbed many Bostonians, but the political crisis generated by the Stamp Act attracted even greater attention during the summer of 1765. Individuals all, the proprietors were not united on this issue. While they were apprehensive about the implications of the Stamp Act, only John Hancock, the newest member of the Standing Committee, was then openly committed to a radical position. On the whole, the proprietors were a conservative lot who supported the government party in politics, a policy which had enhanced the Company's position in the past.[16] But the political situation was changing rapidly, and Governor Francis Bernard was not inclined to support the proprietors in the manner of his predecessors. Company interests in the current court battle might well transcend what were then fading political allegiances in any case. John Hancock's connections among the Boston radicals may have hinted at a solution to Company difficulties.

On August 26, 1765, a mob attacked and destroyed the mansion of Lt. Gov. Hutchinson and laid waste its sumptuous furnishings and irreplaceable manuscripts. On the surface, the outrage appeared merely an incident in the burgeoning Stamp Act protest, which had already led to the destruction of stamp seller Andrew Oliver's Boston home on the fourteenth. The houses of William Story and Benjamin Hallowell, Jr., both customs officials, were sacked on the evening of the twenty-sixth as a prelude to the march on the Hutchinson property. Bostonians thought then, and historians have believed since, that it was the "Loyal Nine," an alliance of artisans and small tradesmen, which was responsible for the violence.[17] This group looked to Ebenezer McIntosh, the shoemaker, for leadership. Government officials knew that John Hancock and his friend Samuel Adams moved in these circles, but they were not openly implicated in the mob attacks. Nor was the Bernard administration able to convict the "Loyal Nine." The mystery grew with the passing years.

In 1788 the Reverend William Gordon published in London a three-volume *History of the Rise, Progress, and Establishment of the Independence of the United States of America*.[18] In this treatment of the Boston Stamp Act riots of 1765, Gordon's comments upon the sacking of Lt. Gov. Thomas Hutchinson's house have aroused much speculation and frustration among historians:

> A certain gentleman of great integrity . . . who fills a place in the judiciary department, with much credit and to the satisfaction of the public, has expressed a strong apprehension, that the mob was led to the house, by a secret influence, with a view to the destruction of certain papers, known to be there, and which, it is thought, would have proved, that the grant to the New Plymouth [Kennebeck] company on Kennebec river, was different from what was contended for by some claimants. The papers were never found afterward.[19]

Though unable to substantiate or disprove the story, historians have often repeated it.[20] Led on by Gordon, it is tempting to go beyond the general motives of intimidation and malicious mischief and to suggest that the leaders of the mob had in mind the elimination of specific documents in the destruction of Hutchinson's papers. Rioters scattered to the winds Admiralty files containing incriminating evidence against smugglers. Could the proprietors have regarded certain items in Hutchinson's papers as a threat to their interests?[21] The evidence is not conclusive, but should not be ignored. The history of the Kennebeck Purchase Company and the complex involvements of its proprietors in law and politics tend to support Gordon's theory. The record of these resourceful proprietors shows that they were not above intrigue in the defense of their interests.

As has been seen, during the early years of Company development proprietors sagely profited from their special relationship with the Massachusetts provincial government. Taking advantage of their voices on the Council and in the House, they both defended and enhanced the Company position. The proprietors had been in an especially favorable position during the administration of Governor Shirley, when at his instigation the Province erected Fort Halifax to guard the upper reaches of their valley.[22] Shirley also assisted in the proprietors' schemes to gain a new explanatory charter.[23] Thomas Pownall had been an equally useful friend to the Company, providing ranging companies on the frontier that further protected the Fort Halifax region, and promising to assist the proprietors upon his return to England.[24] Proprietors such as Thomas Hancock, Silvester Gardiner, and James Bowdoin, intimate friends of the two royal governors, were always able to gain the executive ear. Regrettably for the Kennebeck Company, the relationship which it had enjoyed under two royal governors came to an end under the administration of Francis Bernard, who arrived in Massachusetts in 1760.

For a time it had appeared that the old situation would continue. First, in 1762, the General Court made the new governor a present of Mount Desert Island to help compensate for unusual expenses in assuming his official position.[25] Almost immediately, Governor Bernard began six settlements on the island, thus helping to expand the frontier eastward.[26] Although this was not Kennebeck Company land, the propriety could expect to benefit from the rise in land values and from a governor who had landed interests comparable to their own.[27] But on November 9, 1763, the association between the Company and the governor became even closer when the proprietors granted Francis Bernard Lot No. 21 at Pownalborough for "Encouraging Settlement" in Kennebeck Company territory.[28]

What the Governor had done to merit this generous gift of five hundred acres invites speculation. The anonymous author of *A Strange Account . . . .* smelled corruption. He admitted that Bernard's services were "yet unknown,"[29] but nevertheless presented putative evidence of a patronage deal that the Governor had made with the proprietors. As the pamphleteer explained it, "when desired by a Gentleman to give a Man in our County a Commission for the Peace, he refused, saying he had given the Plymouth [Kennebeck] Company his Word and Honor, that he would not agree to have any, but such as they should approve of."[30] The proprietors had established the precedent with the General Court that they should name the justices and lesser county officials in Lincoln County; Bernard would have been merely confirming the practice.[31] There is no evidence of any collaboration between the Governor and the proprietors. Perhaps the gift was merely an attempt to gain a friend at court. Whatever the relationship was, it is obvious that a rapid cooling soon occurred.

But the man the proprietors hated and feared most of all was not the Governor, but the Lieutenant Governor, Thomas Hutchinson. He acquired his post in 1757, and three years later added to it the position of Chief Justice. The Hutchinsons were an ancient and numerous family, and the Lieutenant Governor saw to it that his friends and relations were well placed. His longstanding opposition to the Kennebeck Company gave the proprietors a tangible reason to distrust him. They still remembered his disastrous interference in the mediation of their quarrel with Clark and Lake in 1757 and his attempts to prevent the incorporation of Bowdoinham in 1762.[32] Family interests in both the Clark and Lake Company and the Pejepscot Company, the threat posed by his possession of a superlative collection of ancient deeds and documents, and his thorough knowledge of the law, all made the Standing Committee fear for the success of their latest and most ambitious attempt to secure the coastal regions of the Kennebec. This was the situation in August, 1765, when the Company's appeal in review before the Massachusetts Superior Court was still pending. Hutchinson's Boston mansion was destroyed by the mob, and the "Loyal Nine" was generally believed responsible for the attack.

The "Nine" was a diverse group of rising merchants, tradesmen, and artisans whose only common bond seemed to be membership in Masonic lodges and radical political clubs in Boston.[33] John Adams, who knew the group well and dined with them on at least one occasion, identified them in his diary: John Avery, Thomas Crafts, John Smith, Henry Welles, Thomas Chase, Stephen Cleverly, Henry Bass, Benjamin Edes, and George Trott.[34] The Reverend William Gordon did not hesitate to lay the blame at their door, and to implicate the Kennebeck Company as well. Some contemporaries of Gordon were inclined to agree with him, at least in part. In a well-guarded statement, Governor Bernard attributed the attack not to political extremism but to personal motives: "The direction of the mob against the Lieutenant Governor must have rose chiefly, if not wholly, from private malice. There was no publick or Popular cause to induce it; at least none adequate to the fury with which it was pursued. It is most probable that many of those who were concerts of the first insurrection [the August 14 attack on Oliver's house] were not privy to the design of the latter."[35] Thomas Hutchinson was less revealing in his account of the affair, perhaps believing that candor on his part might invite future attacks. He contented himself with observing that his losses had included "a great collection of publick as well as private papers . . . ."[36] Although his house and furnishings had been irreparably damaged, he chose to stress the loss of his papers. This loss, whether engineered by the Kennebeck Company or not, must have put the major fears of the proprietors to rest as they proceeded with their plans for the appeal to the Superior Court meeting at Falmouth and the expected ultimate appeal to the King in Council.

Some years ago Edmund Morgan concluded that "If we could establish the connection of Ebenezer McIntosh or the loyal nine with the New Plymouth [Kennebeck] Company, there would be a strong presumption that the assault on Hutchinson's house had purely personal origins."[37] Can "personal origins" be interpreted as springing from economic motives? Actually there exist several links between the "Loyal Nine" and the Kennebeck Company, although none establishes an absolute cause-and-effect relationship. The volatile James Flagg, son of Gershom Flagg and the presumed author of the *Strange Account . . . ,* knew several of the participants intimately.[38] When the pitiful remnant of his estate was settled on August 3, 1773, his brother Gershom, Jr., served as administrator. Joseph North, a surveyor for the Kennebeck Company, James's brother-in-law, and Thomas Crafts, the Boston painter, "Became bound with the said Gershom for his faithful discharge of the said Trust."[39] It is significant that Crafts, one of the most active of the "Loyal Nine," should be close enough to Flagg to serve in this capacity. It is likely that Flagg was acquainted with yet another member of the radical group at the time Hutchinson's house was sacked. Captain Henry Welles married Flagg's sister, Elizabeth, in Boston's First Baptist Church on April 28, 1768, only two years after the riot.[40] Both Flagg and Welles had attended this church for some years prior to the marriage. Captain Welles could have been particularly useful in arranging details of the attack, as he was also brother-in-law of Samuel Adams, the acknowledged manipulator of the Boston mob. If the Kennebeck proprietors wanted to stage a riot that might be mistaken for popular protest, they could not have failed to see that Flagg was in a good position to facilitate the action.[41]

The proprietors had another connection with the "Loyal Nine," but not as close as Flagg's. The printing firm of Edes and Gill, publishers of the most inflammatory newspaper in Boston, had received extensive orders from the Company. Benjamin Edes could have served as a willing instrument to his patrons in planning an attack. Finally, there was John Hancock, a member of the Standing Committee. The summer of 1765 was the only period when he displayed any strong interest in Company operations.[42] He, of all the proprietors, had the closest ties with the Boston radicals; indeed, he was one of them. But incriminating evidence of the kind that might directly link the proprietors with the attack simply does not now exist—if it ever did exist. No present-day historian dares to be so positive as was the Reverend William Gordon in 1788. Whatever the cause of the assault on the lieutenant governor's house, the proprietors still had to go to court.

After many delays caused by the closing of the courts after the Stamp Act crisis, the Jeffries-Donnell case finally came before the Massachusetts Superior Court meeting at Falmouth in June, 1766. Donnell, represented by Daniel Farnham, now became the defendant, and Jeffries assumed the role of plaintiff in this plea of review in a plea of ejectment. It is unlikely that Hutchinson presided at this hearing, and court records do not reveal any startling disclosures. One can only guess whether any adverse evidence had been destroyed in the riots of 1765, whether it had ever existed, or whether Thomas Hutchinson decided to curb his interference in Kennebeck Company affairs.

As the proprietors had expected all along, the court found for Donnell as usual, and assessed David Jeffries £5.7.10 for costs of court.[43] The proprietors had anticipated that the court would refuse to reverse its earlier verdict, but they must have been momentarily disappointed by its denial of the right to appeal to the King in Council. Still, it was no secret that the Superior Court held that cases of ejectment, or others involving real property, were not subject to appeal.[44]

Even this refusal by the Massachusetts Superior Court to allow an appeal to the King in Council had been foreseen by the proprietors in the questions they submitted to Lord Mansfield. Mansfield had been convinced that their appeal could not be denied. The Standing Committee was willing to risk all on his interpretation. Accordingly, they immediately dispatched the complete records of the case to England to be laid in the hands of the best lawyer money could buy.

So far, everything was going as expected. As James Bowdoin confided to former Governor Pownall:

> The issue of this Action is just as we expected it would be, for the prejudices of the People in the Eastern Counties as your Excellency well knows are invariably in favor of those who Claim land by a title similar to their own viz; by Indian deeds real or fictitious, or by possession only; and consequently against such as Claim by Patent.[45]

He frankly asserted that the appeal to the Privy Council seemed by far the best way to gain possession of the coveted seacoast area, and that the Company was in a strong legal position since, in several previous actions, "upon Agreement between the parties they [the issues] were dropt."[46] Bowdoin felt that his Company's grant from the King must be adjudged superior to those of holders under Indian deeds, and would prevail.

The proprietors now began to exploit their contacts in England. Florentius Vassall was conveniently located in London. James Bowdoin, writing for the Company, informed Vassall of the progress of the lawsuit and alerted him to expect receipt of the proprietary State of the Case and its petition of doleance (appeal) which was to be presented to the King in Council. As Agent for the Company, Vassall was to handle the London details, consult with lawyers, coordinate affairs, keep the proprietors informed, and pay the bills. To underscore Vassall's responsibilities, Bowdoin included an itemized account of the various assessments that other proprietors had paid on their shares, but which Vassall had never been pressed to pay. Now the Standing Committee felt it was Vassall's turn. He had contributed little to the Company and was in debt to it for a total of £233.6.8 in "Lawful [Massachusetts] Money," or £175 Sterling.[47]

Piqued at the sudden expense thrust upon him, Florentius Vassall did not immediately reply to Bowdoin's letter, but he did plunge himself into expediting the lawsuit in London. Probably he was the one who selected Thomas Goosetrey to handle the appeal. It is certain he highly approved of Goosetrey, for he commented that "this Gentleman's Chief business is an appeal in which he is very knowing, & in general affairs as good as any, at the Barr."[48] Vassall did caution, however, that Goosetrey would be very expensive.

Meanwhile the Standing Committee sought support from other powerful friends in England. Sir William Baker, a rich London merchant and the recent purchaser of a Company share, and Bowdoin's old crony Thomas Pownall were then members of Parliament. The Standing Committee requested Baker to contact Thomas Goosetrey and help wherever possible. Bowdoin had already notified Pownall about the appeal. Although he held only five hundred acres under the Company, the former governor was more than willing to give advice and use his influence to promote the case. While he fundamentally approved of the action, he did have lingering doubts about its appropriateness. He wrote that the proprietors may have been led "into a process contrary to your charter-rights, and contrary to what many of you would wish to be engaged in."[49] Further, Pownall said he knew of no appeals to the King in Council, only of those to Chancery or the House of Lords.[50] He understood that, under the British Constitution, appeals to the King in Council were established only by charter compact. Thus the Company could appeal only if its own particular type of case was outlined in the Massachusetts Charter. Pownall's commentary was accurate concerning the right of appeal according to charter. Nevertheless, the proprietors went ahead with plans for the appeal. They had been convinced by Company lawyers, Bowdoin assured his friend, that every British subject had the right to appeal to his sovereign regardless of the nature of the case.[51]

James Bowdoin proved to be correct; by an Order in Council dated February 26, 1768, the Privy Council agreed to receive the Jeffries case on appeal.[52] The proprietors were jubilant over the decision, for to them the most crucial phase of their entire strategy had seemed to be to persuade the King in Council to accept the suit. They had few doubts that their cause, once heard, would prevail.

As the hearing was scheduled in the court calendar for November, 1768, the proprietors had little time to lose. The next ship carried their communication advising Thomas Goosetrey that they had immediately dispatched a message to York, Maine, to inform Nathaniel Donnell of the impending case. He, as well as they, must make preparations. As the proprietors explained, "We thought it necessary you should be furnished with such a Certificate lest it should be objected that we have been faulty in not serving said Order on Mr. Donnell as soon as it was in our power."[53] It is clear that the Kennebeck Company would not chance losing such an important lawsuit through ignorance or omission. Taking advantage of the best legal advice in England and America, they played to win.

The Standing Committee, however, had not counted on intransigence on the part of Florentius Vassall, who declined to play his expected financial role. Vassall refused to take the responsibility of paying Goosetrey. The lawyer had successfully completed the first part of the case and naturally expected a partial payment. But Vassall proved obstinate, claiming he had been unjustly treated by his fellow proprietors and demanding a full accounting of past Company expenditures. This the proprietors hastily furnished. In time they might have succeeded in pressing Vassall to pay, but they could not wait. Several of the propriety were rich, but there was always a scarcity of pounds sterling. Their solution was simply that some proprietor who had a favorable account with an English merchant would have to foot the bill. The choice narrowed down to John Hancock, perhaps the wealthiest of all, who happened to have a large sterling balance with George Hayley, a London merchant. Hancock reluctantly agreed to release £50 to Goosetrey and other moneys as they were required, thus solving the immediate problem.[54]

Attention now focused upon obtaining a speedy hearing in the royal court. Because of delays and a full docket, the case did not come up at the November session as originally planned. As the months went by, the proprietors became more apprehensive. In December, 1769, James Bowdoin complained that there was no news from London, and that he had no idea when the appeal would be presented.[55] But Thomas Goosetrey was not neglecting the Jeffries appeal; in fact, he was making methodical preparations for as strong a case as he could offer. This would be costly. In April, 1769, he informed the proprietors that he had decided to print up the Company's side of the case, a precaution suggested by the Attorney General. The collection would include depositions taken over a period of fifty years in support of the proprietary claim, to which Goosetrey planned to add a section of his own composition dealing further with the coastal claims of the Kennebeck Company. The Standing Committee, however, was uneasy about the mounting expense, and commented: "We observe you apprehend from the Printing of the Case and proofs and other Circumstances that the expenses will be enlarged much beyond what you first expected."[56] Nevertheless, Goosetrey's effort was printed in England as the "Appendix to the Appellant's Case," a large tract of eighteen pages. This single aspect of the appeal came to £25.7.8 sterling,[57] and it would represent only a small fraction of the total cost of fighting this colonial case in the courts of Great Britain.

In addition to the printing of depositions, Mr. Goosetrey was studying documents, ordering copies made, preparing his brief, attending court, and applying for summonses; he was also consulting with the Attorney General, with Mr. Forrester, Goosetrey's assistant, and with Sir William Baker and Florentius Vassall, the Company representatives. There were negotiations to be carried on for a hearing before the Privy Council. At every stage of preparation, there were fees to be paid: for messengers, for coach hire, for clerk and doorkeeper expenses, and for gratuities to be given for the searching of records.[58]

Nevertheless, the proprietors told themselves that the mounting outlay was worthwhile. The outcome was far more important than the ownership of four hundred acres of land near Georgetown. As James Bowdoin commented:

> The land in controversy is no object with them [the Kennebeck proprietors]: the expense of attending it is greater than it is all worth. They must have relinquished a very considerable part of their patent, if they had acquiesed in the final judgment here. This obliged them to petition for liberty to appeal, and if the event should be favorable to them it will be equally beneficial to the people that live within the limits of the sd. patent by quieting them in their settlements and preventing a great number of interfering Indian claims which at present lie dormant, from ruining them . . . .[59]

These were fine words, but it is obvious that a successful appeal would do more for the proprietors than it would for the inhabitants of the lower river valley. Because most of these people held land under Indian deeds, a triumph for the propriety would throw the entire region from Woolwich to the coast into confusion. The settlers would then have to negotiate with the Kennebeck Company and pay a second time, as others had done before them. Residents of many other areas of Maine would face the same situation. Thus the verdict would affect many not connected with the Kennebeck propriety.

On July 3, 1771, Thomas Goosetrey sent word of the decision of the King in Council to the expectant proprietors. His letter contained both good and bad news. First, no counsel had appeared for the Donnell interest at the hearing, which was held on June 14. The Donnell family had not been able to afford the costs of such a suit, as the proprietors must have guessed. This was no cause for alarm, however, for the Privy Council agreed in advance to hear the case and the evidence presented whether one or both sides appeared. Dr. Gardiner and his Committee must have been encouraged to learn that "The Lords upon the Stating of the case and considering the Evidence which had been printed here were unanimously of Opinion that the Proceedings in the Court below were erroneous and that the Judgment ought to be reversed, and therefore ordered the same accordingly."[60] But as Goosetrey explained, this meant only that David Jeffries as representative of the Kennebeck Company was entitled to a new trial in the Massachusetts Superior Court. Even this partial victory was a hollow one.

The members of the Council did not give the finality to the case which the proprietors had confidently expected. They decided that the Company had failed to present sufficient evidence of ownership of its tract and, therefore, they omitted any reference to the invalidity of Indian deeds in its reversal.[61] Goosetrey offered the proprietors even more disheartening news: "They [the Privy Council] declared . . . in the State of the proceedings then before them it was not necessary nor proper for them to consider or enter into the Question concerning the extent of the Grant and they desired it might be understood that they had given no Opinion upon that part of the Case."[62]

Finally, Goosetrey informed the proprietors that the wording of their claims was faulty, particularly the contention that an important landmark, the falls at Negumkike, was south rather than north of "the utmost Limits of the Cobboseconte," and that this tended to weaken their case. He therefore suggested that the proprietors find a more positive way to present their claims in a future court.[63] As a postscript, Thomas Goosetrey offered his bill: a total of £351.1.3 Sterling. By Boston standards, it was ruinously high.[64] Considering what the money had bought them, some of the proprietors must have concluded that it was dearly spent. With this letter, Thomas Goosetrey's association with the Kennebeck Company ended.

Although the more daring members of the Standing Committee had every intention of pursuing their grand design further, others must have felt that the time had come for an assessment of their present situation and the prospects for future gains. The gamble taken in appealing the Jeffries case to England and the King in Council had in the long run been a failure. There had been the satisfaction of winning the appeal itself, but without the substance of the Privy Council's backing for their claim to the lower Kennebec and coastal areas, the right to a new trial was meaningless. The proprietors could now proceed with their request for a new trial before the Massachusetts Superior Court; but as they would be facing the same judges and the same attitudes that they had encountered in their last appearance, there was little doubt that the final result would be the same. It was highly unlikely that in a new hearing the Superior Court would confirm David Jeffries' right to four hundred acres of land at Georgetown. Even if it did, it would never render a judgment against the validity of Indian deeds in Maine and thus support the proprietary claims.

On the other hand, if the proprietors should lose in the new trial under roughly the same circumstances, there was always the opportunity for further appeal to the King in Council. In a reappeal, perhaps this highest legal authority could be induced to render a further opinion on the rightful ownership of the disputed lands. Such a hope appeared unlikely, but to Dr. Gardiner and others of the Standing Committee, the expected gains seemed worth a final gamble. Weighing all of these considerations, the Standing Committee decided to proceed with a new trial.

Meanwhile Thomas Hutchinson followed the case with interest. In September, 1771, he wrote his comments on the affair to Francis Bernard, now back in England. Hutchinson believed that Donnell had had a "very clear case"[65] before the appeal was carried to the King in Council, because he knew that the prohibition of Indian deeds applied only to Massachusetts and to "purchases in Marthas Vineyard and Nantucket and do not extend to the Eastern Country."[66] Further, he had "considered the Law before and presently satisfied [his] brethren [of the Superior Court] of the

true construction of it . . . ."[67] Probably his persuasion had
much to do with the original verdict pronounced at Falmouth
Court back in June, 1766. Hutchinson's final comment under-
scored the hopelessness of the Company's position: "Appeals [to
the King in Council] in Real Actions are contrary to [Massachu-
setts] Charter and the Decree for reversing the Judgment in the
Province could never be carried into Execution."[68] Perhaps this
inescapable factor was important in the final proprietary disposition of the case.

After some delays, the Company made plans for a rehearing of
the lawsuit at the Superior Court meeting at Falmouth at the
June, 1773, session. Nathaniel Donnell had died, so the proprietors initiated action against his heirs. In preparation for the rehearing, Company lawyers filed certified depositions with the
court testifying to the authenticity of the claim to the lower
Kennebec River and lands surrounding it "towards the Western
Ocean." The many pages of testimony repeated those included in
Thomas Goosetrey's "Appendix to the Appellant's Case" of
1769.[69] As these statements had been judged compelling enough
to obtain a reversal from the King in Council, the proprietors
hoped they would be equally effective in 1773. When June arrived, however, the case failed to appear on the dockets of the
superior court, and there is no record of its ever coming to trial.[70]

By 1773, political factionalism had badly split the Kennebeck
Company. Dr. Silvester Gardiner, a Tory, stood almost alone in
wishing to pursue the case further. To leading Whigs of the Standing Committee, such as James Bowdoin, James Pitts, and John
Hancock, the suit was an embarrassment. Continuing a highly
unpopular lawsuit successfully appealed to the King in Council
would be unpatriotic in radical Massachusetts, even in 1773.
Strangely enough, Governor Thomas Hutchinson, arch Tory, had
taken the lead in defending the rights of the people in this extremely controversial lawsuit, but his position did not help his
standing in Massachusetts. Whig proprietors, on the other hand,
easily rode out the storm. Nevertheless, by 1773, interests of the
Kennebeck proprietors had shifted. They were now engaged in a
new round of lawsuits, directed toward a more promising objective. It is not surprising that the Company should allow an
enormously expensive and now almost pointless legal action to
lapse.

During the period 1749-1773, the proprietors, both individually and collectively, had been developing their properties on Kennebec River. Their estates were now rising in value, the long-expected fruit of over a decade of careful planning and heavy expense. They held the land upriver, but their most valuable assets were undoubtedly the rich timberlands that covered their tract. Proprietors were already turning their towering white pine into boards, shingles, and ship timbers, and were anticipating the even greater profits they would realize in the future. In exploiting their white pine, however, they clashed with the Wentworths of New Hampshire, uncle and nephew, who as successive Surveyors General of the King's Woods in America, were committed to the opposing course of preserving the larger trees for the Royal Navy. As interest in pursuing their goal of controlling the seacoast waned, the proprietors grew more determined to reap the full benefits of those resources that they regarded as inalienably guaranteed by their ownership of a private tract. Their conflicts with the Surveyor General of the King's Woods would intensify until the very outbreak of revolution in Massachusetts.

NOTES

CHAPTER IX

1 It was true that real estate claims based upon Indian deeds had been invalidated by the governments of both early Plymouth and Massachusetts, but coverage had never been extended to include Maine.

2 See Chapter VII.

3 See H.D. Haseltine, "Appeals from Colonial Courts to the King in Council, with especial reference to Rhode Island," *American Historical Association Report for 1894*, 299-250; and Joseph H. Smith, *Appeals to the Privy Council From the American Plantations* (New York, 1965). Smith's work describes the course of many such appeals, including several aspects of the Jeffries-Donnell case, the central theme of this chapter.

4 Smith, *Appeals to the Privy Council,* 333-334.

5 Akagi, *Town Proprietors of the New England Colonies,* 165-173.

6 *Ibid.,* 173.

7 Smith, *Appeals to the Privy Council,* 164.

8 The proprietors must have acted immediately on Timothy Prout's suggestion to appeal their important cases to the King in Council. (See Chapter VIII.) His letter was dated Dec. 17, 1754. The first King in Council decision favoring Merrill and the Rumford proprietors was announced in England on June 24, 1755, and Lord Mansfield's opinion and reply to the Kennebeck Company is dated Sept. 20, 1755.

9 "Case of the Kennebeck Company and the Opinion of Mr. Attny General J.W. Murray, 20th September, 1755," K.P.P., Printed and Miscellaneous File. Mss. copy of 16 pp. This appears to be a copy of one in the British Museum, Add. Mss., 15488 ff, 113-129.

10 *Ibid.,* 12.

11 *Ibid.,* 15.

12 Statement of Jeffries v. Donnell, c. 1765, Records of the Massachusetts Court of Judicature, Suffolk County Court House, Boston, 1764-1765, 205-206.

13 *Ibid.,*

14 Jeffries v. Donnell, June 25, 1765, Suffolk County Court Files, Suffolk County Court House, Boston, 895, 139592-139620. Point of evidence collected for last stage (1773) of Jeffries-Donnell case. Court costs of £12.18.6 at the June, 1765, hearing, like all other charges, were paid by the Company.

15 The Mass. General Court continued its interest in the case. On May 31, 1769, Nathaniel Donnell appealed to Gov. Bernard, the Council, and the House to address a petition to the King in Council, pleading that the Company appeal to that body be dropped since it must "in its Consequences necessarily effect all the Freeholders of this Government," M.A., XXII, 539-541. The Council agreed to such action on July 1, 1769, and the House on July 15. On Oct. 23, 1769, William Bollan, Mass. agent in England, was instructed by the General Court to use his influence to have the Kennebeck appeal

dismissed. The attempt came too late, for the appeal had already been granted by the King in Council. M.A., XXII, 541-545.

16 See Chapters VII and VIII.

17 Morgan, *Stamp Act Crisis,* 160.

18 William Gordon, a dissenting English clergyman, emigrated to America in 1770, and in 1772 became pastor of the Third Congregational Church in Roxbury, Mass. Four years later, he began to collect materials for a history of the American Revolution which he hoped would be impartial. He returned to England in 1768 and published his *History* two years later. Although it was proved a century afterward that much of his work was plagiarized from the *Annual Register,* he did know the Mass. Whigs well and was active in the revolutionary cause.

19 William Gordon, *History of the Rise, Progress, and Establishment of the United States of America,* 3 Vols. (London, 1788), I, 180.

20 Among historians considering this question are Edmund S. Morgan in "Thomas Hutchinson and the Stamp Act," *New England Quarterly,* XXI (1948), 480, and again in Edmund S. and Helen M. Morgan, *The Stamp Act Crisis: Prologue to Revolution* (Chapel Hill, 1953), 169; G.B. Warden, *Boston: 1689-1776* (Boston, 1970), 166; Clifford K. Shipton *Sibley's Harvard Graduates,* VIII, 174; and Hiller B. Zobel, *Boston Massacre* (Boston, 1970), 36.

21 Warden, *Boston,* 357. Warden states that in 1765 Hutchinson had in his possession "at least two important documents bearing on the Maine land disputes. One was William Bradford's manuscript history of the New Plymouth Colony, which had been kept at the Old South Church by Thomas Prince and later was taken by the British in 1776 to Halifax and England. Hutchinson included an appendix on Plymouth and its grant in the second volume of his *History,* which was in preparation in 1765. A second important document was a map made by Hutchinson's father, who had been a partner of Oliver Noyes, which showed the northern boundary of the Noyes claim." As has been shown in Chap. I, the Kennebeck proprietors were thoroughly familiar with the Hocking story in Bradford's

narrative, and realized its implications. Destruction of the Bradford history and the Hutchinson map could have been considered adequate reason for an attack on the lieutenant governor's house.

22 See Chapter VII.

23 *Ibid.*

24 *Ibid.*

25 Francis Bernard received his royal commission shortly before the death of George II upon payment of the usual fees. Custom demanded that he repeat the fees upon the accession of George III. Bernard found himself badly in need of financial aid and turned to the Province for assistance. William O. Sawtelle, "Sir Francis Bernard and His Grant of Mount Desert Island," *Publications of the Colonial Society of Massachusetts,* XXIV (1923), 199-249.

26 *Ibid.*

27 When the frontier was expanded eastward, the Kennebec Valley became a rear area, and more desirable for settlement. Bernard's development of Mount Desert, however, coincided with the official close of the French and Indian War, after which settlers poured into many previously unplanted areas of Maine.

28 Grant to Francis Bernard of Lot No. 21 at Pownalborough, Nov. 9, 1763, K.P.P., Records, II, 333.

29 _____, *A Strange Account* . . ., 254.

30 *Ibid.*

31 See Chapter VIII.

32 *Ibid.*

33 Morgan, *Stamp Act Crisis,* 160.

34 Adams, *The Adams Papers,* I, 294.

35 Francis Bernard to Lord Shelburne, Jan. 24, 1767, Sparks Manuscripts, New England Papers, II, 23, Houghton Library, Harvard.

36 Hutchinson, *History,* III, 90.

37 Morgan, *Thomas Hutchinson and the Stamp Act,* 470.

38 As "partner" of Dr. Gardiner, James Flagg received several

hundred pounds' worth of merchandise on credit for his store at Gardinerstown. When he failed to pay, Gardiner sued. During the extended court action that followed, both Gardiner and Flagg published pamphlets attacking each other. Gardiner also printed a pamphlet attacking the referees appointed to settle matters at one stage of the case. During this period, the *Strange Account . . .* pamphlet appeared, which attacked the Company in general and Dr. Gardiner in particular. Reference was also made to the Flagg suit.

39 Suffolk County Probate Records, LXXIII, 179.

40 *Boston Marriages, 1752-1809* (Boston, 1903), 61.

41 In addition to knowing John Hancock through the Company, both James and Gershom Flagg had done construction work for him. Young Flagg was living on the Kennebec during the summer of 1765, but he had been in Boston that January. The town was small enough then so that his friends must have been known to other proprietors, especially to John Hancock, who employed many workmen. It is interesting to note that Flagg had other radical connections. His cousin Henry Flagg married Jane Mecom, the niece of Benjamin Franklin. Their son, Josiah Flagg, born in 1760, worked for Franklin. Also, Jane Flagg, James' aunt, married Elihu Greene, the brother of General Nathaniel Greene.

42 John Hancock was elected to the Standing Committee on May 15, 1765, and attended a regular Company meeting on August 15, 1765, which was adjourned for lack of a quorum. He attended a scattering of meetings during the period 1765-1767, most of which were adjourned, and was not active again until the period 1771-1775. His last attendance was on Jan. 18, 1778. He may, however, have attended sessions of the Standing Committee, where the more confidential business was transacted. The one surviving minute book of the Standing Committee, Feb. 15, 1760-May 22, 1765, does not record members' attendance. It may be significant that the minute book ends abruptly two months before the Hutchinson attack, in spite of the fact that not all of the pages had been filled. By the summer of 1765, Silvester Gardiner was an enemy of both Hancock and Flagg. In that year Gardiner had claimed land that two of Hancock's tenants, Henry Layer and Frederick Jacquere, held in Pownalborough. Gardiner ordered the

pair off the land and took the case to court. Jonathan Bowman acted as his cousin's legal counsel in the affair. At about the same time, an attack was made on Gardiner's property on the Kennebec, probably his farm at the "Chops" on Merrymeeting Bay. The attack is described in the *Strange Account . . .*, but because of problems in dating the pamphlet, it is uncertain whether it occurred in 1765 or 1766. Gardiner was in residence during his annual October inspection tour of his properties. One night he was suddenly awakened:

> . . . Oh! The dismal Scene. Savages in human Shape, muffled in the Shade of Night, invested his Abode. Propitious Heaven! defend him against murderous Ruffians, or after all he must fall by dreadful Hands. How great was his Surprise at the unexpected Yell of Indians in the Night, demanding him for their cruel sport? . . . A sudden Shudder seized every Limb, Belshazzarlike, at the Writing on the Wall; but being quick of Leg, as well as Thought, a Window backward presented his View, which, by Favour of the dreadful Night he made his Way.

A Strange Account . . ., 258-259. Apart from this version, no other record exists of the attack on Dr. Gardiner. Certainly he never mentioned it in his correspondence. Nevertheless, there is every reason to believe the pamphlet report is true. Published contemporaneously, the details must have been familiar to many on the Kennebec. The similarity to both the Hutchinson attack and the Boston Tea Party is striking; the use of Indian costume as disguise was common in eighteenth century Boston. Both James Flagg and John Hancock would have had ample motivation to arrange the attack, and Flagg was then living at Gardinerstown.

43 Jeffries v. Donnell, June, 1766, Suffolk County Court Records, Superior Court of Judicature, 1766-1767, 57-58.

44 *Ibid.*

45 James Bowdoin to Thomas Pownall, Dec. 18, 1767, K.P.P., Letter Book I, 12.

46 *Ibid.*, 13.

47 James Bowdoin to Florentius Vassall, Sept. 20, 1766, K.P.P., Letter Book I, 1-2. Vassall had been acting as London agent for the Company since June 6, 1753.

48 Florentius Vassall to Silvester Gardiner, Apr. 6, 1768, K.P. P., Loose Papers (1760-1790).

49 Thomas Pownall to James Bowdoin, Feb. 3, 1769, *Massachusetts Historical Society Collections*, V, 237.

50 *Ibid.*

51 James Bowdoin to Thomas Pownall, May 10, 1769, *Massachusetts Historical Society Collections*, X, 138-139.

52 Order in Council, Feb. 26, 1768: Jeffries v. Donnell, K.P.P., Loose Papers (1760-1790).

53 Kennebeck proprietors to Thomas Goosetrey, Sept. 26, 1768, K.P.P., Letter Book I, 20.

54 Agreement between John Hancock and the Kennebeck Company, Jan. 9, 1768, K.P.P., Loose Papers (1760-1790). The Company would reimburse Hancock for any payments he made to Goosetrey. However, on Dec. 26, 1770, they drew bills for £175 on Vassall through Hayley and Hopkins, thus forcing him to pay Goosetrey.

55 James Bowdoin to Thomas Pownall, Dec. 5, 1769, *Massachusetts Historical Society Collections*, IX, 157.

56 Committee to Thomas Goosetrey, Dec. 18, 1769, K.P.P., Letter Book I, 30-31.

57 Kennebeck Purchase Dr. to Thomas Goosetrey, K.P.P., Day Book, 143. The charges were as follows:

Arranging & settling the proofs & proceedings to be printed by way of Appendix being Four Sheets & half of Letter press	5.5 -
Fair Copy for the printer	3.0 -
Attend him therewith	-6.8
Examining and Correcting the proof Sheet	1.1 -
Paid printers Bills for the Appendix	15.15-
	£25.7.8

58 *Ibid.*, 140-145

59 James Bowdoin to Thomas Pownall, Oct. 22, 1770, *Massachusetts Historical Society Collections*, IX, 212.

60 Thomas Goosetrey to Kennebeck proprietors, July 3, 1771, K.P.P., Loose Papers (1760-1790). Also, official report of the June 14, 1771, meeting of the King in Council, *ibid.*

61 Thomas Goosetrey to Kennebeck proprietors, Oct. 22, 1771, K.P.P., Loose Papers (1760-1790).

62 *Ibid.*

63 *Ibid.*

64 Fees of Boston lawyers for earlier actions of the Jeffries-Donnell case were much more moderate: Jeremiah Gridley: £15; James Otis, Jr.: £20; K.P.P., Day Book, 109-110. John Adams's bill for numerous court appearances, involving much travel during the years 1770-1773, was only £29.7.10. K.P.P., Bills, Receipts (1752-1804).

65 Thomas Hutchinson to Francis Bernard, Sept., 1771, Mayo Typescripts of the Hutchinson Letter Books (Vols. 25, 26, 27 in the M.A.), XXVII, 228-231, M.H.S.

66 *Ibid.*

67 *Ibid.*

68 *Ibid.*

69 The depositions are divided between Court File 139599 and Court File 139641 of the Superior Court of Judicature of the Province of Massachusetts Bay, Suffolk County, Office of the Clerk of the Supreme Judicial Court, Suffolk County Court House, Boston.

70 In the spring of 1773, when their case was ready, the proprietors found it difficult to obtain superior court justices who would hear the case. Thus they were pleased to learn that Joseph Lee and William Browne had been appointed as "Special Judge[s] of the Superior Court in certain Actions wherein we are interested." They begged the new judges to accept the appointments because "those Actions, which have been several years suspended for want of a court, cannot otherwise be tryed." Browne at least accepted, but the proprietors later informed him that his assistance would not be needed. Kennebeck proprietors to Joseph Lee and William Browne, Apr. 28, 1773, K.P.P., Letter Book I, 77; and Kennebeck proprietors to William Browne, June 16, 1773, K.P.P., Letter Book I, 77-78.

X

Masts For The King's Navy

John Wentworth was troubled and angry. The letter before him signed by the proprietors of the Kennebeck Purchase Company, dated October 16, 1769, challenged his authority as Surveyor-General of the King's Woods, a position he held in addition to his commission as Royal Governor of New Hampshire. As Surveyor-General, he was responsible for the preservation of the white pine in New England, an important source of mast trees for the Royal Navy. The dynamic young governor was accustomed to incursions of timber pirates, but he was prepared for complaints from friends concerning royal mast policy. The newly arrived letter gave notice that the extensive holdings of the proprietors on Kennebec River were rapidly being stripped by "divers Persons pretending a License from your Excellency"[1] and that they looked ". . . upon this matter as a very great Grievance and an infringement on the rights of private property . . . ."[2] If Governor Wentworth would not halt the despoiling, the letter continued, the Company would be obliged ". . . to proceed with the trespassers in a Course of Law."[3] Thus began the bitter quarrel between the King's representative and the land company, a dispute that would contribute to the outbreak of the American Revolution and lead to a significant change in the King's Mast policy in America.[4]

John Wentworth assumed his offices in the summer of 1766, when he replaced Benning Wentworth, his uncle. He had been well prepared for his dual role, which by then seemed almost like family property. He grew up in Portsmouth and was well acquainted with the area and its people. After graduation from Harvard in 1755, he went to England to further his career. There, influential Wentworth relatives encouraged him to enter politics. Accordingly, he served with Barlow Trecothick, son-in-law of Charles Apthorp, Kennebeck proprietor, as a joint agent in England for New Hampshire. Wentworth proved useful to the Province and became a hero when he championed the colonial cause in the House of Commons during Stamp Act hearings.[5] Two years later, he returned to New Hampshire as Royal Governor and Surveyor-General. Handsome and personable, John Wentworth made friends wherever he went. Unlike his Uncle Benning, he preferred to build a reputation as an excellent administrator rather than accumulate a fortune. Sincerely interested in reforming the royal forestry system, he showed imagination, courage, and understanding in his approach to timber problems as they arose.[6] His instinctive reliance on tact and persuasion instead of on the threat of force soon became evident in his dealings with the Kennebeck Purchase Company.

With conciliation in mind, Wentworth must have pored painstakingly over the Company letter on that October day in 1769. He reviewed and considered proprietary complaints that depredations of royal mast men within Kennebeck territory were hindering their lumbering, consequently making necessary this appeal to the Surveyor-General. In claiming that all of the white pine in their tract belonged to them by the terms of their grant, the proprietors were well aware that these mast trees were becoming increasingly important to the Royal Navy.

So crucial had the New England white pine become to the mast trade that a whole body of laws controlled the traffic. Regulation began with the stipulation in the Massachusetts Charter of 1691 that "all trees of the diameter of twenty-four inches and upwards at twelve inches from the ground" should be reserved for the Royal Navy.[7] The White Pine Act of 1711 extended the enforcement of this law throughout New England, New York, and the Jerseys.[8] In 1729, this act was further expanded to cover all white pine, regardless of size, that was not located on private property. Meanwhile, the price of mast trees had skyrocketed. By the 1760s, a white pine thirty or more inches in diameter was worth £100 when delivered as a mast to the English

JOHN WENTWORTH (1737-1820)
Portrait by John Singleton Copley. Courtesy of the Frick Art Reference Library.

royal docks. The profit had been going to mast men rather than
landowners, however, so it was inevitable that for many years
landowners had preferred to reduce the trees to lumber rather
than to surrender them for masts. The marks of the "King's Arrow" on these trees made them public rather than private property, so the lumbering of the great white pine had long been illegal.

The cumulative effect of the white pine acts during the
eighteenth century created confusion for both mast men and
property owners. The extension of 1729 made it clear that mast
trees as "private" holdings were exempt from royal control, but
both governor and the property owners must have wondered
what lands were "private" in 1769. Since the beginning of the century, proprietors of large tracts, anxious to keep their holdings in-
tact, had taken the stance that their property was strictly "private" and thus inviolate. It was well known that the "paper townships" of New England had been created in the early 1700s not to
further settlement but to protect the woodlands from the mast
men. In any event, much of the unsettled land in Maine at that
time was in private holdings, some of which had been granted by
royal patents. Because of the royal nature of these grants, proprietors like those of the Kennebeck Purchase Company felt that
their lands were immune from King's mast incursions. For this
reason alone, proprietors for some time had been bold in challenging the forest regulations. The resultant court battles dating
from the turn of the century were significant precedents in 1769,
a time when the mast trees had become of vital importance to
the Kennebeck proprietors.

This was not the first conflict between the Kennebeck Company and a surveyor-general of the King's Woods, as John Wentworth must have known. His uncle, Benning Wentworth, had also
faced the Company's opposition. John might have benefited
from his uncle's experience had their methods of operation not
been so different. Motivated by opportunities for profit, Benning
Wentworth found the means to please nearly everyone and encountered relatively little resistance from the Kennebeck proprietors or from other land speculators. The older man's experience with the proprietors, however, did offer a lesson that could
be useful to his nephew.

Benning Wentworth, the son of an earlier lieutenant governor,
John Wentworth, was a native of New Hampshire and a Harvard

graduate. He had inherited lands at Casco, Maine, and interests in the Pejepscot Company, a rival of the Kennebeck proprietors. In 1741, Benning Wentworth became Governor of New Hampshire and, in 1743, Surveyor-General of the King's Woods, twin offices that placed him in an ideal situation to make a fortune in a hurry. His personal as well as his professional interests inevitably brought him into conflict with the Kennebeck proprietors.

Benning Wentworth succeeded in organizing lumbering affairs in New Hampshire so as to meet naval needs and assure his own profit. He is well remembered for creating scores of new townships within his province and reserving a grant of five hundred acres in each of them for himself.[9] When masts were needed, Surveyor Wentworth sent his agents onto his own lands. After the trees were located, Wentworth as the mast contractor arranged for their delivery and for thriftily cutting the lesser trees in the area into lumber for additional profit. It had, therefore, seldom been necessary for his surveyors to risk trespassing suits as they marked trees with the King's Arrow, or for subcontractors to brave the wrath of judges for cutting them. Benning Wentworth, in effect, turned much of New Hampshire into a private forest preserve, which he could exploit at his leisure. As Surveyor-General, he undertook few prosecutions of mast violators during the decade in which he was able to fill royal mast needs from his own lands.[10] This safe method of operations began to face limitations, however, for only trees located near convenient waterways were readily accessible to the mast men. These were rapidly thinning out, so an assault on previously ignored private holdings seemed necessary. Wentworth's first major encounter was with the Kennebeck Purchase Company.

At about the same time that the Kennebeck patent was reactivated, Benning Wentworth became Governor and Surveyor-General. The inaccessibility of the trees on Company property, as well as Wentworth's moderate forest policies, kept him free from friction with the Kennebeck Purchase Company during his first years as Surveyor-General. By the late 1750s, however, the Surveyor-General began to look more and more to the relatively untouched forests of the Kennebec Valley. In his mind, the Crown had an unassailable right to mast trees there. It was essential for him to act quickly, for the settlers being brought in by the Kennebeck proprietors were rapidly turning the great trees of the region into boards, ship timbers, and barrel staves.

In 1757, twelve years before his nephew was to face a similar encounter, Surveyor-General Benning Wentworth sent his mast men into Kennebeck territory for the first time. The Kennebeck Company Committee to Prosecute and Defend learned of what it considered trespassing violations, and dispatched to Wentworth a respectful but determined letter. After reciting the terms and extent of its grant, the Committee informed him that "divers Persons pretending a License from your Excellency have been and are Cutting down and carrying off a great Number of Masts and making great Strip and Waste of the Timber within the Limits of [the Company's] said purchase."[11] The Committee further emphasized that the terms of its patent reserved the whole growth of timber, as well as the soil, to the patentees.[12] The "divers Persons," presumably the Governor's men, were therefore trespassers, and liable to prosecution. In the foregoing statements, the proprietors were relying for protection on the usual arguments of landholders of the early eighteenth century that the Crown had no timber rights within ancient royal grants. The note also hinted that if mast cutting by the King's surveyor was made worthwhile to the Company, there would be no objections. This was an idea close enough to the one under which Wentworth had been operating at enviable profit in New Hampshire to enlist his sympathies and support.

Strangely enough, Benning Wentworth sent his reply, dated June 24, 1757, to Charles Apthorp, his occasional business partner, rather than to the Committee to Prosecute and Defend. Apthorp, although a full shareholder, had been less active in the Company than had Dr. Gardiner, the leader of the Committee, and such Committee members as James Bowdoin, James Pitts, and Thomas Hancock. Furthermore, the letter was written not by the Governor but by his brother and business associate, Mark Hunking Wentworth. Thus the whole correspondence was given a somewhat less-than-official tone, probably the Governor's intention. Mark Wentworth explained that his brother was unable to write because of the "gout in his right hand" but that he had carefully considered the proprietors' position. Mark Wentworth admitted that he himself, as mast agent, received eleven masts from the Kennebec region but that "those trees were not cutt by virtue of the Surveyor-General's License, neither did I make any Contract for them."[13] He revealed that Captain Samuel Goodwin of Frankfort had received payment for the masts and had even helped haul the trees to water transportation. "As to the wast made," Wentworth taunted, it "is ten trees cutt into Shingles to Clapboards, to one that has been hauled for his Majesty's Service."[14] His comment was undoubtedly correct. The Surveyor-General's office was painfully aware that many white pine trees marked with the King's Arrow were being secretly ripped up for commercial purposes. In revealing that a shareholder of the Kennebeck Company had been at fault in the tree cutting of which they had complained, Mark Wentworth completely turned the tables on the proprietors. Nevertheless, Wentworth promised to keep his mast men out of the Company tract in the future. His parting shot, however, was a telling one: "The Governor . . . is of Opinion by the Act of Parliament the King has the same rights to the Mast Trees there Growing as he has to any in the province of Main."[15]

Benning Wentworth remained true to his word that his men would stay out of the Company territory. The Kennebeck proprietors had no more mast incidents to complain about during the remainder of his term in office. Of course, Wentworth may simply have decided that the mast trees in Kennebeck Company lands were not worth the bother, as there were still sufficient pine trees elsewhere in Maine and New Hampshire, and especially on his own lands.

The proprietors were still uneasy in their control of their forest lands, however, for the property had been subject to raids from timber poachers, who were frequently some of their own settlers. Proprietary records are filled with examples of timber pirating on Company lands. In December, 1763, James Bowdoin wrote to William Cushing, his attorney at Pownalborough, complaining that "for several Winters past and particularly the last Winter a number of People have made great strip and wast on my 3200 Acre Lot no. 24 in Bowdoinham by cutting and carrying away a large number of Pine Logs to the great detriment of Said lot."[16] He specifically accused the Graves family of nearby Topsham of the crime, and directed Cushing to take them to court.[17] The next year Bowdoin informed John McKechnie, Company surveyor, that "if you should meet with any log-paths, I should be glad you would trace them in order to detect any persons that may be cutting Logs within my Tract."[18] He further advised McKechnie to follow the culprits, strike up a conversation, and learn their identities. Bowdoin also ordered that William Cushing should then prosecute the lawbreakers.[19] In 1768 another focus of Company concern was Ponds-Town (later Winthrop). The Company had given Briggs Hallowell, son of a proprietor, power of attorney in order to prosecute offenders and, as an incentive for his services, had even authorized him to seize any cut timber he was able to find.[20] When either the Company or individual proprietors took these cases to court, however, they usually lost. In the few suits that were won, the damages awarded were so trifling that they failed to cover the court costs.[21] Lincoln County juries were notorious in favoring the lawless element. The Kennebeck proprietors, finding that protecting their woodlands from local settlers was a losing battle, naturally struck back against their new challenger, the King's surveyor.

As Governor John Wentworth studied the Kennebeck Company's letter and reviewed the past, it must have been obvious to him that once the proprietors devised a formula for action they stuck to it. The letter of 1757 and the recent one before him repeated a litany familiar in Kennebeck Company legal processes: a recounting of the terms of the Plymouth Colony deed, a balance sheet of services rendered to king and empire in promoting the Kennebec River settlements, and an estimate of the money expended in their development. Both letters contained the expected threats: "We look upon this Matter as a very great Grievance and an Infringement on the rights of private property, and these practices if persisted in, will oblige us to proceed with the trespassers in a Course of Law."[22] In 1757, the proprietors demonstrated a keen knowledge of Massachusetts history, for in their letter then they took the position that Elisha Cooke, Jr., an unscrupulous politician, had assumed in his confrontations with Jonathan Bridger, a surveyor-general in the early eighteenth century. No doubt the proprietors expected the pose to be successful in that dispute with Benning Wentworth because it operated to their mutual interest.

When challenged by Bridger for forming a vast private holding out of the old Gorges tract in southern Maine, a tract that had been exempt from King's mast demands, Elisha Cooke, Jr., posed as the loyal defender of the Crown's interests even as he appealed for popular support in Massachusetts. He answered that he not only had been "Instrumental in Securing His Majesty's Legal and Dutiful Subjects in their Just Right, but also [had] prevented great Stroy and Wast of the woods and preserved them for his Majesty when his occasions Call for them."[23]

In their letter of 1769 to John Wentworth, the Kennebeck proprietors paraphrased Cooke, informing the Governor that:

> Your Excellency must be sensible it is for the Interest of the Proprietors to preserve the Masts for the Royal Navy, and they have and still take all possible care for that purpose, and in a few years it is expected the Settlements on the River will be increased in such a Manner as that Sufficient Assistance can be had in the Neighborhood for procuring the Masts at a reasonable rate when it may be worth while for the Mast Contractors to agree with the Proprietors for the Masts.[24]

This statement of purpose, as well as subsequent ones, leaves no doubt that the Kennebeck Company fully expected to supply masts for the Royal Navy on a contract basis. Such a system would have proved mutually beneficial to the proprietors and the empire. John Wentworth was not moved by the proprietors' stance. Even if his sympathies lay with their point of view, he did not have the authority to make such sweeping changes in royal mast policy.

Deciding not to let a day pass after receiving the proprietors' letter, Wentworth replied on October 19, 1769. He did not apologize but rather expressed surprise that the issue of trespassing had even been raised, as he naturally assumed that the mast trees in the disputed area were the King's. He informed the proprietors that he was merely carrying out the specifications of the royal license in sending in his cutting teams. Exercising his usual tact, he suggested that there did seem to be a question of ownership here and that "if the Mastmen go into private Property it is at their own risque; for my License is only for the King's Woods and if [there are] none on Kennebeck River they should seek elsewhere.[25] Wentworth went on to suggest that since he was only the "executive officer," he was unable to decide on the merits of the Kennebeck proprietors' case and proposed instead: "I will institute a process upon my Trespass."[26] The Admirality Courts, he explained, could then decide who was right. He advised the proprietors to draw up their own state of the case, which he himself would forward to the Admiralty. He added that if the proprietors preferred to propose an alternative plan, he would be willing to listen. Finally, he complimented the proprietors on their public spiritedness in settling the Kennebec region and hoped that they would "amply reap the most desired Lucrations from their large expenditure."[27]

The young governor made the best of a difficult situation. He offered no promise of a solution, but he held the door open for future negotiations. He found himself in a doubly sensitive position, for the Kennebeck proprietors were his friends and members of his own ruling class. His uncle, Benning Wentworth, had been a partner of Charles Apthorp, and the London firm of Apthorp and Trecothick was serving as his own British agent. He looked upon Charles Ward Apthorp, the current head of the Apthorp family and the guardian of its Kennebeck share, as a brother. Charles Ward Apthorp's younger brother, James Apthorp, was married to Wentworth's sister-in-law. Too, John Temple, Wentworth's lieutenant governor, and his brother, Robert Temple of Ten Hill Farm in Charlestown, were Kennebeck Company shareholders. The Governor hoped that some middle way could be found to deliver him from his dilemma. Letting the Admiralty Courts decide seemed the safest course.

The Kennebeck Company's Committee to Prosecute and Defend, however, was hesitant about submitting the matter to arbitration in England for it was already deeply involved in the Jeffries-Donnell case appeal to the King in Council. The Committee knew that opinions from the mother country had often gone against colonial interests. Appealing a hopeless case from Massachusetts to the King in Council was one thing, but the proprietors realized that Provincial courts would support them on the mast issue. Wentworth must also have been aware that his best chance would be to appeal to the Admiralty courts. A case in point was the legal opinion of 1718 concerning mast ownership involving Elisha Cooke, Jr. Cooke had applied to the Lords Commissioners of Trade and Plantations for an opinion regarding the rights of the Gorges patent. The legal authority, Richard West, concluded that any special rights held by private persons in the patent had been erased by the imposition of a new Massachusetts charter in 1691.[28] The West opinion had been most embarrassing to the Massachusetts House, for that body had seized logs within the Gorges patent previously confiscated by Jonathan Bridger, Surveyor-General of the King's Woods at the time. Because the West opinion ruled that Elisha Cooke had no special timber rights in the Gorges patent, the action of the House in seizing the logs from the King's agent appeared to have been illegal. But the

House disregarded the West opinion and continued to support Cooke, a politician with wide backing. In the next election, Cooke's popular party won additional seats in the House, which continued to back Cooke's claims. The Kennebeck proprietors could not expect this partisanship if the Admiralty Courts ruled against them, although popular feeling was on their side.

Rather than submit to the dictates of an opinion like the one of 1718, which ruled against proprietary mast rights in the Gorges tract, the Kennebeck proprietors decided to fall back upon a precedent of their own. In their reply to Governor Wentworth on November 8, 1769, the Committee pointed out that when the same question of mast ownership had been raised in 1757, it had been solved simply by a letter to the Governor's uncle, Benning Wentworth, and asked why it could not be the same again. The Committee thus prepared itself to stand by its old arguments but, at the same time, to try a new approach to the problem.

After describing the Company charter to the Governor, the proprietors posed the "Supposition there had been in the Kennebeck patent an express reservation of Mast Trees [to the King]."[29] They suggested that, assuming for the moment that this unlikely occurrence were so, "yet as it has been wholly by the exertions and great expenditure of the said Proprietors that the said Trees are or may be of any Value for the use of the Royal Navy," did not his Excellency consider it fit and reasonable that "the said Proprietors should have an opportunity even in that supposed Case, to make some Advantage in that way, especially as such Advantage would be in perfect coincidence with his Majesty's Interest and Service, and be promotive of them?"[30] Clearly, the Company was interested in making a profit rather than in the masts *per se,* and was willing to renounce its rights to the masts provided fair compensation could be arranged. Feeling that its proposal was an equitable one which the Governor would accept, the Company suggested that until the details could be worked out the Governor should withdraw the mast license which he had issued for operations within their territory, just as his uncle had done.

John Wentworth felt unable to comply, and reluctantly conceded that negotiations had reached an impasse. He was not surprised that the proprietors insisted on remuneration for their mast trees. This step, however, he refused to consider, and again explained that he lacked the power to grant Company wishes in any case. While he was careful to maintain a forceful appearance, he was conscious of the real weakness of his position.

Realizing that he needed further legal weapons, Wentworth carefully studied old Admiralty records. In a letter of March 20, 1770, the Governor resurrected the specter of another early mast opinion—that rendered by the British Attorney General in 1726.[31] This opinion, an outgrowth of the long-continuing struggle between Elisha Cooke, Jr., and Jonathan Bridger, stated that all pine trees which had a diameter of twenty-four inches at twelve inches from the ground, "whether the same are growing within or without of any Township," were unequivocally the property of the Crown.[32] At the time, this ruling seemed to negate the possibility of any private timber lands being withheld from royal use. Nevertheless, the Kennebeck proprietors were not too much impressed with Wentworth's findings. Their Committee to Prosecute and Defend retorted that, back in 1726, the Attorney General had not been sufficiently well informed to frame a correct opinion. Now the case was different.[33] Feeling secure in the knowledge that a mere legal opinion could not be made binding, even if formulated by the Attorney General, the proprietors settled back to await further developments.

John Wentworth, growing impatient, was less inclined to quibble in what he believed to be a strong case. He took the trouble, however, to re-emphasize the importance of the Attorney General's legal gloss because it echoed an opinion "more fully and explicitly expressed in One given Anno 1716 upon a Memorial of Mr. Elisha Cook."[34] But he also decided to take more direct action. Learning that one of his mast men had received a process for trespassing issued by the Kennebeck Company, Wentworth threatened "to bring this cause into a legal Trial in behalf of the Crown by the first Trespass that I am informed of."[35] The proprietors' complacency was at last shaken. Fending off legal opinions from the dim past had been well enough, but a court action was another matter. They were still paying the bills for the Jeffries-Donnell case. Moreover, unlike an opinion, a trial could set positive legal precedents that might well work against proprietary interests. For the first time, the proprietors felt compelled to take conciliatory action. As they had already agreed to write up their State of the Case and send it to England for a legal opinion, they were in a position to retreat and still save face.[36] The proprietors and the Governor, sensitive toward each other's position, moved to prepare a State of the Case as they gathered forces for the approaching crisis.

A long-continuing, well-fought battle ensued. After the legal dust had cleared, each could look back upon the encounter with the satisfaction that every step necessary to achieve victory had been taken. By then the proprietors had been scattered by the American Revolution, and John Wentworth was an exile in Nova Scotia. Ironically, the struggle between the proprietors and the Crown's Surveyor-General led to a royal mast program with which both could have agreed. The foundations of this program were painstakingly laid by each side as it tenaciously clung to its position while attempting to undermine that of its opponent.

James Bowdoin advanced the proprietors' position. On November 12, 1770, he wrote to his old crony, ex-Governor Thomas Pownall, then living in London and a member of Parliament. Bowdoin explained the crisis, and expressed his uneasiness because the Massachusetts lieutenant governor, Thomas Hutchinson, in a recent speech had blamed proprietors of land companies in eastern Maine for widespread destruction of timber. Bowdoin justified the Company's timber activities, complaining that "If it was made the interest of the land proprietor to preserve the timber for the king's use, there would be no danger of a waste of it, but from the operation of the act of Parliament respecting this matter, it becomes his interest to destroy it as fast as he can."[37] Believing that only Parliament could solve the problem, Bowdoin suggested an idea that the Kennebeck proprietors had as yet only hinted at: their willingness to establish a *reserve* of mast trees for the Crown. Contacting Pownall was a wise move, for the former Governor of Massachusetts still held five hundred acres at Pownalborough.[38] It was convenient in this mast dispute to have a friend in Parliament, especially one whose brother was the influential Secretary of the Board of Trade.[39] If anyone could advance the plan in Parliament, Pownall was the man. Bowdoin closed his letter to Pownall with the request that he forward any useful information that he could unearth in England about the mast case.

Similarly, Surveyor-General Wentworth looked for backing in England. The embroilment with the Kennebeck Company was too momentous to undertake without advice from higher authority. On October 22, 1770, he dispatched his State of the Case, addressed collectively to the Lords Commissioners of the Navy, the Admiralty, and the Treasury, and to Lord Hillsborough, President of the Board of Trade. Wentworth reviewed the circumstances of his quarrel with the Kennebeck proprietors and noted the precedents for his own case—the favorable opinions of 1718 and 1726. He was confident that the Crown's interests would triumph, but he was worried nevertheless about the implications of a victory for his adversary, for if the masts were "thus preserved as private property, whenever they are wanted, the King must pay their own price."[40] He noted in his State of the Case that a direct confrontation had so far been avoided, the proprietors "being most of them Gentlemen of large property and judicious men,"[41] and that they had not yet undertaken any lawsuits. Surveyor-General Wentworth sensibly closed by asking his superiors for special instructions to govern the unusual situation.

John Wentworth next heard from the Kennebeck Committee in December, 1770. The Company leadership accused Edmund Wendell, the mast subcontractor, of wantonly destroying mast trees that the proprietors were doing their best to preserve for the King. After the usual reiteration of their rights to the mast trees growing within their territory, the proprietors complained that the Governor could not expect to negotiate with them while "Mr. Wendell continues to employ Persons to cut Masts within the said Patent without the consent of the particular individuals to whom belong the land thereon."[42] Regardless of this contention, and to show its continuing good faith, the Committee enclosed its State of the Case, which Wentworth had earlier promised to transmit to England.

There were three enclosures in the proprietary State of the Case. The first was "A brief State of the Kennebeck Proprietors Title to the Kennebeck Purchase from the late Colony of New Plymouth."[43] This short account dealt with the original Pilgrim grant, the purchase by the Boston merchants in 1661, and the effects of the Massachusetts Charter of 1691 on this grant. They described the second enclosure as "Containing a State of Facts relative to the Kennebeck purchase from the late Colony of New Plymouth,"[44] actually a detailed chronological history of the Kennebeck Company in ten pages, complete to the year 1771.[45] In this document the proprietors credited themselves with performing an invaluable public service at incalculable expense in developing the Kennebec Valley. The third enclosure condensed into a single page some "Extracts from the last Act of Parliament for the preserving his Majesty's Woods in America," phrases in the White

Pine Act of 1729 which were applicable and showed the Company in a favorable light.[46] Once the necessary legal papers were sent off, Wentworth and the proprietors waited impatiently for a reply.

The opinion arrived from England in good season, but it was disappointing in that it neither dispelled all doubts nor substantially reinforced the claims of either party. The opinion, which was dated June 5, 1771, but probably did not reach New England until late summer, was signed by Richard Jackson, Counsel for the Board of Trade. The name, Richard Jackson, should have inspired confidence among the proprietors, for he was an attorney who had worked on behalf of the colonies for many years. He had served as Massachusetts Agent from 1766 to 1767, and later had also been agent for Pennsylvania and Connecticut.[47] Probably he was personally known by some of the proprietary Council members. And neither would John Wentworth have been unhappy with the signature on the opinion, for Jackson had ably represented the Crown even as he had befriended the colonies.

Jackson's opinion, in several parts, stated that (1) white pine trees on lands which were private property before 1690 could be cut by the owners without special license from the Crown, and (2) (respecting the general preservation of mast trees for use by the Royal Navy) "though the law gives a protection to such trees growing on private property, which they would not otherwise have had, it deprives them at the same time, of another protection [the vigilance and care of the owner] that might, perhaps, have been more efficacious."[48] Therefore, if the proprietors could establish claim to their holding prior to 1690, which appeared easy enough, the mast trees were theirs. Jackson's final statement in the opinion must have pleased the proprietors even more than this, however, for it reiterated their position that if the owner of a tract were compensated for mast trees cut on his property, he would be inclined to take care of them, for himself and the King.

John Wentworth professed to be as well pleased with the Jackson opinion as the proprietors were, probably because he believed that they could not prove that their title predated the 1691 charter. At any rate, he commented to the Earl of Hillsborough that "these reports confirmed me in the Persuasion that all the Pine Timber on the Tract of land lying on both sides Kennebec River, and now held under Grants from the Council of Plymouth belongs to his Majesty, and I have therefore continued to Assert and Maintain the Right of the Crown to be exclusive, and shall persist so to do until I receive his Majesty's final determination on the subject."[49] John Wentworth was forced in all fairness, however, to acknowledge that the proprietors were entitled to some compensation for the loss of their mast trees, and he conceded so to Lord Hillsborough:

> As to their Proposal of getting a Compensation for every Tree cut on the soil, it perhaps may be a measure deserving of Consideration to grant some stated allowance for every good Mast . . . when cut and hauled for the King's Service, not as Matter that they were by Right entitled to, but as a Gratuity for the Timber being found well preserved upon the Land . . . .[50]

In this statement lay the germ of future royal mast policy in the Maritime Provinces.

The proprietors scored yet another point. Wentworth admitted that the Kennebeck Company was correct in its long-standing argument that when the royal mast men invaded its property, it suffered the loss not only of the mast trees but also of the small growth surrounding the great pines. With the favorable Jackson opinion buttressing their claims, the proprietors were now at last ready to petition the Admiralty for compensation for trees cut by the royal mast agents, and this they hastened to do. Wentworth, though he must have smarted from the Jackson decision, agreed to forward the petition himself.[51] The proprietors were in a buoyant mood, but were not encouraged to the extent of submitting the Company title to the courts. The validity of their pre-1691 patent had still not been determined. An adverse ruling here might have affected the pending Jeffries-Donnell case and imperiled their entire position.[52]

The proprietors hurriedly prepared their petition and submitted it to Wentworth for forwarding. Rather than risk their legal ammunition with one carrier,[53] they also asked Governor Hutchinson to transmit a copy to Lord Hillsborough. Naturally, they expected Thomas Hutchinson to endorse the contents, for he was known to favor a liberal mast tree policy. His own land interests made his position a certainty. This request put the Massachusetts governor in a quandary, for he had more than once acted against the interests of the Kennebeck Company. Certainly by 1772 some of the Whig proprietors—at least James Bowdoin, James Pitts, and John Hancock—were his political enemies. Indeed, the governor had recently opposed the Company regarding their appeal to the King in Council.[54] Undercutting their position in this King's Mast suit must have been almost irresistible for him. Too, he probably would not have been averse to assisting a hard-pressed neighboring royal governor. He finally took what appeared to be an equivocal position.

The proprietors soon had reason to question the ambiguity of that position, however. Although the Governor had promised to "say nothing concerning their title,"[55] he made a statement in his covering letter to Lord Hillsborough:

> I am bound to observe to your Lordship that the whole of the Western side of Kennebec River is included in the Patent to Sir Ferdinando Gorges and although this Patent was dated after that which the Kennebec Proprietors Claim from the Council of Plymouth yet it is founded upon a patent or patents from the same council of a prior date to that of the Kennebec Proprietors.[56]

At first glance it appears that Thomas Hutchinson had done stout service to the Kennebeck proprietors by linking at least a part of their holdings with a tract older than their own. The proprietors' claims, however, were quite different from those raised earlier by Elisha Cooke, Jr.[57] Unlike the Gorges patent, the Kennebeck Purchase territory had not been revested in the Crown in 1684, so its title was clear under the new Massachusetts Charter of 1691. In any event, the Gorges link was a dangerous one, for the 1718 and 1726 opinions had run counter to the interests of the Gorges patent. If Hutchinson was aware that the Kennebeck title was clear—and well he might have been since he was an acknowledged authority on New England land titles—he was deliberately misleading the Board of Trade, or at least calling its attention to an unsavory episode in Massachusetts mast trade history. Nevertheless, he did do the proprietors some service, as he favored the principles of compensation of land companies for mast trees. He had commented at length in the second volume of his *History of Massachusetts Bay* on the desirability of making such payment.[58]

Though the proprietors may have felt some chagrin regarding the Governor's action, they were not discouraged. They spread petitions wherever they might do the most good—Lords of the Admiralty, the Board of Trade, and Lord Hillsborough. They also sent a copy directly to Admiral Montagu for forwarding to the Admiralty, perhaps because the preface might be of special interest to a naval hero. The preface stressed the damage done to the King's Masts under the existing system and recommended compensation. Unlike the other petitions, this one was signed only by Dr. Gardiner, who was an acquaintance of the Admiral.[59] In addition, the proprietors made new efforts to contact friends and fellow proprietors in England. Florentius Vassall, who had already been of assistance in the Jeffries-Donnell case, might well be again. The proprietors now requested of him "the favour you will endeavour to obtain a redress of the grievances complained of: the obtaining of which will put a stop to the depredations made on your and the other Lands by the people employed by said Wentworth Agents."[60] James Bowdoin wrote again to Thomas Pownall and asked him to ascertain whether the letters sent to the Admiralty contained "any observations . . . to the disadvantage of . . . the Proprietor' title."[61] If there were any, Bowdoin said, the Company hoped for speedy intelligence. It might not be too late, he reasoned, to send last-minute documents that could strengthen its case. Having then exhausted every means of influencing affairs, the proprietors waited cautiously for a verdict.

In the meantime, Governor Wentworth remained on guard against an adversary that he had come to recognize as wily, devious, and resourceful. Wentworth prided himself that he had conducted his negotiations with Company officials as a gentleman would deal with other gentlemen. It might be years before an answer to the petition would arrive from England, so the Governor probably hoped that the proprietors' recourse to petition would temporarily end their harassment of his agents on the Maine frontier. A truce was not possible, however. From the proprietors' point of view, inaction would have meant allowing mast agents to continue to despoil their valuable timber. To Wentworth, desisting would have meant abandoning the King's Masts to the tender mercies of the proprietors. Neither side could afford to relax, so the notion of commencing lawsuits in the Massachusetts courts became increasingly attractive to each.

John Wentworth was the first to act. During the summer of 1772, he alarmed the proprietors by ordering his deputy, Thomas Scammel, to survey Maine lands "north of Negumkike" on the east side of the Kennebec above Company territory. These were lands claimed by the Company, but they were so far up the river that their practical development was years away. At first the proprietors suspected that their opponent might take possession of the lands in the King's name.[62] This Wentworth did not do, but the surveying did play a role in his future plans for preserving the white pine. The proprietors became increasingly tense and doubly vigilant.

Wentworth despaired of prompt action stemming from the proprietary petition. Accordingly, he filed a lawsuit against the Company when his men discovered mast trees "illegally cut" in the Kennebeck tract.[63] Enraged when he learned that the Company was initiating a countersuit, Wentworth wrote that "not content with this Mr. Silvester Gardiner one of the Committee who signed the Petition on behalf of the Company to the . . . Admiralty, has brought Actions of Damages Against the Persons that have been employed by the Agents of the Contractor."[64] To the Governor, Gardiner as Chairman of the Committee to Prosecute and Defend had become the villain of the whole affair. In a letter to Joshua Loring, Jr., of Boston, Wentworth railed against "the Law-loving and probably Law-losing Dr. Gardiner"[65] for spoiling the season for his mast men. The Surveyor-General swore that if his case was lost in Boston, he would immediately appeal to the British High Court of the Admiralty and would take any measure deemed necessary to protect the King's Woods.[66]

For the next few months, a guarded truce prevailed between Wentworth and the Kennebeck Company. The proprietors commanded their surveyor, Dr. John McKechnie, to increase his vigilance against possible raids on Company timberland by Wentworth's men[67] and wrote a grateful note of thanks to one Jonathan Oakes for informing them of such depredations.[68] Both sides girded themselves for the coming court battle.

The adversaries spared no expense and engaged the best possible legal counsel. Wentworth selected Samuel Fitch, a Tory lawyer, to represent the Crown and, with some misgivings, accepted James Otis, Jr., as Fitch's assistant. Otis, though a Whig, was an authority on land titles. Unfortunately, he had a history of recurring insanity. In communication with Fitch, Wentworth revealed less than complete confidence in Otis when he commented: "You say that he is very calm at present and are of the opinion that he will enter heartily with you in the Matter."[69] Otis proved dependable in this instance. The Kennebeck Company also chose a leading Whig attorney as its counsel, John Adams. Adams had recently worked for Wentworth himself.

John Adams decided that his best defense for the Kennebeck

Company lay in a delaying action. He managed to get the case continued at the Plymouth court through the spring, summer, and fall, much to Wentworth's disgust. The Governor had been hoping for a quick victory, which might frighten off the proprietors from any future actions. Tensions heightened, for the long-awaited reply to the Company petition still had not arrived.[70] Meanwhile the Royal Governor and the radical Whigs among the proprietors were becoming more and more involved in the increasingly strained political situation in New England. It seems logical to conclude that the mast question, involving as it did so many prominent Whigs, such as Bowdoin, Hancock, and Pitts, contributed to this atmosphere of tension.

In spite of the anxieties of the New England political crisis, John Wentworth continued to probe for a solution to the mast preservation problem. The surveying of central Maine and the upper Kennebec suggested a partial answer to him. In these new, unsettled lands, the British government had the opportunity to introduce innovations that were not likely to be opposed. Wentworth, in a clever piece of strategy, wrote to the Lords of the Admiralty and the Treasury recommending that, after the survey was completed, a new government be organized for the area—a government stretching toward Nova Scotia and including present-day New Brunswick. He proposed that, in this new province, in every "township of six miles square one reservation not exceeding 1500 Acres be made, in such places as the Surveyor-General should direct, and the Inspector survey said tract and mark it before the patent passes . . . by reserving such a lot in each township the Crown would of course have the advantage of selecting the best timber."[71] The Governor hoped that settlers would then be attracted to the region and that their labors as lumbermen would bring prosperity to them and to the Crown. Because these forest reserves would be selected in advance, there should be no resentment on the part of the inhabitants. Probably Wentworth knew that the British ministry was already considering the establishment of just such a province by detaching Maine from the authority of Massachusetts and using the Kennebec Valley settlements as a nucleus. The idea had merit, and may have inspired Wentworth's continuing determination to plan for a reservation of mast trees. This idea became very attractive after the outbreak of the Revolutionary War, for British authorities believed that the many loyalists along the Kennebec would support such a government.[72]

The Governor's hopes for the immediate future were dashed by the news on May 3, 1773, that the Kennebeck Company had won its case in the Admiralty Court. John Adams' chief argument had been that the present proprietors formed a solid "chain of ownership" leading back to the original Plymouth grantees of 1629.[73] The Crown attorneys contended that the "chain" was incomplete because of the disruption of settlement on the Kennebec during the Indian wars. They also submitted that only mast trees within organized townships were exempt from royal demands. Adams successfully argued in favor of similar rights for private persons holding grants.[74] Adams' skillful maneuvering was well worth the fees the Company paid him and the time expended. He had appeared in court at least twice before his May performance, yet his total bill was only £12.[75] Because the court accepted the proprietary position that the Kennebeck Company title dated before 1691, its Committee concluded that it had a mandate to the logs earlier seized by the Surveyor-General. For his part, Wentworth immediately appealed the case to the King in Council and, while awaiting a verdict, continued to wage a one-man battle against the foes of the royal forest policy.[76] Unless a reversal could be obtained, it would appear that the Kennebeck Company was on the threshold of a period of enormous financial success to be made possible by the full utilization of its timber.

The Kennebeck proprietors lost no time in exploiting their victory. Led by Dr. Gardiner, they began a suit for trespass against Colonel Bagley, Wentworth's deputy surveyor. In addition to charging Bagley with trespass, Gardiner accused him of committing the worst of crimes for a royal surveyor: selling timber to the mill men for his own gain.[77] Because of the implications of this accusation, the prestige of the King's Surveyor-General would suffer whether or not Bagley was acquitted. John Wentworth could see only a dismal future in store for his office and the white pine policy in America. He complained that "While the claimants to this Timber have a Decree of the Vice Admiralty Court in their favour they will not fail to make their advantage of it by committing every Waste upon the Timber, especially in the agitated state of the Times in this Country."[78] Until a favorable reply to his appeal could reach New England, Wentworth had little power to act.

The Kennebeck Company had triumphed. Even if Wentworth did win his appeal in England, nothing could replace the mast trees sacrificed in the interim. Meanwhile, the worsening political situation had all but made serious discussion of the mast problem mere rhetoric. By the spring of 1775, Maine, like most country areas of New England, was no longer under effective royal control. The mast trees that left port early in 1775 were the last to reach the mother country.[79] While in one sense the opening guns of revolution signaled the final victory of the Kennebeck Company over the Surveyor-General, the war itself prevented the proprietors from capitalizing on their situation. Maine settlers had long been as resistant to outside dominance by speculative land companies as they were to royal authority. By the spring of 1775 the process accelerated, and the country districts drifted away from both British control and proprietary allegiance.

News from Georgetown at the mouth of the Kennebec, a center of the mast industry, was particularly devastating to John Wentworth. Mr. Perry, the Governor's agent at that town, had actually been "seized and confin'd by the Country people at or near Kennebec river, where he was procuring sundry timber, small masts &c., for his Majesty's new yard at Halifax."[80] Furthermore, Wentworth received word that whatever mast trees remained at Georgetown had been secreted in nearby creeks and rivers.[81] The local committees of safety held the whip hand in the north country and decreed that no more mast trees should be delivered into British hands. Governor Wentworth's position was nearly as desperate as Mr. Perry's. Indeed, Wentworth's days were numbered. Soon after the battle of Lexington-Concord, he was besieged in his fort in Portsmouth Harbor by a mob. He eventually escaped aboard a British man-of-war to temporary safety in Boston.

John Wentworth ceased to be royal governor of New Hampshire, but he retained his position as Surveyor-General of the King's Woods. His activities, however, were limited to the Maritime Provinces. In 1778, he submitted a five-point program to the Admiralty that he believed would create effective controls for a future royal mast program.[82] This program was undoubtedly the consequence of his frustrating experience in the Kennebec Valley, and especially with the Kennebeck Purchase Company, 1769-1775.

The cornerstone of the plan was a revision of the idea he had submitted to the Admiralty in 1773. He explained that "The acts of Parliament relative to the preservation of pine timber in America" had in the past been "merely penal and too general" and that they operated "much against the conveniences and even necessities of the inhabitants."[83] He further stated that had he and other surveyors-general followed the letter of the law in regard to the regulation of the mast trees, they would have held back settlement and even retarded the mast trade with England and the West Indies. He was convinced that his new program would have the opposite effect. Wentworth proposed establishing in the Canadian provinces "parishes six miles square," in each of which two lots, or up to six hundred acres, would be reserved for the Royal Navy's use. These lots would be selected by the Surveyor-General.[84] The proposal closely resembled the one made by Wentworth to the Lords of the Admiralty in 1773, but was more comprehensive.

Three points in the proposed five-point program advanced suggestions that would so benefit all parties that the bitter conflict that had arisen in the Kennebec Valley would not raise its ugly head in the Maritime Provinces. Wentworth suggested that, in order that "private interest might be engaged to do all that the nature of the case permits, towards preserving those masts that will be growing on their lands," a compensatory system be created.[85] He thoroughly believed, he said, that "double damages and penaltys [should] be allowed to the proprietors of the lands, and recoverable as other trespassers for cutting and destroying or taking away pine trees from twenty inches and upward, to what the law gives or may give for trespassing upon any other timber."[86] His final point arranged for a bounty system under which property owners would be paid for mast trees felled by royal agents within their holdings. This system would provide compensation ranging from £2 for a tree between twenty and twenty-one inches in diameter to £10 for a thirty-eight-inch mast tree.[87] A property owner would find it well worth his while to deal with the royal mast men. Wentworth's proposal for forest reform was so comprehensive that the Admiralty authorized him to introduce parts of it in Nova Scotia and New Brunswick.

The keynote of John Wentworth's plan was common sense. If the proprietors of the Kennebeck Purchase Company learned of the enactment of the bounty provision into law—as they well may have—the irony must have been apparent to those living in exile, as were Dr. Gardiner and William Vassall, as well as to those in positions of radical leadership, such as John Hancock and James Bowdoin. The proprietors had prodded unrelentingly for compensation for over six years. They would have agreed with John Wentworth at last. The former New Hampshire governor himself must have experienced some bitterness. He understood the motivation of the proprietors and tried to be reasonable in his handling of the mast issue. Forces beyond his control, not the least of which had been the uncompromising attitude of the proprietors, drove him into an untenable position. For this, he was partially rewarded by the British government with the position of royal governor of Nova Scotia. If the mast program later inaugurated in the Maritime Provinces had been adopted in the American colonies before 1775, it undoubtedly would have secured the Kennebeck Company's support, perhaps would have ensured the proprietors' loyalty to the Crown, and most certainly would have eliminated an important cause of the American Revolution.

Yet the mast question was closely interwoven with other revolutionary issues, and with these also the Kennebeck proprietors were deeply involved. By 1775, the Company was almost equally divided between Tories and Whigs, with Dr. Silvester Gardiner and John Hancock representing the opposite poles. These two had important personal differences, as well as economic and political ones. Silvester Gardiner was a vestryman in Boston's prestigious Anglican King's Chapel; John Hancock, a member of wealthy Brattle Square Church, was the son and grandson of Congregationalist ministers. During the last decade before the American Revolution, the strife between Anglicans and Congregationalists embittered many in New England. The Kennebeck propriety, like the society at large, was rent by the same religious struggle that engulfed the northern colonies, and the outcome here was even more devastating.

NOTES

CHAPTER X

1 Kennebeck proprietors to John Wentworth, Oct. 16, 1769, K.P.P., Letter Book I, 26.

2 *Ibid.*

3 *Ibid.*

4 The place of the King's Mast issue in the American Revolution is treated by: Joseph J. Malone, *Pine Trees and Politics: The Naval Stores and Forest Policy in Colonial New England, 1691-1775* (Seattle, 1964), 143; Robert G. Albion, *Forests and Sea Power: The Timber Problems of the Royal Navy, 1652-1862* (Cambridge, 1926), 276; and Bernard Knollenburg, *Origin of the American Revolution, 1759-1766* (New York, 1965), 122-130.

5 Shipton, *Sibley's Harvard Graduates*, XIII, 651-652.

6 For this view of Wentworth, see Lawrence S. Mayo, *John Wentworth, Governor of New Hampshire, 1767-1775* (Cambridge, 1921), 51-52, 60; Malone, *Pine Trees and Politics*, 134, 138-143; and Shipton, *Sibley's Harvard Graduates*, XIII, 652.

7 *Acts and Resolves of the Province of Massachusetts Bay*, I, 20.

8 Malone, *Pine Trees and Politics*, 70.

9 *Ibid.*, 127-128.

10 *Ibid.*, 131-132.

11 Kennebeck proprietors to Benning Wentworth, June 1, 1757, K.P.P., Loose Papers (1640-1759).

12 *Ibid.*

13 Mark Hunking Wentworth to Kennebeck proprietors, June 24, 1757, K.P.P., Loose Papers (1640-1759).

14 *Ibid.*

15 *Ibid.*

16 James Bowdoin to William Cushing, Dec. 23, 1763, Bowdoin-Temple Papers, M.H.S.

17 *Ibid.*

18 James Bowdoin to John McKechnie, Feb. 15, 1764, Bowdoin-Temple Papers, M.H.S.

19 *Ibid.*

20 Kennebeck proprietors to Briggs Hallowell, May 4, 1768, K.P.P., Letter Book II, 15.

21 For example, James Bowdoin accused Thomas and Jeremiah Springer of Bowdoinham of entering his Lot No. 24 in that town in May, 1767, and cutting down and carrying away 200 pine trees, 900 beeches, 900 maples, and 200 oaks, which he valued at £490. Bowdoin lost his case at Pownalborough Court in Lincoln County and appealed to the Superior Court meeting at Falmouth. After a continuance, Bowdoin succeeded in having the decision reversed in June, 1769, and was awarded damages of five shillings. Brief of David Sewall on Case: Bowdoin v. Springer, June, 1769, Legal Papers of David Sewall, M.H.S.

22 Kennebeck proprietors to Benning Wentworth, June 1, 1757, K.P.P., Loose Papers (1640-1759).

23 Elisha Cooke, Jr., *Mr. Cooke's Just and Seasonable Vindication* (Boston, 1720), 7-8.

24 Kennebeck proprietors to John Wentworth, Oct. 16, 1769, K.P.P., Letter Book I, 26-27.

25 John Wentworth to Kennebeck proprietors, Oct. 19, 1769, Wentworth Letter Book I, 300-302, New Hampshire Archives, Concord, New Hampshire, hereafter cited as N.H.A.

26 *Ibid.*

27 *Ibid.*

28 Richard West to the Lords Commissioners of Trade and Plantations, Nov. 12, 1718, *Maine Historical Society Collections*, IX,436-440.

29 Kennebeck proprietors to John Wentworth, Nov. 8, 1769, K P.P., Letter Book I, 29.

30 *Ibid.*

31 John Wentworth to Kennebeck proprietors, Mar. 20, 1770, N.H.A., Wentworth Letter Book I, 335-337.

32 *Ibid.*

33 Kennebeck proprietors to John Wentworth, May 7, 1770, K. P.P., Letter Book I, 35.

34 John Wentworth to Kennebeck proprietors, June 29, 1770, N.H.A., Wentworth Letter Book I, 359-360.

35 *Ibid.*

36 Kennebeck proprietors to John Wentworth, May 7, 1770, K. P.P., Letter Book I, 35.

37 James Bowdoin to Thomas Pownall, Nov. 12, 1770, *Massachusetts Historical Society Collections*, 6th Series, IX, 234-235.

38 Pownall had been granted the land by the Kennebeck Company on May 14, 1760. See Chapter VIII.

39 John A. Schutz, *Thomas Pownall, British Defender of American Liberty* (Glendale, California, 1951), 20.

40 John Wentworth to Lord Hillsborough, the Lords Commissioners of the Admiralty, the Navy, and the Treasury, Oct. 22, 1770, N.H.A., Wentworth Letter Book I, 385-386.

41 *Ibid.*

42 Kennebeck proprietors to John Wentworth, Dec. 11, 1770, K.P.P., Letter Book I, 38. Edmund Wendell of Portsmouth was a grandnephew of Jacob Wendell, a Kennebeck proprietor active in the 1750s.

43 "State of the Case," Numbers 1, 2, and 3, Dec., 1771, K.P.P., Letter Book I, 57-70.

44 *Ibid.*

45 This paper was largely copied from an earlier "State of the Case" sent to England during the appeal to the King in Council in the Jeffries-Donnell case. See Chapter IX.

46 "State of the Case," Number 3, Dec., 1771, K.P.P., Letter Book I, 69-70.

47 Michael G. Kammen, *A Rope of Sand: The Colonial Agents, British Politics, and the American Revolution* (Ithaca, New York, 1967), 324.

48 George Chalmers, *Opinions of Eminent Lawyers on Various Points of English Jurisprudence, Chiefly Concerning the Colonies, Fisheries, and Commerce of Great Britain* (London, 1814), I, 136.

49 John Wentworth to Earl of Hillsborough, Dec. 4, 1771, N.H.A. Wentworth Letter Book II, 3.

50 *Ibid.,* II, 4.

51 *Ibid.*

52 L. Kinven Wroth and Hiller B. Zobel, eds., *The Adams Papers: Legal Papers of John Adams* (Cambridge, 1965), II, 256.

53 Item: "Cash pd: The New Hampshire Carrier for a Package to Govr. Wentworth—1 sh. 2 1/2 p," Dec. 18, 1771, K.P.P., Day Book, 149.

54 See Chapter IX.

55 Thomas Hutchinson to Earl of Hillsborough, Jan 3, 1772. *Maine Historical Society Collections: Documentary History,* XIV, 155-156. As a recognized historian, legal expert, and administrator, Hutchinson's observations would carry weight in England.

56 *Ibid.*

57 *Legal Papers of John Adams,* II, 249.

58 Hutchinson, *History,* II, 91.

59 Silvester Gardiner to Admiral Montagu, June 27, 1772, K.P.P., Letter Book I, 71. Admiral Montagu was stationed in Boston at the time of the Boston Tea Party.

60 Kennebeck proprietors to Florentius Vassall, Dec. 18, 1771, K.P.P., Letter Book I, 53.

61 James Bowdoin to Thomas Pownall, Sept. 29, 1772, *Massachusetts Historical Society Collections,* IX, 296-297.

62 Jonathan Bowman to Kennebeck proprietors, Aug. 10, 1772, K.P.P., Loose Papers, 1760-1790.

63 *Massachusetts Gazette* (Boston), July 16, 1772. According to the newspaper account, the timber seized by Wentworth's men included 573 logs, 424 pieces of timber, and 70,000 feet of boards.

64 John Wentworth to Earl of Hillsborough, Sept. 26, 1772, N.H. A., Wentworth Letter Book II, 36.

65 John Wentworth to Joshua Loring, Jr., Apr. 19, 1773, N.H.A., Letter Book II, 62. Gardiner had a well-earned reputation in Boston for the number of private suits he initiated. It was

true that, as Committee chairman, Gardiner filed the proprietary suits, but James Bowdoin, treasurer of the Company, was nearly as active. He wrote much of the correspondence and also started several private lawsuits in defense of
his own Company-granted lands.

66 John Wentworth to Earl of Hillsborough, Sept. 26, 1772,
N.H.A., Wentworth Letter Book II, 36.

67 Kennebeck proprietors to John McKechnie, Nov. 18, 1772,
K.P.P., Letter Book I, 74-75.

68 Kennebeck proprietors to Jonathan Oakes, Nov. 18, 1772,
K.P.P., Letter Book I, 75.

69 John Wentworth to Samuel Fitch, Nov. 6, 1772, N.H.A.,
Wentworth Letter Book II, 40. Like some of the loyalist Kennebeck proprietors, Samuel Fitch was proscribed and banished in 1778.

70 There is no record that the proprietors ever received an answer to their petition.

71 John Wentworth to the Lords of the Admiralty and Treasury,
January 13, 1773, N.H.A., Wentworth Letter Book II, 41-42.

72 Rumors of British plans to erect such a government persisted
well into the Revolutionary War. In 1781, George Lyde of
London wrote to the Rev. Jacob Bailey of Nova Scotia, formerly of Pownalborough, to say that "There are thoughts of
taking possession of the province of Maine and establishing a
civil government there. Perhaps tis' only talk." Jacob Bailey
Letters, Allen Copies, III, 133, Wiscassett Public Library, Wiscasset, Maine, hereafter cited as W.P.L.

73 *Legal Papers of John Adams*, II, 258.

74 *Ibid.*

75 K.P.P., Day Book, 149. Adams appeared in court on behalf
of the Kennebeck Company on Oct. 23 and Nov. 28, 1772.

76 John Wentworth to Grey Cooper, Oct. 25, 1774, N.H.A., Wentworth Letter Book II, 65-66. In this letter Wentworth lamented that although "Bonds were given to prosecute this Appeal
within the space of twelve Months . . . I have not had the
Happiness of receiving any Advice from their Lordships
whether the Prosecution was going forward or not." Went-

worth's records do not reveal whether he ever received a reply.

77 John Wentworth to Joshua Loring, Jr., July 11, 1774, N.H.A., Wentworth Letter Book II, 62.

78 John Wentworth to Grey Cooper, Oct. 25, 1774, *Ibid.*, 66.

79 William R. Carlton, "New England's Masts and the King's Navy," *New England Quarterly*, XII (1939), 11.

80 John Wentworth to John Durand, May 17, 1775, N.H.A., Wentworth Letter Book III, 91.

81 *Ibid.*

82 Malone, *Pine Trees and Politics*, 140-141.

83 John Wentworth to unknown British official, Oct. 12, 1778, Colonial Office Papers, CO .5/175, 1, Public Record Office, London.

84 *Ibid.*, 2-3.

85 *Ibid.*, 8.

86 *Ibid.*

87 *Ibid.*, 9.

XI

Religious Disaffection

For over three quarters of a century before the American Revolution, New England was torn by dissension between the dominant Congregational Church and a harassed but vocal Anglican minority. The antagonism intensified whenever rumors flew that a bishop was about to be sent to champion the Anglican cause in the colonies. An Anglican bishop would enhance church status, encourage converts, and ease the ordination of native-born missionaries. His presence would contribute immeasurably to the triumph of Episcopacy in New England; in time it might even lead to official establishment of the faith there. Congregationalist leaders feared the consequent loss of their own "religious freedom," and made dire predictions about the cost of an Anglican establishment which they might be taxed to support. Congregationalist fears, dormant for a time, were revived by Thomas Secker, who became Archbishop of Canterbury in 1758. During the next decade, the bishopric issue inflamed New England orthodoxy to such an extent that it has been widely identified as an important cause of revolution.[1] In this drama, the roles played by leaders of the Congregationalist clergy and their radical Whig parishioners are well documented.[2] The controversy permeated the Kennebeck Purchase Company, whose proprietors were themselves closely linked with revolutionary issues. Increasing factionalism among the proprietors can be largely attributed to religious disagreements. Shareholders were in accord on most economic issues confronting the Company, but on religious policy they were not. To Whig proprietors, it appeared that the British conspiracy to destroy Congregationalism and impose an Anglican establishment[3] was being mirrored by similar actions within their own sphere. When the American Revolution came, Congregationalists in the disintegrating Company almost to a man were patriots, while the Anglicans were Tory. The religious imbroglio within the Kennebeck Company from 1760 to 1775 closely paralleled the religious dispute then raging in New England. Because of the influence of the adversaries, the dispute contributed to the shaping of revolutionary tensions in New England. The controversy originated in Company plans to develop its first town at Frankfort.[4]

It was soon apparent to settlers and proprietors alike that Frankfort would never achieve stability and prosperity until a minister was established within its limits. Frankfort citizens recognized that a minister's sermons, religious counsel, and pastoral care, and his occasional doubling as a schoolteacher, were necessities for civilized village life. The absence of a pastor in Frankfort for the first few years was not due to indifference on the part of the proprietors. As early as December 11, 1754, only two years after the founding of Frankfort, they resolved that the first settled minister would receive two hundred acres for his needs and that the church would be endowed with one hundred acres.[5] The townspeople, however, would have to build their own church and make their own salary arrangements. The settlers, hardly able to sustain themselves, could not have supported a clergyman at that time.

Ambitious Congregationalist divines showed little interest in a Maine frontier post. They gave Frankfort a wide berth in their search for a pastorate, for once officially settled, they would expect to remain for life. At Frankfort, the poverty of the settlement and the dangers of Indian attack discouraged even the most dedicated minister from volunteering his services. The multiplicity of denominations in the town and the likelihood of religious discord were also deterrents to prospective ministers. Recognizing the importance of a pastor to the settlers and to the success of the town, the proprietors frantically sought to fill the post, and would have accepted almost anyone, at least temporarily.

The proprietors found the answer to their problem in the person of the Reverend William MacClenachan, recently assigned to nearby Georgetown by the Society for the Propagation of the Gospel, the Anglican missionary organization. Governor Shirley himself had recommended MacClenachan for the post. The fact that he was an Episcopalian would be appreciated by the High Church proprietors, and his religious views were unorthodox enough to be acceptable to the Congregationalists. He could easily assume the obligations of a Frankfort minister in addition to those of his Georgetown parish. Furthermore, he would cost the proprietors nothing; his salary would be paid by the Society for the Propagation of the Gospel. The Company's acceptance of MacClenachan and his successor marked the beginning of a long struggle on the Kennebec between Congregationalists and Anglicans. MacClenachan himself contributed to the controversy.

William MacClenachan's tenure as missionary at Georgetown was unsatisfactory to all concerned—the Kennebeck proprietors, the minister, and the inhabitants. Although MacClenachan, as the only minister on the river, was useful to the Company, the proprietors disagreed on his official status. They refused to strengthen his position by granting him their glebe lands, probably because Frankfort was not his missionary station. Instead, they established the MacClenachan family in nearby Fort Richmond, a deteriorating set of buildings. Although backed by the Anglican proprietors, the missionary petitioned in vain for the church lands and even failed to induce the proprietors to repair his living quarters.

MacClenachan, a former Presbyterian minister of considerable gifts, should have been able to win support among the people. He was a stirring preacher, but his congregation found his habits intemperate. It was said that "when Mr. Macclenachan was in the pulpit he ought never to come out of it and when he was out of the pulpit he ought never to go into it."[6] In 1758, tired of the anomalous position, MacClenachan abandoned his spartan lodgings at Fort Richmond and withdrew to the congenial atmosphere of Philadelphia.[7]

The ministerial vacancy at Georgetown caused tension among the proprietors. The Congregationalists among them feared the encroachments of Anglicanism, and it was rumored that the Society for the Propagation of the Gospel had selected a bishop for America. Because New England Congregationalists had triumphantly defeated earlier attempts to implement the Society's scheme,[8] it was to be expected that these descendants of the once-persecuted Puritans would view with suspicion the founding of an Anglican station on the Kennebec. Most of them, parishioners of the liberal and wealthy Brattle Square Church in Boston, a leading opponent of Anglican expansionism, would be alert to the implications of the Society for the Propagation of the Gospel's move.

The Congregationalist proprietors included many powerful Boston merchants who were among the richest inhabitants of that city. In 1771, £41,000 of the £104,000 then out at interest in Boston was held by four members of the Brattle Square Church: James Bowdoin; John Hancock; Hancock's widowed aunt Lydia; and Bowdoin's father-in-law, John Erving, Sr.[9] The first three were Kennebeck proprietors. The Bowdoin family had attended the Brattle Church for generations. James Bowdoin, James Pitts, William Brattle, and Benjamin Hallowell had been married in the church, as had many of their relatives.

These wealthy proprietors and their families dominated the Brattle Square Church, which was founded by the son of one of the original proprietors. They were also intimate friends of the pastor, the Reverend Samuel Cooper, an activist in the anti-bishop struggle as well as a strong Whig. Relations among Congregationalists, however, were not entirely without friction. When the old Brattle Square Church needed rebuilding in 1772, James Bowdoin offered family property nearby for a new building site. John Hancock countered with the offer of a generous contribution if the structure was rebuilt on the original location. He had his way.

The next year Hancock made a welcome offer to some Congregationalists then attempting to organize their own society at Pownalborough, the former Frankfort. The terms are not clear; they may have included financial support for a minister, the building of a meeting house, or both. Although the offer was not implemented, it caused great uneasiness among Anglicans. The Reverend J. Wingate Weeks, Anglican missionary at Marblehead, complained to his brother-in-law, the Reverend Jacob Bailey, then missionary on the Kennebec that "As to Hancock's bounty, no reflections can be too severe; but it is just of a piece with the whole conduct of the Dissenters, who it is my serious opinion had they the power, would tolerate no religious sect but their

own."[10] Weeks had good reason to complain. Though Anglicans
had been grudgingly allowed to build their first Boston church as
early as 1688, they continued to be the victims of discrimination.
Few Anglicans held elective office in the town. Opposition to
Episcopalianism had become militant among the Congregationalist members of the town meeting. And so it was at the Brattle
Square Church. The seating plan in the new building, which
placed Kennebeck Company proprietors such as the Pitts, Hancock, and Bowdoin families in dominant positions along the center aisle, reads like a roll of the leaders of the Congregationalist
establishment.

The Anglican King's Chapel in Boston, as fashionable and nearly as wealthy as its Brattle Square rival, sheltered leaders of the
pro-bishop faction in Massachusetts. In 1771, the Anglican stronghold could boast that 66% of those members owning real
estate—the most accurate gauge of wealth at that time—held
property renting at more than £30 a year. Only 30% of Boston
property owners could make such a claim.[11] Prominent among
the Anglican leaders were Kennebeck proprietors, who could be
seen at the church services in the centrally located pews. Here,
Dr. Silvester Gardiner might nod to such nearby fellow proprietors as the Apthorps, the Tailers, the Vassalls, the Tyngs, and
the Shirleys; to the Company lawyers, Benjamin Prat and Robert
Auchmuty; as well as to many family connections. These kinfolk
included members of the well-known Hutchinson, Erving, Trecothick, Wendell, Temple, Nelson, Bulfinch, Dumaresq, and
Hallowell families. Proprietors who occupied pews in King's
Chapel held the largest fortunes in that parish; their influence ri-
valed that of members of the Brattle Square Church.

One of the most prosperous of the Kennebeck proprietors was
Charles Apthorp, merchant and paymaster of British forces in
America, as well as friend and business associate of Thomas Hancock.[12] Apthorp's sixteen children helped cement marriage alliances with many prominent colonial families. In 1747, Apthorp
contributed heavily to the rebuilding of King's Chapel where he
is commemorated by an elaborate marble wall monument.[13] The
most significant Apthorp commitment to Anglicanism, however,
was that of one of Apthorp's sons. In 1760, East Apthorp, after
years of study in England, returned to Boston upon the death of
his father. As he had been given an expensive education, he received little from the estate,[14] which may explain why he respond-

ed to the entreaties of the Society for the Propagation of the Gospel to serve as missionary to Cambridge. In this sensitive post, he precipitated a new episode in the campaign to establish an American bishopric.[15]

Rumors began to circulate that East Apthorp would soon be appointed bishop, and thus, as had long been feared by the Congregationalists, the creation of this position would become a reality. Certainly, Apthorp's educational background gave evidence of grooming for the role. As a classical scholar with two degrees from Jesus College, Cambridge, East Apthorp was eminently qualified. Few Anglican clergymen in America possessed his credentials: education, family, and social position. The possibility of quick advancement in the church must have been the irresistible inducement that brought about his return to Massachusetts and acceptance of the Cambridge mission.

To New England Congregationalists, sending Anglican missionaries to places like suburban Cambridge, rather than to the frontier to minister to settlers or to convert the savages, exemplified all that they distrusted about the English church. They would also have feared the conversion of Harvard students to Anglicanism. East Apthorp's special qualifications made him particularly controversial, for in Congregationalist eyes, Apthorp had the stature to become bishop. Unfortunately for him, the young missionary commenced building a handsome mansion in Cambridge, and thus strengthened the impression that his appointment was imminent. The mansion, soon dubbed the "Bishop's Palace,"[16] became a symbol of Anglican encroachment.

The conflict between the elegant missionary and such Congregationalist champions as the Reverend Jonathan Mayhew is too familiar to bear repeating.[17] A brief pamphlet war with Mayhew terminated in Apthorp's hasty decision to abandon his mansion and the small but equally showy Christ Church in Cambridge and return to England. Vilified by unfavorable publicity, East Apthorp had become a liability, and could no longer expect to become bishop—if indeed he had ever been given such a promise. The Cambridge mission was faltering, and could not support him in the style to which he was accustomed. This and the pamphlet warfare may have been enough to force the fashionable missionary to withdraw. Later, life in England at the vicarage of Croyden and a subsequent position as prebendary at St.

Paul's must have provided the tranquillity for a writing career that he had been denied in Cambridge.

At the same time that the son of an Anglican proprietor was experiencing harsh treatment as missionary to Cambridge, the Society for the Propagation of the Gospel was preparing to send one of his fellows to minister to the inhabitants of Frankfort. A year after the Rev. MacClenachan's departure, the settlers themselves had seemingly taken the initiative in seeking a new pastor. On November 24, 1759, they had sent a petition containing fifty-four signatures to the Society for the Propagation of the Gospel formally requesting the "sending [of] a Missionary to this truly necessitous place,"[18] and making extravagant promises for his support. They would place at his disposal the "mansion house" of Fort Richmond, which they described as being in the midst of "very valuable" farmlands valued at £20 a year, see that he was endowed with glebe lands, and soon construct a church and parsonage. They then informed the Society that "one Mr. Bailey, a sober, prudent and well disposed young man, is willing to undertake this Mission, and with the approbation of the Rev. Clergy of Boston will proceed to England for Holy Orders and offers himself to this service."[19] They prayed that Bailey would be acceptable to the Society so that they might again have the comfort of the Christian religion in their isolated valley.It seem unlikely that this petition originated with the settlers themselves, who could not have known Bailey or details of his availability. Jacob Bailey, who served briefly as a schoolmaster in the Massachusetts towns of Rowley and Kingston and the New Hampshire village of Hampton following his graduation from Harvard, was only then being encouraged by Boston Anglicans to defect from the Congregationalism of his youth. His readiness would, however, have been known to Dr. Henry Caner, rector of King's Chapel, and to his determined vestryman, Dr. Silvester Gardiner. It would be in the doctor's interests to fill the Frankfort vacancy with an Anglican minister.

Dr. Gardiner's family had been staunch Episcopalians in Rhode Island for generations. Gardiner's brother-in-law, the Reverend James MacSparran, rector of St. Paul's Church, Kingston, Rhode Island, was an Anglican protagonist in an earlier stage of the bishopric controversy. Dr. John Gibbins of Boston, Gardiner's father-in-law, had been a vestryman of King's Chapel. It was to be expected that Silvester Gardiner would take whatever steps he deemed necessary to establish Anglicanism on the Kennebec, such as sponsoring Jacob Bailey for the missionary post.

The speed with which Jacob Bailey was eased into Anglican Church membership, the ministry, and a missionary station at Frankfort in that era of sluggish transportation and communication seems remarkable, particularly since Bailey himself must have represented rather unpromising missionary material. He came from a poor Rowley family of strict Puritan background, and had not entered Harvard until the age of twenty, where he stood at the foot of the Class of 1755. After indifferent success as a schoolmaster, he must have considered life as an Anglican cleric, even on the frontier, as a distinct advancement. As the protégé of Dr. Caner, Bailey accepted the call to the ministry in September, 1759, and backed by the approval of the Society for the Propagation of the Gospel, sped around Cambridge and Boston gathering recommendations for ordination. The Apthorps and Gardiners were helpful. Charles Ward Apthorp, now head of the Apthorp clan, signed a letter of recommendation. Dr. Gardiner gave advice and lent religious works.[20] New England orthodoxy reacted differently. President Holyoke of Harvard, himself a Congregationalist minister, refused to endorse the apostate, but lionizing by the Gardiners and the Apthorps helped make up for this slight. Zealous for ordination, Jacob Bailey decided to brave a disagreeable winter crossing, and left for England on the *Hind* on January 10, 1760.

Bailey arrived at Spithead on February 16, and hastened up to London. The Bishop of Rochester conferred upon him the order of the Diaconate on March 2; he was ordained to the priesthood on the sixteenth, and had a brief audience with the Archbishop of Canterbury on the seventeenth. He received the traditional bounty of £19.7.6 and was appointed a missionary by the Society for the Propagation of the Gospel at £50 per year. By the end of the month, he was bound for America. On May 28 he was again in Boston, and by July 1 in residence at his new post on the Kennebec. After this heady, event-crammed half year, he was now ready to face the adventure of the Maine frontier.

The Rev. Mr. Bailey's goals in his new life were few and modest: to build a church, construct a comfortable house for his family in the raw, backwoods village, and plant a string of missions along the Kennebec. He expected that the church at Frankfort, now renamed Pownalborough in honor of the governor, would be only the first of many. As the seat of the new Lincoln County, Pownalborough seemed certain to grow rapidly, and Episcopalianism would thrive with it.

Important proprietors supported Bailey in his goals, and the settlers informed him that "if Missions were established at convenient distances, especially upon the Kennebec River, in such a manner as people might generally attend service, that it would meet with almost universal acceptance, and conduce greatly to serve the interest of religion and morality."[21] To some extent, Bailey achieved his ambition. The young missionary was willing to go wherever he was needed; he preached sermons at Georgetown, Fort Western, Gardinerstown, and elsewhere along the river, as well as at Pownalborough.

A first step in establishing himself should have been to obtain the long-promised church glebe lands for the Pownalborough mission. The Company, however, was not willing to dispense the church lands at this time. Through the intercession of Dr. Gardiner, the proprietors did grant him the "Liberty to possess and improve Richmond House & Farm"[22] on the site of old Fort Richmond, about two miles below Pownalborough. They also granted him a one-hundred-acre lot in town, half that due him as the first settled minister, but only if he remain as preacher for ten years and improve the land during that time.[23] This gift was no more than the ordinary settlers received. His position in the town was a far cry from what he had expected. In spite of their earlier promises, his parishioners now insisted they were too poor to pay Bailey a salary. Forced to rely entirely upon his £50 income from the Society for the Propagation of the Gospel, he and his family were hard put to survive. He accepted the situation, though probably with reluctance. Bailey undoubtedly realized that much of his success in the region would depend upon his relationship with his congregation and the reservoir of good will he could build up there. As there was no money available to build a church, he conducted religious services in the courtroom of the newly completed Pownalborough Court House. In time, he must have hoped, the proprietors would recognize his good works and grant the church lands that would make possible the construction of his own house of worship.

Bailey's own account of the townspeople's religious preferences reveals built-in differences that would inevitably lead to fragmentation. Denominations by heads of families included:

Presbyterians	5
Catholics	7
Lutherans	15
Churchmen (Anglicans)	25
Independents (Congregationalists)	23
Quakers	3
Calvinists	2
Baptists	3
No preference	1
	84[24]

Because Bailey identified each family by name, it is possible to generalize about the nationalities represented. The "Independents" were from old New England stock; the Presbyterians were more recent Scotch-Irish immigrants; the Catholics were Irish; and the Lutherans, Calvinists, and "Churchmen" were mainly of German and Huguenot background. The difficulties of providing a common religion must have seemed insurmountable to the new pastor. Nevertheless, as he and the Kennebeck proprietors hoped, any Protestant faith would to some extent be acceptable to most of the inhabitants.

The hopes for unity were not fulfilled. Religious factions formed soon after Bailey's arrival. One group composed of Anglicans was joined by Lutherans, Calvinists, and the handful of Catholics. It was natural for the Lutherans to identify themselves with Anglicanism, a worship not unlike their own. The Catholics, at a disadvantage in the Protestant New World, also must have opted for the High Church because of its similarities to their own faith. This coalition formed the core of Bailey's little flock. Presbyterians and Congregationalists made up the second faction. Neither the Anglican nor the Congregationalist contingents had a clear-cut majority. To this religious dissension were added difficulties stemming from cultural and language differences. The almost unanimous agreement necessary for the conduct of town affairs, so common in older Massachusetts towns, was lacking in Pownalborough.[25] Perhaps the proprietors were wise in refusing to become involved in the squabble and in denying the promised church lands.

One probable reason for the refusal of the Congregationalist proprietors to grant Pownalborough Anglicans the glebe lands was the defeat of their own attempts to create a religious society rivaling the Society for the Propagation of the Gospel. James Bowdoin had been a leader in this abortive movement. In January, 1762, the Massachusetts General Court received a petition praying leave to incorporate an organization to be styled the Society for the Propagation of Christian Knowledge Among the Indians of North America. The petitioners emphasized the political and economic benefits which could be reaped now that the French had been defeated in North America by "endeavouring to spread the knowledge of Protestant Religion."[26] They described the procedures to be followed in holding meetings and electing officers, but did not include a plan of operation. They did promise that the Society would provide frontier ministers, "men of reputed piety loyalty prudence gravity knowledge and literary and of other Christian or necessary qualifications suited to their respective Stations. [27] The proposal was endorsed by so many influential Congregationalist ministers and laymen that it could not be easily ignored by the General Court.

At first the petition fared well. Among the more than one hundred signatures, appear those of the best minds and fortunes of the Congregationalist establishment. Many were members of the House and Council. Among the Kennebeck proprietors, James Bowdoin, James Pitts, William Brattle, Benjamin Hallowell, Thomas Marshall, and Thomas Hancock—all members of the Brattle Square Church—signed their names, as did many of their important family connections. With such support the petition quickly passed the House and Council and was signed by Governor Bernard, then a close friend of several of the proprietors.

Although the bill cleared all local hurdles, like every colonial enactment it was subject to approval in England. Here the Congregationalists expected opposition. The Reverend Jonathan Mayhew confided his fears: "We are not without apprehension that our *good Friends* of the Church of England will endeavor to obstruct this scheme, but hope, to no purpose."[28] Mayhew's fears were well founded. New England Episcopalians already planned to contest the bill. Working through the influence of Archbishop Secker, Dr. Caner of King's Chapel swayed the Board of Trade to disapprove the proposed Society. On the Board's recommendation, the King in Council declared the act null and void on May 20, 1763.[29] Such a move could not help but alienate a large and influential group in the New England colonies.

No specific reason was given for the action, but James Bowdoin, as a Council member, was in a position to learn how it had come about. He was notified of Archbishop Secker's behind-the-scenes dealings by Jasper Mauduit, then English agent for Massachusetts. Mauduit, himself an English dissenter, attempted to save the bill. At first Bowdoin was incredulous that Anglican interests were responsible, for he believed that "This opposition was least to be expected from a Society, the end of whose institution so much coincided with that of ours."[30] If he was shaken when he learned that the act had been disallowed, he would never be so naive again. This disagreeable experience with the Church of England in 1763 must have been a significant factor in Bowdoin's eventual decision to join the revolutionary cause.[31]

The defeat of the bill was a setback for Bowdoin and the other Congregationalist proprietors. The proposed organization had aimed at pre-empting the Society for the Propagation of the Gospel in an area where it had been notoriously inefficient—the missionary field.[32] William MacClenachan and Jacob Bailey were exceptions in venturing to the very fringes of settlement. Most Anglican missionaries, like East Apthorp, had located in established towns where the pluckings for conversion from Congregationalism seemed ripest. The propaganda impact for Congregationalism, if the proposed society had prevailed in planting effective Indian missions on the frontier, would have been enormous. Even more important, Congregationalist missionaries financed by the new Society could have moved into towns like Pownalborough, where no regular minister would venture, and effectively hold them for New England orthodoxy, thus eliminating the Anglican menace in those areas. In less controversial wilderness regions, the missionaries might have brought about the conversion of Indian tribes. In their wholehearted support of this Society, Kennebeck proprietors would have been able to realize both ends.

The failure to establish the new Society meant that Congregationalist shareholders still were faced with the threat of spreading Anglicanism in the Kennebec valley. This danger was personified in the Reverend Jacob Bailey, indefatigable missionary at Pownalborough. During the remaining years of his tenure on the Kennebec, Bailey's enemies harassed him unmercifully.

Unfortunately, the Anglican missionary in a series of incidents took foolhardy positions that contributed to his growing unpopularity. Personally bound to Dr. Gardiner, his benefactor, Bailey became involved in the highly controversial lawsuit between the doctor and James Flagg.[33] Gardiner was not above using Bailey as a tool in achieving victory, and Bailey could not deny his assistance.

The case reached a crisis when Dr. Gardiner charged that Flagg had deliberately destroyed his dam at Gardinerstown, and then used Bailey's evidence to establish a favorable predisposition of kindness to Flagg before the court action began. The testimony of the McCausland brothers, employees of Gardiner and witnesses of the damage to the dam, was especially critical in the lawsuit. Bailey was acquainted with the McCauslands' way of doing business. In November, 1766, he wrote to Dr. Gardiner, volunteering information and thus making his own position vulnerable. Bailey recalled:

> . . . when these men [the McCauslands] seriously threatened Mr. Flagg for cutting away the mill dam at Cobbosseecontee, I remember in general you endeavoured to make them easy and to discourage them from prosecution. I have likewise heard the McCauslins (though attached to your interest) complain of your partiality to Mr. Flagg notwithstanding he was no friend and always secretly opposed the settlement of the [Anglican] church in these parts.[34]

The letter shows that Flagg, himself a Baptist and accustomed to religious persecution, was connected with the local church dispute.

Gardiner's instructions to the Rev. Mr. Bailey clearly show the power he wielded over his protégé. He directed the missionary to rewrite his evidence: "If you will be so kind as to put it into a statement leaving out what I have erased, it will be, I think, of great service to me, and I beg of you will be so kind as soon as this comes to your hand you will proceed with it to Gardinerstown to . . . get it done with some other evidence . . . and send them up to me."[35] Bailey's willingness to change his story in a court action to suit his benefactor stopped short of perjury, as it only eliminated information. The doctor's dictation was never aired in public. Bailey's final statement was produced at the trial in Boston, and was subsequently printed and circulated during the Gardiner-Flagg pamphlet war. Through it, Bailey himself contributed to the decrease in his popularity at Pownalborough, where young Flagg was well liked.

By his testimony in Gardiner v. Flagg, as well as in other incidents, Bailey aligned himself with Silvester Gardiner against John Hancock, Jonathan Bowman, and Charles and William Cushing. In 1765 and again in 1769, Hancock had occasion to go to court when Dr. Gardiner ordered his tenants off land that the older man claimed.[36] Relations rapidly cooled between the two. Jonathan Bowman and the Cushings were also drawn into the imbroglio, for they owed their important courthouse positions to the Hancock family.[37] Judge Bowman was Hancock's first cousin, and his legal representative at Pownalborough. Although Bowman and Charles Cushing had been Bailey's classmates in college, they did not hesitate to persecute the missionary. In doing so, they were showing their opposition to Dr. Gardiner. James Bowdoin and his brother-in-law, James Pitts, whose religious affiliations and increasingly radical sympathies coincided with Hancock's, may also have indirectly opposed Bailey and Gardiner.[38] It is difficult to imagine how the religious struggle at Pownalborough could have proceeded without at least their tacit approval.

Parson Bailey further incurred the displeasure of his enemies at Pownalborough and within the Kennebeck Company by actively seeking out ties with the Massachusetts Tory leadership at a time when relations with Great Britain were rapidly worsening. Bailey naturally chose the politics of his church and his patron, Dr. Gardiner. In November, 1767, he applied for a subscription to the *Boston Chronicle,* printed by John Mein, a Scotsman who was adept at dispelling Whig propaganda and at discouraging the Non-Importation Agreements.[39] Bailey, who learned about the paper and its aims from Dr. Gardiner, lost no time in writing to the controversial printer, applauding his efforts and observing that he had no doubt Mein "would be able to support a paper without those pieces of dirty scandal with which some of our public prints have lately abounded."[40] To encourage this good work, the minister took out a subscription and persuaded some of his Pownalborough neighbors to do the same. In addition, he promised to send "any anecdotes [he could] furnish from this remote corner of the world"[41] as his own contribution to the success of the cause. Bailey's subscription was to be sent to Dr. Gardiner's shop in Boston, where it would be forwarded to the Kennebec, "sealed under cover."[42] Whether he actually contributed any articles to the *Boston Chronicle* remains unknown, but even in subscribing to the paper, Bailey risked his own security. The printer, John Mein, was driven out of Boston as early as 1770. As a subscriber, Jacob Bailey could not have hoped to remain undetected at Pownalborough.

The missionary was foolish to risk the displeasure of the Congregationalists just when he and his Anglicans were renewing their demands for the glebe lands. This time, Dr. Gardiner was determined that the proprietors should make the grant, regardless of any ill feelings that resulted. Before any action could be taken, Pownalborough's Congregationalist faction, having learned that the Anglicans were about to petition again, decided to circumvent this effort by presenting their own petition. Capably organized by Jonathan Bowman and Charles Cushing, the group prepared an appeal signed by over fifty petitioners and, on January 9, 1769, sent it to the proprietors. The petitioners described themselves as "not of the Persuasion of the Church of England."[43] They pointed out that the Bailey flock was about to submit its own request, and lamented that if Bailey had his way, "the greater part of the Inhabitants upon the West Side of the Town would be excluded from all Advantages of a Parsonage Lot."[44] They then requested several three-acre lots within the town limits which might serve "for the use of such a Minister as the Majority of us shall choose."[45] This minister would, of course, be a Congregationalist. The petition, modest though it appeared, was not granted.

The proprietors were deadlocked about the glebe lands and did not propose to endow both religious factions. Silvester Gardiner alone had enough power to squelch the Congregationalist request. On April 12, 1769, at a proprietary meeting held at the Royal Exchange Tavern in Boston, Gardiner finally secured the glebe lands for Bailey and his congregation. He did it in such an audacious way, however, that he created further division among the proprietors, and also among the already factious people of Pownalborough. Dr. Gardiner gained his objective simply by using proxies that he had collected from Charles Ward Apthorp of New York City and Florentius Vassall of London and calling for a vote. Most likely he also had the concurrence of Benjamin Hallowell, whose son Robert was soon to marry Gardiner's daughter. As the attendance at the meeting was poor, his surprise move met with no opposition.

Gardiner presided at this meeting, which later became a focus of much controversy. The agenda reveals a routine granting of standard lots to new settlers at Ponds Town (Winthrop), the donation of an old blockhouse to the county for use as a jail, and the long-delayed granting of the glebe lands. The disputed lands were "voted Granted and assigned to the Minister and Church Wardens for the time being of the Episcopal Church in Pownalborough . . . One hundred Acres of land."[46] Some years later, Gardiner's political and religious foes in the Kennebec Valley issued their version of what happened that afternoon in April:

> . . . finally the Doctor took . . . advantage of the other Gentlemen of the Company, attended one of the Meetings exactly at the hour the Meeting was adjourn'd to, with a design to make this grant, he had already cut and dried & only he and Mr. Hallowell . . . Voted the land away as they did, & a Record was made of it in an instant. Immediately upon it, one of the principal Gentlemen of the Company [James Pitts] came in, & finding what had been done he reproved the Doctor severely for his Conduct.[47]

Silvester Gardiner's presumptuous action must have stunned the Congregationalist proprietors. The loss of one hundred acres was of scant monetary significance, but the concession that had been involuntarily exacted from them was galling: Congregationalist leaders of the Kennebeck Purchase Company had seemingly gone on record as subsidizing the hated Church of England.

Dr. Gardiner probably argued that his action was within his rights, and that a New England land company could grant church lands to any denomination. He was not the first member of his family to try to secure glebe lands for the Anglican Church. In the earlier case of MacSparran v. Torrey, Dr. Gardiner's brother-in-law had gone to court for the same reason. In that instance, Anglican James MacSparran and the Congregationalist Joseph Torrey, pastors in South Kingston, Rhode Island, had tested the strength of their respective denominations when each claimed a gift of glebe lands designated by will for an "orthodox minister."[48] When the Rhode Island courts ruled against MacSparran, he appealed to the British Privy Council. Unfortunately for the Anglican cause, in 1752, after a struggle of many years, the Privy Council awarded Torrey the land on the grounds that the intent of the original donors had been to benefit a Congregationalist church.[49] In New England, at least, the Congregational Church would continue to be regarded as the "orthodox" one, despite the fact that Episcopalianism was established by law in the mother country and several American colonies.[50] Although the Rhode Island test had failed, Dr. Gardiner was willing to risk much the same position at Pownalborough. One immediate result of awarding Bailey the glebe lands was to increase the opposition to him.

Judge Bowman and Charles Cushing attacked Bailey repeatedly during the next decade for a number of reasons. Bowman, the son of a Congregationalist minister, may have felt compelled to undertake the destruction of Bailey's mission as a kind of personal crusade. Both he and Cushing would have struck at Bailey for being the protege of Dr. Gardiner. In any event, Bowman knew that his actions would win the veiled approval of the Congregationalist proprietors, an approval that would benefit him professionally. Bailey later reported that Colonel Cushing had informed him in 1772 that "had not my attachment to Dr. Gardiner been so great, I should not have an enemy in Pownalborough, and he hinted that it was yet in my power to secure the friendship of every one."[51] The ill-treatment that he suffered from the hands of Judge Bowman ranged from the petty to the sadistic. On occasion, obscenities were shouted at him as he passed the Bowman mansion; foul language was scribbled in his Bible and *Book of Common Prayer;* he was locked out of his church on Sunday mornings; and he found soap, scraps of paper, and playing cards in the collection plate.[52] Dr. Gardiner's patronage had become a millstone around his neck.

The minister offered occasional resistance, but directed most of his energies toward building a church. Dr. Gardiner intended that the glebe lands would be put to immediate use for this construction. On April 17, 1769, Bailey recorded in his journal that "Capt. Callahan arrives here, with a large packet from Dr. Gardiner, containing a Plan of a Church."[53] This was only five days after he had received the glebe lands. While Bailey wanted a proper church building, he did not wish to exercise such undue haste. His parishioners were needy, and much help would be necessary from outside sources; but he was duty-bound to follow Gardiner's wishes. On the few occasions when he opposed the doctor, Bailey received almost as much abuse as he had come to expect from his enemies. He did not presume to incur his patron's wrath if he could avoid it. As he wrote in 1772 to Samuel Goodwin, his confidant, "both of us have by reason of our connection with the above gentleman [Dr. Gardiner] often to act contrary to our sentiments and inclinations."[54] Samuel Goodwin, a minor proprietor, was deeply in debt to the doctor and caught in the same web. The church was completed as Dr. Gardiner desired.

The new church, named St. John's, was moderate in size, sixty by thirty-two feet. Silvester Gardiner predicted that it would be "one of the prettiest in the Province, and a bigger one you can't build."[55] St. John's did not have the architectural distinction of Apthorp's Christ Church in Cambridge, but was elaborate for frontier construction. It contained glass windows, still rare in Pownalborough, and may have had a tower. Inside it was graced by a pulpit set off with fringe and tassels. Gardiner donated £50 toward the costs, and other King's Chapel families made contributions. The Rev. Mr. Bailey and five of his congregation, however, were compelled to give their bonds to Dr. Gardiner for construction costs. When the church was completed, the parishioners, although already overburdened financially, helped Bailey erect a parsonage nearby. He was at last achieving his goal.

This was the last period of real calm that Bailey was to know along the river. During the building of the parsonage he was free to indulge his dreams of laying out an orchard and a formal flower garden. He transplanted native wild flowers from the forest to the building site. Here, also, were to be found daffodils, crocuses, violets, tulips, and English pinks. Legend has it that Bailey's pink roses and white lilacs are yet blooming on the Kennebec.[56] An amateur writer and naturalist, the minister even found the leisure to write some verses and speculate about the origins of the local Indian tribes. His days of peace and contemplation came to an end with the completion of his parsonage home.

Just as life was becoming easier for Bailey and his flock, his foes struck. The title to the land on which the church buildings stood was defective, and could be claimed by Samuel Goodwin. When Judge Bowman learned of this, he somehow extracted the deeds from Goodwin and forced Bailey to surrender the church and parsonage to him. Probably the judge expected to use the buildings to attract a minister to the Congregationalist society he had been planning for Pownalborough. Dr. Gardiner immediately contested his claim, and an involved legal battle followed.

Although Gardiner knew the title was faulty before ground was broken, he now blamed Bailey for much that went wrong, alternately encouraging and scolding him. Naturally outspoken himself, he could not understand how Bailey could be intimidated. Once he reprimanded the missionary for supposedly treating a townsman unfairly: "It is such behavior that makes you so many enemies, and a sufficient reason for me to wash my hands clean of having any further to do with [the building of] your house."[57] Thus spoke a man whose own foes were legion. The next summer, he counseled the minister that "your enemies know your weak side and throw out these [threats] on purpose to plague and worry you. If you would take no notice of them, but treat them with the contempt they deserve they would leave off."[58] When Silvester Gardiner felt himself abused, he struck back with all of his formidable resources.

Bailey was not in a position to follow the doctor's example. The final step in the worsening relationship between the doctor and the minister came when Bailey agreed to take out a six-month lease on his own parsonage from Judge Bowman. Gardiner was enraged and demanded that the minister proceed with a lawsuit against Bowman, even upon evidence which Bailey felt was thin. At the next general church convocation in Boston, Bailey experienced the full force of Dr. Gardiner's wrath:

> I had a most melancholy time. The Doctor made his complaints against me to the clergy, accused me of sacrilege, and, if I understand the matter, endeavoured to obtain their interest against me with the Society [for the Propagation of the Gospel]. Two or three gentlemen were very severe against me, and an equal number were in my favour. At length the matter dropped without any representation of the affair to the Society.[59]

In due time Dr. Gardiner won his court battle, thus reclaiming the church and parsonage for the Pownalborough Anglicans. In spite of his outburst against Bailey, he forgave the minister and continued to support him until the outbreak of revolution. Actually, Gardiner had little choice, for Anglican ministers were difficult to come by in the colonies. In any event, it was a natural alliance; their religious and political feelings united them.

As with other Anglican ministers, Bailey's position became increasingly difficult as the war approached. While returning from a trip to Boston in 1774, he was caught by a mob at Brunswick and forced to run for his life.[60] Political and financial problems began to take their toll when Jacob Bailey's salary from the Society for the Propagation of the Gospel stopped with the war. Somehow he contrived to feed a large family from his meager savings and garden produce, supplemented only by infrequent gifts from neighbors. Enemies in the town despoiled his orchard and shot his cattle. Nevertheless, the missionary was determined to remain at Pownalborough, although the political opinions which he often voiced, and his steadfast allegiance to the king, made living there almost unendurable.

Paradoxically, while his personal difficulties increased, Bailey helped expand Anglicanism in the valley. After the departure of the Reverend William Wheeler, a fellow missionary stationed for a time at Georgetown, Bailey was the only minister on the river, and his attention was badly needed. He conducted services at Georgetown as often as he could. Meanwhile, Dr. Gardiner had erected a church at Gardinerstown, which he called St. Ann's. Jacob Bailey also held services there, and at Ponds Town. The pews of his Pownalborough church were usually filled, sometimes even with his opponents. But mob action and repression by the local revolutionary government often accompanied this spreading of Episcopalianism in the early days of the American Revolution.

On May 24, 1776, the Pownalborough Committee of Correspondence, Inspection, and Safety called Jacob Bailey before it to answer complaints. He was charged with being "unfriendly to the Cause of Liberty;"[61] his accusers stated that "he had given great Reason to believe that he does not wish Success to our Struggle for Freedom."[62] The evidence was real enough, but overdrawn. Bailey had refused to read the proclamations for fast days issued by the Continental and Massachusetts Provincial Congresses. For this offense, the Committee required him to post a bond of £40, almost a year's salary in normal times, and notified him that he would soon be called to account for his crimes. In the interim, he was to obey all acts and directives and refrain from aiding "the despotic Measures of our unnatural Enemies, or by any Ways and Means directly or indirectly assist them in their Designs of enslaving the . . . colonies."[63] Bailey chose the path of defiance. He continued to pray for the king at church services, although forbidden to do so. The consequence was another call to appear before the Committee of Safety, this time to explain the prayers and his refusal to read the Declaration of Independence before his congregation. Bailey now had an opportunity to offer proof of why he was not "a most inveterate and dangerous Enemy to the Rights and Liberties of these United States."[64] When he faced the Committee on October 2, 1776, Bailey was well prepared. He freely admitted the truth of the accusations against him, offering as his defense the taking of religious orders which required a sworn oath of allegiance to the King. This oath, Bailey proudly announced, could not be dissolved. In addition to giving proof of his good character, he asserted that he had never acted to help the British cause. He asked, "Can any Person without Money, without Influence, without Authority, without opportunity, in such a remote Corner, do any Thing to obstruct the wheels of Government, or to determine the Operations of the War?"[65] His refusal to comply with the revolutionary government's edicts sprang "not from any Contempt of Authority, but from a Principle of Conscience."[66] Jacob Bailey's appearance before the revolutionary committee may well have been his finest hour. The Committee was not convinced, however. Bailey's actions had not been as pure as his statements indicated. Surviving letters show that he had done what he could in the King's interest, thereby endangering his own situation and that of his congregation.[67]

Jacob Bailey's parishioners were at that moment being deprived of their civil rights because of their religious convictions. The Congregationalists, now a majority, soon denied them the right to vote in town meeting, and on March 17, 1777, the Anglicans petitioned the Massachusetts General Court for redress. The twenty-five signers of the petition emphasized that the "great part of them [the petitioners] are french and Dutch German Protestants, who came into America . . . Upon the Incouragement given by the Massachusetts Government, that they should enjoy their religious privileges."[68] That solemn promise had been violated in 1773, when they had withdrawn from the town meeting in protest after losing their voting rights.

Since 1776, the Pownalborough Anglicans had been taxed for the support of a nonexistent Congregationalist church. Where the money went, no one knew. The Anglicans demanded justice from the legislature, assuming the Lockean position that "it is the unalienable right of mankind to worship the Supreme being according to the Dictates of a well-informed conscience."[69] The signers appealed for a legislative act freeing those of their church from being assessed for ministerial rates, especially since there was no Congregational church within town limits. Their petition was not ignored. As usual in cases of complaint, the General Court notified the accused, identified in this instance as "the inhabitants of the West Parish of Pownalborough," to show cause why the petition should not be granted.

West Parish, probably led by Jonathan Bowman, replied with a lengthy indictment of its own, in which it accused Jacob Bailey of being party to a conspiracy plotted by Dr. Gardiner, now a Tory refugee, Samuel Goodwin, and the missionary himself. Gardiner, they stated, fraudulently induced the Kennebeck Company to grant the glebe lands to the Episcopalians in the first place. They charged that Samuel Goodwin and the "pious Mr. Bailey" were guilty of persuading "the good People of this Precinct to renounce the pure and undefiled Religion & instead thereof to embrace Episcopacy."[70] They went on to assert that "the greater Part of the People of this Precinct who signed that Petition are not conscientiously Churchmen, but only profess themselves such, to avoid paying Taxes toward the support of the gospel . . . [and] the granting their Petition will have a tendency to encourage People to go over to the [Anglican] Church to save their taxes."[71] They warned that if the petition of the Episcopalians was granted, it would further delay the establishment of a Congregational meeting house in the town.

The issue was not a new one nor peculiar to Pownalborough. That this situation was not more widespread can be explained only by the small number of Anglican congregations extant. Certainly New England Separate Baptists, far more numerous than the Anglicans, and struggling for the same kind of religious freedom, were meeting the same discouraging treatment.[72] What was unusual in the situation on the Kennebec was the relative apathy toward religion of any denomination. The Congregationalist group was probably correct in saying that many "Anglicans" professed this denomination in an attempt to avoid paying the ministerial rates. As Episcopalians they escaped supporting the established church, but they also failed to make payments to their own.[73] The Congregationalists were nearly as lethargic. They lacked the strength and energy to build a church or attract a pastor, in spite of their access to the parish rates. The result was an impasse.

Neither group of petitioners received satisfaction from the Massachusetts General Court. It seldom intervened in a local quarrel,[74] and it was not likely to sponsor the Anglican cause during the war years. The situation worked to the advantage of the Congregationalists, and by 1779 the Rev. Mr. Bailey was ready to concede the hopelessness of the struggle. The missionary would have left Pownalborough earlier, but the terms of his bond for £40 forbade the move. He had ample reason to leave even in the face of the court order. Certainly his family would have been more comfortable elsewhere, for this was a time of famine on the river; but to have slipped quietly away would have meant breaking his word as well as forfeiting his bond. He continued to suffer harassment from his enemies. At times it was even necessary for him to go into hiding. Finally, in July, 1778, he made a difficult journey to Boston and petitioned the General Court for a safe conduct pass to Nova Scotia. He tearfully explained that he had not been paid by his Society for three years, that his congregation could not help him, and that he had "been obliged to dispose of almost all his moveable Effects to support himself."[75] Because his continued residence could only be a burden on the state, he hoped for permission to leave. The General Court granted him the safe conduct in October; owing to bad weather, however, the Bailey family remained at Pownalborough until June 9, 1779. Bailey, grown old after almost twenty years on the Kennebec—and a scarecrow of a figure in patched, rusty black coat, bedticking breeches, and greasy moth-eaten wig—sailed with his family for Halifax.

The Anglican missionary work started by Jacob Bailey was not continued after he left. Services were halted, and the churches at Pownalborough, Georgetown, and Gardinerstown decayed and soon disappeared. Their end, however, did not mean the installation of an orthodox Congregational church. Twenty-one years elapsed before the long-awaited meeting house arose in the town. When another Episcopal church was erected at Pownalborough in the early 1800s, hostility to Anglicanism had disappeared.

The conflict between Congregationalism and Anglicanism in New England, which was an intermittent issue from 1688 until the American Revolution, was a special irritation during the 1760s, the period of greatest expansion of the Kennebeck Company. During these years, an Anglican heir-presumptive to an American bishopric was routed from the field, and a proposed

Congregationalist society rivaling the Anglican Society for the Propagation of the Gospel was defeated, largely through the efforts of New England Episcopalians. Even though Congregationalist outnumbered the Anglicans by thirty-to-one in New England, they remembered the religious persecution of their Puritan ancestors and reacted. The longstanding distrust between the two denominations lingered and festered. Facing continued harassment during the period, the Anglicans had naturally turned to the King for protection, and thus had been inevitably drawn to the unpopular side in the revolutionary struggle.[76] When the Revolution finally erupted, many, like Dr. Gardiner, were forced into exile.

Much of the converging of Episcopalianism and political allegiance was due to the antagonism built up during the long span of the bishopric controversy. Kennebeck proprietors, their families, and their friends played a significant role in this controversy. East Apthorp and his aborted missionary effort, the aggressive actions of the Society for the Propagation of the Gospel, and the thwarting of the Congregationalist attempt to establish a rival society—each contributed to the intensifying of the religious question and helped to make it an important cause of revolution.

Religion was a divisive force in the Kennebeck Company from at least 1759, when Jacob Bailey was first considered as missionary to a proprietary town, until the outbreak of the Revolution. The Apthorp case and James Bowdoin's hopes for a counterforce to the Society for the Propagation of the Gospel had left their mark. Dr. Gardiner's persistence and eventual success in establishing an Anglican church within Company territory was a decisive factor in splitting the proprietors into warring camps. Jacob Bailey, a courageous but sometimes foolhardy man, was an agent as well as victim of this cleavage. By 1775, friction among the proprietors, for religious reasons as well as other causes, reached the point where corporate activity had almost ceased. The Hancocks, Bowdoins, and Pittses—all influential Congregationalists in the Company—faced their Anglican rivals, led by Gardiners and Apthorps, across the proprietary board in much the same manner as they opposed each other in Massachusetts politics. The religious question provided substantial tinder igniting the broader conflagration.

NOTES

CHAPTER XI

1 Knollenberg, *Origin of the American Revolution,* 76-86; Carl Bridenbaugh, *Mitre and Sceptre: Transatlantic Faiths, Ideas, Personalities, and Politics, 1689-1775* (New York, 1962), xix-xx; Sweet, *The Story of Religion in America,* 173.

2 See, for example, Bridenbaugh, *Mitre and Sceptre,* 239-243.

3 The colonists' idea of a British conspiracy to deprive them of their liberties inevitably tied together Church and State. For the conspiracy viewpoint, see Bernard Bailyn, *The Origins of American Politics* (New York, 1969), 11-14.

4 See Chapter IV.

5 Company Resolution, Dec. 11, 1754, K.P.P., Records, II, 81.

6 Bartlett, *The Frontier Missionary,* 254.

7 Many years later, while living in Philadelphia, MacClenachan assisted the proprietors in a proposal to send Pennsylvania residents to Maine. The plan was never executed. James Bowdoin to William MacClenachan, Apr. 9, 1765, James Bowdoin Letter Book (1759-1797), 109, M.H.S., hereafter cited as J.B. L.B. MacClenachan, as the only Anglican minister in the American colonies to encourage revivalism, proved to be as controversial in Philadelphia as he had been on the Kennebec. The Reverend Robert Jenney refused him further use of his pulpit because of his "Extemporary Prayer & Preaching, [and] his railings and revilings," as well as "his aspersions of the Whole Body of our Church and Clergy, their Doctrines and Principles, their Lives & Writings . . . ." Presbyterians in the area naturally supported MacClenachan, who had formerly been a minister of their faith. Although denied a license to preach by the Bishop of London in 1760, MacClenachan persisted in his efforts, and established St. Paul's Church, Philadelphia. William S. Perry, ed., *Historical Collections Relating to the American Colonial Church,* II—*Pennsylvania* (Hartford, 1871), 305-311, 319-324, 341, 354-355, 364-365, 392-393, 413-414.

8 Bridenbaugh, *Mitre and Sceptre,* 54-116.

9 Bruce E. Steiner, "New England Anglicanism—A Genteel Faith?" *William and Mary Quarterly*, 3rd Series, XXVII, 123.

10 J. Wingate Weeks to Jacob Bailey, Apr. 1, 1773, Jacob Bailey Letters and Diaries, Allen Copies, W.P.L.

11 Steiner, "New England Anglicanism," 123.

12 See Chapter V.

13 Henry W. Foote, ed., *Annals of King's Chapel* (Boston, 1882-1896), II, 118.

14 Will of Charles Apthorp of Boston, probated May 25, 1759, Suffolk County Probate Records, LVI, 68, No. 11871. East Apthorp's share of the real estate was only £580.17.6, but he had earlier been educated at great expense in England, and may have had other income.

15 Bridenbaugh, *Mitre and Sceptre*, 211-213; 240-242.

16 Wendell Garrett, *Apthorp House, 1760-1960* (Cambridge, 1960), 118.

17 Bridenbaugh, *Mitre and Sceptre*, 239-243; Knollenberg, *Origin of the American Revolution*, 80-81; 84-85.

18 Allen, *History of Dresden*, 256-257. This copy of the petition is said to have been made by Jacob Bailey.

19 *Ibid.*

20 Bartlett, *Frontier Missionary*, 45.

21 *Ibid.*, 90.

22 David Jeffries to Jacob Bailey, Sept. 25, 1760, K.P.P., Loose Papers (Nov. 1757-Apr. 1768).

23 Grant of Lot No. 19 at Pownalborough to Jacob Bailey, June 10, 1761, K.P.P. Records, II, 278.

24 Allen, *History of Dresden*, 350.

25 Zuckerman, *Peaceable Kingdoms*, 108. Zuckerman contends that most New England towns deliberately excluded those of foreign national or religious origin as a means of avoiding unnecessary controversy and maintaining a broad consensus. In this respect, Pownalborough was at a disadvantage from the start.

26 Petition to the Massachusetts General Court for the formation of a religious society, Jan. 20, 1762, M.A., XIV, 289-291.

27 "An Act to Incorporate Certain persons by the name of the Society for propagating Christian Knowledge Among the Indians of North America," Jan. 27, 1762, M.A., XIV, 300-305a.

28 Jonathan Mayhew to Thomas Hollis, Apr. 6, 1762, *Massachusetts Historical Society Proceedings,* LXIX, 130-131.

29 Proceedings of the King in Council, May 29, 1763, M.A., XIV, 345-346.

30 James Bowdoin to Jasper Mauduit, Apr. 25, 1763, J.B.L.B., 49.

31 James Bowdoin must have had a number of reasons for joining the radicals, including a personal dislike for Gov. Bernard, his intrigues to gain the governorship first for himself and later for his brother-in-law George Scott, and his partisan support for his son-in-law John Temple, a customs official. See Chapter XII.

32 Joseph J. Ellis, III, "Anglicans in Connecticut, 1725-1750: The Conversion of the Missionaries," *New England Quarterly,* XLIV, 81, demonstrates the feeble growth of Anglicanism in Connecticut, 1740-1750, despite determined missionary effort.

33 See Chapter IX.

34 Jacob Bailey to Silvester Gardiner, Nov. 12, 1766, Bailey Letter Books, Allen Copies, 246, W.P.L.

35 Silvester Gardiner to Jacob Bailey, Nov. 12, 1766, Bailey Letter Books, Allen Copies, 18, W.P.L.

36 Hanson, *History of Gardiner, Pittston, and West Gardiner,* 82.

37 See Chapter VIII.

38 James Bowdoin never contributed to Bailey's church at Pownalborough, but in 1775 he donated the window glass to a new, rival Congregational church at nearby Bowdoinham.

39 Philip Davidson, *Propaganda and the American Revolution, 1762-1783* (Chapel Hill, 1941), 171; 307.

40 Jacob Bailey to John Mein, Nov. 19, 1767, Bailey Letter Books, Allen Copies, 250, W.P.L.

41 *Ibid.*

42 *Ibid.*

43 Petition to the Committee of the Kennebeck proprietors, Jan. 9, 1769, K.P.P., Loose Papers (Nov. 1757-Apr. 1768).

44 *Ibid.*

45 *Ibid.*

46 Resolution, Apr. 12, 1769, K.P.P., Records, II, 8.

47 "Answer of Inhabitants of the West Precinct in Pownalborough to a Petition of certain Persons calling themselves members of the Episcopal Church & Inhabitants of said West Precinct & adjacent," June 27, 1777, M.A., CLXXXIII, 60-70.

48 Bridenbaugh, *Mitre and Sceptre,* 44; Charles E. Clark, "A Test of Religious Liberty: The Ministry Land Case in Narragansett, 1668-1752," *A Journal of Church and State,* XI, 295-319.

49 Clark, "A Test of Religious Liberty," 318-319.

50 Bridenbaugh, *Mitre and Sceptre*, 44-45.

51 Jacob Bailey to J. Wingate Weeks, Nov. 7, 1772, Allen, *History of Dresden*, 343.

52 Bartlett, *Frontier Missionary*, 94.

53 Extract from Bailey's journal for Apr. 17, 1769, Allen, *History of Dresden*, 339. Callahan, a Catholic and future loyalist, was a member of Bailey's church.

54 Jacob Bailey to Samuel Goodwin, Dec. 18, 1772, Bailey Letters, Allen Copies, IV, 44, W.P.L.

55 Bartlett, *Frontier Missionary*, 86.

56 Elizabeth Coatsworth, *Maine Memories* (Brattleboro, Vt., 1968), 69.

57 Silvester Gardiner to Jacob Bailey, Nov. 22, 1771, Bailey Letters, Allen Copies, 12, W.P.L.

58 Silvester Gardiner to Jacob Bailey, July 22, 1772, Bailey Letters, Allen Copies, 17-18, W.P.L.

59 Jacob Bailey to William Wheeler, Oct. 15, 1772, Bartlett, *Frontier Missionary*, 353; 342.

60 Extract from Bailey journal, Bartlett, *Frontier Missionary*, 350.

61 "Complaint against Rev. Jacob Bailey," May 24, 1776, *Maine*

Historical Society Collections, Documentary History, 2nd Series, XIV, 349-350.

62 *Ibid.*

63 *Ibid.*

64 *Maine Historical Society Collections, Documentary History,* 2nd Series, XIV, 389-390.

65 *Ibid.,* 393.

66 *Ibid.*

67 For example, when General McLean sailed from Halifax to invade Castine in 1779, he was supplied with a list of British sympathizers prepared by Bailey indicating Loyalist support in the Maine towns of Bristol, Broad Bay, Woolwich, Georgetown, Pownalborough, St. George's, Bowdoinham, Hallowell, Topsham, and Winthrop. Bartlett, *Frontier Missionary,* 172-173.

68 "Petition of Church People" to the General Court, Mar. 17, 1777, William Vassall Papers, M.H.S.

69 *Ibid.*

70 Allen, *History of Dresden,* 365.

71 *Ibid.,* 369.

72 William G. McLoughlin, *Isaac Backus and the American Pietistic Tradition* (Boston, 1967), 136-166.

73 Jacob Bailey to the Boston Convention of the Society for Propagating the Gospel in Foreign Parts, Boston, 1772. In this report he stated that "I never received any salary from the people." Bartlett, *Frontier Missionary,* 95.

74 Zuckerman, *Peaceable Kingdoms,* 35-38.

75 Allen, *History of Dresden,* 361.

76 Edwin S. Gaustad, *The Great Awakening in New England* (Chicago, 1968), 116-119.

XII

Political Disruption

Serious political disruptions accompanied religious disaffection as, from 1765 onward, tensions between the colonies and Great Britain mounted. This unrest affected the Kennebeck Company at two levels. First, individual proprietors became involved in political intrigues and factions, these interests ultimately overriding those of the Company; relationships within the propriety disintegrated as war approached. Second, the proprietary settlements along the Kennebec used the revolutionary agitation to free themselves not only from British control, but also from the control of the Kennebeck Company itself.

Revolutionary issues directly affected the lives and relationships of leading proprietors such as John Hancock, James Bowdoin, Benjamin Hallowell, James Pitts, and Silvester Gardiner. Lesser Company personnel such as John Temple and Thomas Marshall were also involved in disruptive activity. The story of these crises and their effects on the propriety begins with Francis Bernard's accession to the governorship of Massachusetts in 1760.

Although for the most part proprietary contacts with Governor Bernard were cordial until at least 1763,[1] the governor aroused animosities in the province almost immediately by his selection of Thomas Hutchinson as Chief Justice in 1760. James Otis, Sr., had been promised the post by both William Shirley and Thomas Pownall.[2] William Brattle, a former proprietor, also had aspired to the office.[3] James Otis, Jr., the popular young lawyer often em-

ployed by the Company,[4] swore to avenge his father, and began
to embarrass both the governor and Hutchinson in House actions.
Hutchinson was particularly vulnerable. He was fair game for
Otis's charges of plural officeholding. Otis formed an opposition
party to the governor that eventually included William Brattle,
Samuel Adams, John Hancock, and James Bowdoin, all powerful
figures in the House and Council. The coalition became known
as the Popular Party, and provided an agency under which enemies of Governor Bernard could unite against Crown policies.

Surprisingly, a Crown official—but a Crown official who was
also a minor proprietor—first focused public dissatisfaction on
the unfortunate Bernard. John Temple, the son of Captain Robert
Temple, who had been so influential in reorganizing the Company in the early 1750s, was serving as Lieutenant-Governor of
New Hampshire under John Wentworth when he received the important appointment of Surveyor-General of the Customs, stationed in Boston. Temple was frank in his determination to make
a reputation for himself. Writing to his old friend, Thomas Whately of the Treasury Office, he remarked, "I told my friends that I
came abroad not to make a fortune, but to make a character, so I
am in hopes that my services in America may recommend me to
future favor at home."[5] He soon unearthed corruption in the customs service which extended to the governorship.[6] Historians
have disagreed upon the amount of smuggling then going on in
New England.[7] They are certain that the opportunities for profits
among port authorities and the administration were enormous;
customs men, the governor, and the province shared equally the
returns from ship seizures under provisions of the Navigation
Acts. Temple openly accused Governor Bernard of encouraging
seizures for his own gain, and especially of connivance with
James Cockle, a customs collector. In 1764, Temple commented
to Whately that James Cockle had:

> . . . given me more trouble in keeping him tollerably to his
> duty than all the other offices in the district together, which he has
> been encouraged to do by Governor Bernard, whose insatiable
> avarice exceeds anything that I have yet met with . . . Mr. Ber-
> nard was instrumental in getting [Cockle] appointed to be Collec-
> tor of Salem, and it is not doubted here that he receives the great-
> est part of the gratuitys which I have no doubt Mr. Cockle has
> often taken.[8]

These may have been unsubstantiated accusations; but Temple
was outraged, not so much because of the customs evasion as be-

cause the governor was subverting Temple's control over his own customs men, making him look inefficient and damaging his career. To add insult to injury, Bernard was profiting handsomely in the process. The Surveyor-General—no doubt with promotion at least partially in mind—took prompt action.

On September 28, 1764, John Temple suspended James Cockle as Collector for the Port of Salem. In doing so, he earned the lasting gratitude of New England merchants, at whose expense Cockle had been profiting. Although he was a royal official, Temple moved among the merchants as one of them and was regarded as a stout-hearted Whig who held America's interests foremost. For the time being, moreover, he managed to please his superiors in England as well. John Temple alone of the customs officials in the colonies was accepted at both ends of the political spectrum—Whig and Tory—though he and Governor Bernard remained bitter enemies to the end. The feud between Temple and Bernard is an example of how the political tension exacerbated personal quarrels. It also illustrates the way in which men such as Temple used a popular cause to further their own ambitions.

The son of another Kennebeck proprietor also became enmeshed in the conflict with Bernard. Briggs Hallowell, one of several sons of old Benjamin Hallowell, settled on the Kennebec and developed the family holdings.[9] The family had maritime interests, and Briggs was no exception. He was a merchant and owned his own sloop, the *Oliver Cromwell*. His brothers, Benjamin, Jr., and Robert, also felt the call of the sea, but sought their fortunes in the customs service, as John Temple was doing. Not content with managing three thousand acres, Briggs also did odd jobs for the proprietors, especially during their quarrel with John Wentworth,[10] and took occasional voyages to England. Briggs Hallowell was a maverick Whig in a family of Tories. His radical stand inevitably led to estrangement from the other Hallowells. This alienation was repeated in other proprietary families.

During one of his visits to England in the early 1760s, Briggs Hallowell did some casual detective work that won him praise from the radicals in Massachusetts. While visiting the Plantation Office in London, he came across a set of depositions concerning customs violations that had been sent there by Governor Bernard. At least one of these documents was notarized by Thomas Hutchinson. Briggs returned to Boston in the summer of 1764 with copies of these depositions, which he knew could be explo-

sive if placed in the right hands. He later wrote, "I found out
when I was in London in 1763 and 1764 the plans which was
formed by Governor Bernard and that Wicked [prerogative]
party to Ruin this Country, with Great Pains and Cost I procured
the Coppys of their papers, and sent them to James Otis Esqr by
which means their design was found out."[11] Otis and Samuel
Adams printed the papers and distributed them, channeling the
wrath of the Boston mob against Thomas Hutchinson. On August
15, 1765, the windows of the Chief Justice's mansion in Garden
Court Street were smashed—only a hint of what was in store for
him later that month.[12] Briggs Hallowell's part in the affair was
not generally known, but it came to light many years later by his
own admission.[13] His role would cost him dearly after the outbreak of revolution. During the early 1760s, however, the publication of the depositions Briggs had found did much to inflame the
people of Boston against British navigation policies, and provided
additional motivation for the Stamp Act rioting.

After the Stamp Act became effective on November 1, 1765,
the King's representatives in the province were panic-stricken,
each hesitating to do business without the hated stamps, but unwilling to take the further drastic step of closing the port of Boston. Both actions had to be taken temporarily to uphold the authority of the King and Parliament, but neither Governor Bernard
nor Surveyor-General of the Customs John Temple would rule on
whether resumption of business was proper once it was clear that
the stamps could not be sold. Adroitly, they left the decision to
Deputy Collector William Sheaffe and Comptroller Benjamin
Hallowell, Jr., the brother of the radical, Briggs Hallowell.[14] In refusing to render a decision, John Temple retained the affections
of both Whigs and Tories; Sheaffe and Hallowell, finding themselves abandoned, bowed to radical pressure. Boston radicals lost
all fear of the wavering customs officials, and in time forced the
opening of the port of Boston and the courts, even before the odi-
ous Stamp Act was repealed by Parliament on March 18, 1766.
Shortly after the repeal, a series of search and entry cases en-
tangled the customs service and John Hancock in further strained
relations between Crown and Province.

The first search occurred on September 24, 1766, when Sheaffe
and Hallowell, armed with a writ of assistance, ransacked the
home of Captain Daniel Malcom of the North End, Boston, in a
hunt for imported liquor. Upon gaining entry, they failed to find

the liquor and were halted before a locked door, which Malcom refused to open claiming that the property inside the room belonged to another. The two harassed customs men then obtained a search warrant, but Malcom still refused them entrance, nor would he admit Sheriff Stephen Greenleaf, who had been summoned.[15] Greenleaf, left to carry the day alone, even tried to form a posse from the crowd that had gathered around the house. To a man, the group declined to join him. Malcom backed as he was by the citizens of Boston, escaped punishment. Daniel Malcom was a native of Maine and held three islands near the mouth of the Kennebec granted him by the proprietors.[16] He was also a close friend of John Hancock. Suddenly a hero and now personally involved in the customs war, Malcom was actively supported by Hancock and the other radicals in the continuing struggle. The fact that Malcom and Hancock were opposed by Benjamin Hallowell, Jr., is further evidence of disintegrating relationships within the Kennebeck Company. Political loyalties now overrode proprietary ties.

Because he was an outstanding Whig and probably the richest merchant in Boston, Hancock now became the special target of the customs officials in their persecution of smugglers. Customs men seized his ship *Lydia* on April 8, 1768, after they had been forcibly ejected by Hancock's crew upon boarding the vessel. Attorney General Jonathan Sewall declared the search illegal, however, on the grounds that the customs men lacked the authority to go belowdecks.[17] Undaunted, on June 10, 1768, customs officials boarded and seized the *Liberty,* another of Hancock's ships, one month after it had entered Boston Harbor loaded with a cargo of wine. They alleged that the wine had been illegally loaded at Madeira during the previous voyage. A search of this kind one month after a vessel had arrived in port was unprecedented. No wine was found, but unfortunately for Hancock, the customs men were presented with an unusual opportunity.[18] Hancock had neglected to obtain a loading permit for the oil and tar that had just been openly loaded by the crew. The Customs Board immediately accused him of having smuggled the cargo into the country, and confiscated both the ship and its contents on August 1, a move which caused a frightful riot at dockside. Hancock and five merchants, charged with unloading one hundred pipes of wine valued at £700 from the *Liberty* on the night when it had first entered port,[19] were prosecuted for a total of £54,000, an enormous sum for such a suit.[20] What proof existed for such an accusation is unclear, but there is evidence that Governor Bernard and the admiralty judges were rewarded for prosecuting the case.[21] In spite of extraordinary measures taken to gain a conviction, the Crown dropped its suits against Hancock *et al* on March 25, 1769, no doubt because of the alarming reaction stirred up in New England. The merchants of Boston, aware of common danger, rallied behind Hancock, and with them hundreds of sailors and dock workers. Customs officials and their families became so unnerved that they took refuge aboard the *Romney,* a man-of-war then lying in Boston Harbor.

John Temple alone of the customs men remained in perfect safety in the town. Fortunately for him, his role as a customs official had been diminished by the home office before the rioting broke out, and his authority had not been put to the test in the *Liberty* riot. A new Board of Customs Commissioners with headquarters in Boston had been created as a provision of the Townshend Acts of 1767. Benjamin Hallowell, Jr., continued as Comptroller, with his younger brother Robert as his deputy. But John Temple was demoted and his salary halved as punishment for his earlier sympathy with the radicals. Possibly disgruntled because of his demotion, Temple had been able to remain aloof during the *Liberty* proceedings and continue on amicable terms with Whig leaders.[22] He was an astute politician, and continued to walk the tightrope between Crown responsibilities and colonial approval.

Benjamin Hallowell, Jr., on the other hand, played a significant part in the proceedings. It was Hallowell who had located the informer whose report led to the initiation of the case and then had taken charge of the seizure arrangements. He also had gone to England to testify before the House of Lords with the aim of rallying British public opinion to the side of the colonial customs commissioners. Hallowell's involvement put an end to his popularity in America.

Governor Bernard was similarly feeling the pressure of unfavorable public reaction. He negatived eleven hostile councillors elected by the House, one of them James Bowdoin, and appealed for British troops in a desperate effort to regain political control after the repercussions of the *Liberty* affair. He succeeded only in increasing antagonism against himself. The *Liberty* suit, characterized as one of the most spectacular examples of customs racketeering during the colonial period; his mass negativing of councillors; his appeal for British troops; and protests by influential Whig merchants—all led to the recall of the governor. Boston celebrated wildly on the day of Bernard's departure, July 31, 1769.[23] He was replaced by the Lieutenant Governor, Thomas Hutchinson, who was perhaps even more generally hated.

Even lesser proprietary figures were caught up in the radical movement. Thomas Marshall, sometime clerk of the Kennebeck Company, achieved a measure of Whig acclaim for his attack upon John Mein, British-financed publisher of the *Boston Chronicle*. Mein had become a special irritation to the radicals through his series of exposures of violators of their Non-Importation Agreement, effective in Boston after January 1, 1769. He held up to ridicule the "Well Disposed" as hypocrites, who were secretly trading with England in spite of Non-Importation. His printing of recent cargo manifests had shown that "friends of government" were freely importing British goods and, more important, that such Whigs as James Bowdoin and his father-in-law, John Erving, Sr., were doing the same thing.[24] John Hancock, archpatriot, had often been listed in Mein's columns.[25] Such leading radicals were responsible for enforcement, and were highly embarrassed at being exposed as violators themselves. The publisher defied his political adversaries to shut him up, and there were many who were willing to take him at his word. It was Thomas Marshall, however, who achieved that dubious honor on October 28, 1769. Mein narrowly escaped death in the street when Marshall swung at him with a shovel, and fled into a nearby guardhouse, where he was finally arrested for firing a pistol into the mob that had assembled to take his life.[26] Marshall escaped prosecution, for he had friends and influence in Boston, and his action won overwhelming public approval.

Thomas Marshall is an example of how the exigencies of the moment changed the lives of proprietors. He had been influential in Company activities during the 1750s, but afterwards he declined in importance.[27] Marshall was a tailor who, by way of a series of fortunate marriages, managed to increase his estate and rise to the position of colonel in the Boston regiment. In the 1760s he was living next door to the Customs House in King Street, a key location for one with his radical affiliations. Long before 1769 he had made his political choice. Perhaps it was easier for him to make a decision of this kind than it was for such great proprietors as James Bowdoin and Dr. Gardiner. To some extent, however, all of them were victims of circumstances, and the final and undoubtedly agonizing decision of whether to stand by the King or to join the insurgents in an unpredictable course was a personal one.

Bowdoin's and Gardiner's experiences highlight the political conflicts in which proprietors were caught up. Both of these men had prospered in Massachusetts, Gardiner through his own efforts and Bowdoin through the development of an inherited estate. They had close family connections among both Whigs and Tories and, consequently, must have viewed the disorders of the late 1760s and early 1770s with increasing alarm as they reassessed their political positions. Contemporaries believed that Bowdoin's consistent ambition determined his shifting politics. As one of Boston's delegates to the House and later as a Council member, he supported the prerogative party and endorsed Governors William Shirley and Thomas Pownall, associations that helped the Kennebeck Company to thrive. By the 1760s, however, Governor Bernard and the prerogative party began to stand in his way, and he gradually swung to the radical camp. In contrast, Dr. Silvester Gardiner, his good friend and associate, had compelling interests that he could not back away from and, therefore, could not have changed his political allegiances if he had wanted to. Affiliations with New England Anglicanism, promotion of his own Episcopal church at Pownalborough,[28] business interests, his position as a large landowner, and especially his many lawsuits, all aligned him with the prerogative government and later ranged him on the side of the Loyalists. Not surprisingly, diverging interests—some connected with revolutionary developments and others not —forced a cleavage between the two friends.

James Bowdoin's schemes to advance himself and his family connections in public office helped drive the first wedges in his political allegiance to the mother country and in his friendship with Gardiner. By 1767, the political situation in Massachusetts was becoming very warm for Governor Bernard, and Bowdoin was contributing to this state of affairs. James Bowdoin's first major scheme was aimed at the removal of Bernard. He saw his opportunity in Captain George Scott, who had married one of his sisters-in-law. In 1763, Captain Scott secured the governorship of Grenada, a sugar island post yielding immense profits, and he had invested in sugar. A short time later, Bowdoin congratulated him upon his opportunity, observing that "Ten thousand pounds is no foolish thing. Count Brown says you made at least that sum before he came away. This with £3000 per annum, ordinary produce, will make your Situation not only preferable to Don Francisco's [Governor Bernard's] but any Don's on the continent."[29] The island governorship became even more preferable when this territory was extended to include nearby Dominica; this gave Scott more absolute power than any other continental colonial governor, since there was no representative assembly to check his ambitions. Bowdoin even admitted that "This is a Situation I would like mighty well, tho (I think) in a latitude more northerly."[30] He must have been referring to Massachusetts, and assumed that Scott would feel the same way. He later wrote Scott that "supposing you should offer an exchange with Governor B [Bernard]—perhaps he may not be averse to it, especially as you say, *you* would not change *yours* for one and a half of his in point of income."[31] Bowdoin began to fondly hope that Bernard would not object to exchanging his province for a colony so remunerative and uncontroversial as Dominica. He advised Scott, "you may depend I shall use every argument my cranium can furnish to induce him to accept it."[32]

Rumors that Grenada would soon become a free port encouraged Bowdoin's dream. Grenada would then be a prize much desired by any governor. The enactment of the Townshend duties, however, changed the picture, for according to plan, its revenues would guarantee the governor of Massachusetts a salary of £2000 Sterling per year. This was a princely income indeed, and it was not to be subject to the whims of an intransigent assembly. Bowdoin reluctantly warned Scott that "If this shall turn out a Fact, I fear there will be no chance for an exchange between you and Mr. Bernard."[33] In any event, time ran out when Scott died unexpectedly in the fall of 1767. James Bowdoin had to transfer his king-making activities to another candidate.

Bowdoin's new choice for political advancement became John Temple, who married his daughter Elizabeth in the Brattle Square Church on January 20, 1767. Before the wedding, Bowdoin had not been close to Temple, in spite of an early association in proprietary affairs with the younger man's father. He must have regarded John Temple as eminently suitable as a son-in-law since the marriage brought together two of the most prominent

families in New England. Moreover, Temple was in line for an
English baronetcy. The alliance brought an abrupt change in
Bowdoin's politics, evident especially in the Council, where Bowdoin's opposition to the governor became open. Thomas Hutchinson noticed this change and wrote that "Mr. Temple, the surveyor-general of the customs, having married Mr. Bowdoin's
daughter, and having differed with Governor Bernard, and connected himself with Mr. Otis, and others in the opposition, Mr.
Bowdoin, from that time, entered into the like connection."[34]
Temple had perhaps more to gain from the new relationship than
did Bowdoin. As Peter Oliver, an enemy of Bowdoin, phrased it,
Temple "had a rich Father in law to support him in Resentment."[35] Oliver added of Bowdoin that "He was a Man, who had
his full share of Pride, Wealth and Illnature, and had been
soothed, by that Son in Law, into Perswasion of his being appointed to a Government."[36] Both Hutchinson and Oliver, themselves friends of government and not without bias, saw the motivation for Bowdoin's change of colors as ambition, not patriotism.

By 1768, Governor Bernard was complaining about Bowdoin in
dispatches to the Earl of Hillsborough. Bernard's description of
Bowdoin as the "perpetual President, Chairman, Secretary and
Speaker of this new Council"[37] clearly showed Bowdoin's power.
To make matters worse, Bowdoin insolently published documents that he and his fellow councilmen had promised the governor to keep confidential. Bernard angrily confronted Bowdoin,
but received no satisfaction. The enraged governor later reported
that "Upon my observing that they had promised to keep no
Copies of the Papers they had used upon the last Occasion, he
[Bowdoin] answered that the Publication was not from Copies
but the Originals."[38] This episode confirms the deviousness in
Bowdoin's character that Peter Oliver emphasized.

Bowdoin organized the Council so that it operated in close cooperation with an even more radical House—not a difficult task,
for the Council then included his brother-in-law, James Pitts, and
his father-in-law, John Erving, Sr. He also rendered considerable
service to the Whig cause as a propagandist. Using skills he had
developed in writing tracts for the Kennebeck Company, he deliberately composed an inaccurate and highly inflammatory account of the Boston Massacre. The *Short Narrative*, as it is titled,
is an edited compilation of ninety-six depositions describing the
events of that tragedy. The work was printed and circulated in

advance of the trials of Captain Preston and his soldiers, making an unbiased hearing impossible.[39] During 1768-1769, Bowdoin's contributions to the *Journal of the Times,* a radical propaganda publication, alerted the American colonies to the latest political incidents occurring in Boston. The printing of his *Additional Observations on a Short Narrative* helped to heighten tensions as the Revolution approached.[40] When it came, Bowdoin was securely entrenched at the top level of Massachusetts radical leadership, and in a position to achieve the power to which he had always aspired.

Meanwhile his associate, Dr. Gardiner, was rapidly sinking within Tory ranks. Though he was a devout vestryman of Boston's Anglican King's Chapel and, therefore, of the same religion as Governor Bernard and many other supporters of the Crown, Gardiner was often incompatible with them in business and personal matters. Disliked and feared by many, he had the reputation of being an excellent surgeon but a harsh and unsympathetic businessman. Gardiner had no love for Bernard, and a notation in a recipe book compiled by the first Mrs. Gardiner in the 1760s suggests that she supported her husband. Among her methods for preparing fish, she included a recipe "To pickle Salmon the Newcastle Way, according to a Receipt procured from England, as it is said by the infamous Sir Francis Bernard."[41] But Dr. Gardiner had many Tory connections. When the first Mrs. Gardiner died in 1771, the next year he selected as her successor Mrs. Abigail Eppes of Salem, the mother of grown children and the widow of William Eppes. It could not have helped Gardiner with the radicals that his second wife was the sister of Benjamin Pickman, a prominent Salem merchant and a Loyalist.[42] Neither could it have helped that a daughter of his "young wife" had married Richard Routh, Collector of Customs at Salem, and a Tory.[43] Nor were the doctor's misfortunes limited to this family involvement.

Gardiner and his sons-in-law, Robert Hallowell and Philip Dumaresq, probably sealed their political fates in the province when they ill-advisedly signed the famous *Address to Thomas Hutchinson* upon his departure for England in 1774. Robert Hallowell, in addition, had succeeded his brother Benjamin as Comptroller of the Customs in Boston. By 1774, his very life was endangered by the radicals. Philip Dumaresq also earned the resentment of the Whigs when he served as a juror during the first Boston Massacre trial and helped free Captain Preston.[44] By his own actions and those of his relatives, Dr. Gardiner reached a position where there was no turning back; he was wholly committed to the Loyalist position.[45]

Dr. Gardiner and his family remained within British lines during the siege of Boston, for by that time they had no· other choice. During these months, Abigail Gardiner displayed her political feelings openly. As Attorney John Gardiner, the eldest of the doctor's sons, and a Whig, later commented: "the whole Conduct of your late Wife, during the Seige, is mentioned even by your Friends, with uncommon Asperity."[46] Dr. Gardiner himself was guilty of further political indiscretions. His son John later remarked that "Your Plaudits to the Soldiers, when they had returned from the Islands in this [Boston] Harbour, and had boasted of the Number of Rebells (as they called them) which they killed, are mentioned here much to your whole Disadvantage."[47] Dr. Gardiner also tended British wounded after the Battle of Bunker Hill and, with his sons-in-law, signed the *Address to General Gage* upon Gage's being relieved by Lord Howe in 1775. It is not surprising that Gardiner, Hallowell, and Dumaresq were deemed arch-enemies of the radical cause.

The three were proscribed and banished by the Massachusetts General Court in 1778, but they had already fled to Halifax with the British Army after the evacuation of Boston in March, 1776. Dr. Gardiner managed to leave with £500 Sterling, which he had set by for just such an emergency.[48] The cold weather and the high cost of living in Halifax did not suit the doctor, so he soon embarked with the British Army for New York City. By 1778, he was ready to bid goodbye to America, and sailed for England. At Poole, a coastal town in Dorsetshire, he sat out the war, fretting about his inadequate pension and the condition of his Kennebec River estates.

Meanwhile, his old friend, James Bowdoin, was elected to the first Continental Congress and, years later, would become governor of Massachusetts, a position he had long coveted. Thus, irreversible stands taken by Dr. Gardiner, Company moderator, and James Bowdoin, treasurer, well before the Revolution began, determined their fate in the Bay Colony as well as in the Kennebeck Company. Other important members of the propriety had taken similar steps, with equally devastating or rewarding results.

From the frigid evening of the Boston Massacre onward, proprietors and their relations were more than just participants in the turbulent events of the times—indeed, they were leaders in the crisis. Thomas Marshall and Dr. John Jeffries, like James Bowdoin, were key figures in the Boston Massacre trials. John Temple appears to have stolen some highly controversial letters. James Bowdoin, John Hancock, and Lendall Pitts were principals in the events of the Boston Tea Party, a milestone in the revolutionary timetable. The fortunes of war shattered the Kennebeck Company more effectively than intracompany bickering of the 1760s had ever been able to do.

Weeks of unrest and mob action were punctuated by the Boston Massacre on the evening of March 5, 1770, when Captain Thomas Preston and his British regulars, responding to the taunts and threats of the mob, opened fire in front of the imposing Customs House.[49] Thomas Marshall and Dr. John Jeffries, son of David Jeffries, the proprietor, were among those attracted to the scene by the commotion. Marshall, who watched the shootings from his front steps, served as a witness for the prosecutors during the separate trials of Preston and his men. Marshall testified that he had observed groups of British soldiers yelling "Fire!" and that there had been time between the discharge of the first and last volleys for Preston to have halted his men. Philip Dumaresq, a pro-British juryman and Dr. Gardiner's son-in-law, expressed the conviction before the trial began that Preston was innocent, and the acquittal was never in doubt. The extreme Whigs were thwarted in this attempt to gain a conviction because John Adams, counsel for the defense as well as engaged in a cover-up of radical participation in the event, skillfully "packed" the jury to avoid an embarrassing verdict.[50] Even in the face of Marshall's damning evidence, Adams obtained Preston's release.

Nor was the acquittal of Preston's men ever in question. Dr. John Jeffries attended Patrick Carr, a participant in the rioting who had been mortally wounded but lingered on for nine days after the shooting. According to Jeffries, Carr exonerated the British, stating that they had fired in self-defense. The court accepted the hearsay evidence because it was believed to be the testimony of a dying man.[51] All but one of the troopers were released; the one held pleaded "benefit of clergy," and was set free after being branded on the thumb. The British Army prudently hustled all of the men out of the country. Extreme Whig leaders, like Samuel

Adams, were less than satisfied by the verdicts, which had been largely political.

A deceptive calm followed the trial and continued until 1773, when the affair of the "Stolen Letters" was revealed in England and in the American colonies. Thomas Hutchinson and others in the colonies had written confidential dispatches to various British officials in the conduct of their duties. These had become the property of Thomas Whately, British official and friend of John Temple. As nearly as can be determined, Temple, who had been holding a minor customs post in England since 1769, sometime after Whately's death on May 26, 1772, had borrowed the papers from William Whately, his brother's executor. Temple is believed to have passed the papers on to Benjamin Franklin, agent for Massachusetts and Postmaster General for the American colonies, though this has not been proved. In any event, the correspondence finally ended in the hands of Thomas Cushing, Speaker of the Massachusetts House and kin of Pownalborough's William and Charles Cushing. Although the letters revealed little that was new or inflammatory, the Boston radicals wrung the last possible measure of propaganda from them.[52] John Hancock dramatically announced the receipt of the letters to the House, where the decision was made to publish them.[53] Governor Hutchinson's popularity plunged to a new low, and he became a distinct liability to the British government.

The correspondence severely damaged the political careers of John Temple and Benjamin Franklin.[54] Temple's seeming duplicity ruined his future in the customs service, and William Whately challenged him to a duel. The encounter took place in Hyde Park on December 11, 1773, an affair that might have been tragicomic if Whately had not been badly wounded.[55] At this juncture, Franklin came forward and generously took the blame, announcing in a letter to the London *Public Advertiser* that "the letters were never in the possession of Mr. Whately, after his brother's death; and that he [Franklin] alone was the person who obtained, and transmitted them to his constituents."[56] At the same time, Franklin curiously condemned those who had made the letters public. His disclosure saved neither Temple nor himself; after a brief hearing, the Privy Council dismissed them both.

In a letter written to his father-in-law in America shortly afterwards, Temple professed to be ignorant of the cause of his re-

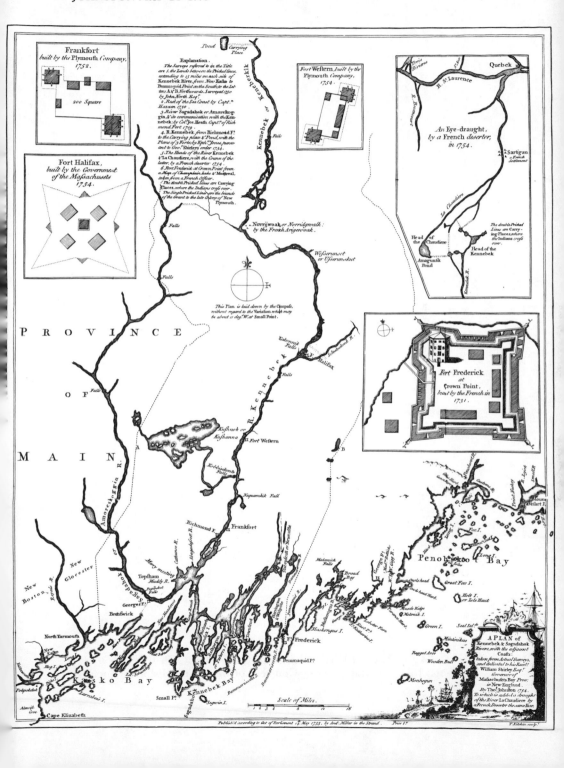

moval. He complained that "with all the interest I can make, I cannot gain information what my fault is . . . .Everyone else, as well as myself, are at a loss to conjecture what I am dismissed for, unless it be that I am tho't a friend to the American claims."[57] He also commented that "I have been advised to lay still and say not a word."[58] It is significant that Temple did not protest his innocence, only that he did not know the cause of dismissal.

By 1779, John Temple was eager to return to Boston, if only for a brief visit. He was still regarded with suspicion by Whitehall, and it was uncomfortable to be stationed in British-held New York City. He needed a pass to go through enemy lines and sought help from his old friends, even if it meant taking the credit for the earlier theft. Back in Massachusetts, influential relations and intimates, namely James Bowdoin, Samuel Adams, Thomas Cushing, the Reverend Charles Chauncey, and the Reverend Samuel Cooper, were only too happy to write a testimonial for him and eager to share the credit for the exploit. These radical leaders stated that Temple had indeed stolen the now almost legendary letters and that they themselves had been a part of the plot. They concluded that John Temple had "a Claim in Reason and equity to a compensation for his great Sufferings in the zealous service of [his native country] and [should] be regarded by it with patriotic gratitude and respect."[59] Cushing, Adams, and the others were in a position to know the truth, and Temple did not deny their assertion. His longstanding opposition to Governor Bernard and his influence on the politics of his father-in-law, James Bowdoin, gives the radical disclosure credence.

The next pre-Revolutionary crisis involving proprietors was triggered by Parliament's passage of the East India Tea Act in 1773. The tax provision caused a disturbance in Boston equal to the panic of the Stamp Act of 1765. As tea ships began to reach the port of Boston in November, Governor Hutchinson called upon his Council for advice: What should be done to protect the newly arrived tea from mob action, and how might he regain his flagging control of the provincial government? As it had done so often in the past, the Council refused aid in a reply drafted by James Bowdoin. Without the support of some branch of his government, Hutchinson could do nothing. The situation worsened. As a direct result of town meeting action on December 16, 1773, "Indians" destroyed the tea on Boston Harbor. John Hancock and his associates were almost certainly present at the Tea Party.[60]

Members of the "Loyal Nine" were also there. Lendall Pitts was said to have been in command.[61] British authorities raised no hand against the participants in the Tea Party, but the radicals feared that retaliation was sure to follow.

Governor Hutchinson felt confident that paying for the tea would soften the blow. The town of Boston refused to make compensation, even though George Erving personally volunteered to pay £2000, a quarter of the cost.[62] Parliament then countered with the Boston Port Act, accompanied by other well-known restrictive acts which punished not only Boston but the whole province. It also brought military rule to Massachusetts when Thomas Hutchinson was replaced by General Thomas Gage. The General brought with him a list of new Mandamus Councillors as replacements for members who formerly had been chosen by the House. Among those listed were Thomas Flucker, John Erving, Jr., and George Erving, all brothers-in-law of James Bowdoin, and William Vassall.[63] These mandamus councillors immediately became scapegoats, and were subjected to abuse even while British troops were stationed in Boston.

Councillor Vassall, like many others, refused to serve, probably because he anticipated what was in store for him. Even in good times he had refused public office, and in 1774 officeholding was particularly hazardous. Ironically enough, it was his cousin, Florentius Vassall of London, who had secured the post for him. Writing to William on May 31, 1774, "Cousin Flory" exulted in the appointment he had wangled, certain that William would "be an honour to the family to be amongst the first of the Councillors appointed by the King for that Province of Massachusetts."[64] William Vassall, Jr., then in England, echoed his uncle's approval, for he felt "satisfy'd that your Advice as a Councillor will be of great Service to the Province.[65] Also, he added, the post will "be the Means of your Name being handed down to Posterity, with that Honour as a publick Officer, which it so well deserves as a private Gentleman."[66] William Vassall's relations were woefully out of touch with public sentiment in America, and he appears to have known it. Although he refused the "honour," he could not avoid becoming a marked man. Unwillingly, he was pushed into the Tory camp.

By now, sides had been drawn up and events began to move rapidly toward open warfare. Avowed Loyalists and even British sympathizers no longer dared live in the country districts without the benefit of military support. As General Gage reported to Lord Dartmouth, "People are daily resorting to this town [Boston] for protection for there is no security for any person deemed a friend to Government in any part of the Country, even places always esteemed well affected, have caught the infection."[67] Dr. Gardiner, fortunately in Boston at that time, had to forego his annual visit to his properties on the Kennebec. The Kennebeck Company's activities on the river were deeply affected by the unrest.

The political upheaval heightened tensions among Kennebeck proprietors, already badly split by religious disputes, disagreements over the prosecution of court cases, and private quarrels. Shareholders found it increasingly difficult to reach a consensus. Boston was becoming more and more isolated from the rest of the province, so it was almost impossible for those living outside the town to put in an appearance at Company meetings. Even some living within the metropolis did not choose to attend. Henry Allyne, Company clerk and a Whig, dutifully appeared for every scheduled meeting and, for most of them, recorded the names of the few members present and regretfully noted adjournment due to lack of a quorum.

John Hancock did not favor the Company with his presence after June 9, 1773. He may have been too busy with more important affairs, or he may have objected to meeting with some of the Tory proprietors, especially Dr. Gardiner. Other leaders of the Company, however, in an effort to transact business, continued to attend meetings until after the outbreak of the Revolution in April, 1775.[68] James Bowdoin, Silvester Gardiner, James Pitts, William Vassall, and William Tailer generally attended. Gardiner and Bowdoin, still serving respectively as moderator and treasurer, were the most faithful of all. They continued to cooperate in transacting proprietary business, in spite of political differences, until well after the battle of Lexington-Concord. The last regular meeting of the propriety, and an important one, was planned for March 22, 1775.[69] Here the proprietors divided among themselves 72,000 acres that they had previously voted to make available for purchase by members.[70] The propriety did not assemble again until a new warrant was obtained, and that did not take place until after the British evacuation of Boston.[71] At this meeting, on June 13, 1776, vacant seats around the tavern table marked the places of Tory proprietors, having fled to safer regions. In these early days of the American Revolution, the proprietors were becoming increasingly aware that their dominance of the Kennebec Valley was fast eroding.

In addition to dividing Company members into Whigs and Tories, the revolutionary agitation weakened the Company's control over its own settlements along the Kennebec. As, one by one, their towns were incorporated, the people took control by way of town meetings. Many settlers previously granted land by the Company were indebted to it, and were finding the weight of its mortgages crushing. They, and also settlers whom the proprietors had alienated, now had the opportunity to strike back. They decided on church rates, the building of roads and other improvements, and support for schools. They voted regular taxes, based on land ownership that were almost confiscatory for the largest landowners, most of them absentee Company proprietors. The local committees of safety encouraged a new spirit of independence which denied a return to proprietary control. The hydra of patriotism in the Kennebec Valley thus manifested two heads: opposition to British rule and antagonism to proprietary control.

Settlers could best demonstrate their opposition to British rule by terrorizing Tories living in the area. The Reverend Jacob Bailey, Samuel Goodwin, the Callahan family, and other prominent Tories were vilified, physically attacked, and sometimes jailed. Most of them were unfortunate enough to be Anglicans as well as Tories, and were therefore persecuted for both religious and political reasons. Chief among the sufferers was William Gardiner, the son of Dr. Gardiner. Left behind to guard the family estates, William endured trial and imprisonment and barely escaped transportation.[72] Twenty-two persons in Lincoln County alone applied to the British claims commission for losses suffered during the Revolution; fifteen claimed losses of £1000 or less.[73]

The American Revolution offered settlers an opportunity to even old scores against the Tory proprietors and avenge themselves against the propriety in general. The evolution of the new towns as self-governing entities rendered the Company impotent in this battle. As taxes sky-rocketed, great and small proprietors debated whether to sell their lands cheaply or to accept the mounting assessments and hope for a final profit when lands appreciated. Although James Bowdoin was distraught about his tax rates, he was careful to meet all of his obligations. In 1778, he commissioned Charles Cushing of Pownalborough to attend to "the unreasonable taxes lately imposed on Wastelands" because "the unjust advantages taken in the sale of these lands makes it needful to have a friend in the place where they lie."[74] Cushing also acted for John Temple and ex-Governor Pownall. His prompt attention saved Bowdoin, Temple, and Pownall lands from confiscation. Nevertheless, John Temple, an expatriate at the time, found meeting the rates more than he could bear. In 1780, Robert Hallowell informed Silvester Gardiner, his father-in-law, that "mr. [John] Temple has sold all his property in America—the taxes on his unimproved Kennebeck lands last year was £300—and he supposes that in a year or two there will not be One Acre left for the proprietors."[75] Nor was damage suffered by the proprietors limited to excessive taxes. Lumber pirates—most of the adult male population could be numbered among them—were free to ravage the valuable woodlands. "Strip and waste" was everywhere. The proprietors who held on to their lands were powerless to prevent great losses. Townspeople also suffered, however. In exploiting the great white pine they neglected to grow crops and, instead, purchased high-priced provisions in Boston. When winter came and ice blocked the river, many settlers were in want, and some starved. Because of the townspeople's contentious spirit, proprietors steered clear of the Kennebec—even John Hancock and James Bowdoin, who had a following at Pownalborough. Misery and famine stalked the river.

The proprietors were so caught up in the revolutionary conflict that they had little time to concern themselves with their Kennebeck Company investment. Undoubtedly they hoped that once the war was over, they could regain their position of dominance in the valley. But this they never did. The American Revolution set into motion forces that led to a strengthening of local control, which would have come about in any case. When the scattered proprietors assembled in 1783, they could do little but preside over the dissolution of their shattered empire.

NOTES

CHAPTER XII

1 See Chapters VIII and IX.

2 John J. Waters, Jr., *The Otis Family in Provincial and Revolutionary Massachusetts* (Chapel Hill, 1968), 118-120; Peter Oliver, *Origins and Progress of the American Rebellion,* eds. Douglas Adair and John Schutz (Stanford, Cal., 1961), 27-28; Zobel, *Boston Massacre,* 7-10; Hutchinson, *History,* III, 62-64.

3 Robert E. Brown, *Middle-Class Democracy and the Revolution in Massachusetts, 1691-1780* (New York, 1969), 178.

4 With Gen. John Winslow, Gamaliel Bradford, William Tailer, his brother-in-law, James Warren, and others, Otis received the Company grant of Winslow (site of old Fort Halifax) in 1766. By 1773, the terms of the grant had been fulfilled, and the town proprietors received full possession.

5 John Temple to Thomas Whately, Sept. 10, 1764, *Bowdoin and Temple Papers, Massachusetts Historical Society Collections,* 6th Series, IX, 27.

6 John Temple to Thomas Whately, Oct. 3, 1764, *ibid.,* 29.

7 See Oliver Dickerson, *The Navigation Acts and the American Revolution* (New York, 1951), 63-103, 276-278, for arguments that smuggling was minimal under the Navigation Acts and the later restrictive acts enacted by Parliament after 1763.

8 John Temple to Thomas Whately, Oct. 3, 1764, *Bowdoin and Temple Papers, Massachusetts Historical Society Collections,* 6th Series, IX, 29.

9 Gardiner, *Earl Recollections,* 7.

10 See Chapter X.

11 Petition of Briggs Hallowell to the Massachusetts General Court, Apr. 25, 1779, *Documentary History of the State of Maine,* 2nd Series, XVII, 366.

12 Zobel, *Boston Massacre,* 32. See Chapter IX for details of the August 26 destruction of Hutchinson's home.

13 Petition of Briggs Hallowell, 367. Overtaken by financial reverses shortly before the Revolution, Hallowell, like others

on the Kennebec, had been forced to mortgage his lands to
Dr. Gardiner. During the siege of Boston, 1775-1776, while
the British Army occupied the town, Gardiner obtained a
judgment against Hallowell, and had him jailed. After the
evacuation, Hallowell petitioned the radical General Court for
redress, asserting that Gardiner had defrauded him of his
property. He claimed that he had been punished by Gardiner
and his brother (either Benjamin, Jr., or Robert) for his patriotic actions of 1764. The General Court awarded him the
lands.

14 Morgan, *Stamp Act Crisis,* 176-182. In this crisis, Temple
by-passed the issue by referring his customs men to the Attorney General for a ruling; he in turn sent them back to
Temple, who again refused responsibility. By his refusal to
take a stand, Temple managed to keep the favor of Bostonians at the expense of enforcing the law.

15 Zobel, *Boston Massacre,* 51-54. Sheriff Greenleaf was the
father-in-law of John Apthorp, a son of Charles Apthorp.

16 Grant to Captain Daniel Malcom of Boston, Feb. 1, 1758,
K.P.P., Records, II, 139-140.

17 Dickerson, *The Navigation Acts and the American Revolution,* 235.

18 *Ibid.,* 237-238.

19 *Ibid.,* 242.

20 At this time, the income of a wealthy man in the colonies was
only about £500 per year.

21 Dickerson, *The Navigation Acts and the American Revolution,* 246-248. Dickerson offers a most convincing case for
Crown-sanctioned customs racketeering aimed at ruining
Hancock as an example to other radicals. In Boston, Gov.
Bernard and the Robinson-Hulton-Paxton faction of the Customs House are depicted as advancing the scheme, which
also promised substantial personal reward.

22 Warden, *Boston, 1689-1775,* 180; Morgan, *Stamp Act Crisis,* 23.

23 Warden, *Boston,* 225.

24 *The Boston Chronicle* (Boston), Jan. 13 and Feb. 5, 1770.

25 *Ibid.*

26 Zobel, *Boston Massacre,* 157.

27 Marshall initially managed the Company shares of several proprietors who later became active themselves. See Chapter III. Although he had not worked closely with the proprietors for 20 years, "in full Consideration for all his services done for this Propriety," he received in 1774 a grant of 400 acres at Winthrop. Grant to Thomas Marshall, May 11, 1774, K.P.P., Records, III, 101.

28 See Chapter XI for Gardiner's strategy in obtaining the glebe lands at Pownalborough for Jacob Bailey's church.

29 James Bowdoin to George Scott, Mar. 1, 1763, James Bowdoin Letter Book (1759-1797), 43, M.H.S.

30 *Ibid.*

31 James Bowdoin to George Scott, May 20, 1765, Bowdoin Letter Book, 116-117.

32 James Bowdoin to George Scott, May 8, 1767, Bowdoin Letter Book, 176.

33 James Bowdoin to George Scott, July 10, 1767, Bowdoin Letter Book, 179.

34 Hutchinson, *History,* III, 211. Hutchinson also observed that after 1765 Bowdoin influenced the Council to concur with the more radical actions of the House.

35 Oliver, *Origins and Progress,* 66.

36 *Ibid.,* 70.

37 Francis Bernard to Earl of Hillsborough, Oct. 14, 1768. Bernard Papers, VII, 78, Sparks Manuscripts, Houghton Library, Harvard.

38 *Ibid.,* 78-80. Bowdoin misquoted Bernard for his own purposes on more than one occasion. See Bernard to Hillsborough, Nov. 30, 1768, Bernard Papers, VII, 109-110, Sparks Manuscripts, Houghton Library, Harvard.

39 Zobel, *Boston Massacre,* 213; Francis G. Walett, "James Bowdoin, Patriot Propagandist," *New England Quarterly,* XXIII (1950), 329.

40 Walett, "James Bowdoin, Patriot Propagandist," 332-336.

41 *Mrs. Gardiner's Receipts from 1763* (Hallowell, Me., 1938), 332-336.

42 Pickman fled Salem and spent the Revolutionary War years engaged in profitable trade in England. Because he fared so well, he was denied a pension by the British government.

43 George F. Dow, *The Diary and Letters of Benjamin Pickman (1740-1819) of Salem, Massachusetts* (Newport, R.I., 1928), 19. Richard Routh eventually became Collector of Customs and finally Chief Justice of Nova Scotia.

44 Zobel, *Boston Massacre*, 245-246.

45 Apart from Dr. Gardiner's son, John, the family was entirely Loyalist in its sympathies. Gardiner's daughter, Anne, had married John Brown, the second son of the Earl of Altamont, an Irish peer. Anne cherished hopes that her husband would inherit the title from his sickly older brother, but this never occurred. Instead, the brother eventually became the Marquis of Sligo. Nevertheless, Anne must have spent many pleasant hours at the palatial family seat, Westport House, in County Mayo. Her son John married a daughter of Lord Howe.

46 Foote, *Annals of King's Chapel*, II, 360.

47 *Ibid.*

48 E. Alfred Jones, *The Loyalist of Massachusetts, Their Memorials, Petitions, and Claims* (London, 1930), 146. According to Gardiner's memorial to the British government, dated Oct. 10, 1783, he sold his furniture in New York and his silver in London. He tried in vain to sell medicines to the British Army at New York, and accused Gen. Washington of pilfering the medical supplies he had left behind him in Boston. While in England, he received a government pension of £100 per year.

49 The Customs House was leased from Grizzel Apthorp, the widow of Charles Apthorp, and had formerly been occupied as a residence by the family.

50 Zobel, *Boston Massacre*, 243-246.

51 *Ibid.*, 285-286.

52 Warden, *Boston*, 270. Warden shows that in his unpublished correspondence Hutchinson displayed a contempt for the people, and a predilection for the use of force against them if it proved necessary. See Hutchinson Correspondence, M.A.

53 Hutchinson, *History*, III, 284.

54 Franklin was removed from his position of Postmaster General in the American colonies.

55 Cecil B. Curry, *Road to Revolution: Benjamin Franklin in England, 1765-1775* (Garden City, N.Y., 1968), 324. Curry's work, although chiefly concerned with Franklin's role as a large-scale colonial land speculator, is useful regarding aspects of his London years as colonial agent.

56 Hutchinson, *History*, III, 298.

57 John Temple to James Bowdoin, Mar. 15, 1774, *Massachusetts Historical Society Collections*, 6th Series, *Bowdoin and Temple Papers*, IX, 357-358.

58 *Ibid*.

59 "Certificate of James Bowdoin and Others," May 21, 1779, *Massachusetts Historical Society Collections*, 6th Series, *Bowdoin and Temple Papers*, IX, 434-435.

60 Esther Forbes, *Paul Revere and the World He Lived In* (Boston, 1942), 198.

61 Benjamin W. Labaree, *The Boston Tea Party* (New York, 1964), 143. Lendall Pitts was the son of James Pitts, who died in 1776. Lendall's brother John served on Boston's Committee of Correspondence.

62 *Ibid*., 229. George Erving, a Tory, was the brother-in-law of James Bowdoin. His father, John Erving, Sr., was a moderate Whig.

63 William H. Whitmore, *The Massachusetts Civil List for the Colonial and Provincial Periods, 1630-1774* (Albany, 1870), 64.

64 Florentius Vassall to William Vassall, May 31, 1774, Vassall Papers, Houghton Library, Harvard.

65 William Vassall, Jr., to William Vassall, July 13, 1774, Vassall Papers, Houghton Library, Harvard.

66 *Ibid*.

67 Thomas Gage to Lord Dartmouth, Sept. 20, 1774, Sparks Manuscripts, "British Papers Relating to the American Revolution," 43, I, 195-196, Houghton Library, Harvard.

68 On Apr. 26, 1775, Dr. Gardiner wrote to Jonathan Pinkham
of Mount Vernon, Me., to confirm the grant of a tract of land
to Pinkham and his associates. In typical Gardiner fashion,
the doctor warned Pinkham "not to admit any drunken people" to the land and wished him good success. This is the
last pre-revolutionary transaction of which any record remains in Company papers. Silvester Gardiner to Jonathan
Pinkham, Apr. 26, 1775, K.P.P., Loose Papers (Aug. 1769-
July 1793).

69 Proprietary meeting, Mar. 22, 1775, K.P.P., Records, III,
119. Unsuccessful attempts were made to form quorums on
Apr. 12, Apr. 26, and July 12, 1775.

70 See Chapter V for details on these land sales.

71 Eighth Warrant, May 25, 1776, K.P.P., Records, III, 122-124.

72 William Gardiner to Silvester Gardiner, Dec. 29, 1777, Silvester Gardiner Papers, Me. H.S.

73 Wallace Brown, *The King's Friends: The Composition and
Motives of the American Loyalist Claimants* (Providence,
R.I., 1966), 24. Lincoln County, a hotbed of Loyalist sympa-
thies, was surprisingly enough one of the poorest counties in
Mass.

74 James Bowdoin to Charles Cushing, Dec. 16, 1778, Bowdoin
Collection—Special Collections, Bowdoin College Library,
Brunswick, Me. The heavy town tax rates were to some de-
gree prompted by the equally oppressive state taxes which
were levied on the towns. In 1777, for example, the town of
Augusta (Fort Western) was assessed a state tax of £149.6.11,
a sizable amount for a struggling town on the frontier. North,
History of Augusta, 139.

75 Robert Hallowell to Silvester Gardiner, Aug. 24, 1780, Silvester Gardiner Papers, Me. H.S. Both Hallowell and Gardiner were then in exile, but had sources of information in
America. It is not known whether Temple did in fact sell all
of his Kennebeck lands at this time.

XIII

Dissolution

The erosion of proprietary power, which became apparent in the late 1760s and accelerated during the American Revolution, persisted after the war. During the Revolution, the Kennebeck Company continued to operate under the leadership of its Whig proprietors. The Company attempted to assert control over the settlers who were rapidly filling its lands, and engaged in the customary litigation—with the usual lack of success in the courts. It did win one notable victory in obtaining its claims to the northern boundary. In the long run, however, it was a losing struggle. The growth of local political power and the increased demand of Maine residents for separation from Massachusetts created dilemmas for the Company that could be solved only by dissolution.

The Whig proprietors attempted to hold the line during the war years. Although the Gardiners, Hallowells, Vassalls, and Apthorps had defected to the enemy,[1] seriously reducing Company effectiveness, the remnant convened for a meeting under the eighth Company warrant on June 13, 1776, and proceeded as under previous warrants. There were the usual articles: to choose a moderator, treasurer, clerk, and other officials; to continue surveys; to plan new land divisions; to sell or lease property; and to choose a new Standing Committee.[2] Proprietary elections held on June 20, 1776, mirrored the political changes that had occurred in the province. James Bowdoin continued as treasurer and member of the Committee, as was probably expected, and he now became moderator as well.[3] Bowdoin, John Hancock, John Pitts, David Jeffries, and James Thwing—Whigs all—were elected to the Standing Committee.[4] New representatives from among the lesser proprietors took office, but they played no more important a part in Company affairs than had their forebears. Bowdoins and Pittses continued to dominate.

The proprietors were called together twenty-five times during the Revolution. Fourteen of these meetings were adjourned for lack of a quorum. At the eleven functioning meetings—three in 1777, one in 1779, one in 1780, three in 1781, and three in 1782[5]—no important business was transacted. The Standing Committee, empowered to carry on Company operations, must have formulated whatever decisions were made in the interim.[6] Even as late as 1783, proprietors seldom assembled. It made little difference, for by this time prospective settlers were taking the lead and requesting the granting of townships and individual tracts.[7] The proprietors gladly honored the requests, probably reasoning that settlers occupying the land would save it from squatters and lumbermen.

As the threat of war receded from northern Maine, settlers—many of them Revolutionary War veterans—began to pour into the Kennebec region.[8] They sought out the land they wanted, and occupied it. Later, many dickered with the Company for titles. On March 13, 1777, following a lull of several years in the granting of lands, the proprietors awarded Samuel and John Ball two hundred acres within the settlement of Balls-Town (Whitefield) which they were creating.[9] They also made extensive grants in Winthrop and Vassalborough that year. By 1781, the proprietors were granting land in the townships of Norridgewock and Canaan. Here, twenty settlers received two hundred acres each on the same day.[10] Titles to all of these lands were obtained according to the customary terms: clearing five acres within three years, building a dwelling house with dimensions at least eighteen by twenty feet, and living on the land for seven years. Company records indicate that the settlers in each case were already living in the townships where the land was being granted. Settlers who did not negotiate with the Company for lands were the source of endless litigation during the post-Revolutionary years. Fortunately for the proprietors, some prospective landholders sought grants through the established channels.

Typical of settlers who negotiated for lands before attempting development were "Joseph Nye of Sandwich, Esq., and Joseph Dimmuck of Falmouth, Esqr.," who became tenants in common of a tract ". . . on [the] West Side of Kennebeck River above Fort Halifax." Their bargaining with the Company led to a major real estate transaction involving sixty lots, size unspecified, but probably at least one hundred acres, "at £30 lawful Silver money each." The terms were £300 down, the rest to be paid later.[11] The Company also granted new lands "above Norridgewalk, on the Easterly side of Kennebeck River," and "above Norridgewalk, on the Westerly side of Kennebeck."[12] This unprecedented expansion on the river seems remarkable considering the hardships and disorders of the Revolutionary period, and it must have been an incentive to the proprietors to exert themselves on their own behalf.

Among the proprietors, this was a period of making up deficiencies and adjusting inequities. In 1782 James Bowdoin received Back Lot No. 20, a total of 4800 acres, "to make good a deficiency" in lands he had purchased from the Company for £160 on December 1, 1774. At the same time, the Company granted him 2524 acres "adjoining to the other" to make up a further deficiency.[13] The Company had ignored Captain Robert Temple's heirs after his death in 1754. John Temple, British placeman though he was, was now in high favor in Massachusetts and had James Bowdoin's backing in the propriety. On April 23, 1783, the heirs of "Paschal Nelson of London, dec., and Robert Temple, Sen., Esq., and his wife Mehitable, heirs of Sir Thomas Temple, dec.," received lands in different townships totaling 14,600 acres.[14] Other neglected proprietors received similar grants. Those who did not receive their just due realized that land accession came as a reward for Company service and thus became more highly motivated to pursue further Company development.[15]

With the signing of the Treaty of Paris in 1783, the proprietors, many of whom had been in exile, began to assemble in Massachusetts, reconstituting the Company to a remarkable degree. Some Tory shareholders did not return. Dr. Gardiner was unable to do so, and proprietary meetings lacked the bombast and enthusiasm he had once supplied. William Vassall was too prudent to return, and in 1793 he sued the Commonwealth of Massachusetts for his confiscated estate but at that time failed to get possession. Governor John Hancock blocked his claims at a special session of the legislature called to consider the case.[16] John Temple had no such difficulties, but he preferred to have his father-in-law manage his proprietary interests. Although he lived in America, he was much too busy to attend Company meetings. In 1780, he had succeeded to his baronetcy and now was serving as British consul at New York, where he remained until his death in 1798. During the postwar years, he continued to enjoy the best of two worlds—esteemed in England and always welcomed in Boston by his Whig friends and Bowdoin connections. Samuel Goodwin and Jonathan Reed, two of the smaller shareholders, remained in retirement at Pownalborough and also looked to Bowdoin for direction. Goodwin was now heavily in debt, but he occupied the courthouse with his family until his death.[17] James Bowdoin served as Governor of Massachusetts during the troubled period of Shays' Rebellion, and maintained his place as Company moderator. Bowdoin dominated meetings until his death in 1790, when his son, James, Jr., replaced him for a time.

Silvester Gardiner, in involuntary retirement at Poole in England, dreamed of returning to America to resume his business career. Reports from New England about his property and Company affairs whetted his appetite. A letter from his son William in 1783 carried both depressing and exciting news. In assessing the condition of his father's estate on the Kennebec, William had noted ruin everywhere, and he now informed the doctor that

> . . . as far as Strip and waste can render [the land] injured they are so—Gideon Gardiner's hav no Lumber on it within two miles [of the] river of any worth . . . great destruction of timber on the diamond Lott have been made. All your other Estates are in the same situation, without the Least improvement, and every thing growing worse.[18]

He also described an unparalleled expansion in the valley:

> . . . this last winter Norridgewock alone sold one thousand bush. Grain. We have Settlements as far as the great carrying place, five hundred famileys between that & ft. Halifax . . . Sandy River is settled about 50 famileys on at present & every Lott taken up . . . & eight Mile above is began another Settlement on said River . . . The land above ft. Halifax West Side & Norridgewock on the road is sold & settled by 60 famileys from Cape Cod—a number [of] famileys are on Sebastacok 25 Mile Pond—Jones plantation are full, & so is west side Vassalboro—the back lotts of Hollowell & Vassalboro are settled. Win-

throp is over running—Washington also Pinckham are most
full—60 famileys are on the lands back Cobbise[conte], quite over
to Ameriscogging, where likewise is great Settlements.[19]

These tidings convinced Silvester Gardiner more than ever that
his presence, as well as his business skill, was needed at home,
and he began his campaign to return to Boston.

Gardiner dispatched impassioned letters to anyone in New England who might expedite the end of his exile—to his sons, William and John; to his son-in-law, Oliver Whipple;[20] and to his
former confidant, James Bowdoin. He did not approach John
Hancock, who in 1778 had denounced him on the floor of the
Massachusetts House.[21] In any event, Hancock was remaining
aloof from proprietary affairs at this period.[22] Gardiner always received the same answer: the time was not yet ripe for his return.
William Gardiner, having suffered much abuse at Gardinerstown
during the war, cautioned, "for God's sake, think not of returning
untill the State here, have repealed all criminal Acts and Statutes
[against Tories]."[23] John Gardiner added that "It would be mad-
ness for you to think of attempting to return here at least until
matters were more settled, & the passions of men were
cooled . . . ."[24] A month later, James Bowdoin was no more optimistic, but he did promise the doctor that on his return "be it assured it will give me the greatest pleasure to see my old friend."[25]
Oliver Whipple could offer no hopes in 1784. He could only comply with the doctor's request for a detailed account of the damage done to Gardiner's Maine estates.

Whipple journeyed to the Kennebec to assess the situation for
himself. During his seventeen-day visit, he was greeted with hostility by squatters living on tracts showing destruction and neg-
lect. Typical was his reception at Brown's Farm, a Gardiner holding where a Dr. Flitner had taken possession. Whipple described
Flitner as "poor and miserable, and insolent withall, he conceived
at first, the Place was his; and looked on us as Intruders."[26] After
much persuasion, Flitner conceded that he was indeed a tenant
of Gardiner's, and signed a new lease.[27] Typical also were the
Smiths and Coburns, whom Whipple called "four very notable
Trespassers." These men had erected a sawmill and had "Sawed
about one hundred Thousands of Boards, some of which Logs
they purchased of Gideon Gardiner [another tenant] and some of
other People on the River."[28] These intruders, too, agreed to accept leases for the land they had preempted. And so the story

went. Clearly, a strong hand was needed to supervise the Gardiner properties.

Whipple was glad to note, however, that William Gardiner had not been remiss in protecting his father's property.[29] The son had leased the Cobboseconte grist and fulling mills to advantage and had rented a Gardiner farm there for use as a tavern, where he lived. Whipple also was relieved to learn that little of the Gardiner land on the Kennebec had been sold for taxes. William Gardiner had somehow contrived to keep up the payments.[30] Whipple's account increased the doctor's determination to return to America.

Silvester Gardiner was still not welcome in Massachusetts; but in Rhode Island, where the family roots were deeper, he found a haven. It was quite a different man who left England for Newport, probably in 1785.[31] He had been saddened by his second wife's death at Poole in 1781 and, now nearly eighty, lacked his old vitality. Once in Newport, Gardiner attempted to straighten out his muddled financial affairs, and chose as his third wife Catherine Goldthwaite, a woman nearly forty years his junior. Dr. Gardiner never succeeded in returning to Boston or his Maine estates. He died in Newport on August 8, 1786, and was buried at Trinity Church. His double share passed to his children and grandchildren.

Dr. Gardiner's children assumed their places in the propriety. William, a bachelor, lived on at Gardinerstown. John, the Whig barrister who had helped defend John Wilkes at his trial in 1765, practiced law on the Kennebec; served as representative to the General Court; supported Hancock, his father's enemy, in politics; and forsook Anglicanism for Unitarianism. He drowned in the wreck of the packet *Londoner* off Cape Ann on October 17, 1793.[32] Robert Hallowell, Dr. Gardiner's son-in-law, retained a British pension for his services as Comptroller of Customs but lived in Boston, where he helped recover the Gardiner and Hallowell estates.[33] He lived down his Tory past, took his place on the proprietary board and, when he died in Gardinerstown in 1818, was highly respected.[34] In accordance with Dr. Gardiner's will, Robert's son changed his name to Robert Hallowell Gardiner and inherited much of the Gardiner estate in Maine.[35] Unfortunately, he and others of the new generation of proprietors reaped much difficulty and little success from their shares in the Kennebeck Company.

An immediate problem confronting the proprietors following the American Revolution was to establish a legal right to the northern boundary of the Company tract. The proprietors had always insisted that it lay as assigned in the original grant to William Bradford and his associates: at ". . . the Utmost Limits of Cobbisconte, alias Comaseconte, which adjoineth to the river of Kennebeck . . . ."[36] For more practical purposes, however, they had fixed upon the Wesserunsett River as their boundary. In the early days of Company exploitation, this northern limit had been of little consequence to anyone; but by the end of the Revolution, hordes of settlers, most of them not licensed by the proprietors, were pushing into the area, thus making an exact boundary crucial to Company prosperity. Led by James Bowdoin, the propriety petitioned the Massachusetts General Court for a determination of the exact limit. Nathan Dane, Nathaniel Wells, and Samuel Phillips, Jr., were appointed members of the legislative committee on October 28, 1783, to study Company documents, Indian deeds, agreements with other land companies, and depositions from early settlers. On June 15, 1785, they presented their recommendations to the General Court:

> That the general course of Kennebeck-river shall be pursued up to the mouth of Wesserunsett—that a line shall be drawn through the mouth of the said Wesserunsett, at right angles with the said course of Kennebeck-river; that another right line shall be drawn parallel to the said right line, passing through the mouth of Wesserunsett, six miles above it, on a perpendicular distance between the said lines, and extended into the woods fifteen miles on each side of the said Kennebeck-river; and that the said upper line shall be the northern boundary line of the Company's claims . . . .[37]

The legislature accepted this final determination on November 25, 1785. It was highly satisfactory to the proprietors, because it followed the lines upon which they had always insisted. The controversial lands now officially belonged to the Company—a great victory, on paper at least.

It was one thing for the General Court to assign a northern boundary to the proprietors and quite another for the Company to enforce it. The process of obtaining the "submission" of the settlers alone took several years. The first step was to survey lands in townships falling within the line. Next, the settlers had to "make submission" to the Company. A commission of "disinterested persons" appointed by the Governor and Council then fixed prices on the individual holdings.[38] The commissioners operated arbitrarily in many instances. Farmers of the region, feeling themselves wronged, responded with bitterness and, when they could, with open resistance.

The experience of settlers in the town of Industry, located near the border, seems representative. One of these settlers, William Allen, complained that:

> My lot cost me two hundred and seven dollars and forty-two cents, in 1804. I was able, by selling my oxen and all my grain, and by appropriating my wages for teaching school, to raise the necessary sum within ten dollars, and Elijah Fairbanks, of Winthrop, voluntarily lent me that sum to complete the payment. I then took a receipt and demanded my deed, but was refused for some time, till I paid the two dollars required by the agent and took a deed without a warranty.[39]

Complaints and resentment spread to the more settled lower areas of the Company tract. On their part, the proprietors pressed their court suits and distributed eviction notices.

Sometimes the settlers had sufficient backing to print their own pamphlets disputing Company actions. The most noteworthy example of such pamphleteering was the effort published by Samuel Ely in Boston in 1796, which demonstrated that the old revolutionary spirit was still alive. His title explicitly conveyed the libertarian theme: *The Deformity of a Hideous Monster, Discovered in the Province of Maine, By a Man of the Woods, Looking After Liberty.*[40] Like the *Strange Account* pamphlet of the 1760s, this work was "printed near Liberty Tree, for the Good of the Commonwealth," a warning that old issues could be revived if occasion warranted. The basic message of Ely's publication related to the illegal nature of the Kennebeck Purchase title, not a new argument but still an effective one: the charter granted to Bradford and his associates had never been signed by the King, thus "they remained without a [legal] charter until they were incorporated with the Massachusetts in the year 1691 or 1692."[41] If the Pilgrims and, after them, the four merchant purchasers of 1661 had functioned without a valid charter, it was argued, the propriety was an illegal operation and thus without power to enforce its claims on the people of the valley. The pamphlet contained a thinly veiled justification for the use of violence against the Company. Between the resentment spawned by the pamphlet and the Company's continued actions against the settlers, tension increased in the valley.

A crisis was reached on September 8, 1809, when squatters shot
Paul Chadwick, a surveyor employed by the proprietors at Malta
(Windsor) on the Sheepscot River.[42] Thus began the "Malta War."
Shortly after the seven men held responsible for the act were imprisoned in the Augusta jail awaiting trial, an armed mob dressed
as Indians braved a militia patrol and attempted to storm the pri-
son. The movement failed, however, because of strong popular
support. The seven accused men were acquitted when they went
before the bar in November on a charge of murder.[43] The Chadwick murder was naturally of concern to the proprietors, but
they kept their feelings to themselves for many years. Few references to the case, the mob action, and the trial appear in Company files. Several years later, the propriety openly discussed the
event and prepared to offer compensation—an almost unprecedented action for them. On February 14, 1811, they acknowledged that Chadwick, an employee of the Company, had been
"inhumanly and barbarously beset and fired upon by persons
disguised as Indians, in which attack . . . Chadwick was so
wounded that he soon after died." Because they learned that Paul
Chadwick's widow had "since had issue a child of the said Chadwick named Lois"[44] and the infant's mother and grandparents
were needy, the proprietors granted the child Lois a parcel of
land in Malta, which was her home as well as the scene of her
father's murder. The proprietors recorded this generous gift of
162 1/4 acres in their files as "consideration of the unhappy and
melancholy murder of her Father, while employed in the service
of this propriety."[45] The Chadwick murder became linked with
the statehood issue in local politics, with pro- and anti-separation
leaders taking sides, the proprietors aligning themselves with the
latter group.[46]

As Ronald F. Banks has recently observed, it is significant that
it was in the towns carved out of the old Kennebeck Purchase tract,
still the strongholds of anti-Company feelings, that the movement
for statehood was strongest. The question of statehood for Maine
had been raised several times in the early 1800s, and in 1816 the
clamor for separation became so strident that the issue was submitted to the towns for action. Separation was defeated, but the
towns of Sidney, Vassalborough, Augusta, Harlem (China), Fairfax (Albion), Winslow, Unity, Freedom, and Palermo, all located
in Company territory, returned 747 yea's (for separation) as opposed to only 179 nay's.[47] These towns had endured absentee rule

by a speculative land company from their founding, and were therefore more anxious for statehood and independence than the towns in more favored areas. Banks attributes this attitude to the bitter, longstanding quarrel between proprietors and inhabitants over land ownership.[48] The Chadwick case demonstrates that the people of the valley were surfeited with proprietary interference and that other instances of open resistance could occur if conditions did not change. The final compromise, however, like the drawing of the Company's northern boundary line, had to come from the state legislature.

A commission appointed by the Commonwealth of Massachusetts to divide disputed lands between inhabitants and proprietors made an award, which the General Court endorsed on February 23, 1813. To the proprietors' dismay, the settlers received all of the controversial acreage. This was a fair decision for the residents in view of their efforts to improve the land and the inflated prices they would have had to pay for it if the proprietors had won. The Company, for its part, was compensated with a six-mile-square unimproved township above Moosehead Lake called Soboomook.[49] The new township offered the advantage of a clear title; but the proprietors would have to bear the expense of developing land located in an inaccessible area, where the chance for profit was slight. Thus, although the proprietors accepted this grant, they really achieved only the satisfaction of knowing that a festering disagreement had been settled at last. It may have been this court award that finally discouraged the propriety enough to decide to dissolve the Kennebeck Company.

On June 22, 1815, the proprietors assembled for what was surely one of their most important meetings. Shareholders were so keenly aware of the gravity of the proceedings that several who could not attend sent lawyers or judges to represent them.[50] The names of those in attendance illustrate the continuity of leading families in the Company. Robert Hallowell Gardiner, whose name united those of two earlier leaders, served as moderator. There were two Pittses present (John and Thomas), as well as two Hancocks (Ebenezer and John).[51] William Sullivan Apthorp appeared, as did Ward Nicholas Boylston, a Hallowell heir.[52] Benjamin Goodwin, a descendant of Samuel Goodwin, was also present. Robert Hallowell Gardiner opened the meeting and proceeded to the business at hand.

At issue was the dispersal of unsold lands in certain townships of the Kennebeck tract. The first item on the agenda was surveying Soboomook, the land recently granted the Company by the General Court. This was to be completed by the twentieth of the following October. Next, the proprietors voted that "On Monday the twenty second of January, eighteen hundred and sixteen, there shall be a sale and disposition of all the property and estate of this propriety including the judgements, bonds, notes, &c., belonging thereto."[53] During the interim, the Company was to advertise the auction in the states of Connecticut, New Hampshire, and Massachusetts, and the District of Maine, through seven newspapers. On the appointed day, the sale of the six-mile-square tract of Soboomook and eighty thousand acres of land spread through Somerset, Lincoln, and Kennebec counties was to take place at the proprietors' rooms in the Suffolk Building, Boston. The towns located within these lands, in addition to Soboomook, were Malta (Windsor), Palermo, Patrick Town (Somerville Plantation), Harlem (China), Fairfax (Albion), Madison, Industry, Mercer, Rome, Waterville, Augusta, Canaan, Dearborn (once included Rome), Belgrade, Winthrop, Wayne, Starks, Hallowell, and Freedom. The proprietors later decided that the Company's judgments, bonds, and mortgage notes would be sold at a later date. The auction, a highly important one for the period, proceeded as planned and yielded receipts which totaled $40,160.62.[54]

Profits were not distributed at this time, nor was the Company liquidated. The proprietors plodded on through a succession of meetings, granting and selling lands and tidying up details of management. The outstanding mortgages and notes were sold at auction on February 21, 1822. Probably by then the bulk of what the Company had held had already been disposed of, for the sale brought only $1,809.50.[55] Affairs of the Company now were drawing rapidly to a close.

At a meeting on April 24, 1822, the final reckoning was posted, and the Company's treasury was divided. A total of $48,555.60 was distributed to the shareholders.[56] The amount they received, though welcome, was small compared with the profits that the proprietors had received in land distributions and incidental returns during the seventy-three years of Company operation. The propriety held two more meetings—on April 25 and 26.[57] On the 26th, the final details of liquidation were arranged, records and legal documents were assigned permanently to the last treasurer,[58] and the books of the Kennebeck Purchase Company were closed forever.

Although its operations had been controversial, the Company's contributions to the development of Maine were meaningful. No doubt its most notable achievements occurred during the crisis years of the 1750s, when central Maine was the frontier and forts, inspired by the propriety, defended not only the Kennebec valley but much of northern New England. After the French and Indian War ended, the proprietors, free to concentrate upon reaping the vast riches now available to them, pursued an aggressive policy of land development. Here the Company's real problems began, for in exploiting the land, it conflicted with the claims of others—inhabitants, rival land companies, and even the prerogatives of the Crown. The proprietors' audacious policies won them few friends and many enemies.

The end of the Kennebeck Purchase Company brought to a conclusion the dreams of its founders. The Company had not been as successful as the proprietors had hoped, it declined in part because of factors beyond their control. Yet, it achieved its objective in settling central Maine, even if its reasons were hardly in the public interest. Perhaps the proprietors were not entirely dissatisfied in the long run, for many had become wealthy through their association with the Kennebeck Company. It stands as an example of early American business enterprise in its ruthlessness, its use of political influence, and its relation to the role that greed and ambition played in the settling of this country. The death of the Kennebeck Company in 1822 was long overdue, but the dissolution of the propriety did not mean that other speculative land companies would not continue to flourish, intrigue, aggrandize, and, incidentally, serve the people in their time and place.

NOTES

CHAPTER XIII

1 For details of the flight of the Gardiners and Hallowells, see Chapter XII. William Vassall was living in his luxurious Bristol, R.I., summer home when the Revolution came. Driven out

by a mob, he took refuge briefly at Nantucket. He was then forced to make a difficult choice. If he fled New England, he would lose his valuable properties to the radicals; if he remained there, as a rebel his Jamaica estates would be forfeited to the Crown. Tainted by Toryism as he was, he decided to return to England. Charles Ward Apthorp, a wealthy Loyalist who was a member of the New York Council, lived out the Revolution in comfort in British-occupied New York City. William Brattle, important proprietor in the 1750s, became a refugee. A leading Whig until he switched allegiances at the zero hour, he had no alternative but to embark with the British Army for Halifax when it evacuated Boston. He died in Halifax in 1776 at the age of 74. John Adams believed that Brattle had been bribed to join the government party in 1773 by his appointment to a major-generalship in the militia. Shipton's *Sibley's Harvard Graduates,* VII, 19-21. James Bowdoin's Erving in-laws (but not his father-in-law) also left the country, as did another brother-in-law, Thomas Flucker, last Secretary of the Province.

2 Eighth Warrant, May 25, 1776, K.P.P., Records, III, 122-124.

3 Proprietary Meeting, June 20, 1776, K.P.P., Records, III, 125-126. Bowdoin soon found the dual office more than he could handle. On Jan. 14, 1778, he resigned as treasurer, retaining the more important post of moderator. His nephew, John Pitts, was elected treasurer. Proprietary Meeting, Jan. 14, 1778, K.P.P., Records, III, 132.

4 Proprietary Meeting, June 20, 1776, K.P.P., Records, III, 125-126.

5 Proprietary meetings, Mar. 13, 1777-Aug. 14, 1782, K.P.P., Records, III, 128-163.

6 Records of the Standing Committee have not survived for this period, but the Eighth Warrant authorized the Committee to employ surveyors, lease lands or millstreams, and prevent the cutting of Company timber.

7 As a case in point, the first settlers of Farmington, in Sandy River valley, believing that their area was not a part of the Kennebeck Purchase, began clearing land in 1777. It was not until 1780 that they contacted the proprietors and petitioned for a grant. The land was then surveyed by Joseph North for

the Company, and settlers took up their individual tracts. They never obtained title to the land, however, preferring that this process be delayed until a final determination of the Company's northern boundary was made. When a Mass. commission finally set the boundary, it was learned that Farmington did indeed lie outside Company territory. The inhabitants then petitioned the General Court for a title. The town was incorporated in 1794. Thomas Parker, *A History of Farmington, Me., From Its Settlement to 1846* (Farmington, Me., 1846), 9-17; 45-49.

8 William Collins Hatch, *A History of the Town of Industry, Franklin County, Maine* (Farmington, Me., 1893), 24-39. Unlike Farmington, nearby Industry fell within the Kennebeck Purchase. The settlers were regarded as squatters by the proprietors, and were forced to pay prices many considered exorbitant for their land. Hatch presents a sympathetic view of their plight.

9 Grants to Samuel and John Ball of Balls-Town, Mar. 13, 1777, K.P.P., Records, III, 128.

10 Grants at Norridgewock and Canaan, Feb. 7, 1781, K.P.P., Records, III, 145-151.

11 Grant to Joseph Nye and Joseph Dimmuck, Oct. 4, 1781, K.P.P., Records, III, 155-156.

12 Resolution, Feb. 7, 1781, K.P.P., Records, III, 152.

13 Grant to James Bowdoin, Aug. 14, 1782, K.P.P., Records, III, 161-162.

14 Grants to the heirs of Paschal Nelson and Robert and Mehitable (Nelson) Temple, Apr. 23, 1783, K.P.P., Records, III, 166-170.

15 Settlers in the new townships opened during the war complained that more than half of the land was reserved for proprietors, leaving little for them. Hatch, *A History of Industry*, 29.

16 Shipton, *Sibley's Harvard Graduates*, XIII, 444. William Vassall later recovered his Me. lands and in 1797 sold them for £3090. See Chapter II.

17 Samuel Goodwin died in 1802 at the age of 86, but his de-

scendants lived in the courthouse until well into the 20th cen-tury.

18 William Gardiner to Silvester Gardiner, May 14, 1783, Silvester Gardiner Papers, Me. H.S.

19 *Ibid.*

20 Oliver Whipple, a Portsmouth, N.H., lawyer, had Loyalist inclinations but escaped banishment.

21 Bartholomew Sullivan to Silvester Gardiner, Nov. 22, 1778, Gardiner-Whipple Mss., II, 87, M.H.S. Hancock's speech must have been made before the General Court proscribed and banished a large number of Loyalists in 1778, including Gardiner, Robert Hallowell, and Philip Dumaresq.

22 One reason may have been that he and James Bowdoin had become political enemies before the latter's death in 1790.

23 William Gardiner to Silvester Gardiner, May 14, 1783, Silvester Gardiner Papers, Me. H.S.

24 John Gardiner to Silvester Gardiner, July 14, 1783. Foote, *Annals of King's Chapel,* II, 360.

25 James Bowdoin to Silvester Gardiner, Aug. 10, 1783, Gardiner-Whipple Mss., II, 89, M.H.S. Bowdoin also wanted Gardiner's aid in a lawsuit that John Tyng of Dunstable, one of the heirs of Edward Tyng I, had recently commenced against the Company. John Tyng, the son of Eleazer Tyng, the grandson of Jonathan Tyng, and the great-grandson of Edward Tyng I, one of the four purchasers of the Kennebeck tract in 1661, sued the Company on the grounds that his grandfather, Jonathan, had been excluded from his father's will, while three other children divided the family's Kennebeck shares. Tyng now claimed his portion under devise of his grandfather. The proprietors finally acknowledged his claim on June 16, 1784. John Tyng and John Lowell, who had purchased a part of his right, were admitted as proprietors, received compensatory land grants, and in 1822 at the liquidation of the Company, received the sum of $1,548.00 as their 3/4-share right in the propriety. North, *History of Augusta,* 283.

26 Oliver Whipple to Silvester Gardiner, Nov. 8, 1784, Silvester Gardiner Papers, Me. H.S.

27 *Ibid.*

28 *Ibid.*

29 Dr. Gardiner distrusted his son, believing him to be scheming to take the estate for himself. During the war, William Gardiner falsified papers deeding his father's Gardinerstown property to himself, thinking to save it from confiscation. His father turned against him upon learning of his action. Hanson, *History of Gardiner,* 102-103. Dr. Gardiner's daughter, Abigail Whipple, and her husband took a somewhat similar action during the Revolution. On Sept. 12, 1781, the Whipples petitioned Gov. John Hancock and the General Court for a portion of Gardiner's confiscated Boston estate. Their grounds were that, at their marriage, Gardiner had promised Abigail a dowry of £500. Because of the war, the sum was not paid. Accordingly, the Whipples petitioned for a "Child's Share or Portion of her Father's Estate . . . ." The issue of this petition is unknown. Petition of Oliver Whipple to Governor Hancock, Sept. 12, 1781, Ms Am 1582 (758), Houghton Library, Harvard.

30 Oliver Whipple to Silvester Gardiner, Nov. 8, 1784, Silvester Gardiner Papers, Me. H.S.

31 Surviving evidence is hazy regarding the exact day of Gardiner's return to America. One early authority states that it was 1785. Webster, *Silvester Gardiner,* 7. If so, it must have been very early in that year. Receipts for supplies purchased by Dr. Gardiner in London in August, 1784, suggest that he was preparing for a long sea voyage. Gardiner-Whipple Mss, II, M.H.S.

32 Shipton, *Sibley's Harvard Graduates,* XIII, 602.

33 Gardiner's Kennebec lands were saved by a legal technicality during the Revolution, because the Mass. Attorney General found the action for confiscation of his property to be illegally prosecuted. A new action was still in process when . the war ended. Hanson, *History of Gardiner,* 89.

34 Jones, *The Loyalists of Massachusetts,* 160.

35 Gardiner, *Early Recollections,* 4. Robert Hallowell Gardiner was only four at the death of his grandfather.

36 Grant of Council of Plymouth to William Bradford and his associates, *Farnham Papers, Maine Historical Society* Publications, I, 108-116.

37 *Statement of the Kennebeck Claims, by the Committee ap-pointed By a Resolve of the General Court of the 28th of Oc-tober, A.D., On the Subject of unappropriated Lands in the County of Lincoln; And, among other Things, to ascertain the Extent and authenticity of private claims to Lands in that County* (Boston, 1786), 27-28.

38 Members of the commission were Peleg Coffin, state treasur-er; Elijah Bridgham, a justice of the Court of Common Pleas; and Col. Thomas Dwight. The commission fixed prices on the land without viewing it, and the valuation ranged from $125 to $225 for a one-hundred acre plot. Settlers were to pay all charges, including back interest, in specie or bank bills, within an allotted time limit. Landholders complained that the prices set were higher than the value of good land in adjoining towns. Hatch, *A History of the Town of Industry*, 28-37.

39 *Ibid.*, 37.

40 Samuel Ely, *The Deformity of a Hideous Monster, Discover-ed in the Province of Maine, By a Man of the Woods, Looking After Liberty.* Printed near Liberty Tree, for the Good of the Commonwealth (Boston, 1796).

41 *Ibid.*, 31.

42 Williamson, *History of the State of Maine*, II, 613-614.

43 *Ibid.*, 615. Gardiner, "History of the Kennebeck Purchase," *Maine Historical Society Collections* (Portland, Me., 1847), II, 289.

44 Resolution, Feb. 14, 1811, K.P.P., Records, IV, 488-489.

45 *Ibid.*

46 Ronald F. Banks, *Maine Becomes a State* (Somersworth, N.H., 1973), 47-48.

47 *Ibid.*

48 *Ibid.*, 84. Maine finally achieved statehood in 1820.

49 Gardiner, "History of the Kennebeck Purchase," 292. Soboo-mook is still an unorganized township, which in 1960 had a population of four persons.

50 Proprietary Meeting, June 22, 1815, K.P.P., Records, V, 172.

51 These were probably nephews of the patriot. By this time,

the direct Bowdoin line had died out, so the surviving family members were represented by lawyers.

52 Ward Nicholas Boylston (1749-1827) was the son of Benjamin Hallowell, former Comptroller of the Customs, and Mary (Boylston) Hallowell, but took the name of Boylston to inherit a large fortune from an uncle, a rich London merchant. Boylston Market in Boston bears his name.

53 Proprietary Meeting, June 22, 1815, K.P.P., Records, V, 172.

54 Sale of proprietary lands, Jan. 22, 1816, K.P.P., Records, V, 211-214.

55 Sale of mortgages and notes, Feb. 21, 1822, K.P.P., Records, V, 211-224.

56 Proprietary Meeting, April 24, 1822, K.P.P., Records, V, 272-273. The money was distributed as follows:

To the heirs and assigns of:	Shares	Amount
James Bowdoin	20 1/5	$ 5,160.00
William Bowdoin	16	4,128.00
Thomas Hancock	16	4,128.00
Silvester Gardiner	16	4,128.00
Benjamin Hallowell	16	4,128.00
James Pitts	16	4,128.00
Charles Ward Apthorp	8	2,064.00
Samuel Goodwin	8	2,064.00
Sir William Baker	8	2,064.00
Tyng and Lowell	6	1,548.00
Gershom Flagg	4	1,032.00
David Jeffries	4	1,032.00
Edward Goodwin	4	1,032.00
William Vassall	4	1,032.00
Robert Temple	4	1,032.00
Jacob Wendell	2	516.00
Nathaniel Thwing	2	516.00
Samuel Fowle	2	516.00
Nathan Stone	2	516.00
Habijah Weld	2	516.00
Jonathan Fox	2	516.00
Jonathan Reed	2	516.00
Francis Whittemore	2	516.00
William Brattle	1	258.00

William Tailer	8	2,064.00
Thomas Temple or Paschal Nelson	13 1/5	3,405.00
	188 2/5	$48,555.60

Under this distribution, the heirs of William Brattle and Jacob Wendell, who had lost interest in the Company after 1754, and sold most of their holdings shortly thereafter, were remembered. The only obvious omission is Florentius Vassall, an absentee whose New England estate was confiscated during the American Revolution. His heirs continued to press for restoration of their rights for many years after 1822, but failed to gain them. See Chapter V. Proprietary Meeting, April 24, 1822, K.P.P., Records, V, 272-273.

57 Proprietary meetings, April 25 and 26, 1822, K.P.P., Records, V, 273.

58 Reuel Williams, an Augusta, Me., lawyer.

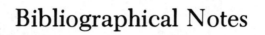

Bibliographical Notes

BIBLIOGRAPHICAL ESSAY

Looking back upon the experiences of a lifetime, the aged Robert Hallowell Gardiner sat down to write a brief "History of the Kennebeck Purchase," which was subsequently published in Volume II of the Maine Historical Society *Collections* (Portland, Me., 1847). He had served for years as the last Company moderator, and Silvester Gardiner and Benjamin Hallowell, his grandparents, had been important leaders during the early years of the propriety. Robert Hallowell Gardiner had been born in exile during the last years of the American Revolution, and had encountered the mistrust and hatred that was the lot of all Loyalist returnees. As a latter-day Kennebeck proprietor, he was in a doubly sensitive position, for the animosities generated by Company policies had persisted to his own era. By 1847, however, old memories were dying, and Gardiner must have believed that the time was propitious to write a vindication of Company actions from the proprietary viewpoint. Although Gardiner admitted that the Company had made mistakes, he believed the proprietors to have been the benefactors of the Kennebec region. Thus Gardiner created the legend of the Kennebeck propriety which has endured until the present. Gardiner's "History" remained as the only work to deal with the Kennebeck Company as a whole until the present effort. The "History" was scholarly for its day, and was based upon official Company records which were available to Gardiner.

GENERAL MANUSCRIPTS

The Kennebeck Purchase Company Papers are still undoubtedly the best source for an understanding of this corporate body. After the liquidation of the Company, the Papers were entrusted to Reuel Williams of Augusta, last proprietary treasurer. Upon his death in 1863, Joseph H. Williams, in obedience to his father's wishes, presented the collection to the Maine Historical Society. The Papers comprise nineteen bound volumes and fourteen boxes of "Loose Papers," and include: Records, I-IV (1749-1822); Letter Books, I-III (1766-1820); Ledger Book (1754-1800); Waste Book (1754-1814); Titles Traced; Land Accounts; Money Accounts; Share of Proprietors (1754-1795); Shares of Proprietors in 1753, 1756, and 1757; and several Books of Grants (1777-1819). The "Loose Papers" contribute a wealth of material to round out an understanding of Company activities, including correspondence, accounts, contracts, petitions, claims, grants, bills, and receipts. Such treasures as the plan of Fort Western (1754) and the deerskin pouch used to carry proprietary dispatches have been carefully preserved. In short, the collection must have represented the prime possession of men who could not bear to throw anything away. The Maine Historical Society is also rich in maps relating to the propriety. Especially valuable are John North's surveyor's plat of 1751, measuring 6'6"x9'6"; "A Copy of a plan of great Lotts in the fifth Division," dated 1761; and Thomas Johnston's *Plan of Kennebec and Sagadahock Rivers,* printed in London in 1755.

The papers of several influential proprietors, some in the Maine Historical Society and others elsewhere, shed additional light on the workings of a great speculative land company. At the Maine Historical Society, these include the Silvester Gardiner Papers, especially numerous for the years of the Doctor's exile in England. Here also are the Robert Hallowell Gardiner Papers; these, however, are disappointing, in that they concentrate almost entirely on Gardiner's later private, industrial and real estate interests. The Waldo-Knox-Flucker Papers contain several documents pertaining to the division of the estate of James Bowdoin I, a division that made possible his heirs' heavy investment in the Kennebeck Company. The Jabez Fox Account Books (1743-1745 and 1745-1754) reveal something of the business methods of an early Falmouth merchant who occasionally sold supplies to other proprietors and to the Company. Of unusual value are the Pejepscot Papers, the residue of a speculative land company rival to the Kennebeck propriety. The Pejepscot Company's correspondence and records of meetings reveal the opposing view in several important land controversies.

Similarly revealing are the John Wentworth Letter Book Copies, located at the New Hampshire Archives in Concord,

New Hampshire. This correspondence affords an opportunity rare in historiography: that of matching letters written by both parties during the mast tree controversy.

Probably the richest source of the papers of proprietors is the Massachusetts Historical Society. The Bowdoin and Temple Papers go far toward explaining the transformation of James Bowdoin from an upholder of the prerogative into a radical Whig, and the James Bowdoin Letter Books (1759-1797) underscore Bowdoin's preoccupation with the surveying and development of his Kennebeck Company lands. Here also are the Gardiner-Whipple Papers; Volume II contains letters written by Dr. Gardiner and other members of his scattered family during the revolutionary era. The thirty volumes of David Jeffries Papers, discovered under the floorboards of Jeffries's old office in Faneuil Hall, tell much about the long-time Company clerk's personal, business, and religious interests, but little about his proprietary involvements. Some of the letters in the slim packet of William Vassall Papers concern Vassall lands on the Kennebec. Israel Williams was not a proprietor, but his Papers include several letters from Thomas Hutchinson that describe the state of the defenses of the Kennebec valley, 1751-1754. The John Winslow Letter Book contains material relating to the Kennebec expedition of 1754 and Winslow's own expense account. The Parkman Papers, XL, hold several letters written by William Shirley to Thomas Robinson, Secretary of State, and to other Whitehall officials concerning the defense of central Maine, and also their replies. In addition, at the Massachusetts Historical Society are the Mayo typescripts of Hutchinson Correspondence. (The originals, almost illegible, are in the Massachusetts Archives.) Hutchinson, implacable foe of the Kennebeck proprietors, wrote several letters commenting upon the precedent-breaking Jeffries-Donnell case. Earlier letters describe the arrival of German and Huguenot immigrants in Boston during the winter of 1751. Many of these immigrants found their way to the Company town of Frankfort (Pownalborough), only to endure the hardships of frontier fighting during the French and Indian War.

One of the finest primary sources relating to the defense of central Maine by William Shirley and Thomas Pownall is to be found in the Massachusetts Archives. The Archives collection is also important for other phases of Company history: the importation of German and Huguenot immigrants, church history, and certain episodes of the Jeffries-Donnell case. The Bowman Papers and the Goodwin Papers, part of the extensive collection of the Pownalborough Court House Papers, Lincoln County Cultural and Historical Association, Wiscasset, Maine, provide documents relating to the celebrated Gardiner vs. Flagg lawsuit and the Jeffries-Donnell case. Unquestionably, however, the best collection pertaining to both cases is to be found in Early Court Files and Papers, Office of the Clerk of the Supreme Judicial Court for Suffolk County, Boston. In this office is located the complete file of Dr. Gardiner's many lawsuits. Nearby, in the volumes of the Suffolk County Probate Records, rest the wills and inventories of several prominent proprietors.

Vassall papers are scattered. In addition to the modest William Vassall Papers at the Massachusetts Historical Society, there are important William Vassall items among the Lloyd, Vassall, and Borland Papers, Houghton Library, Harvard. A small but highly significant collection of the papers of Florentius Vassall is in the Vassall Correspondence, New York Public Library. Finally, the Allen-Bartlett copies of the Jacob Bailey Letters and Diaries are to be found in the Wiscasset Public Library, Wiscasset, Maine.

PRINTED SOURCES

While the original sources available for the writing of a history of the Kennebeck Purchase Company are rich, varied, and relatively plentiful, they have necessarily been augmented by an even larger collection of published works, many pertinent to the operation of the Company and others indispensable in placing this speculative venture in the proper context of the world of the eighteenth century. During this period, central Maine was still the frontier; several recent works provide the framework for the wilderness milieu that the proprietors encountered and subdued. Charles E. Clark's *The Eastern Frontier: The Settlement of Northern New England, 1610-1763* (New York, 1970) examines old Falmouth, Maine, 1727-1764, a center of the mast trade and the residence of several early proprietors. Douglas E. Leach's *The North-*

ern Colonial Frontier, 1607-1768 (New York, 1966) offers a valuable chapter on the nature of speculative land companies in New England. The classic source for both town and land company proprietorships is still Roy Hidemichi Akagi's *The Town Proprietors of the New England Colonies* (Philadelphia, 1924). A flood of recent town studies, demographic in approach, illustrate proprietary planning in selected New England towns, which is sometimes applicable to the Kennebeck Company experience. These include: Philip Greven, Jr., *Four Generations: Population, Land, and Family in Colonial Andover, Massachusetts* (Ithaca, N.Y., 1970); Kenneth Lockridge, *A New England Town: The First Hundred Years* (New York, 1970); Sumner C. Powell, *Puritan Village: The Formation of a New Town* (Middletown, Conn., 1963); and Charles Grant, *Democracy in the Connecticut Frontier Town of Kent* (New York, 1961).

PUBLIC RECORDS AND BIBLIOGRAPHIES

The following standard sources and bibliographies are indispensable aids to the writer in the area of the colonial history of Maine. Elizabeth Ring's *A Reference List of Manuscripts Relating to the History of Maine* (3 Vols., Orono, Me., 1938-1941) is a logical starting point. Unfortunately for this writer, Charles E. Clark's exhaustive compilation of *Maine During the Colonial Period: A Bibliographical Guide* (Portland, Me., 1974) was not available until his work was completed. *The Province and Court Records of Maine* (Vols. I and II edited by Charles T. Libbey, Portland, Me., 1928-1931; Vol. III edited by Robert E. Moody, Portland, 1947; and Vols. IV and V edited by Neal W. Allen, Jr., Portland, 1958-1960) are useful concerning early lawsuits involving proprietary families. *The Documentary History of the State of Maine* (Vols. I-XXIV, Portland, Me., 1869-1916) contains many original printed sources relating to Kennebeck Company history. Equally helpful are the *Publications* of the Colonial Society of Massachusetts; *Collections* of the Massachusetts Historical Society; *York Deeds* (Vols. I-XVIII, Portland, Me., 1887-1910); *The Probate Records of Lincoln County, Maine, 1760-1800,* edited by

William Patterson (Portland, Me., 1895); and *The Acts and Resolves, Public and Private, of the Province of Massachusetts Bay*, A.C. Goodell *et al*, editors (Boston, 1869-1922).

CHAPTER I. THE LURE OF THE VALLEY

The Kennebeck Purchase Company had its roots in the Council of Plymouth's grant to William Bradford and his associates in 1629-1630. The text of the original grant can be found in the *Farnham Papers*, I, Maine Historical Society *Publications* (Portland, Me., 1901), but the proprietors also published their own version as *A Patent for Plymouth in New-England, To which is annexed Extracts from the Records of that Colony, etc.* (Boston, 1751). Two of the best editions of Bradford's *History*, which describes the Hocking incident so worrisome to latter-day proprietors, are *William Bradford's History of Plymouth Plantation, 1620-1647* (2 vols., Boston, 1912), edited by Worthington C. Ford, and *William Bradford's Of Plymouth Plantation* (New York, 1970), edited by Samuel Eliot Morison. George D. Langdon's *Pilgrim Colony: A History of New Plymouth, 1620-1691* (New Haven, 1966) and George F. Willison's *Saints and Strangers* (New York, 1945) provide readable accounts of Pilgrim interest in the Kennebec River fur trade, while John Demos's *A Little Commonwealth: Family Life in Plymouth Colony* (New York, 1970) illustrates the personal lives, customs, and religious orientation of the Pilgrims. In *Records of the Colony of New Plymouth* (12 vols., Boston, 1855-1861), edited by Nathaniel Shirtleff and David Pulsifer, the history of the Pilgrim trading operation at Cushnoc can be traced through its rise, decline, and eventual sale with the rest of the Pilgrim patent in 1661.

William Bradford and his friends, like the later Kennebeck proprietors, had to come to terms with the Indians of the valley. Charles C. Willoughby's *Antiquities of the New England Indians* (Cambridge, 1935) proved useful in establishing the background of the Kennebec Indians, and Roger Ray's compilation, *The In-*

dians of Maine: A Bibliographical Guide (Portland, Me., 1972), would have been invaluable if it had been available then. A popular written work by Stanwood C. Gilman and Margaret C. Gilman, *Land of the Kennebec* (Boston, 1966), is especially helpful for its identification of Indian place names on the Kennebec River.

The Pilgrim associates were by no means the first Europeans to settle in Maine. Henry S. Burrage's *The Beginnings of Colonial Maine, 1602-1658* (Portland, Me., 1914) and Henry O. Thayer's edited volume, *The Sagadahock Colony, Comprising the Relation of a Voyage into New England* (Portland, Me., 1892), present several English explorers' early impressions of the Kennebec River. Two classic works, William D. Williamson's *History of the State of Maine* (Hallowell, Me., 1832) and James Sullivan's *History of the District of Maine* (Boston, 1795), are still useful for their accounts of early Maine history. Although once employed as a lawyer by the Kennebeck proprietors, Sullivan was capable of describing Company actions with detachment. Robert E. Moody's unpublished Yale dissertation, "The Maine Frontier, 1607-1763" (1933), chronicles the horrors of the Indian wars and the establishment of the great proprietary holdings along the Maine coast.

The four wealthy Boston merchants who purchased the tract from the Pilgrims were unable to develop the property because of unsettled conditions, but their descendants and assigns did so several decades later. *The New England Historical and Genealogical Register* proved of great worth in tracing their family lines, as did Edward Harris's *An Account of Some of the Descendants of Captain Thomas Brattle* (Boston, 1867), Justin Winsor's *Memorial History of Boston (Including Suffolk County, Massachusetts), 1630-1880* (4 vol., Boston, 1880), and William Goold's *Portland in the Past, with Historical Notes of Old Falmouth* (Portland, Me., 1882). Bernard Bailyn's masterful study, *New England Merchants in the Seventeenth Century* (New York, 1964), clarifies the political, economic, and social positions of Tyngs, Brattles, and Winslows in the Boston of their day.

CHAPTER II. OPPORTUNITY ON THE FRONTIER

Although the new group of proprietors of 1749 often exceeded their legal rights and prerogatives, they worked within the law when it was possible or convenient to do so. They incorporated, published notices and agendas of Company meetings, elected officers, and distributed land divisions as provincial laws directed. Roy Hidemachi Akagi's *The Town Proprietors of the New England Colonies* (Philadelphia, 1924) compares the Kennebeck experience with that of other speculative land companies of the colonial era. Charles S. Grant's *Democracy in the Connecticut Frontier Town of Kent* (New York, 1961) offers a useful comparison of the workings of a town proprietorship of the same period. Individual histories of some of the towns created within the Kennebeck Purchase—James W. North, *The History of Augusta, With Notices of the Plymouth Company* (Augusta, 1870); John W. Hanson, *History of Gardiner, Pittston, and West Gardiner* (Gardiner, Me., 1852); and Silas Adams, *History of the Town of Bowdoinham, 1752-1912* (Fairfield, Me., 1912)—furnish more pertinent information. The *Papers of the Lloyd Family of Lloyd's Neck, New York, New York Historical Society Collections,* II (New York, 1927), reveal the attitudes of a minor proprietary family toward the Kennebeck Company during its early stages of development. The anonymous *A Strange Account of the Rising and Breaking of a Great Bubble* [*With Amendments and Enlargements*] (Boston, 1767?), reprinted in the *Magazine of History,* Extra Edition, 1928, presents a mine of information regarding popular hostility to the Company from its reactivation until shortly after the passage of the Stamp Act. In general, however, records of the Company and of individual proprietors are most rewarding with reference to the early days of reorganization.

CHAPTER III. THE PROPRIETY: LEADING LIGHTS

The proprietors who assumed leadership of the Kennebeck Company in 1749 were, for the most part, educated men. Clifford Shipton's volumes in the *Sibley's Harvard Graduates* series furnish voluminous detail and useful bibliographies concerning the lives of William Bowdoin, Jabez Fox, David Jeffries, William Brattle, Edward Winslow, and others. Two works by Temple Prime, *Some Account of the Bowdoin Family* (New York, 1894) and *Some Account of the Temple Family* (New York, 1894), trace the genealogies of these two great proprietary families. The *Early Recollections* (Gardiner, Me., 1930) of Robert Hallowell Gardiner offers a personal evaluation of the Gardiner family which cannot be matched elsewhere. Henry T. Webster's *Silvester Gardiner* (Gardiner, Me., 1913) is less useful, presenting an uncritical view of the Doctor's life and career. For the same reason, Evelyn L. Gilmore's *History of Christ Church, Gardiner, 1793-1962* (Gardiner, Me., 1962) is useful for background but not for interpretation. It is always helpful to be able to visualize one's subject. Jules Prown's magnificent *John Singleton Copley* (2 vols., Cambridge, Mass., 1966) presents portraits of many of the proprietors and their families. The Bowdoin portraits at Bowdoin College, Brunswick, Maine, painted by Robert Feke and other early masters, offer an opportunity to become familiar with likenesses of family members, and possibly even a chance for insight into their characters.

CHAPTER IV. "TO ENCOURAGE SETLERS . . ."

In the early 1750s, the proprietors' hopes centered upon the success of their struggling town of Frankfort, and their encouragement of German-Huguenot immigration saved the day. The literature of colonial immigration is impressive. Abbott E. Smith's monograph, *Colonists in Bondage: White Servitude and Convict Labor in America, 1607-1776* (Chapel Hill, 1947), examines every phase of an infamous trade, including the perilous sea voyage. Lucy F. Bittinger's *The Germans in Colonial Times* (Philadelphia, 1901) and Lucy J. Fosdick's *The French Blood in America* (New York, 1906) are especially useful. Here, in describing the hardships of the Frankfort immigrants, Charles E. Allen's *History of Dresden* (Augusta, Me., 1931), an almost encyclopedic work, is an unparalleled source. Nearly as valuable is Erna Risch's "Joseph Crellius, Immigrant Broker," *New England Quarterly,* XII (1939), which outlines the career of the unscrupulous agent who brought the Frankfort settlers to Boston.

CHAPTER V. THE PROPRIETY: OTHER LUMINARIES

After the Company's success in organizing the town of Frankfort in 1752, enthusiastic new faces appeared at the proprietary board. Several of the new shareholders would exert considerable influence upon policy-making. Chief among these were Thomas Hancock and James Bowdoin. Hancock's mercantile career, like that of his famous nephew, John Hancock, is chronicled in William T. Baxter's *The House of Hancock: Business in Boston, 1724-1775* (Cambridge, Mass., 1945). For Bowdoin, see Clifford Shipton's notable study in *Sibley's Harvard Graduates.* See also Francis Walett's "James Bowdoin, Patriot Propagandist," *New England Quarterly,* XXIII (September, 1950); "The Massachusetts Council, 1766-1774," *William and Mary Quarterly,* Third Series, VI (October, 1949); as well as his unpublished Ph.D. dissertation, "James Bowdoin and the Massachusetts Council," (Boston University, 1948). Sketches of the lives of Habijah Weld, Nathan Stone, William Vassall, and Paschal Nelson also appear in Shipton's *Sibley's.* John Adams confided to his *Diary* his impressions of several of the Kennebeck proprietors in *The Adams Papers: Diary and Autobiography of John Adams,* ed. L.H. Butterfield, 4 vols. (Cambridge, Mass., 1961).

CHAPTER VI. CONSOLIDATING COMPANY GAINS

The story of the development of Frankfort during the later

1750s is largely told through Company records—its letter books, account books, waste books, and day books. Corroborating evidence, however, is available in several other sources, notably Charles E. Allen's *History of Dresden, Maine* (Augusta, Me., 1931), and also in such older works as William S. Bartlett's *The Frontier Missionary: A Memoir of the Life of the Rev. Jacob Bailey* (Boston, 1855). *American Population Before the Federal Census of 1790* (New York, 1932), by Evarts B. Green and Virginia D. Harrington, fixes the populations of Frankfort (Pownalborough) and other Kennebec River towns at two dates before the American Revolution. William D. Patterson's compilation of *The Probate Records of Lincoln County, Maine, 1760-1800* (Portland, Me., 1895) provides invaluable information concerning the estates left by several early settlers of Frankfort.

CHAPTER VII. PROTECTING THE VALLEY

Governor William Shirley's Kennebec expedition of 1754 highlighted the early years of proprietary history. The reader might well begin his study of this episode by examining John A. Schutz's *William Shirley, King's Governor of Massachusetts* (Chapel Hill, 1961). *The Correspondence of William Shirley: Governor of Massachusetts and Military Commander in America, 1731-1760* (2 vols., New York, 1912), edited by Charles H. Lincoln, includes several important letters relating to the expedition. *The Boston Weekly News-Letter* (Boston) for September 12 and 26 and October 3, 1754, affords an insight into the kind of laudatory reporting of the Shirley exploit that can probably be duplicated in other colonial newspaper files. The tone is much more earthy in "John Barber's Journal of the Kennebec Expedition, May 30-August 17, 1754," *New England Historical and Genealogical Register,* XXVII (1893). George Dow's *Fort Western on the Kennebeck* (Augusta, Me., 1922) contributes an unhurried view of what is today regarded as a proprietary monument, while Joseph Williamson's "Materials for a History of Fort Halifax," Maine Historical Society *Collections,* VII (1876), assembles the original sources describing the building and maintenance of Fort Western's sister fort, constructed by the Province in 1754.

Like William Shirley, Governor Thomas Pownall befriended the Kennebeck propriety. His career, like Shirley's, is chronicled by John A. Schutz, this time in the excellent *Thomas Pownall, British Defender of American Liberty: A Study of Anglo-American Relations in the Eighteenth Century* (Glendale, Cal., 1951). Pownall's Penobscot expedition, which parallels Shirley's Kennebec effort, is described by the Governor in "Journal of the Voyage of His Excellency Thos. Pownall, Esq., Capn General and Governor In Chief in and over His Majesty's Province of the Massachusetts Bay, to Penobscot, and of his Proceedings in Establishing Possession of His Majesty's Rights There in Behalf of Said Province," Maine Historical Society *Collections*, V (1857). Thomas Pownall's advice to James Bowdoin concerning Company policies should not be overlooked in the *Bowdoin and Temple Papers*, Massachusetts Historical Society Collections, 6th Series, IX.

CHAPTER VIII. DEFENDING THE TITLE

During the last two decades before the American Revolution, much of the proprietors' time and money was expended in the court actions that they initiated against rival land companies—the Clark and Lake Company, The Pejepscot Company, the Brunswick Proprietors, and others—for control of the mouth of the Kennebec River and adjacent coastal areas. Although the Kennebeck proprietors did not win these battles, they did exact concessions from their opponents which spurred them on to even greater efforts. The reader might well begin by studying the original charter granted to the Pilgrims by the Council of Plymouth, which is reproduced in the *Farnham Papers, Maine Historical Society Publications,* I. He will soon become aware of the difficulties involved in fixing boundaries based upon such inexact reference points. Nevertheless, it does appear that the Kennebeck proprietors' claim to the river mouth was extremely tenuous. Many of the events of a long series of lawsuits are described in

Company records, often in broadsides printed by those involved in the lawsuits. These include: *Plaintiff's State of the Case; the Proprietors holding under Lake and Clark, Plaintiffs, against Proprietors from Plymouth-Colony, Defendants* (Boston, probably Dec., 1756); *The Award and Final Determination of the Referees respecting the Claims of the Proprietors of the Kennebeck Purchase from the late Colony of New-Plymouth, and the Company holding under Clark and Lake, relative to the Lands on each Side Kennebeck River* (Boston, Aug., 1757); and *Remarks on the Plan and Extracts of Deeds lately published by the Proprietors of the township of Brunswick (as they term themselves) agreeable to their Vote of January 27th 1753* (Boston, Jan. 31, 1753). Probably the best treatment of the clash between the Kennebeck and Brunswick proprietors can be found in Lawrence C. Wroth, "The Thomas Johnston Maps of the Kennebeck Purchase," *In Tribute to Fred Anthoensen, Master Printer* (Portland, Me., 1952).

CHAPTER IX. APPEAL TO THE KING IN COUNCIL . . .

If William Gordon is to be believed in his *History of the Rise, Progress, and Establishment of the Independence of the United States* (4 vol., London, 1788), the Kennebeck proprietors were caught up in the turmoil of the revolutionary struggle as early as 1765 through their planning of the attack on Thomas Hutchinson's house. Certainly circumstantial evidence points in that direction. The following later historians have considered Gordon's theory: Edmund S. Morgan, "Hutchinson and the Stamp Act," *New England Quarterly,* XXI (1948), and again in Edmund S. Morgan and Helen M. Morgan, *The Stamp Act Crisis: Prologue to Revolution* (Chapel Hill, 1953); G.B. Warden, *Boston, 1689-1776* (Boston, 1970); Clifford K. Shipton, *Sibley's Harvard Graduates*, VIII; and Hiller B. Zobel, *Boston Massacre* (Boston, 1970). Proprietary involvement seems to hinge upon the Company's crucial Jeffries-Donnell case, which was appealed to the King in Council. The case can be followed in "Early Court Files and Papers," Office of the Clerk of the Supreme Judicial Court for Suffolk County, Boston, but for aspects of the process of appeal, see Joseph H. Smith's *Appeals to the Privy Council From the American Plantations* (New York, 1965) and H.D. Heseltine's "Appeals from Colonial Courts to the King in Council, with especial reference to Rhode Island," American Historical Association *Report for 1894.*

CHAPTER X. MASTS FOR THE KING'S NAVY

In dealing with the King's Mast controversy, the historian is most fortunate to have access to both the original Company correspondence with John Wentworth, Surveyor-General of the King's Woods, and his replies to the proprietors. A considerable body of specialized literature sheds further light on the controversy. A pioneer work, still potent, dealing with Royal Navy needs is Robert G. Albion's *Forests and Sea Power: The Timber Problem of the Royal Navy, 1652-1862* (Cambridge, 1926); more specific is Joseph J. Malone's *Pine Trees and Politics: The Naval Stores and Forest Policy in Colonial New England, 1691-1775* (Seattle, 1964). For an understanding of the intricacies and problems of the mast trade, see Leonard B. Chapman, "The Mast Industry of Old Falmouth," Maine Historical Society *Collections,* 2nd Series, VII (1896), and William R. Carlton, "New England's Masts and the King's Navy," *New England Quarterly,* XII (1939). Lawrence S. Mayo's *John Wentworth, Governor of New Hampshire, 1767-1775* (Cambridge, 1921). presents a sympathetic view of Wentworth's role as Surveyor-General of the King's Woods. *Mr. Cooke's Just and Seasonable Vindication* (Boston, 1720) written by the Boston politician and land speculator, Elisha Cooke, Jr., offers some convincing arguments for private ownership of the great white pine that were later utilized by the Kennebeck proprietors in their own quarrel with the King. Bernhard Knollenberg, in *Origin of the American Revolution* (New York, 1965), deals with the King's Mast issue as an important cause of revolution. John Adams was employed as a lawyer by the proprietors in their suit against Wentworth; his briefs are analyzed in *The Adams Papers: The Legal Papers of John Adams* (2 vol., Cambridge, Mass., 1965) by Kinvin L. Wroth and Hiller B. Zobel, the editors. The opinion of Richard Jackson, Counsel for the Board of Trade, regarding one aspect of the mast tree controversy is reprinted in George Chalmers, *Opinions of Eminent Lawyers on Various Points of English Jurisprudence, Chiefly Concerning the Colonies, Fisheries, and Commerce of Great Britain* (2 vols., London, 1814).

CHAPTER XI. RELIGIOUS DISAFFECTION

The Kennebeck proprietors plunged from one crisis into another, but the religious controversy between Anglicans and Congregationalists came closest to splitting the Company. Secondary works explain the bitterness which permeated all of New England. Bernhard Knollenberg examines the religious issue in *Origin of the American Revolution* (New York, 1965). In *Mitre and Sceptre: Transatlantic Faiths, Ideas, Personalities, and Politics, 1691-1780* (New York, 1962), Carl Bridenbaugh traces the entire history of the bishopric campaign in America, with special attention to the role of East Apthorp. Henry W. Foote's edited *Annals of King's Chapel* (3 vols., Boston, 1882-1896) concentrates on the Anglican church's parishioners, many of whom were proprietors, while Bruce Steiner's "New England Anglicanism—A Genteel Faith?", *William and Mary Quarterly*, XXIII (1970), not only scrutinizes the incomes of these parishioners, but compares them with those of members of the equally wealthy Brattle Square Church, attended by several Congregationalist proprietors. Charles E. Clark's "A Test of Religious Liberty: The Ministry Land Case in Narragansett, 1668-1752," *A Journal of Church and State*, XI, clarifies a famous lawsuit between Congregationalists and Anglicans which may have influenced Dr. Gardiner, the brother-in-law of a participant, in his plans for a Company-endowed Episcopal Church at Pownalborough. Wendell Garrett's little volume, *Apthorp House, 1760-1960* (Cambridge, Mass., 1960), explores the career of the Reverend East Apthorp and the building of his "Bishop's Palace." In contrast, Ellis Motte's *The Manifesto Church, Records of the Church in Brattle Square, 1699-1872* (Boston, 1902) examines the history of a liberal church supported by the Congregationalist proprietors. Much has been written about Anglicanism on the Kennebec during the pre-revolutionary period, which centered on the missionary efforts of the Reverend Jacob Bailey. William S. Bartlett's *The Frontier Missionary: A Memoir of the Life of the Rev. Jacob Bailey, Missionary at Pownalborough, Maine, Cornwallis and Annapolis, Nova Scotia* (Boston, 1853) includes documents relating to the career of the missionary that are not available elsewhere. Charles E. Allen's versatile work, *History of Dresden, Maine* (Augusta, Me., 1931), is equally useful here. In *History of Christ Church, Gardiner, 1793-1962* (Boston, 1966), Evelyn L. Gilmore tells the story of the church founded by Dr. Gardiner, and supported by his descendants.

CHAPTER XII. POLITICAL DISRUPTION

For a deeper understanding of the revolutionary crisis in Massachusetts, the reader would do well to consult such authorities as: Edmund S. Morgan and Helen W. Morgan, *The Stamp Act Crisis* (New York, 1967); Robert E. Brown, *Middle-Class Democracy and the American Revolution in Massachusetts, 1691-1780* (New York, 1969); Jackson T. Main, *The Social Structure of Revolutionary America* (Princeton, 1965); Arthur M. Schlesinger, *Prelude to Independence: The Newspaper War on Britain, 1764-1776* (New York, 1965); John J. Waters, *The Otis Family in Provincial and Revolutionary Massachusetts* (Chapel Hill, 1968); and Hiller B. Zobel, *Boston Massacre* (New York, 1970). John Shy's *Toward Lexington: The Role of the British Army in the Coming of the American Revolution* (Princeton, 1965) is helpful in demonstrating that the political affiliations of such proprietary families as the Apthorps and Hancocks could depend upon the retaining of British Army and Navy contracts. For everyday life in revolutionary Boston, see Carl Bridenbaugh's *Cities in Revolt: Urban Life in America, 1743-1776* (New York, 1955) and G.B. Warden's *Boston: 1689-1775* (Boston, 1970). For contemporary opinions regarding several of the leading proprietors during the revolutionary period, see Thomas Hutchinson's *The History of the Colony and Province of Massachusetts-Bay,* ed. Lawrence S. Mayo (3 vols., Cambridge, Mass., 1936); Peter Oliver's entertaining *Origin and Progress of the American Revolution,* eds. Douglas Adair and John Schutz (Stanford, Cal., 1961); and John Adams, *The Adams Papers: Diary and Autobiography of John Adams,* ed. L.H. Butterfield (4 vols., Cambridge, Mass., 1961).

Several of the Kennebeck proprietors were Loyalists who were exiled during the American Revolution. Their experience is described in such works as: Wallace Brown, *The King's Friends: The Composition and Motives of the American Loyalist Claimants* (Providence, R.I., 1966); Alfred E. Jones, *The Loyalists of Massachusetts, Their Memorials, Petitions, and Claims* (London, 1930); and James H. Stark, *Loyalists of Massachusetts* (Boston, 1910).

CHAPTER XIII. DISSOLUTION

From the close of the American Revolution until the dissolution of the Kennebeck Company in 1822, the proprietors fought to preserve their tract from the encroachments of squatters and other claimants. Apart from Company records, local histories—generally useful throughout this study—are especially valuable. Among the best are: Silas Adams, *History of the Town of Bowdoinham, 1762-1912* (Fairfield, Me., 1912); Cyrus Eaton, *Annals of the Town of Warren, In Knox County, Maine* (Hallowell, Me., 1877); George Wheeler, *History of Brunswick, Topsham, and Harpswell, Maine* (Boston, 1878); Charles E. Nash, *The History of Augusta* (Augusta, Me., 1904); James W. North, *The History of Augusta, With Notices of the Plymouth Company* (Augusta, Me., 1870); William E. Hatch, *A History of the Town of Industry, Franklin County, Maine* (Farmington, Me., 1893); Thomas Parker, *A History of Farmington, Maine, From Its Settlement to 1846* (Farmington, Me., 1846); Henry W. Owen, *History of Bath, Maine* (Bath, Me., 1936); and, of course, Charles E. Allen, *History of Dresden* (Augusta, Me., 1931). Finally, Ronald F. Banks, in *Maine Becomes a State* (Middletown, Ct., 1970), presents some fascinating speculations upon the relationship between political attitudes of the old Kennebeck Purchase towns and the movement for statehood.

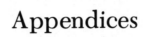

Appendices

APPENDIX I

Charter of the Plymouth Colony to Lands on the Kennebec River, January 13-23, 1629-1630

To all to whom these presents shall come Greeting; Whereas Our Late Souveraigne Lord King James for advancement of a Collony & Plantation in the Country Called or known by the name of New England in America By his Highness Letters Pattents under the great Seale of England bearing date att Westminster, the Third Day of November in the Eighteenth yeare of his Highnesses Reigne of England &c., Did giue grant & confirme unto the Right Honble Lodwick late Lord Duke of Lenox George late Lord Marques of Buckingham James Marques Hamilton Thomas Earle of Arundell Robert Earle of Warwick Sr fferdinando Gorges Knt & divers others whose names are Expressed in the sd Letters Pattents, and their Successors that they should be one Body Politique and Corporate Perpetually Consisting of forty persons & that they should have perpetuall Succession and One Comon Seale to Serve for the said body and that they and their Successors should be Incorporated Called and knowne by the name of the Councill Established att Plymouth in the County of Devon for the Planting Ruling ordering and governing of new England In America, And also of his Speciall Grace Certaine Knowledge and meere motion did give grant and Confirme unto the said President and Councill, and their Successors for Ever, under the Reservations Limitations and Declarations in the said Letters Patents Expressed All that part and portion of the Said Country now Called New England in America, Scituate Lyeing and being In breath from forty Degrees of Northerly Latitude from the Equenoctiall Line to forty Eight Degrees of the said northerly Latitude Inclusively, and in Length of and in all the Breadth aforesaid throughout the maine Land from Sea to Sea together also with all the firme Lands Soyles Grounds Creeks Inletts Havens Ports Seas Rivers Islands Waters ffishings Mines and Mineralls Pretious Stones quarries and all and Singular the Commodities Jurisdictions Royalties Priviledges ffranchises & Preheminences both within the said Tracts of Land upon the Maine as also within the said Islands adjoyning, To have hold possess and Injoy; all and Singular the aforesaid Continent Lands Territorys Islands Hereditaments and Precincts Seawater ffishing with all and all manner Commodities Royalties Previledges Preheminences and Proffitts that shall or may arise from thence with all and Singular their appurtenances and Every part and parcell thereof unto the said Councill and their Successors and assignes for Ever To be holden of his Majesties his heires and Successors as of his manner of East Greenwich In the County of Kent In ffree and Comon Soccage & not in Capite not by Knight Service. Yeilding and payeing therefore unto the late Kings Majesties his heires & successors a ffifth part of the Oare of Gold and Silver

which from time to time and att times from the Dates of the said
Letters Pattents Shall be there gotten had and Obtained for and in
Respect of all and all manner of Dutyes Demands and Services
whatsoever to be Done and paid unto his s^d Late Matie his heires
and Successors as in and by the said Letters Pattents amongst Sundry other Priviledges and matters therein Contained more fully
and att Large it doth and may appeare Now Know yee that the
said Councill by Virtue and Authority of his said Majesties Letters
Pattents for and in Consideration that William Bradford and his Associates have for these nine yeares lived in New England aforesaid
and have there Inhabited and planted a Towne Called by the
Name of New Plym^o at their Owne proper Costs and Charges and
now Seeing that by the Speciall Providence of God and their Extraordinary Care and Industry that have incressed their Plantation to
neere three hundred People and are upon all Occasion able to re-
leive any new Planters or other his Majesties Subjects who may fall
upon that Coaste Have Given granted Bargained and Sold
Enfeoffed allotted assigned and Sett Over and by these presents
Doe Clearely and Absolutely Give grant Bargaine Sell Allien in
ffeeof alott Assign and Confirme unto the said Wm Bradford his
heires associates & assignes all that part of New England in America aforesaid and Tract and Tracts of Land that lyes within or betweene a certaine Revolett or Runlett there commonly called Cohasett alias Conahasett towards the North and the River commonly
called Narragansett River towards the South and the great Western
Ocean towards the East, and betweene, and within a Streight Line
directly Extending up Into the Maine Land towards the west from
the mouth of the said River called Narragansett River to the utt-
most bounds of a Country or place in New England Commonly
called Poconockett alias Sawnonsett; westward and an other
Streight line Extending it Self Directly from the mouth of the said
River called Cohasett als Conahasett towards the West So farr up
into the Maine Land Westwards as the Utmost Limmits of the said
place or Country Comonly called Poconockett als Sawamsett Do
Extend together with one half of the s^d River called Narragansett
River and the s^d Revolett or Runlett called Cohasett als Conahasett
and all Lands Rivers waters havens Ports Crecks ffishings fowlings
and all hereditaments Proffitts Comodityes and Imoluments Whatsoever Scituate Lyeing and being or ariseing within or betweene
the said Limitts or bounds or any of them and for as much as they
have no Convenient Place either of Trade or of ffishing within
their Owne precincts where by after Soe Long travell and great
pains so hopefull a plantation may Subsist, as also that they may
be incouraged the better to proceed in soe pious a worke which
may be Especially tend to the propagation of Religion, and the
great Increase of Trade to his Majesties Realms, and advancement
of the publick Plantation, the said Councill hath further Given
granted Bargained sold Enfeofef a Lotted and Sett over and by
these presents doe Clearely and absolutely give grant bargaine Sell
Alien Infeoffe a Lott assigne and Confirme unto the said Wm Brad-

ford his heirs Associates and Assignes all that Tract of Land or part
of New England in America afores d which lyeith within or betweene and Extendeth it Self from the utmost of Cobestcont alias
Comasecont Which adjoyneth to the River Kenibeck alias Kenebeckick towards the Western Ocean and a place called the falls of
Nequamkick in America aforesaid and the Space of fifteen English
milles on Each Side of the said River Comonly called Kenebeck
River and all the said River Called Kenebeck that Lyes within the
said Limmits and Bounds Eastward Westward Northward and
Southward Last afore mentioned, and all Lands Grounds Soyles
Rivers Waters ffishing hereditaments and profitts whatsoever Scituate Lying and being arising hapening and accrueing or which shall
arise hapen or Accrue in and within the said Limitts and bounds or
either of them togeather with free Ingress; Egress & regress with
Shipps Boats Shallops and other Vessels from the Sea Commonly
Called the Westerne Ocean to y e s d River called Kenebeck and
from the River to the said Westerne Ocean togeather with all
prerogatives Rights Royalties Jurisdictions Priviledges ffranchises
Libertyes and Emunities; and also Marine Lyberty with the
Escheats and Causalityes thereof (the Admiralty Jurisdiction Excepted) with all the Interests Rights titles Clame and Demand
whatsoever which the s d Councill & their Successors now have or
ought to have and Clayme and may have and acquire hereafter in
or to any of the s d Portions or Tracts of Lands hereby mentioned
to be granted or any of the preheminences; In as free Large Ample
& benefitial manner to all Interests and purposes Whatsoever, as
the Said Councill by virtue of his Majesties Letters pattents may or
can grant TO HAVE AND TO HOLD the said Tract and tracts of
Land and all and Singuler Y e premisses above mentioned, to be
granted with their & every of their appurtenances to the said Wm
Bradford his heires associates and assignes for Ever to the Onely
proper and absolute use and behoof of the s d W m Bradford his
heires Associates and assignes for Ever. Yeilding and payeing unto
Our lat Soveraigne Lord the King his heires and Successors for
Ever One fifth part of the Oares of the Mines of Gold and Silver,
and one other fifth part thereof to the president and Councill,
which shall be had possest & obtained within the precincts aforesaid for all Services & demands Whatsoever And the said Councill
Do further Grant And agree to and With the said W m Bradford his
heires associates and assignes and Every of them his and their
ffactors Agents Tenants and Servants and all such as he or they
shall send or Imploy about his s d perticular Plantation Shall and
may from time to time freely and Lawfully Trade and trafique as
well with the English as any of the Natives within the precincts
afores d with the Liberty of ffishing upon any Part of the Sea
Coasts and Sea Shores of any of the Seaa or Islands ajacent & not
being Inhabited or otherwise disposed by order of the said president and Councill & also to Import Export and transport their
Cattle and Merchandise att their Will & pleasure paying Onely
such Duty to the Kings Majestie his heires & Successors as the said

president and Councill doe or ought to pay, without any other
taxes Impositions Burdens or Restrictions upon them, to be I
pressed, And further the said Councill doe grant and agree, to &
with the said Wm Bradford his heires Associates and Assignes, that
the Persons transported by him or any of them shall not be taken
away Imployed or Comanded Either by the Governour for the
time being of New England or by any other Authority there from
the Bussiness and Imployements of the said Wm Bradford and his
Associates his heires and assignes; Nessasary deffence of the Country Preservation of peace Supresseing of tumults with in the Land,
Tryalls in matters of Justice by appeall upon a Speciall Occassion
only Excepted, also it shall be Lawfull and free for the said Wm
Bradford his associates heires and assignes att all times hereafter to
Incorporate By some usuall and fitt name and title him & themselves or the people there Inhabiting under him or them, with Liberty to them and their Successors from time to time to frame and
make Orders Ordinances and Constitutions as well for the better
government of their affaires here and the Receiving or admitting
any to his or their Society, as Also for the better Government of
his or their People and affaires in New England or of his and
people att Sea in goeing thether or Returning from thence and the
Same to be put in Execution by such Officers and Ministers as he
and they shall Authorize and Depute Provided the said Laws and
Orders be not repugnant to the Lawes of England or the forme of
Governm^t by ye President and Councill hereafter to be Established; And further itt shall be Lawfull and free for the said Wm
Bradford his heires Associates and Assignes to transport Cattle of
all kinds and powder Shott Ordinances and amunition from time
to time as shall be necessary for their Strength and Safty hereafter;
for their Severall Deffences and Safty to Encounter Expulse repell
and resist by force of Arms as well by Sea as by Land by all
Wayes and means whatsoever, and by Virtue of Authority to us derived by his Late Majesties Letters Pattents To take apprehend
Seize and make prisse; of all such persons their Shipps and goods
as shall attempt to Inhabit and trade with the Savages people of
that Country within the Severall precincts and Limitts of his and
their Severall plantacons or shall Interprisse or attempt att any
time destruction Inusion detrement or annoyance, to his or their
plantations the one moyety of which goods so Seized or taken it
shall be Lawfull for the Said Wm Bradford his heires Associates &
assignes to take to their Owne use and behoofe and the other
moyetie thereof to be delivered by the said Wm Bradford his heires
associates and assignes to such Officers as shall be appointed to receive the same for his Majesties Use and the said Councill doe
hereby Covenant and Declare that it is their Intent and meaning
for the good of the plantations that the said Wm Bradford his
heires associates his or their heires and assignes shall have and
Injoy whatsoever priviledge or priviledges of What Kind so Ever
as are Expressed or intended to be Granted in and by his said Late
Majesties Letters Pattents and that In as Large and ample manner

as the said Councill thereby now may or hereafter Can grant (Coyning of money Excepted) and the Said Councill for them and their Successors Do Covenant and grant to & with the said Wm Bradford his heires Associates and assignes by these presents that they the said Councill shall att any time hereafter upon Request, att the onely proper Charge and Costs of the said Wm Bradford his heires associates and assigns Do make Suffer Execute and Willingly Consent unto any other Act or Acts Conveyances assurance or assurances, whatsoever; for the good and perfect Investing assureing and Conveyeing and Sure making of all the aforesaid Tract or Tracts of Lands Royaltyes mines and Mineralls Woods ffishings and all & Singular their appurtenances unto the said Wm Bradford his heires associates and assignes as by him or them or his or their heires and Assignes or his or their Councill Learned in the Law shall be devised advised or required and Lastly KNOW Ye that wee the Councill have made Constituted and Deputed authorized and appointed, Captn Miles Standish or in his absence Edward Winslow, John Howland and John Alden or any of them to be Our true and Lawfull Attorney & Attorneys Joyntly & Severally in Our Name and Steed to enter into the said Tract or Tracts of Land & their premisses with their appurtenances or into Some part there of in the name of the whole for Us and in Our name to take possion and Seizen there of and after such possession & Seizen of all & Singular the sd mentioncd to bc granted premisses unto the said Wm Bradford his heires associates and assignes or to his or their Certaine attorney in that behalf Ratifieing allowing Confirming all whatsoever Our said attorney shall doe in or about the premisses IN WITNESS whereof the Councill established att Plymo in the County of Devon for the Planting ruling Ordering and Governing of New England In America have hereunto put their hand and Seale this thirteenth Day of January in the fifth yeare of the Reigne of our Soveraigne Lord Charles by the Grace of God King of England Scottland ffrance & Ireland yc Deffender of the faith ye Anno Domini 1629./

Robert Warwick L.S.

Mary Farnham, comp., *The Farnham Papers: Collections* of the Maine Historical Society, VII (Portland, Me., 1901), pp. 108-117.

APPENDIX II

Indenture for the Purchase of Lands on the Kennebec River, by
the General Court of Plymouth

October 27
November 6' 1661

This Indenture of the Twenty Seventh day of Octob'r Anno
Domini One thousand Six hundred Sixty & One made between the
General Court for the Jurisdiction of Plymouth in New England in
America in the behalfe of the s d Collony on the One p t and
Antipas Boys Edw d Tynge Thomas Brattle and John Winslow of
the Town of Boston in the County of Suffolk in the Jurisdiction of
the Massachusets in New England Afores d Merch ts on the Other
part Witnesseth that Whereas our Late Soveraign Lord King James
for the Advancem t of a Collony & plantation in this Country
Called or known by the Name of New England in America by his
highness letters Pattents under the Great Seal of England bareing
date At Westminster the third day of Novemb r in the Eighteenth
year of his highness reign of England &c did give grant & Confirm unto the R dt Hon ble Lodowick L d Duke of Lenox George
Late L Marquess of Buckingham James Marquess Hambleton
Thomas Earle of Arundel Robert Earle of Warrick S fferdinando
Gorges Knight and divers others whose Names Are Expressed in
the s d Letters Pattents & their Successo r that they should be One
body polotick & Corporate perpetually Consisting of forty psons
&c a And further Also of his Special Grace Certaine Knowledge &
Meer Notion did give grant & Confirm unto the s d president &
Council And their Successors forever und r the reservations Limita-
tions & Declarations in the s d Letters pattents Expressed all that
part & portion of the s d Country Now Called New England in
America &c a Together Also with all the firm land Soyles grounds
&c As by the s d Letters Pattents doth more Largely Appear, where-
upon the s d Councill by Vertue & Authority of the s d Late Maj tys
Letter Pattents And for & in Consideration that William Bradford
And his Associates for this Nine years have lived in New England
Afores d And have there Inhabited & planted a Town Called by
the Name of New Plymouth at their own proper Cost & Charges
&c And upon other Considerations As is more Largely Expressed
in a deed under the s d Councills Seale bareing date the thirteenth
day of Jan ry in the fifth year of the reign of Our Latg Soveraign
Lord Charles the first by the grace of God King of England Scot-
land france & Ireland Defender of the faith &c a Annoq, Domini
1629 Have given granted bargained & Sold Enfeoffed Aliened
Assigned and Set over unto the s d W m Bradford his heirs Associates & Assigns All that Tract or Tracts of Land that by within or
between a Certaine river or rundlet there Comonly Called Cohas-
set or Conahasset towards the North & the river Comonly Called

Narraganset Towards the South as by the s^d Charter may more
fully Appear And whereas the s^d Councill in Consideration that
the s^d Wm Bradford & his Associats have no Convenient place
Either of Trading or ffishing within their own prescints whereby
after So long a Travell and great pains So hopefull a plantation
may Subsist As Also that they may be Encouraged the better to
proceed in So Pious a work wch may Especially Tend to the
propagation of religeon & the Great Increase of trade to his
Maj^tys realms & Advancem^t of the Publick plantation did give
grant bargaine Sell Enfeoffe Allot Assigne & Set over unto the s^d
Wm Bradford his heirs Associates & Assigns All that tract of land or
part of New England in America afores^d which lyeth within or between And Extendeth its Selfe from the utmost Limits of Cobbaseconte Al^s Conaseconte which Adjoyneth to the river of Kenebeck
Al^s Kenebeckick Towards the Western Ocean & a place Called
the falls at Nequamkick in America Afores^d And the Space of fifteen English miles on both Sides s^d river Comonly Called Kenebeck river And All the s^d river Called Kenebeck river that lyeth
within the s^d Limits & bounds Eastward Westward Northward
and Southward & All lands grounds Soyles rivers tradeing ffishing
heridttm^ts & profits whatsoever Scittuate lying & being Ariseing
happening or Accrewing or which shall happen or Accrew in or
within the s^d Limits or bounds or Either of them Together with
free Ingress Egress & regress with their Boats Shallops & other vessells from the Sea Comonly Called the Western Ocean to the s^d river Called Kenebeck & from the s^d river to the s^d Western Ocean./
Hereupon the s^d Court & Collony of New Plymouth by vertue &
Authority of the s^d deed granted to them by the Councill Afores
for & in Consideration of the Sum of four hundred pounds Star-
ling to us in hand paid by the s^d Antipas Boyes Edwd Tynge
Thomas Brattle & John Winslow Wherewith we do Acknowledge
Our Selves Satisfied Contented & fully paid & thereof & of Every
part & parcell thereof Exonerate Acquit and discharge the Afores^d
Antipas Boyes Edwd Tying Thomas Brattle & John Winslow them
their heirs Ex^rs Adm^rs & Assigns forever by these presents Have
freely & Absolutely bargained Alienated and Sold Enfeoffed &
Confirmed And by these p^rsents do bargaine Sell Enfeoffe & Con-
firm from us the s^d Collony & Our heirs to them the s^d Antipas
Boyes Edwd Tynge Thomas Brattle & John Winslow & their heirs
& Assigns forever All those our lands lying & being in the river of
Kenebeck bounded As followeth vizt All that our Tract of Land in
America which Lyeth in or between & Extendeth from the Utmost
bounds of Cobbaseconte Al^s Comaseconte which Adjoyneth to the
river of Kenebeck Al^s Kenebeckick towards the Western Ocean
and a place Called the falls in Nequamkick in America Afores^d
And the Space of fifteen English Miles on both Sides the s^d river
Comonly Called Kenebeck river And all the s^d river Called Kenebeck river that lyeth within the s^d Limits & bounds Eastward Westward Northward & Southward & also All lands grounds Soyles rivers Tradeing ffishing heriditam^ts & profits whatsoever Scittuate ly-

ing & being Ariseing hapening or Acrewing or which shall hapen
or Accrew in or within the s d Limits or bounds Together with free
Ingress Egress & regress with Ships boats Shallops or other vessells
from the Sea Comonly Called the Western Ocean to the s d river
Called Kenebeck & from the s d river to the s d Western Ocean As
Also All the lands on both Sides of s d river from Cushena upwards
to Weserunscut bought by us of Munguim Al s Matahameada As
Appears by a deed bareing date Aug st the Eighth One thousand
Six hundred forty & Eight And Consented unto by Essemenosque
Agadodemagus & Tassuck Chief men of the place & proprietors
thereof To Have & To Hold the Afores d lands lying & being in
the river of Kenebeck bounded as afores d And Also the Afores d
Lands on both Sides the s d river from Cushena upwards to
Weserunscut Together with All the grounds Soyles rivers Tradeing
fishing heriditam ts & profits benefits & Priviledges thereunto belonging or Accrewing or which Shall hapen or Accrew in or within
the s d Limits or bounds or Either of them to the s d Antipas Boyes
Edw d Tynge Thomas Brattle & John Winslow to them & their
heirs & Assigns forever the s d premisses with All our s d lawfull
right in the hands Abovementioned Either by Purchase or pattent
with All & Singular the Appurtenances priviledges and Imunitys
thereunto belonging to Appurtaine to them the s d Antipas Boyes
Edw d Tynge Thomas Brattle & John Winslow to them & Every of
them their & Every of their heirs & Assigns forever to be holden
of his Maj ty his Manor of East Greenewick in the County of Kent
in free And Comon Soccage And not in Capite Nor by Knights
Service by the rents & Services thereof & thereby due & of right
Accustomed Warranting the Sale thereof Against All People whatsoever that from us or und r us the s d Collony of New Plymouth or
by Lawfull right & Title might Claime Any right & Title there-
unto/ To and for the performance of the premisses We have hereunto Affixed the Seal of Our Governm t this Twenty Seventh of
Octob r One thousand Six hundred Sixty and One

                                                    Tho Prince Governo r

Signed Sealed & Deliv-
  ered the ffifteenth day
  of June Anno Dom.
  1665

[*L.S.*]

Mary Farnham, com., *The Farnham Papers, Collections* of the
Maine Historical Society, VII (Portland, Me., 1901), pp. 296-301.

APPENDIX III

Governor William Shirley's Letter to the Board of Trade Recommending That a New Patent Be Granted the Kennebeck Purchase Company, December 31, 1754.

Boston New England, Decm. 31st 1754—

My Lords—

I have endeavoured to set forth in former Letters to your Lordships the importance of the River Kennebeck in His Majesty's Colonies in North America—As on the one hand it affords the shortest and most practicable Passage to the French from Canada into the Eastern part of New England and to it's Sea Coast upon the Atlantic Ocean and on the other the most commodious place near the Head of it for the English to Erect a large Fort upon, which would not only secure this Pass against the French but put it into the power of the English to make a discent from thence to Quebec itself thro' the River Chaudiere with a large body of Troops and Train of Artillery in a few days—

It was with this View that I availed myself of the Alarm that the French had built or were building a Fort upon the Carrying place between the Chaudiere and this River to set on Foot and carry into execution the late Expedition upon the Kennebeck and to Erect there Two Forts at Cushnoc & Taconnoc Falls—

This was the Utmost that could be done the last Summer: —The length of the River, Distance of it's head from the Settlements from whence a Fort there could be supplyed with Provisions and stores, together with the Difficulty of the Navigation Fifty miles above Cushnoc, made it impracticable to carry a Fort higher up without first building these two Intermediate Forts for it's support: But I am in hopes that the next advance which is made upon this River may carry us up to a proper spot for erecting a Fort upon, which may be capable of holding a Garrison strong enough to curb the French and secure this principal pass into the Heart of Canada against the whole Force of Quebec——

How greatly such a Number of Settlements upon this River in the neighbourhood of the Forts as would be able to raise Grain and other Provisions sufficient for the Garrisons in them and to reinforce them upon any sudden Emergency would contribute to their Security and Strengthen our possession of the River, I need not observe to your Lordships—

The Consideration of this Circumstance is what hath induced me to transmitt to Your Lordships the Inclosed Petition and Papers with the following Account of the Proposalls made to me by the Subscribers in behalf of themselves and their Partners in the Patents under which they claim—

A Few days after my return from England a large Number of this Company, who have of themselves sufficient ability and Spirit to People this River waited upon me to acquaint me with the Settlements they had begun upon it in my absence and desired of me what incouragement and protection I could give them: As the settlement of the Kennebeck had seemed to me a great object ever since I have been concerned in the late Publick Disputes with the French. I promised them if their Title to what they claimed should appear to me a good one I would afford them all the support in my Power, upon this they lay'd the inclosed State of their Case before me; which, upon the Perusal of it and the Vouchers seems to me as far as I can judge to have so fair foundation as to justifye my transmitting it to Your Lordships and to Recommend their Petition to Your Lordships favourable consideration. What hath still more ingaged my Attention to this Affair is, that upon finding myself under a Difficulty to carry a Fort as high up the Kennebeck last Summer as Taconnoc Falls (which was the point of the River I had determined to Erect one upon) unless an intermediate Fort was built at Cushnoc which is Eighteen miles short of Taconnoc and communicating it to some of the Principal Gentlemen of this Company they readily offered to do it at the Companys Expence in order to enable me to build one at Taconnoc and accordingly effected it at a considerable Charge, This Proof, My Lords, of their Ability and Spirit, with the good Consequences to His Majesty's Service at that conjuncture, the expediency of Strengthening this River with Numerous Settlements as soon as may be and my dispair of it's ever being done unless they do it, induced me to make a proposal to them for settling a Thousand Families upon the River (including those they have already settled there) at the Companys charge, which they have undertaken to do provided their Title to the Lands they claim there shall be confirmed to them by a New or Explanatory Patent from the Crown, or in any Manner so as to put an end to the Continual Interruptions they meet with in their present Settlements. Five hundred of these Families to be settled in three years and the other five hundred in seven years after, provided peace shall continue so long between the two Crowns and in case of a Warr's intervening, the Company to be allowed such a Protection from the Government as will cover the Settlements whilst they are making or in default thereof so many Years of Peace after the End of the Warr as shall make up those two Periods—

If a new Patent can be Granted to this Company upon these Conditions consistant with Justice to such as set up pretentions to the Land claimed by them, it seems evident My Lords, that it would be a most happy Circumstance for his Majesty's Service; It is clear that together with the Forts erected on Kennebeck, and that proposed to be erected, it would absolutely secure to the Crown the Possession of the most important River in New England for stopping the Incroachments of the French on that side and gaining at the same time the Principal Pass into their Country—

The French have for some Years extended their Settlements twelve miles in length on each side the River Chaudiere within Thirty Miles of the Carrying place between that and the Head of the Kennebeck; and we have had intelligence, which seems not to be doubted, from the Indians, that they design'd to erect a Fort before now on the Carrying place itself: It is the Settled Policy of the French in North America to possess themselves of as many of the Principal Lakes, Rivers and Passes in the Country as they can, by first building Forts upon them and then strengthening them with settlements; Thus they have Built Forts upon Lake Champlain and been several Years propagating Settlements in the Country adjacent to their Main Fort upon a Point at the End of that Lake commonly called Crown Point; they did the same thing several Years ago upon the Great Lakes, and Passes between them, and are executing the same Scheme now upon the Ohio, where they have lately begun a Settlement with three hundred Families; Their Scheme is the same upon the River St. John's in the Bay of Funda; [sic] upon the Isthmus of the Peninsula of Nova Scotia; and the River Chaudiere; The Charge of making all these Settlements, which is large is constantly at the Expence of the Crown; But his Majesty hath now an Oppertunity of doing it upon the Kennebeck at the Expence of this Company; and this further advantage might result to the Crown from renewing their Patent; It may be a Question now whether the White Pine Trees upon that River and within fifteen Miles on each side of it, fit for Masting the Royal Navy, of which there is a great plenty of fine ones there, belong to the Crown or not as the Reservation of the White Pines growing within the Province of the Massachusetts Bay, to the use of the Crown, was not, I believe made untill the granting of their present Charter in 1692, which is many Years subsequent to the Grant under which the Company claims; But if their Patent is renewed, a reservation may be now made of them—

The Difficulties which this Company, My Lords, labour under, are these; The Grant under which they claim the lands upon this River, are undoubtedly elder than those of their Competitors and the Title they set up to those which are as high up the River as Taconnoc & Cushnoc was accompanied with an Ancient possession, But the Lands extending on each side the River from a place called Cobbiseconte to the Mouth of it, not having their Limits very clearly described in the Grant, that hath giving occasion to the New Settlers under them being harrassed with little Actions of Trespass which are tryed in a County where the Judges, Juries, and Witnesses are generally more or less interested as they represent to me in the claims made against them; the Strength of which as I understand consists in, the imperfect Description of the Limits in the Companys Patent, more than any Title they pretend to set up to them: But if the matter was to be decided by the plain Intent of the Original Patent from the Council Established at Plymouth in Devonshire by King James the first under which the Company claims, it seems clear as far as I understand it that the Merits are with the Company—

Whether, if that should appear to be the Case to Your Lordships, and Your Lordships should be of Opinion that the strengthening of this River with Settlements deserves the Notice of the Crown, there may not be room from the Covenant of the Council of Plymouth here inclosed for his Majesty's Granting a New Patent of them to the Company in Order to put an End to these innumerable and Endless Disputes in the Law, which will be a perpetual Obstacle to the Settlement of the River, I would humbly submit to Your Lordships—

It seems pritty certain that if the Company is prevented from Settling the River it will never be done; As to any Lands actually Improv'd by Persons who may have sate [sat] down upon them, tho' without Title those Lands might be saved to them in the New Patent with an hundred Acres adjacent. The Company I understand have desired Mr. Florentius Vassall a Gentleman largely interisted in these Lands to wait upon Your Lordships on this Occasion and Mr Bollan to sollicit their Petition

I am with the highest respect My Lords, Your Lordship's most humble and most Obedient Serv [t]

Copy

(S) W Shirley

Public Record Office CO.5 / 887, London, England.

APPENDIX IV

Board of Trade's Reply to Governor William Shirley Concerning a New Patent for the Kennebeck Purchase Company, August 6, 1755.

1755
August 6th

To William Shirley Esq. Governor of the Massachusets Bay

Sir,

Since Our Letter to you dated the 5th of July 1754, We have received yours of the 19th of August, 8th of November, 31st of December and 12th of January last, and the several Papers transmitted with them.

The first of these Letters, which is dated from Falmouth in Casco Bay, contains a very particular Account of your Proceedings upon the River Kennebeck; The securing of which and preventing any designs the French might have of taking Possession of it, was a Service of the greatest importance. The steps you took to obtain the Consent and Assistance of the Indians to build two Forts upon this River, were very wise and prudent, and the whole of the Expedition appears to us to have been executed with great Spirit and Discretion. We agree with you in Opinion, that the building a Fort at the head of this River would tend greatly to the future Security of all His Majesty's Colonies in that part of North America, and in case of a Rupture with France, might greatly facilitate any measures, which might be thought expedient for dispossessing them of their Possessions on the River St Lawrence; and We shall think it Our Duty to do every thing within Our Province towards promoting this important Service. As We are fully convinced, from the Assistance which you say you received from the Proprietors of the Kennebeck Grant in building the two Forts at Cushnock and Taconnac Falls, that they may be of great Service, whenever it shall be thought adviseable to build the other Fort at the Head of the River; We shall, as soon as their Agents here are prepared to attend Us, take their case into Our serious Consideration. We must however observe to you, that it appears to Us, upon a general View of it, that the Difficulties, which the Proprietors alledge they are under from the Claims and Pretensions of others, who have settled within the Limits of their Grant, and which is the principle Reason assign'd by them for applying for a new Grant, may, when the matter comes to be particularly discuss'd, operate as a Reason against it, or at least may render such new Grant ineffectual for the purposes for which it is desired, because it cannot set aside any Right or Interest, which the Province of the Massachusets, by their Charter, or any Persons, by particular Grants, may have in the said Lands; and therefore in this general view of it, it appears to Us, that the most effectual measure, which the Proprietors could take, would have been to have brought an Action of Ejectment against some one of the private Claimants in Possession, upon a Trial of which in the Provincial Courts, or upon an appeal before This Majesty in Council, the whole of the matter might be finally determined in a judicial method.

The Reasons, which you offer in your Letter of the 12th of January in support of the Excise Act, convinced Us so clearly of the Inexpediency of repealing it, that We thought it Our Duty, after having heard what the Agents for the Province and for the Towns of Boston, Marble head and Gloucester had to offer upon it, to lay it before the Lords Justices for their Approbation, leaving it to the Representatives of the People, who in this case are the best judges of what may be for their Interest and Convenience to determine on the Propriety or Impropriety of renewing the like Tax, when the present Act shall be expired.

It gave Us great Concern to find by Letters, which We have received from New York, that great Disputes have arisen concerning the true Boundary Line between your Province and that, and that it had been attended with Riot and Bloodshed upon the borders. It is very much to be lamented, that the internal Peace of Government should be disturbed by trivial Disputes of this kind, at a time when the Colonys are so loudly called upon to exert, with the greatest unanimity, their utmost Strength in their own Defence, and in vindication of His Majesty's Right. We are well convinced, from the nature of the dispute and from the experience of what has happened between New York and New Jersey upon the same occasion, that it cannot be finally or effectually put an end to, but by a Commission from the Crown; and We Should hope both Provinces would readily concurr in this measure.

We heartily wish you success in the Vigorous measures, which have been undertaken for the defence of the Colonys against the Invasion and Encroachments of a Foreign Power. So We bid you heartily farewell, and are your

very loving Friends
and humble Servants,

Dunk Halifax
J. Pitt
J. Grenville

Whitehall——
August 6: 1755

Public Record Office CO. 5/918, London, England.

Index